CENTRAL STATISTICAL OFFICE

330005478 X

KV-513-549

.... CLASS No. ....

.... BOOK No. ....

FOR USE IN LIBRARY ONLY
WESTMINSTER COLLEGE

WITHDRAWN
LIBRARY

Social
Trends

1992 Edition

Editor: TOM GRIFFIN

Associate Editor: PHILIP ROSE

Chapter Authors: BRENDA STURGE
BRIAN SALERNO
DARREN SHORT
ELOISE CRITCHLEY
RICHARD ADSHEAD
KATHY MARSH

A publication of the Government Statistical Service

London: HMSO

Contents

CLASS NO 310 SOC REF
ITEM NO 33000 5478X
THE LIBRARY
WESTMINSTER COLLEGE
OXFORD OX2 9AT

Introduction

This new edition of *Social Trends* updates its broad description of British society. The material in it is arranged in 13 chapters, corresponding closely to the administrative functions of Government. The focus in each chapter is on current policy concerns, as the primary user of *Social Trends* remains Government.

Article

This year *Social Trends* includes an article on the use and misuse of crime statistics by Chris Lewis of the Home Office. The article includes sections on the definition of crime, variations in the reporting and recording of crime, presentation of crime statistics and future developments.

New Features in Social Trends 22

To preserve topicality, nearly a third of the 231 tables and over a third of the 159 charts in *Social Trends 22* are new compared with the previous edition. There is a new chapter in this years *Social Trends*. Following on from the initial expansion in *Social Trends 21* of the environment section of Chapter 9, *Social Trends 22* now has separate chapters on the environment and on transport. Chapter 9 now contains even more information on the environment and the new Chapter 13 contains the expanded transport section. In all chapters the source of the data is given below each table and chart, and published sources are named where appropriate. *Social Trends 22* also includes chapter bibliographies, directing readers to other published sources of data (both government and non-government). As many people use *Social Trends* as a first point of reference, these bibliographies should be a useful addition. Regional and local authority analyses of much of the information in *Social Trends* may be found in the CSO's publication *Regional Trends*.

Contributors

The Editor and Associate Editor wish to thank all their colleagues in the Government Statistical Service and their contributors in other organisations, without whose help this publication would not be possible. Within the Central Statistical Office the *Social Trends* production team was: Brenda Sturge, Brian Salerno, Darren Short, Eloise Critchley, Richard Adshead, Kathy Marsh, Carlton Brown, Adeline Fadugba and Naeema Sharief. Thanks are also due to Ian Goode who was closely involved during the early stages of preparation of this edition, and to our colleagues in the Graphic Design Unit, Word Processing Unit and Typesetting Unit.

Appendix

This edition of *Social Trends* again includes an Appendix, giving definitions and general background information, particularly on administrative structures and legal frameworks. Anyone seeking to understand the tables and charts in detail will find it helpful to read the corresponding entries in the Appendix. Statistical notes are also included as footnotes to the tables and charts. A full index to this edition is included at the end.

Social Statistics Branch
Central Statistical Office
PO Box 1333
Millbank Tower
Millbank
London SW1P 4QQ

Symbols and conventions

Reference years. Because of space constraints, it is generally not possible to show data for each year of a long historical series. When a choice of years has to be made, the most recent year or a run of recent years is shown together with past population census years (1981, 1971, 1961 etc) and sometimes the mid-points between census years (1976 etc). Other years may be added if they represent a peak or trough in the series shown in the table.

Rounding of figures. In tables where figures have been rounded to the nearest final digit, there may be an apparent discrepancy between the sum of the constituent items and the total as shown.

Billion. This term is used to represent a thousand million.

Provisional and estimated data. Occasionally data for the latest years shown in the tables are provisional or estimated. To keep footnotes to a minimum, these have not been indicated; source departments will be able to advise if revised data are available.

Non-calendar years. Unless otherwise stated, the symbol - represents financial years (eg 1 April 1989 - 31 March 1990). In Chapter 3 the symbol / represents academic years (eg September 1989 / July 1990).

Italics. Figures are shown in italics when they represent percentages.

Symbols. The following symbols have been used throughout *Social Trends:*

    . .   *not available*   *not applicable*
    —   *negligible (less than half the final digit shown)*   0   *nil*

List of Tables and Charts

Numbers in brackets refer to similar items appearing in
Social Trends 21

Social Trends 22, © Crown copyright 1992

4: Employment

5: Income and Wealth

Social Trends 22, © Crown copyright 1992

Crime statistics: their use and misuse

Chris Lewis

Home Office

- Crime rate shows biggest fall since 1950s
  (Daily Telegraph 4 April 1989)

- Crime 'Challenge to civilisation'
  (Independent 4 May 1989, quoting Mrs Thatcher)

- Fear of crime 'Can cripple lives'
  (Independent June 1989)

- Call for more police as crime soars by 17.4 per cent
  (Daily Telegraph 27 March 1991)

- Crime rise linked to depth of recession
  (Daily Telegraph 28 March 1991)

- Crime total has doubled since 1979
  (Observer 15 September 1991)

Note

This article has been written on the law and crime recording systems in England and Wales. While there are important differences in both the legal systems and crime recording systems in Scotland and Northern Ireland, the general principles on the use and misuse of crime statistics also apply there.

Introduction

All official statistics are used by different groups for different purposes. Crime statistics are no exception. Authorities use the figures to inform, guide and justify their policies while critics use them in their attacks.

Commentators react to a rise in the figures by calling for more police or tougher penalties. Pressure groups use the figures to plead for greater resources for their special interests or for changes in the law. Statisticians try to explain that crime figures should not be interpreted in a simplistic way whilst growing groups of academics and leader writers rubbish the figures without having any clear alternatives to offer.

What are the public to make of all this? The problem is how to formulate crime figures in a way which is not misleading and informs and improves our understanding of crime. This article attempts to explain some of the uses and misuses of crime statistics and provide a basis for critically assessing claims made using them.

What is crime ?

In every society the state defines certain rules which should not be broken. Many rules are relatively minor, such as not parking one's car in a particular place. This article is not concerned with the statistics of such offences but with the more serious crimes against the person or against property. In most cases, eg murder, rape or robbery, it is well accepted that an incident is a crime, but the definitions also cover incidents which not all people consider serious, such as not paying income tax or vehicle licences.

Changes in society bring the need to devise new rules, for example, the large number of offences connected with the motor car or more recently the computer. Simple crimes such as theft turn up in more subtle forms: eg using electricity without paying, travelling without a ticket and taking money by means of computer.

Moreover, changes in the law redefine crime. The last generation has seen the end of crimes such as attempted suicide and most homosexual activity but introduced crimes concerned with environmental damage and keeping certain breeds of dog.

The definition of crime varies as society changes. The complexity of society tends to increase the huge range of activities labelled as crime. It is important to realise that the murders, assaults and robberies that the term conjures up in people's minds are a very small part of the total.

What the public knows about crime

The average citizen's personal experience of serious crime will be fairly limited. However, the Home Office British Crime Survey (BCS), which we shall consider in more detail later, tells us that in 1987 about one in three people experienced one or more of the offences covered in the survey. But people are also influenced by the experiences of friends, by contact with the judicial authorities, particularly the police, and by the way the media portrays crime. The media role is particularly important since it is ever present in most people's lives; so that if the information the media use is wrong or misinterpreted, then this could lead to misconceptions about crime and justice issues.

There is also a need for the media to treat crime in a balanced way. Thus, if Monday's news mentions briefly a 7 per cent fall in local crime because of a police initiative while Tuesday's papers are full of a gruesome murder in another part of the country, the retained image is likely to be the murder rather than the local reduction in crime.

The *true* amount of crime

True crime is a difficult concept. It represents the total amount of crime which takes place in the country whether or not it is recognised as crime and whether or not it is reported to and recorded by the police. The crime figures quoted in the media most often and those which form the basis of the headlines at the opening of this article do not show the amount of *true* crime. They are simply statistics of *recorded* crime: ie. crimes which have been reported to the police or discovered by them and which they regard as genuine. These figures are the most readily available and they form the basis of the regularly published statistics[1].

The relationship between *true* and *recorded* crime is complex; it is only in recent years that the BCS has enabled us to make estimates of this for certain crimes. If an event is to be recorded as a crime, the first thing that must usually happen is that someone (eg a witness or a victim) must consider that a crime has been committed. Secondly, the incident must be reported to the police. Thirdly, only if the police accept the report as genuine, and consider that a successful prosecution could in principle be brought is the incident counted in the official statistics. But sometimes information turns up at a later stage which shows that the police decision was wrong; eg the victim of a reported theft later finds the item. In such cases, where it is still practicable, the original incident is deleted from the statistics, but this may not always occur.

Steps involved in recording crime

Incident

Victim/witness judges incident to be a crime

Crime reported to the police

Crime recorded by the police

Crime counted

Further information showing incident was not a true crime

Crime deleted from count

What incidents are included in recorded crime

There are many thousands of possible offences ranging from murder to not paying one's TV licence. However, the expression *recorded* crime only includes particular types of offences, those defined as notifiable offences. Broadly speaking, these are the more serious offences. Thus, all theft, criminal damage, burglary, robbery, fraud and sexual and violent offences are notifiable; but illegal parking, minor assaults, speeding, licence evasion, prostitution, use of cannabis and drunkenness are not notifiable.

Because the nature of crime is continuously changing, the definition of what is and what is not a notifiable offence needs to be regularly reviewed. A balance has to be struck between including new types of offences and maintaining consistency in the statistical series. In the 1980s the series remained almost unchanged, with only drug trafficking, gross indecency with a child and a small number of public order offences being added in. Thus the observed changes in the recorded crime figures for the 1980s have been influenced very little by changes in definitions.

The value of victim surveys

The discussion so far could well lead the reader to ask:

> If statistics of *recorded* crime could be shown to be a poor guide to what has actually happened are there alternative measures of the *true* level of crime?

> Can we improve our understanding about what is going on by finding out why people do not report crime?

> Can we find out to what extent people are anxious about crime?

Good answers to these questions can be inferred from sample surveys in the community, usually known as victim surveys. During the 1980s our understanding of the recorded crime figures in England and Wales has been greatly helped by the results of the Home Office British Crime Survey (BCS), which has asked people about their experiences of crime in 1981, 1983 and 1987[2]. In particular the BCS has, for the first time, given us a measure which is independent of the processes designed to control crime.

The extent to which understanding of crime increased during the 1980s can be seen by looking at the articles by Glennie and Bruce in Social Trends 1976[3]. There were no victim survey results to add to the authors' understanding of recorded crime data.

Given that a victim survey such as the BCS can produce such useful insights why do we not concentrate entirely on victim surveys?

The first point to note is that while statistics of recorded crime have been available for over a hundred years only in the 1980s, with the availability of computers to facilitate analysis and the refinement of survey methodology, did victim surveys become practicable.

Secondly, statistics of recorded crime are a by-product of the administrative system run by the police for recording incidents reported to them. The cost of recorded crime statistics is probably no more than £100,000 a year; but the cost of one sweep of the BCS is considerably higher.

The fact that recorded crime statistics are obtained from an administrative system means that we have been able to obtain regular, consistent and timely series, with comparisons over time and across police forces. Victim surveys tend to give information only on a regional basis, cannot cover all notifiable crime, give limited information about trends and produce results a year after the crimes to which they refer.

Surveys also have various technical limitations: in particular because crime surveys question only a sample of the population results are subject to sampling error. And, for various reasons certain types of offence are not well reported: there is little doubt that BCS counts of sexual offences and domestic or non-stranger violence are underestimates[4]. Thus, the two sources are not alternatives but rather complement each other. Even when they are used together we do not obtain anything like a full picture of crime. Indeed, the situation has been likened to a dark stage with two spotlights which illuminate part of the action extremely well while other areas remain in semi-gloom.

Reporting crime

Having discussed the two main sources of crime data we can return to the steps involved in reporting crime. Putting together our two sources of statistics we can determine that the statistics of recorded crime often considerably underestimate the level of crime. This is simply because, for a variety of reasons, many offences are not reported to the police. Victim surveys show examples such as sexual offences, rape, domestic violence, theft from shops, fraud and drugs offences. For each type of offence covered the BCS gives estimates of the proportion of the true amount of crime which is reported and recorded.

Indeed the survey shows three fifths of all crimes recalled by respondents to the BCS in 1988 had not been reported to the police. However, some of the offences reported do not get recorded, or, if they are recorded, may be placed in different crime categories by the police. For example, the BCS estimates that the police record only about two thirds of property offences known to them.

The extent of reporting and recording varies considerably between offences (Chart A.1). Theft of a vehicle is very likely to be reported since the ownership of a recovered vehicle is easily discovered by the police. Offences against the person such as wounding are less well reported but a high proportion of these, although reported, are not recorded by the police. Theft and criminal damage are less likely to be reported than burglary.

A.1 Recorded and unrecorded crime: by type, 1987

England & Wales

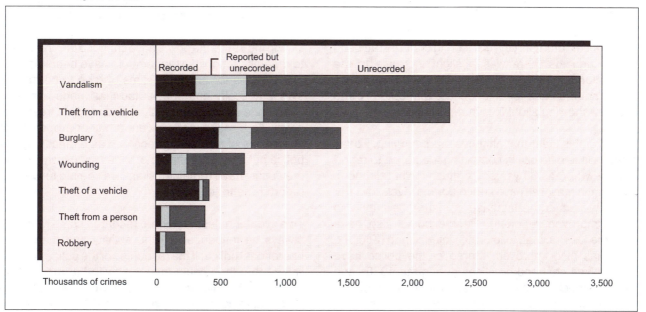

The main reason for not reporting crime in 1988 was that people thought it was too trivial or that there was little loss/damage (Chart A.2). However, one in three victims said that the police would not be interested or could do nothing. Examples here may be some burglaries and much domestic violence. About one in ten victims said they would deal with the matter themselves. An example here may be theft from shops, especially by very young people.

A.2 Unreported crime: by reason for not reporting[1], 1987

England & Wales

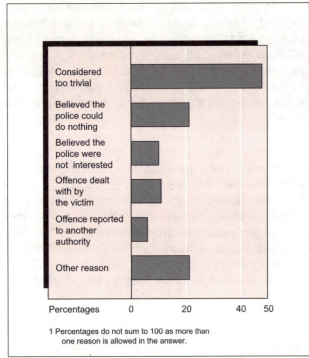

Percentages 0   20   40   50

1 Percentages do not sum to 100 as more than one reason is allowed in the answer.

The British Crime Survey, measuring crime in 1981 and 1987 suggests there was a slight increase in the proportion of offences reported (Chart A.3). However, this is not the case for all offences, with burglary and robbery showing slight falls in reporting.

However it is clear that attitudes are changing. Today there is little difficulty in contacting the police to report a crime whereas 30 years ago much lower telephone ownership may well have kept reporting levels low. For property crimes the increase in insurance may also have improved reporting. People could also have become less inclined to tolerate violence and reporting here has also improved. Moreover the police have themselves changed practices during the 1980s and are now much more likely to take reports of domestic violence or sexual abuse seriously and to record such incidents as crimes[5].

A.3 Percentage of crimes reported to the police: by type of offence, 1981 and 1987

England & Wales

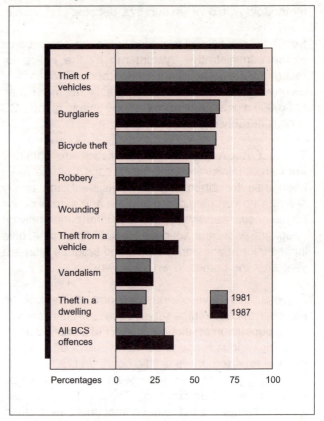

| | 1981 |
| | 1987 |

Percentages   0   25   50   75   100

The policing of crime

Most crimes are reported to the police and only a proportion are discovered by them. However, for certain kinds of offences, the activity of the police themselves can affect recorded crime rates. For example, the number of recorded crimes of rape has risen from 1,200 in 1980 to 3,300 in 1990. There is widespread acceptance that this considerably overstates the true rise in the number of offences of rape actually committed.

During the 1980s the police have changed their response to rape allegations: arrangements have been made in many forces for alleged victims of rape to be treated sympathetically and special facilities made available for interviews to be conducted, and medical treatment given. As a result, not only are a higher proportion of allegations of rape being recorded as offences by the police but a higher number of rape victims who would previously have remained silent are coming forward to report rape to the police.

To a greater or lesser degree recorded crime rates will always be influenced by the activity and number of operational police. If the resources of the police were so limited that they could only deal with the most major offences, it is likely that people would simply stop reporting minor incidents as they learned that nothing was being achieved by doing so.

At the other extreme, if the police force were increased dramatically there would be more resources to deal with behaviour which in other circumstances might not attract much attention. This would not mean that the actual crime rate had changed, even though the number of recorded crimes had increased. Although such extremes have not occurred; there was a considerable increase in police manpower durimg the 1980s which needs to be taken into account when considering the crime figures for England and Wales.

Changes in the way police deal with crime can therefore change the level of recorded crime without there being any change in the number of criminal incidents - though variations in reporting by the public are thought to have had a bigger impact in recent years.

Counting rules

Most criminal incidents are not clearcut events. A group of three men with knives might attack another group of five men at a bus-stop, injuring two of them, robbing all of them of ready cash and stealing all their credit cards which are passed on and used to buy goods. There is room for discussion as to how many offences have been committed. To cover such complexities and ensure consistency the Home Office issues *Counting Rules* to define how many crimes arising from such incidents are to be recorded.

Interpreting and understanding crime rates

As we have seen, recorded crime figures are affected by a number of factors. They can reflect real changes in crime levels but they are also shaped by people's willingness to report offences and by the behaviour of the police. Another important factor affecting the number of crimes recorded by the police is the size of the population and its age distribution.

Not surprisingly, a police force with a larger population living, working or visiting its area is likely to have more crime. For instance, one would expect there to be more crime in West Yorkshire than in West Sussex. Similarly one would expect the number of crimes in England and Wales to have increased simply because the population has increased or the proportion of young men has risen. Since males aged 15-25 are the most likely offenders and the number of such people is projected to fall over the 1990s a fall in the true level of crime is likely to come about because of this demographic change. However, this effect is small. It has been estimated, using projections of the population that the effect on recorded crime will be no more than one per

cent a year. Since improvements in reporting and recording are pushing up recorded crime by an average of 5 per cent a year, the demographic effect over the 1990s will probably be simply to mitigate a continuing upward trend. When making such comparisons it is thus much more meaningful to discuss crime figures in a standard way which relates them to size of population. Chart A.4 shows such crime rates for each police force in England and Wales.

Relative to resident population, the recorded crime rate was generally much higher in metropolitan than in non-metropolitan areas (11.4 and 7.6 per 100 population in 1990.) However, as the map shows there are exceptions. Nottinghamshire has always been near the top of the league table for recorded crime, although victim surveys have suggested levels of crime in adjacent counties were only slightly lower and that the high crime rates in Nottinghamshire could be largely attributed to distinctive recording practices of the local police[6].

A.4 Crimes recorded by the police: by police force area, 1990

England & Wales

Crimes recorded per 100 population

- 13.1 and over
- 10.1–13.0
- 7.1–10.0
- 7.0 and under

A.5 Homicide rate

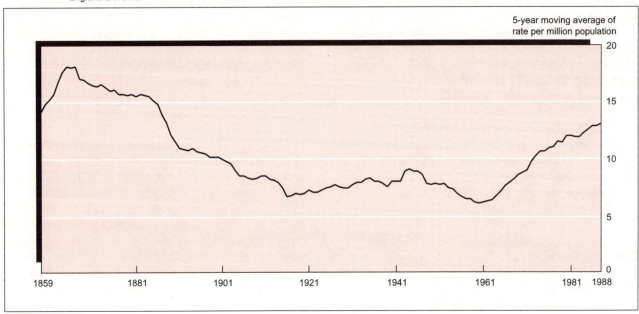

England & Wales

5-year moving average of
rate per million population

A further example of the use of crime rates is to compare the growth in the extent of crime over time. It is generally accepted that the police come to know about a very high proportion of homicides. Chart A.5 shows that the number of homicides recorded by the police as a proportion of the population was much lower in the 1980s than it had been in the 1880s. In fact the peak rate was reached in the late 1860s, followed by a long-term decline to under half the peak rate by 1920, a fairly static situation up to 1960 and a steady rise over the last 30 years. The advance in medical science will affect our interpretation of this trend: it is likely that more victims escape death in the 1980s because of medical intervention - though conversely, advances in forensic science may have lead to more crime being detected.

A.6 Burglaries recorded by the police

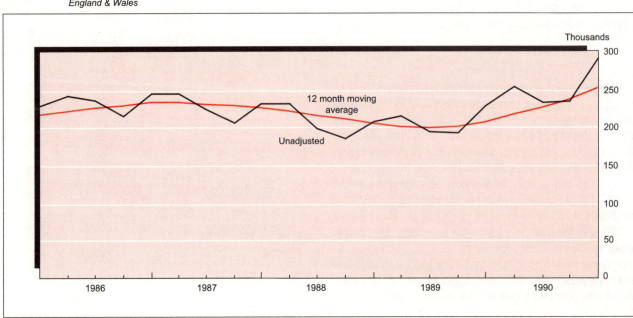

England & Wales

Thousands

12 month moving average

Unadjusted

Analysing crime trends

Even when recorded offences provide a reliable picture of the incidence of crime we must be careful in assessing crime trends over short periods because of frequent short-term fluctuations of unknown cause. No one expects that rapes or robberies occur at exactly the same rate every year and so a change might be part of a trend or simply a random variation.

Much of the variation in recorded crime is seasonal. Criminal activity varies according to the weather, hours of light, the chances of people being away on holiday etc. Thus in order to make comparisons over time we need to make an adjustment to the raw recorded crime figures to allow for seasonal variation. Many such adjustments are possible but the variation easiest to explain is the average number of offences which have been recorded during the last 12 months. Since each season is covered the seasonal effect can thus be removed from any comparisons. For example, the short term fluctuations in the quarterly figures in Chart A.6 can be misleading: eg. the falls in recorded burglaries from the first to the second quarters of 1989 and 1990 were purely seasonal effects. The chart also shows the 12-monthly moving average, which does not mislead.

A.7 Residential burglaries involving loss

England & Wales

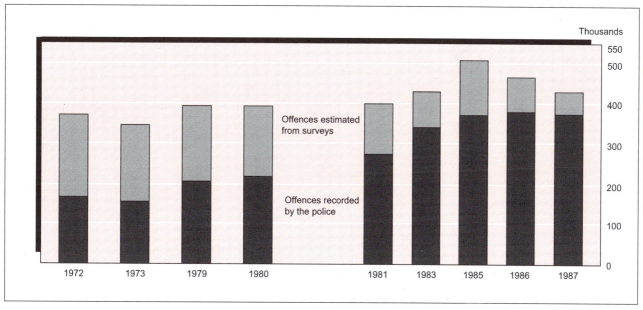

The vast majority of recorded offences are property crimes and many of these concern property of low value which has been damaged or stolen. The suggestion is made from time to time that incidents involving property of value less than a specified cut-off point are too trivial to be counted as crimes. In general this idea has been resisted because to introduce a cut-off point would require that point to be revalued each year with the rise in prices to avoid artificial growth. On the occasions where there is a cut-off point; eg. when criminal damage is quoted as 'being over £20', the trend in such figures can be misleading unless inflation is taken into account.

Longer term trends in recorded crimes can also be misleading because of changes in reporting systems. Since 1972 the General Household Survey has included a question on burglary with loss. Putting the GHS results with later BCS figures allows a long-term comparison to be made with recorded offences. Chart A.7 shows the result.

BCS estimates of the number of burglaries rose by 17 per cent over the 15-year period 1972-1987 while recorded offences rose by 127 per cent, nearly 8 times more. Increased reporting helps to explain this, partly driven by changing patterns of insurance. In only 19 per cent of burglary incidents was property stolen covered by insurance in 1972, whereas the figure was 58 per cent in 1987. The police also record a higher proportion of offences reported to them, partly because of increased manpower, standardised recording practices and computerisation. The best estimate is that 45 per cent of burglaries committed ended up as recorded offences in 1972 but by 1987 the figure was 73 per cent.

Abuse of crime statistics

Commentators on crime statistics occasionally use completely misleading methods of presentation. For example, a national newspaper used the following graph above the heading 'Death Toll: how the murder figures have soared'.

By starting the graph at 600 and finishing at 680 and without showing any years in between they have produced a totally alarming picture. A more balanced form of presentation would be Chart A.8, looking at homicides related to population. This could have been entitled 'Death Toll: how the homicide rate may be inching up'.

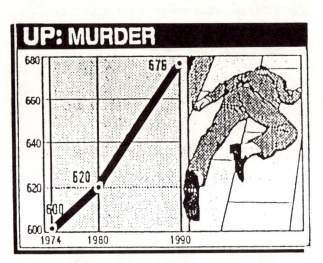

DEATH TOLL: How the murder figures have soared

A.8 Homicides

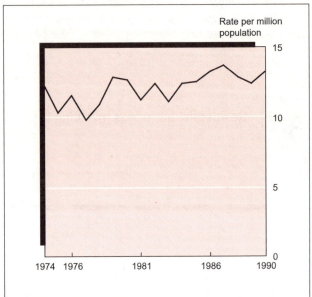

England & Wales

Crime and economic trends

The relationship between crime levels and population has been mentioned but there is also a criminological theory that crime may have economic causes. In this theory wealth in society is thought to represent both an incentive and a disincentive to property crime. It is an incentive in that, with wealth, there are more goods to steal, and a disincentive in that wealthy people have less need to steal. The most recent study on these lines is the work of Simon Field of the Home Office Research and Planning Unit and his first results were published in 1990[7].

The work indicates that the relationship between crime and the state of the economy is a very complex one. Over short periods there has been a very close relationship between changes in the growth of consumption rates (the annual growth of real personal consumption per head) and changes in the growth of recorded crime rates. Property crime has increased more quickly when the rate of increase in personal consumption has slowed: it increased slowly or even decreased (as in 1988) when personal consumption increased more rapidly. There was no clearcut evidence that unemployment and property crime were related on a national level.

Personal crime (violence against the person and sexual offences) increased more quickly when personal consumption increased rapidly and increased more slowly or declined when the growth in personal consumption slowed. There was also a very strong relationship between changes in the consumption of beer and changes in the rate of crimes of violence against the person.

This analysis included data up to 1988. Since that time the growth in personal consumption has declined and as predicted property crime has risen quickly and personal crime has either increased more slowly or actually declined.

Dr Field's work says little about the long-term increase in recorded crime. Although it seems common sense that the greater opportunity to commit crime (because a lot more goods are in general circulation) has an influence on the long-term growth there is little hard statistical evidence to support this.

Presentation of crime statistics

This article contains very few actual statistical series on crime but the figures are very easy to find. Chapter 12 of this issue of Social Trends gives the trends in recorded crime up to the middle of 1991 together with some results from the 1988 BCS. Further figures can be found in the short 80-page digest of statistics on crime and the justice system published by the Home Office in 1991 and to be updated in 1992[8].

More detail is given in the reports of each British Crime Survey. A video of the 1988 survey has recently been made. (For details contact Mrs P Mayhew of the Home Office Research and Planning Unit)

Finally, the annual volumes of *Criminal Statistics, England and Wales*, give much more detail in Chapters 2 to 4 on crimes recorded by the police and, in recent years, some discussion on the relation of these figures to BCS figures. A supplementary volume gives detail for each police force area[1,9].

International comparisons

The problems of data collection are common to all countries, although different methods have been used to produce crime estimates. Nearly all countries take advantage of their police administrative systems to collect the equivalent of recorded crime data but not all countries have as tight a centralised control of reporting standards as we do. Some countries have problems in putting together police figures from different areas to produce consistent national figures: others, such as the USA, concentrate police recording on the most serious half a dozen or so types of offence.

Only the USA has an ongoing crime survey which gives a regular series of crime estimates from the victim's point of view. Other countries, such as Canada and the Netherlands have crime surveys from time to time which they use to complement their police statistics in the same way as we do.

Comparisons with other countries are very difficult. Except for offences such as homicide it makes little sense to compare recorded crime figures for different countries, even after allowing for differing population. Firstly, the laws will be different and even when the laws are broadly equivalent the definition of what seems to be the same offence, may well differ from one country to another. The police procedures in recording and the counting rules will almost certainly vary even if national

guidelines exist at all while the propensity of people to report crime to the police will vary from country to country. After all, comparisons between England and Wales and Scotland are difficult.

Comparison of victim surveys might in principle be thought likely to yield more sensible results but in practice differences in survey methods and question format upset easy comparisons and by no means all countries have conducted national surveys in any case. A new technique has recently been tried, of conducting victim surveys by telephone at the same time in several countries with the same questions being asked. These results are likely to be more comparable. Chart A.9 shows that fewer than one in five of the population of England and Wales were the victims of one or more crimes in 1988 as measured by the International Telephone survey (ITS)[10].

A.9 Victims of one or more crimes: international comparison, 1988

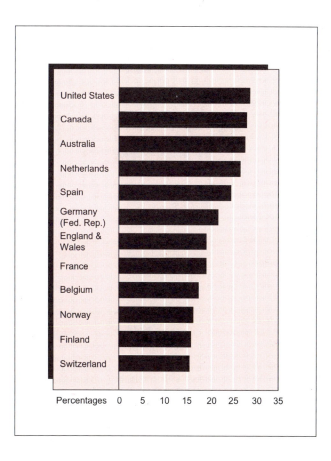

The position is very different if we consider different types of offence (Chart A.10). The ITS showed England and Wales as being the country with the lowest rate of non-sexual assault, at barely one half of one per cent compared with over 3 per cent in Australia and about 2.5 per cent in the USA. However, for those who reported they had been the victim of a car theft in 1988 the differences are reduced with the figure for England and Wales, at nearly 2 per cent being closer to those in Australia, France and the USA where the figure was just over 2 per cent.

A.10 Victims of assaults and car thefts: international comparison, 1988

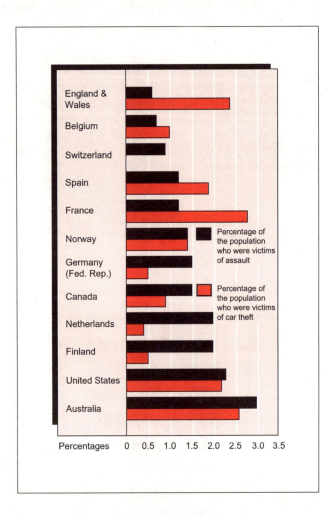

There is no doubt that, because of the relative cheapness of recorded crime statistics, they will continue to be collected and published as the measure of the amount of crime with which the police are faced. It is highly likely that these figures will continue to show upward growth as people increase their rate of reporting criminal incidents to the police. It is also likely that the growing complexity of life, especially the growing use of computers will lead to a growth in the numbers of crimes analogous with the numbers of offences (mostly not notifiable) associated with the spread of the use of the motor-car from the 1930s to the present day. In particular the number of ways of depriving other people or institutions of some form of money or property will probably continue to grow. For many of these types of offence, which could perhaps be broadly categorised as fraud a simple count of the number of offences may not be relevant and the loss, or potential loss, in money terms, might have to be substituted.

The most likely improvement in crime statistics, in statistical terms, is the growing reliance on the detail that police record on their computers as distinct from simple counts of how many crimes have been recorded.

Once police forces are using standard computer systems, with common technical and data standards, the potential exists for this information to be available on a general network for use generally within the criminal justice system: for operational and investigative use by the police, for criminal justice use by the prosecution service, the courts and the prisons, but also for statistical and research use by all agencies, not only to measure trends in known crime but to isolate patterns in crime, both locally and nationally, which can lead to better crime prevention measures, changes to the social environment and new measures of dealing with offenders.

Future developments

The last ten years have seen considerable developments in the measurement of crime both in this country and throughout the world. The rapid progress in the use of victim surveys has been noted, both at home and abroad. Victim surveys will probably become more used in the future depending on the availability of resources.

The next BCS will be held in 1992, relating to crime experienced in 1991. Thereafter the survey is to be put on a more regular footing, with at least three-yearly repeats and possibly an increased sample size. A repeat of the International Crime Survey is probable in 1992. Various countries which did not take part in the initial round have expressed interest, although not all previous participants are likely to be able to afford to conduct a repeat.

Conclusions

Reports of crime figures, though useful, should always be regarded critically. The relationship between the level of recorded crime and the level of real crime is influenced by community attitudes, levels of policing, legislative change and the statistical definitions used. The relationships between these factors are complex and changing. The one thing that can be said is that police recorded crime statistics *do not* provide a simple picture of trends in crime. Despite all this, statistics on recorded crimes, together with the results from the British Crime Surveys remain the only regular basis on which we can infer crime trends. If they can be analysed with all the considerations discussed here kept in mind, they can yield valuable insights into crime trends and the demands on police and criminal justice resources. If, however, they are analysed carelessly they simply foster uninformed public debate.

NOTES

---

1   *Criminal Statistics, England and Wales*. Cmnd 1322. HMSO, 1990. The latest in an annual series dating back to the 19th century. *Notifiable Offences Recorded by the Police in England and Wales April 1990 - March 1991*. Home Office, 1991. The latest in a series of quarterly statistical bulletins dating back to the late 1970s.

2   Hough, M. and Mayhew, P. *The British Crime Survey: first report*. Home Office Research Study No. 76. HMSO, 1983. Hough, M. and Mayhew, P. *Taking Account of Crime: findings from the second British Crime Survey*. Home Office Research Study No. 85. HMSO, 1985.

3. Glennie, C. Crime in England and Wales, *Social Trends No.7*. HMSO, 1976. Bruce, D. Crime In Scotland, *Social Trends No.7*. HMSO, 1976.

4   Mayhew, P. Elliott, D. and Dowds, L. *The 1988 British Crime Survey*. Home Office Research Study No. 111. HMSO.

5   Smith, L.J. *Concerns about Rape*. Home Office Research Study No. 106. HMSO, 1989. Smith L.J. *Domestic Violence*. Home Office Research Study No. 107. HMSO, 1989.

6   Farrington, D.P. and Dowds, E.A. *Disentangling criminal behaviour and police reaction*. In Farrington, D.P. and Gunn, J. (Eds) *Reaction to crime: the public, the police, courts and prisons*. John Wiley, 1987.

7   Field, S. *Trends in crime and their interpretation: a study of recorded crime in post-war England and Wales*. Home Office Research Study No. 119. HMSO, 1990.

8   Barclay, G. (ed.) *A Digest of information on the Criminal Justice System. Crime and Justice in England and Wales*. Home Office, 1991.

9   Table S3.1 of Supplementary Volume 3 of *Criminal Statistics, England and Wales*. Home Office, 1990. The latest in an annual series dating back to 1982.

10 Van Dijk, J., Mayhew, P. and Killias M. *Experiences of Crime across the world, Key findings of the 1989 International Crime Survey*, Kluwer, 1990.

Population Trends

Population Trends is the journal of the Office of Population Censuses and Surveys. It is published four times a year in March, June, September and December. In addition to bringing together articles on a variety of population and medical topics, Population Trends contains regular series of tables on a range of subjects for which OPCS is responsible.

These include

* **Population**	* **Vital statistics**
* **Live births**	* **Expectation of life**
* **Deaths**	* **Abortions**
* **International migration**	* **Internal migration**
* **Marriage**	* **Divorce**

Population Trends is available from HMSO Bookshops or accredited agents, or from HMSO Publications Centre, telephone 071 873 9090

* Annual subscription £28.00 (including postage)

* Single issues £ 7.25 net

Chapter 1: Population

Population structure and changes

- By the year 2030 it is projected that there will be more deaths than births, so the United Kingdom will have a natural decrease in population for the first time since 1976. *(Table 1.3)*

- The elderly account for an ever-increasing proportion of the population. *(Table 1.5)*

- The white population is much older than the ethnic minority population. One in five of the White population is aged over 60, compared with only one in twenty of the ethnic minority population. *(Table 1.8)*

- Britons are mobile. During 1989, over one million people moved to live in a different region of the country. *(Table 1.11)*

Births and deaths

- Flu is still a killer disease. At the height of the flu epidemic just before Christmas 1989, the number of deaths (over 21.5 thousand) was the highest recorded weekly figure since the peak of the 1969 epidemic. *(Chart 1.16)*

Migration

- Applications for asylum in the United Kingdom have increased very rapidly. The increase is particularly marked for applicants from African and South Asian countries. Only one quarter of total cases processed were found to have a well-founded fear of persecution. *(Chart 1.18)*

International comparisons

- The world's population continues to grow at an ever faster rate. It took over a century for the population to grow from one billion to two billion, but it is now growing by almost one billion per decade. *(Page 36)*

- The United Kingdom is one of the most densely populated countries in the EC, exceeded by only Belgium and the Netherlands, although taking England alone it is more densely populated still. *(Table 1.22)*

1.1 Births and deaths

United Kingdom

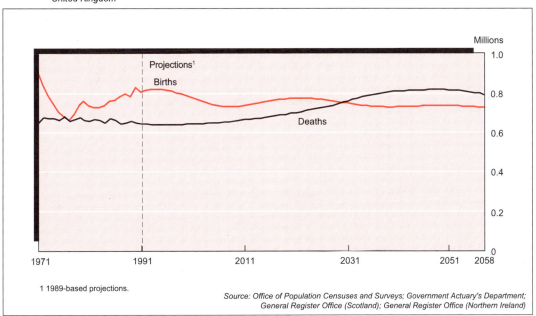

1 1989-based projections.

Source: Office of Population Censuses and Surveys; Government Actuary's Department; General Register Office (Scotland); General Register Office (Northern Ireland)

Population structure and changes

Chart 1.1 shows that the number of births in the United Kingdom is projected to peak at around 810 thousand in 1994. Thereafter the annual number of births is projected to fall as the large generation born in the 1960s passes the peak of their child bearing age. The number of deaths is projected to remain at about 650 thousand a year for the next 20 years. After around 2011 deaths will increase because the larger generations born after World War II will be approaching old age.

The annual number of births is projected to remain higher than the number of deaths over the next 40 years leading to a natural increase in population. However, it is projected that around the year 2030, deaths will start to exceed births, meaning a natural decrease in population. If the long-term assumption that the same number of people leave the country as enter it also holds, the population of the United Kingdom would then start to fall.

The latest Census of population was held on 21 April 1991. The provisional count of the population present in the United Kingdom on Census night was 55.5 million, around 0.3 per cent less than the 1981 Census (Table 1.2). This provisional figure is likely to be subject to an upward revision when the final census count is published, suggesting some growth between the two censuses.

Population increases by births and by people moving to live in the country and decreases by deaths and by people moving to live outside the country. Table 1.3

1.2 Population at each Census

Thousands

	1951	1961	1971	1981[1]	1991[2]
England	41,159	43,461	46,018	46,221	46,170
Wales	2,599	2,644	2,731	2,790	2,798
Scotland	5,096	5,179	5,229	5,117	4,957
Great Britain	48,854	51,284	53,979	54,129	53,925
Northern Ireland	1,371	1,425	1,536	1,532	1,583
United Kingdom	50,225	52,709	55,515	55,661	55,508

1 Including estimate of non-enumeration.
2 Preliminary figures based on enumerator returns. Changes between figures from successive censuses arise partly from variations in under-enumeration.

Source: Office of Population Censuses and Surveys;
General Register Office (Scotland);
General Register Office (Northern Ireland)

shows how these different factors - births, deaths and migration - changed between 1901 and 1990 and how they are projected to change up to the year 2025. Between 1989 and 1990 the population is estimated to have increased by 174 thousand; this was similar to the average annual increase between 1984 and 1989. The total United Kingdom population is projected to increase to slightly over 59 million by 2001 and to almost 61 million by 2025. It should be noted that these projections depend on a number of assumptions, for example, about future birth rates which can be very difficult to predict accurately.

1.3 Population change: actual and projected[1]

United Kingdom

Thousands

	Population at start of period	Average annual change					
		Live births	Deaths	Net natural change	Net civilian migration	Other adjustments[2]	Overall annual change
Census enumerated							
1901-1911	38,237	1,091	624	467	−82	.	385
1911-1921	42,082	975	689	286	−92	.	194
1921-1931	44,027	824	555	268	−67	.	201
1931-1951	46,038	785	598	188	25	.	213
Mid-year estimates							
1951-1961	50,290	839	593	246	−9	15	252
1961-1971	52,807	963	639	324	−32	20	312
1971-1981	55,928	736	666	69	−44	17	42
1981-1989	56,352	749	655	94	14	3	111
1989-1990	57,236	782	664	118	47	9	174
Projections[3]							
1991-1996	57,561	810	639	170		0	170
1996-2001	58,413	790	638	152		0	152
2001-2006	59,174	747	645	102		0	102
2006-2011	59,681	725	655	70		0	70
2011-2016	60,033	740	670	69		0	69
2016-2025	60,379	763	697	66		0	66

1 See Appendix, Part 1: Population and population projections.
2 Changes in numbers of armed forces plus adjustments to reconcile differences between estimated population change and the figures for natural change and net civilian migration.

3 1989-based projections.

Source: Office of Population Censuses and Surveys;
General Register Office (Scotland); General Register
Office (Northern Ireland); Government Actuary's Department

1.4 Population: by selected age bands

United Kingdom

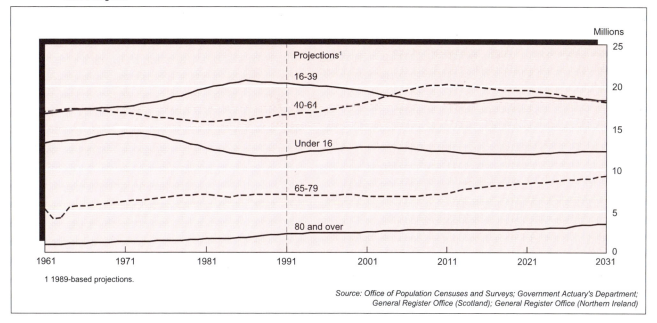

Millions

Projections[1]

16-39

40-64

Under 16

65-79

80 and over

1961   1971   1981   1991   2001   2011   2021   2031

1 1989-based projections.

Source: Office of Population Censuses and Surveys; Government Actuary's Department; General Register Office (Scotland); General Register Office (Northern Ireland)

The elderly will form an increasing proportion of the United Kingdom population over the next 40 years (Chart 1.4). By the year 2031 those aged 80 and over are projected to number 3.4 million - over 60 per cent more than in 1990 and 3.5 times more than in 1961. Although the population aged under 16 has fallen quite sharply during the last 20 years (from 13.1 million to 11.6 million) it is projected to rise steadily during the 1990s to reach a peak of about 12.6 million early in the next century. There are more young men than young women, but more elderly women than elderly men (Table 1.5). In 1990 there were nearly 1.4 million more females than males. By 2025 it is expected that the excess of females over males will have narrowed to 0.6 million, mainly due to changing age structures of the population.

1.5 Age and sex structure of the population[1]

United Kingdom

Millions

	Under 16	16 – 39	40 – 64	65 – 79	80 and over	All ages
Mid-year estimates						
1951	. .	. .	15.9	4.8	0.7	50.3
1961	13.1	16.6	16.9	5.2	1.0	52.8
1971	14.3	17.5	16.7	6.1	1.3	55.9
1981	12.5	19.7	15.7	6.9	1.6	56.4
1986	11.7	20.6	15.8	6.8	1.8	56.8
1990	11.6	20.3	16.5	6.9	2.1	57.4
Males	6.0	10.3	8.2	3.0	0.6	28.0
Females	5.7	10.0	8.3	3.9	1.5	29.4
Mid-year projections[2]						
1991	11.7	20.3	16.5	6.9	2.2	57.6
1996	12.3	19.9	17.1	6.8	2.4	58.4
2001	12.6	19.3	18.1	6.7	2.5	59.2
2006	12.5	18.4	19.5	6.7	2.6	59.7
2011	12.1	18.0	20.2	7.0	2.7	60.0
2025	12.0	18.5	19.0	8.6	2.9	61.0
Males	6.1	9.5	9.5	4.0	1.1	30.2
Females	5.8	9.1	9.5	4.6	1.8	30.8

1 See Appendix, Part 1: Population and population projections.
2 1989-based projections.

Source: Office of Population Censuses and Surveys; General Register Office (Scotland); General Register Office (Northern Ireland); Government Actuary's Department

1.6 Population aged 16-19

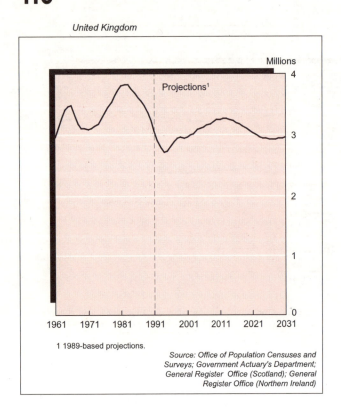

United Kingdom

Projections[1]

1 1989-based projections.

Source: Office of Population Censuses and
Surveys; Government Actuary's Department;
General Register Office (Scotland); General
Register Office (Northern Ireland)

1.7 Population of pensionable age[1]

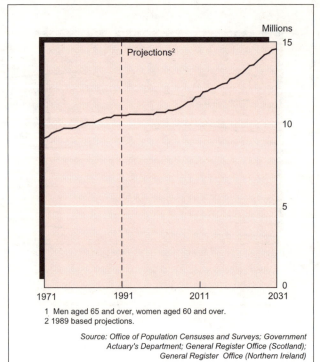

United Kingdom

Projections[2]

1 Men aged 65 and over, women aged 60 and over.
2 1989 based projections.

Source: Office of Population Censuses and Surveys; Government
Actuary's Department; General Register Office (Scotland);
General Register Office (Northern Ireland)

Population changes in the age group 16 to 19 are shown in Chart 1.6 and illustrate the projected increase in the size of this section of the population from the mid-1990s. This is attributable to previous trends in the number of births. Thus the peak in the number of 16 to 19 year olds reached in the early 1980s reflects the high number of births in the mid-1960s. These projected changes will have an effect on the flow of young persons into higher education and into the work force and could lead to consequent problems as the labour market will need to adjust. An influx of a large number of young persons can lead to high youth unemployment while a scarcity of school leavers may result in increased economic activity amongst older persons and married women.

Chart 1.7 illustrates how the population of pensionable age (men aged 65 and over and women aged 60 and over) has risen since 1971 and how it is projected to increase over the next 40 years. In 1990 there were 10.5 million people in this category - a rise of over 1 million since 1971. Numbers are expected to reach over 14.5 million by 2031 - a rise of nearly 40 per cent on the 1990 figure.

1.8 Population: by age and ethnic group, 1987-1989

Great Britain

Percentages and thousands

	Age group (percentages)					All ages (= 100%) (thousands)
	0 – 15	16 – 29	30 – 44	45 – 59	60 and over	
Ethnic group						
West Indian or Guyanese	24	32	17	21	8	482
Indian	30	26	24	15	5	779
Pakistani	45	23	19	10	2	433
Bangladeshi	47	25	14	12	2	112
Chinese	28	26	31	11	4	132
African	30	29	28	10	2	127
Arab	24	31	30	11	4	72
Mixed	53	25	12	6	4	284
Other	27	28	28	10	6	149
All ethnic minority groups	34	27	21	13	5	2,569
White	19	22	21	17	21	51,600
Not stated	29	24	17	13	18	498
All ethnic groups[1]	20	22	21	16	21	54,666

1 Including White and Not Stated.

Source: Labour Force Survey, Office of Population Censuses and Surveys

Social Trends 22, © Crown copyright 1992

1.9 Ethnic minority population: by age and whether UK - born or overseas - born, 1987-1989

Great Britain

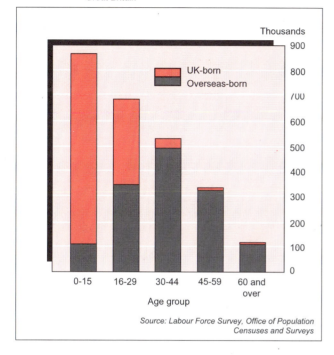

Source: Labour Force Survey, Office of Population Censuses and Surveys

1.10 Population growth: by region, mid 1981-1990

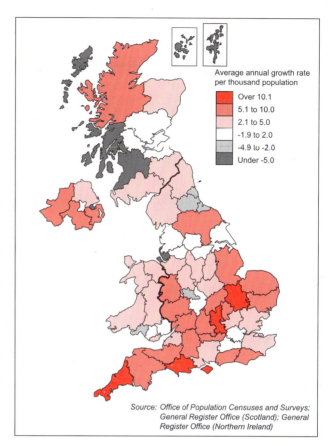

Average annual growth rate per thousand population

- Over 10.1
- 5.1 to 10.0
- 2.1 to 5.0
- -1.9 to 2.0
- -4.9 to -2.0
- Under -5.0

Source: Office of Population Censuses and Surveys; General Register Office (Scotland); General Register Office (Northern Ireland)

The age structure of the population is an important factor in population change over time and it is important to note that most of the ethnic minority groups have markedly different age structures from that of the White population (Table 1.8). In the late 1980s, one in five of the White population was aged 60 or over compared with only one in twenty of the ethnic minority population. Correspondingly those aged under 16 formed a smaller proportion of the White population than they did of the ethnic minority populations - one in five compared with one in three for the ethnic minority groups.

Individuals in the ethnic minority population can of course have been born in the United Kingdom or have been born overseas. Chart 1.9 illustrates the marked difference in age structure between these two groups of the ethnic minority population. Most of the overseas-born group arrived as young adults, or as dependants while those born within the United Kingdom are the descendants of these earlier immigrants. Not surprisingly, this means that the ethnic minority population born in the United Kingdom tends to be a young population: two-thirds are aged under 16 and only one in twenty is aged over 29. In contrast, only 8 per cent of the overseas-born population are aged under 16 while over two-thirds are aged over 29.

Chart 1.10 shows how population is changing in the different parts of the United Kingdom. The counties that are shaded red on the chart are those with increasing populations while those shaded grey have falling populations. The counties with the fastest growing populations were Buckinghamshire and Cambridgeshire at 1.3 per cent per annum between 1981 and 1990.

Belfast and the Islands of Scotland experienced the largest fall in population (both 0.7 per cent per annum). Generally, the chart confirms a movement from metropolitan to non-metropolitan areas. The fastest growing counties tend to be non-metropolitan ones and those with falling populations are metropolitan or the more urban non-metropolitan counties.

Births and deaths are estimated accurately because there is a system of registration. The other factor in shifting population patterns, migration - that is people moving from one region to another or to/from abroad - is much more difficult to estimate. Table 1.11 shows movement of doctors' patients between Family Health Services Authorities (FHSAs) within England and Wales and Area Health Boards (AHBs) within Scotland to estimate internal migration patterns in the United Kingdom. Over 1 million people moved to live in a different region of the United Kingdom during 1989. The South East region had a net loss of 41 thousand people to other parts of the United Kingdom with 292 thousand leaving the region compared with 251 thousand moving to live in it. The most notable change in 1989 was net migration between Scotland and the rest of the United Kingdom which showed a net gain to Scotland of 6 thousand, compared with losses of 14 thousand in each of the previous two years. The net outflow from the South East and the net inflow to Scotland in 1989 may, however prove to be untypical of the early 1990s. More detailed information on the regional variations within the United Kingdom can be found in the CSO publication *Regional Trends*. A further analysis is also made in the article *Movement* *within England and Wales during the 1980s, as measured by the NHS Central Register* from the OPCS publication *Population Trends No 65*.

1.11 Migration[1] within the UK: inter-area movements, 1989

Thousands

	United Kingdom	North	York- shire & Humber- side	East Mid- lands	East Anglia	South East	South West	West Mid- lands	North West	Eng- land	Wales	Scotland	Northern Ireland
						Area of origin							
Area of destination													
United Kingdom	.	55	90	88	52	292	106	96	106	131	51	59	16
North	54	.	10	4	2	16	3	4	8	47	1	6	1
Yorkshire & Humberside	95	10	.	15	4	28	7	8	15	86	3	5	1
East Midlands	95	4	15	.	7	35	7	12	9	88	3	4	1
East Anglia	59	2	4	6	.	32	4	3	3	54	1	3	—
South East	251	17	25	26	23	.	50	29	33	203	17	24	7
South West	128	3	6	7	4	71	.	14	9	114	8	5	1
West Midlands	85	3	7	10	3	29	11	.	11	74	7	3	1
North West	103	8	15	9	3	32	8	12	.	87	8	6	2
England	118	47	81	79	46	242	89	82	87	.	48	56	13
Wales	63	1	3	3	2	22	10	9	10	61	.	2	—
Scotland	65	6	6	5	3	24	6	4	7	62	2	.	2
Northern Ireland	10	—	1	1	—	4	1	1	1	9	—	1	.

1 Data are based on patient movements recorded by the National Health Service Central Registers at Southport and Edinburgh and the Common Services Agency in Belfast.

Source: Office of Population Censuses and Surveys; General Register Office (Scotland); General Register Office (Northern Ireland)

Births and deaths

Table 1.12 shows that births to mothers born outside the United Kingdom fell from 12.2 per cent of all live births in 1981 to 11.0 per cent in 1990. Of all births to women born outside the United Kingdom in 1990, 60 per cent were to women born in the New Commonwealth and Pakistan (NCWP), a rise of 10 percentage points since 1971. In the text accompanying Table 1.8 the point was made that the ethnic minority populations have markedly different age structures to that of the White population. The trends in birth rates partly reflect these differences. It is important to remember, however, that ethnic group does not necessarily equate with birthplace of mother.

In particular, there are an increasing number of women from the ethnic minorities in the younger childbearing ages who were themselves born in this country and births to such women would be included in those to mothers born in the United Kingdom. Conversely, some women, although born in countries of the NCWP, are not of ethnic minority descent. Analysis of the question on ethnicity in the 1991 Census will provide a better estimate of the fertility of ethnic groups.

1.12 Live births: by country of birth of mother

Great Britain — Thousands and percentages

Area/country of birth of mother	Live births (thousands)			
	1971	1981	1989	1990
United Kingdom	777.3	617.3	667.7	686.9
Percentage of all live births	*88.9*	*87.7*	*88.9*	*89.0*
Outside United Kingdom				
Irish Republic	22.5	8.6	6.8	6.6
Old Commonwealth	2.7	2.6	3.0	3.3
New Commonwealth and Pakistan				
India	13.7	12.6	9.0	8.7
Pakistan and Bangladesh	8.5	17.0	17.9	18.5
Caribbean	12.6	6.3	4.1	3.8
East Africa	2.2	6.7	6.9	6.7
Rest of Africa	3.0	3.6	4.8	5.1
Other New Commonwealth	6.2	8.4	8.3	8.3
Total New Commonwealth and Pakistan	46.2	54.6	50.9	51.2
Other European Community	20.4	6.1	7.8	8.0
Rest of the world		14.1	15.0	16.0
Total with mother born outside United Kingdom	91.8	86.0	83.4	85.1
Not stated	4.8	0.2	0.1	0.0
Total live births	869.9	703.5	751.2	772.1

Source: Office of Population Censuses and Surveys; General Register Office (Scotland)

There were nearly 800 thousand live births in the United Kingdom in 1990 (Table 1.13), 22 per cent more than the trough in 1977 but over 21 per cent fewer than the post-1950 peak year for births in 1964. These changes are reflected in the three most widely used measures of fertility: the crude birth rate (CBR), the general fertility rate (GFR) and the total period fertility rate (TPFR). In 1990 the TPFR, which is independent of the number and age structure of the female population of childbearing age, was 1.84 births per woman - 9 per cent more than the trough in 1977 and 4 per cent less than the 1964 peak rate.

Overall fertility rates fell between 1971 and 1981 in England and Wales, and have since remained stable. However, rates for overseas-born women have in general continued to fall since 1981 (Table 1.14). The total period fertility rate for women born in India almost halved between 1971 and 1990 to stand at 2.2. A similar decrease occurred over the same period for women born in Pakistan and Bangladesh, although in 1990, the rate was over twice that for women born in India. The total period fertility rate for all women born in the New Commonwealth and Pakistan fell from 3.8 in 1971 to 2.9 in 1986 and to 2.6 in 1990.

The percentage of births outside marriage has increased dramatically since 1971, and there were large variations in 1990 according to the mothers' country of birth. In 1990, 28 per cent of all live births were outside marriage, this had increased from only 8 per cent in 1971. Figures ranged, in 1990, from only 1 per cent of births to mothers born in Pakistan and Bangladesh to 48 per cent of births to mothers born in the Caribbean. The percentage for mothers born in the Caribbean had actually fallen slightly between 1981 and 1990. Chapter 2 contains further details on births outside marriage.

1.13 Live births and age of mother

United Kingdom

	Total live births (thousands)	Crude birth rate[1]	General fertility rate[2]	Total period fertility rate[3]	Mean age of mother at birth (years)
1951	797	15.9	73.0	2.15	28.4
1956	825	16.1	78.8	2.36	28.0
1961	944	17.9	90.6	2.80	27.7
1964	1,015	18.8	94.1	2.95	27.3
1966	980	17.9	91.5	2.79	26.9
1971	902	16.1	84.3	2.41	26.2
1976	676	12.0	61.3	1.74	26.4
1977	657	11.7	58.9	1.69	26.5
1981	731	13.0	62.1	1.81	26.8
1986	755	13.3	61.1	1.78	27.0
1987	776	13.6	62.3	1.82	27.1
1988	788	13.8	63.2	1.84	27.2
1989	777	13.6	62.4	1.81	27.3
1990	799	13.9	64.2	1.84	27.5
Projections[4]					
1991	800	13.9	64.5	1.84	27.6
2001	769	13.0	64.6	1.99	28.6
2011	728	12.1	64.1	2.00	27.8
2025	763	12.5	68.3	2.00	28.1

1 Total births per 1,000 population of all ages.
2 Total births per 1,000 women aged 15-44. Also includes births to mothers aged under 15 and 45 and over.
3 The average number of children which would be born per woman if women experienced the age-specific fertility rates of the period in question throughout their child-bearing life span.
4 1989-based projections.

*Source: Office of Population Censuses and Surveys;
General Register Office (Scotland);
General General Office (Northern Ireland);
Government Actuary's Department*

1.14 Fertility rates and births outside marriage: by country of birth of mother

England & Wales   Rates and percentages

Area/country of birth of mother	Estimated total period fertility rates					Percentage of live births outside marriage				
	1971	1981	1986	1989	1990	1971	1981	1986	1989	1990
United Kingdom	2.3	1.7	1.7	1.8	1.8	*8.1*	*13.4*	*22.9*	*28.9*	*30.3*
New Commonwealth and Pakistan										
India	4.1	3.1	2.9	2.4	2.2	*1.7*	*1.2*	*1.7*	*2.1*	*2.4*
Pakistan and Bangladesh	8.8	6.5	5.6	4.7	4.7	*0.8*	*0.5*	*0.6*	*1.0*	*1.0*
Caribbean	3.3	2.0	1.8	1.6	1.6	*36.3*	*50.0*	*48.3*	*48.1*	*47.8*
East Africa	2.4	2.1	2.0	1.9	1.8	*3.7*	*2.4*	*3.4*	*5.6*	*6.2*
Rest of Africa	3.8	3.4	2.8	4.2	4.1	*4.6*	*13.0*	*22.1*	*27.0*	*31.1*
Other New Commonwealth	2.6	2.0	2.0	1.8	1.7	*5.2*	*6.3*	*9.9*	*13.0*	*12.0*
Total New Commonwealth and Pakistan	3.8	2.9	2.9	2.7	2.6	*11.9*	*8.4*	*8.4*	*10.0*	*10.2*
Rest of the world	2.7	2.0	1.9	1.9	2.0	*8.9*	*9.4*	*13.7*	*17.4*	*18.4*
All countries	2.4	1.8	1.8	1.8	1.9	*8.4*	*12.8*	*21.4*	*27.0*	*28.3*

Source: Office of Population Censuses and Surveys

1.15 Deaths: by age and sex

United Kingdom   Rates and thousands

| | Death rates per 1,000 in each age group | | | | | | | Total deaths (thousands) |
	Under 1[1]	1-14	15-39	females 40-59 males 40-64	females 60-79 males 65-79	80 and over	All ages	
1961								
Males	24.8	0.6	1.3	11.8	66.1	190.7	12.6	322.0
Females	19.3	0.4	0.8	4.9	32.2	136.7	11.4	309.8
1971								
Males	20.2	0.5	1.1	11.4	59.9	174.0	12.1	328.5
Females	15.5	0.4	0.6	4.8	27.5	132.9	11.0	316.5
1976								
Males	16.4	0.4	1.1	11.1	60.4	183.4	12.5	341.9
Females	12.4	0.3	0.6	4.7	28.0	140.8	11.7	338.9
1981								
Males	12.7	0.4	1.0	10.1	56.1	167.5	12.0	329.1
Females	9.6	0.3	0.5	4.4	26.4	126.2	11.4	328.8
1986								
Males	10.9	0.3	0.9	9.1	54.0	158.2	11.8	327.2
Females	8.1	0.2	0.5	3.7	25.7	120.5	11.5	333.6
1989								
Males	9.5	0.3	1.0	7.8	50.5	149.6	11.5	320.2
Females	7.2	0.2	0.5	3.4	25.1	117.0	11.5	337.5
1990								
Males	8.8	0.3	1.0	7.6	49.2	143.7	11.2	314.6
Females	6.8	0.2	0.5	3.3	24.3	111.9	11.1	327.2

1 Rate per 1,000 live births.

Source: Office of Population Censuses and Surveys;
General Register Office (Scotland);
General Register Office (Northern Ireland)

1.16 Deaths[1] per month: Mid 1989-1990 and 1990-1991

Great Britain

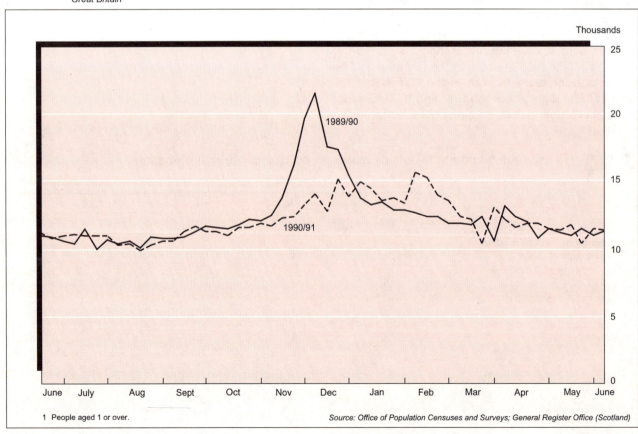

1 People aged 1 or over.   *Source: Office of Population Censuses and Surveys; General Register Office (Scotland)*

Social Trends 22, © Crown copyright 1992

There were just under 642 thousand deaths in the United Kingdom in 1990, a drop of 16 thousand over the 1989 figure (Table 1.15). The crude death rate, which takes no account of the age structure of the population, was 11.2 deaths per thousand population for males and 11.1 deaths per thousand population for females in 1990. There were declines in the death rate for all age groups and both sexes between 1961 and 1990, although men had higher death rates than women at all age groups. The most dramatic falls in death rates have been in the under 1 year age group (where the rate has dropped by almost two thirds) and in the elderly (80 and over) where the death rate has fallen by up to one fifth. Chapter 7 gives information on life expectancy at different ages, causes of death and infant mortality.

The number of deaths at different times of the year are affected by, among other factors, the weather and by epidemics. Chart 1.16 shows the number of weekly deaths in Great Britain for two one-year periods: mid 1989 to mid 1990 and mid 1990 to mid 1991. The 1990/91 line shows a typical annual pattern of deaths with weekly numbers around 11 thousand in summer rising to nearly 16 thousand in the coldest part of the winter. The 1989/90 line however, shows an unusual fluctuation caused by the influenza epidemic occurring during November, December and January 1989/90. In the week ending 22 December 1989, 21,532 deaths were registered, compared with only 14,090 in the corresponding week of 1990 (a 35 per cent decrease). Deaths registered in that week of 1989 were the highest figure recorded since the peak of the 1969/70 epidemic, in December 1969. Information on causes of death is contained in Chapter 7. An analysis of the 1989/90 'flu epidemic is made in the article *Deaths in Great Britain associated with the influenza epidemic of 1989/90* in the OPCS publication *Population Trends No 65*.

Migration

1.17 International migration into and out of the United Kingdom[1]: by country of last or next residence[2] (annual averages)

Thousands

	1975-1979			1980-1984			1985-1989		
	Inflow	Outflow	Balance	Inflow	Outflow	Balance	Inflow	Outflow	Balance
Country of last or next residence									
Commonwealth countries									
Australia	21.1	28.4	− 7.3	12.7	34.8	− 22.1	18.3	35.3	− 17.0
Canada	6.9	22.5	− 15.6	5.7	14.4	− 8.6	6.1	9.3	− 3.3
New Zealand	8.6	9.7	− 1.1	6.2	8.6	− 2.4	10.7	7.1	3.7
African Commonwealth	17.0	11.7	5.3	14.1	10.0	4.0	11.5	6.3	5.2
Bangladesh, India, Sri Lanka	15.6	3.9	11.8	15.5	3.9	11.6	14.0	4.0	10.0
Pakistan	12.7	1.9	10.8	10.8	1.6	9.2	9.5	2.5	7.1
Caribbean	4.5	3.3	1.3	3.5	3.2	0.3	3.4	3.2	0.2
Other	16.2	9.7	6.5	15.5	15.6	−	17.0	15.2	1.8
Total Commonwealth	102.6	91.1	11.6	84.1	92.0	− 8.0	90.6	82.9	7.7
Non-Commonwealth countries									
European Community[3]	28.5	36.5	− 8.0	37.8	36.7	1.1	57.8	51.2	6.6
Rest of Europe	5.0	7.9	− 2.9	7.0	6.0	1.1	10.7	10.4	0.3
United States of America	14.8	23.0	− 8.2	20.3	28.6	− 8.3	26.4	30.4	− 4.1
Rest of America	4.0	3.9	0.1	3.3	3.8	− 0.5	3.3	3.1	0.2
Republic of South Africa	10.6	13.8	− 3.2	6.1	15.7	− 9.6	12.2	4.3	8.0
Middle East	10.3	18.3	− 7.9	13.1	22.8	− 9.7	15.4	15.1	0.3
Other	10.7	13.2	− 2.6	14.6	8.3	6.2	15.7	10.5	5.1
Total Non-Commonwealth	83.9	116.6	− 32.7	102.3	121.9	− 19.6	141.5	125.0	16.5
All countries	186.6	207.7	− 21.1	186.3	213.9	− 27.6	232.1	208.0	24.1
of which:									
British citizens	79.3	140.6	− 61.2	82.9	145.2	− 62.3	104.5	127.2	− 22.7
Non-British citizens	107.2	67.1	40.1	103.4	68.7	34.7	127.6	80.8	46.8

1 Excludes the Channel Islands and the Isle of Man from 1988.
2 Excludes migration with the Republic of Ireland.

3 Figures for the European Community have been revised for all the years in this table to show the community as it was constituted in 1989.

Source: Office of Population Censuses and Surveys

Over the period 1985-1989 as a whole more migrants (who include British citizens returning to live in the United Kingdom) entered the United Kingdom than left (Table 1.17). The number of migrants entering from other European Community (EC) countries doubled between 1975-1979 and 1985-1989, while the number leaving for EC countries increased by two-fifths. Similarly, there was an increase of four - fifths in the number of migrants entering from the USA compared with only a one-third increase in the number leaving for the USA.

1.18 United Kingdom[1]: net balance from international migration: by country and region, 1989

Thousands

	All countries	Old Common-wealth	New Commonwealth		European Community	Rest of the world
			Indian[3] sub-continent	Other		
Region of United Kingdom						
United Kingdom	44.3	− 6.4	17.8	7.0	9.7	16.3
North	− 1.2	− 0.3	0.5	− 0.2	0.1	− 1.3
Yorkshire & Humberside	2.9	0.7	1.2	0.2	2.8	− 2.0
East Midlands	7.3	− 1.5	1.1	0.7	4.0	3.0
East Anglia	4.9	− 1.6	− 0.1	0.6	0.5	5.4
South East	34.0	3.8	9.8	2.9	6.3	11.4
South West	− 6.0	− 4.6	—	0.8	− 2.0	− 0.2
West Midlands	− 2.8	− 1.4	2.6	− 1.0	− 4.2	1.1
North West	2.5	0.9	2.4	1.2	0.4	− 2.5
England	41.5	− 4.0	17.6	5.3	7.8	14.9
Wales	0.5	− 0.4	0.1	1.0	− 0.1	− 0.2
Scotland	4.0	− 1.2	—	1.3	2.0	1.9
Northern Ireland	− 1.7	− 0.7	—	− 0.7	—	− 0.3

1 Excluding the Channel Islands and the Isle of Man.
2 Excluding Irish Republic.

3 Bangladesh, India, Pakistan and Sri Lanka.

Source: International Passenger Survey
Office of Population Censuses and Surveys,

Estimates of the effect of overseas migration on the size of the population are made annually by the Registrar General. At any one time there are a very large number of people (including holiday makers) moving between the United Kingdom and other countries. For demographic purposes they therefore use an internationally agreed definition of migrants, such that an 'immigrant' is someone who, having lived abroad for at least twelve months, declares an intention to reside in the United Kingdom for at least twelve months. The definition of an 'emigrant' is the converse. Estimates are derived from the small International Passenger Survey which is one of the main sources of data on international migration. They do not cover migration with the Republic of Ireland.

Analysis of these movements by citizenship shows that the migration trends mainly reflect the movement of

1.19 Acceptances for settlement: by category of acceptance

United Kingdom

1 Includes Pakistan.

Source: Home Office

1.20 Applications[1] for asylum in the United Kingdom

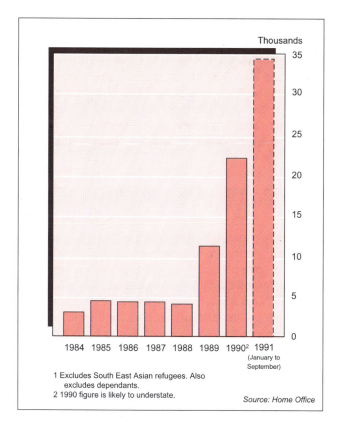

Thousands

1 Excludes South East Asian refugees. Also
  excludes dependants.
2 1990 figure is likely to understate.

Source: Home Office

British citizens. Between 1980-1984 and 1985-1989 there was a fall in the number of British citizens leaving the country as migrants while the number of those returning, having left the United Kingdom in earlier years, increased. Both the inflow and the outflow of non-British citizens increased, but the net inward balance remained fairly constant.

Migrants entering and leaving the United Kingdom affect regional as well as national population. Table 1.18 shows the net effect of international migration on the population of the regions of the United Kingdom. The South East, which usually accounts for about half the total number of migrants, had a larger net gain in 1989 than in recent years.

An alternative measure of longer term immigration of non-British citizens is the number of people accepted for settlement (ie allowed to stay indefinitely) in the United Kingdom under the *Immigration Act 1971* (Chart 1.19). This is on a different basis from the International Passenger Survey (IPS). It includes people who are initially admitted for a shorter period and then later accepted for settlement, but excludes persons not subject to immigration control, such as those who have the right of abode in the United Kingdom. In 1990, 52 thousand people were accepted for settlement, 3 thousand more than in 1989 but 29 thousand less than in 1976. Figures in recent years have however been reduced by a procedural change and the temporary effects of changes to the immigration rules.

Citizens from the New Commonwealth accounted for nearly half of those accepted for settlement in 1990 and half of these were wives and children of men who are British citizens, or are settled or are settling in the United Kingdom. When analysed by country of origin a quarter of total acceptances in 1990 were from the Indian sub-continent, 20 per cent from the other parts of Asia, 16 per cent from Africa and 13 per cent from the Americas. Acceptances from Africa have increased substantially in recent years.

A significant aspect of recent international migration flows has been the increased numbers seeking to migrate to Western Europe and a particularly large increase in applications for asylum. The numbers seeking asylum in the United Kingdom have risen very rapidly. Excluding dependants, the total rose from 4,000 in 1988 to over 22,000 in 1990 (over 30,000 including dependants) and 34,000 in the first nine months of 1991 (Chart 1.20). The increase has been particularly marked for African and South Asian countries and these accounted for about 60 per cent and nearly 25 per cent of total applications respectively in the first nine months of 1991. There have been large rises for asylum seekers from Zaire and Angola.

Table 1.21 shows the decisions taken in selected recent years on asylum applications. Only about a quarter of the cases processed in 1990 were found to have a well-founded fear of persecution under the terms of the *1951 UN Convention* and so were granted asylum. The main nationalities granted asylum were Somalians, Turks and Ethiopians. In total, an estimated 4 thousand decisions (excluding dependants) were made in 1990. This was less than the high figure of 7 thousand in 1989, because of the problem of handling the large increase in applications, though still more than in earlier years. A large increase in staff resources to process applications was announced in April 1991.

1.21 Decisions taken on applications for asylum[1,2]

United Kingdom					Numbers
	1984	1986	1988	1989	1990
Decision taken					
Granted asylum	460	370	640	2,220	970
Granted exceptional leave	630	2,120	1,590	3,930	2,410
Refused asylum or exceptional leave	350	540	450	820	610
Total decisions	1,440	3,020	2,680	6,970	3,990

1 See Appendix, Part 1: Refugees.
2 Decisions in a particular year do not necessarily relate to applications made in that year.

Source: Home Office

International comparisons

The United Nations (UN) estimated that in 1974 the world's population was 4 billion: 13 years later the UN designated 11 July 1987, 'Day of 5 Billion' as the symbolic focus of a world-wide recognition of the day the world population reached that figure. By comparison it took around 35 years to grow from 2 billion in the middle of the 1920s to 3 billion in 1960 and more than a century to grow from 1 billion to 2 billion. It is projected that the world's population will reach 6 billion by 1999, 7 billion by 2010 and 8 billion by 2022.

Table 1.22 compares data for the European Community and selected other countries. Among EC countries in mid-1989, Germany (including, following re-unification, the former German Democratic Republic) had the largest population (78.8 million) followed by Italy (57.5 million) and the United Kingdom (57.2 million). Of the countries where data were available, Belgium, the Irish Republic and Italy are all expected to have slightly smaller populations in the year 2010 than they had in 1989. Of the non-EC countries shown, the population of India is projected to increase the most between 1988 and 2010 (by 54 per cent), when it will reach almost 90

per cent of the Chinese figure. The highest birth rate of the countries shown in Table 1.23 was in India (33 live births per thousand population) followed by China (21) and the USSR (20). Japan had the lowest death rate (6 deaths per thousand population). In 1989 the highest population densities shown in the table were in the Netherlands (363 people per square kilometre); and Belgium (325). Within the United Kingdom England had a population density of 366 people per square kilometre, slightly greater than the Netherlands.

Chart 1.23 shows total fertility rates in 1988 measured as the average number of children a woman will bear during her lifetime given prevailing age-specific fertility rates. Generally, fertility rates have fallen since 1970 in most developed, and the largest developing, countries. There are however exceptions, Ethiopia for example - one of the 16 largest developing countries - has seen its total fertility rate rise from 5.8 in 1970 to 6.5 in 1988. Most African and Middle Eastern states had total fertility rates of 5 or more in 1988 whilst almost every European and North American country had total fertility rates of less than two.

1.22 Population and population structure: selected countries[1]

	Estimates of mid-year population (millions)			Projections (millions)		Birth rate[2]	Death rate[3]	Population density (per sq km)	
	1971	1981	1989[5]	2000	2010	1990[4]	1990[4]	1960	1989[5]
United Kingdom	55.9	56.4	57.2	59.0	60.0	13.9	11.2	213.7	234.1
Belgium	9.7	9.8	9.9	9.9	9.7	12.4	10.5	298.1	325.4
Denmark	4.9	5.1	5.1	5.2	5.1	12.4	11.9	106.0	119.1
France	51.3	54.2	56.2	57.9	58.8	13.5	9.3	82.8	101.6
Germany[6]	78.4	78.4	78.8	..	..	11.3	11.5	202.9	219.6
Greece	8.8	9.7	10.0	..	..	9.9	9.2	62.9	75.9
Irish Republic	3.0	3.4	3.5	3.5	3.4	15.1	9.1	40.3	50.1
Italy	54.1	56.5	57.5	57.6	56.4	9.8	9.3	166.0	190.9
Luxembourg	0.3	0.4	0.4	0.4	0.4	13.0	9.9	121.0	145.0
Netherlands	13.2	14.2	14.9	15.9	16.4	13.2	8.6	279.5	362.5
Portugal	8.6	9.9	10.3	10.6	10.8	11.2	9.9	97.4	111.5
Spain	34.2	37.8	38.9	39.4	39.1	10.2	8.6	60.1	77.0
European Community	322.4	335.8	342.7	..	..	11.9	10.1	124.8	144.3
China	787.2	1,007.8	1,104.0	1,285.9	1,382.5	21	7	..	115
India	550.4	683.8	796.6	1,042.5	1,225.3	33	11	..	242
USSR	245.1	267.7	283.7	307.7	326.4	20	10	..	13
USA	207.0	229.8	246.3	266.2	281.2	16	9	..	26
Japan	104.7	117.6	122.6	189.1	131.7	11	6	..	325

1 EC countries; natural increase for China, India, USSR, USA and Japan.
2 Live births per 1,000 population.
3 Deaths per 1,000 population.
4 Data for USSR, China, India, USA and Japan are for 1989.

5 Data for USSR, China, India, USA and Japan are for 1988.
6 Figures shown include both the Federal Republic of Germany and the German Democratic Republic.

Source: Statistical Office of the European Communities; United Nations Demographic Yearbooks; Government Actuary's Department

1.23 World total fertility rates[1], 1988

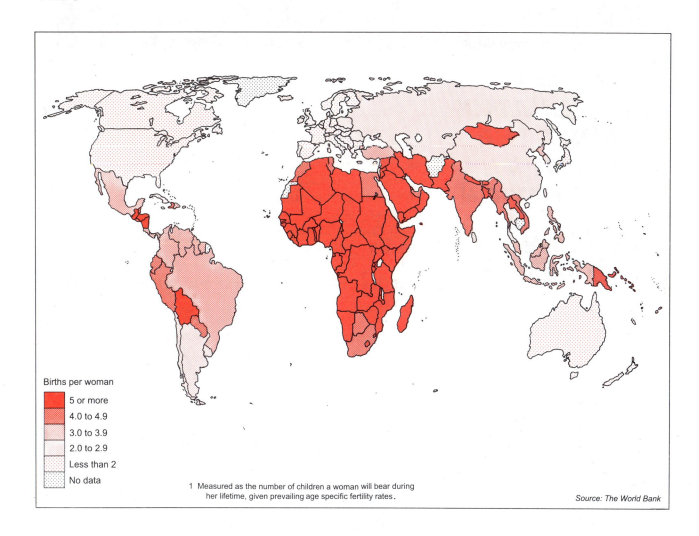

Births per woman

- 5 or more
- 4.0 to 4.9
- 3.0 to 3.9
- 2.0 to 2.9
- Less than 2
- No data

1 Measured as the number of children a woman will bear during her lifetime, given prevailing age specific fertility rates.

Source: The World Bank

BIBLIOGRAPHY

The following list contains selected publications relevant to Chapter 1: Population. Those published by HMSO are available from the addresses shown on the back cover of Social Trends.

Annual Report of the Registrar General for Northern Ireland, HMSO
Annual Report of the Registrar General for Scotland, General Register Office (Scotland)
Birth Statistics (Series FM1), HMSO
Demographic Statistics, EUROSTAT
Demographic Yearbook, United Nations
International Migration Statistics (Series MN), HMSO
Key Population and Vital Statistics (Series VS/PP1), HMSO
Labour Force Survey, HMSO
Mortality Statistics for England and Wales (Series DH1, 2, 3, 4, 5, 6), HMSO

OPCS Monitors, Office of Population Censuses and Surveys
Population Estimates, Scotland, HMSO
Population Projections 1989-2029 (Series PP2 No 17), HMSO
Population Projections for the Counties of Wales (1987 based), Welsh Office
Population Projections, Scotland (for Standard Areas), General Register Office (Scotland)
Population Projections 1985-2001: area - England (Series PP3), HMSO
Population Trends, HMSO
Regional Trends, HMSO

CENSUS 1991

VALUABLE INFORMATION ABOUT THE NATION'S POPULATION

COUNTY REPORTS

The results of the **1991 Census** will provide reliable and valuable statistical information about the nation. A series of reports for each county in England and Wales and each region in Scotland will be published by HMSO – some **County Reports** are already available. These reports will be preceded by summary results, in the **Census Monitor** series, published by OPCS but still available from HMSO.

Each **County Report** is in two parts and includes the following information:

Part One (information from an analysis of all Census forms)

* Demographic and economic characteristics of the population: eg, age group, sex and marital status, country of birth, ethnic group and economic position

* Housing, tenure and amenities: eg, availability of central heating, use of cars and number of people per room

* Households and household composition: eg, households with dependent children, pensioners, households by ethnic group

* Household spaces and dwellings: eg, households in permanent and non-permanent accommodation, shared dwellings, tenure of dwellings

Part Two (information from an analysis of a 10% sample of Census forms)

* Economic and employment status; occupation and hours worked; industry and employment status; working parents; travel to work, etc

For further information and ordering details on Census publications, and to find out which **County Reports** are already available, write to HMSO Publicity, Dept B, St Crispins, Duke Street, Norwich NR3 1PD.

For more details of the **Census Monitor** series, contact OPCS Information Division, St Catherine's House, 10 Kingsway, London WC2B 6JP.

HMSO books are available from HMSO Bookshops, Agents (see Yellow Pages) and through all good booksellers.

HMSO Books

Chapter 2: Households and families

Households

- The number of people living alone continues to increase. In 1990, more than one quarter of households in Great Britain were one-person households. *(Chart 2.2)*

Families

- The average number of children per woman has fallen in all EC countries over the past two decades. In both 1971 and 1990, the Irish Republic had the largest number of children per woman. *(Table 2.11)*

Marriage and divorce

- The United Kingdom has one of the highest marriage rates and one of the highest divorce rates in the EC. *(Table 2.12)*

- The seven year itch still applies - the most likely time for a couple to divorce is still between 5 and 9 years of marriage. *(Table 2.17)*

Family building

- The proportion of births outside marriage has risen sharply in recent years - from less than 11 per cent in 1979 to nearly 28 per cent in 1990. *(Chart 2.22)*

- As the number of births outside marriage increases, there is some evidence that many of these births are within a stable relationship. In 1990, one in five births outside marriage were registered by both parents, compared with only one in 25 in 1971. *(Chart 2.23)*

- Most married couples are now waiting longer to start a family than they did in the early 1970s - an average of 27 months after marriage in 1990 compared with 20 months in 1971. *(Table 2.26)*

- There has been a slight decline in the use of contraceptives since 1983, but 72 per cent of women aged 18-44 still practised some form of contraception in 1989-90. *(Table 2.29)*

2.1 Proportions[1] of all families with dependent children headed by lone mothers and lone fathers

Great Britain

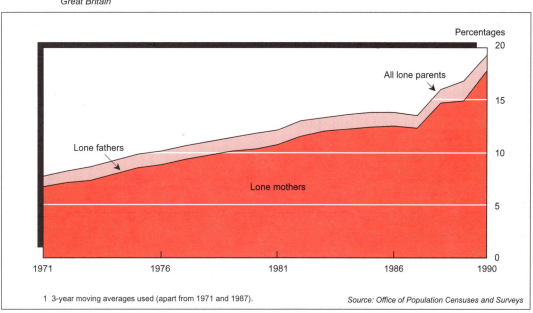

1 3-year moving averages used (apart from 1971 and 1987).

Source: Office of Population Censuses and Surveys

Households

2.2 One-person households as a percentage of all households: by age and sex

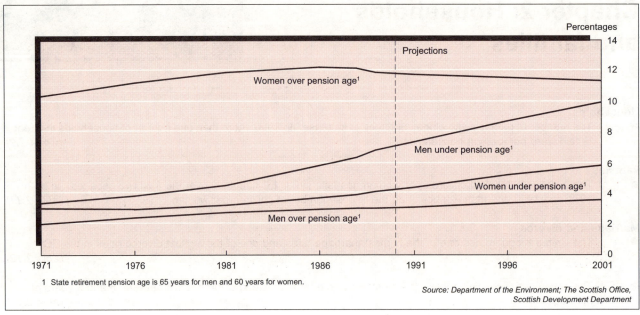

Great Britain

Percentages

Projections

Women over pension age[1]

Men under pension age[1]

Women under pension age[1]

Men over pension age[1]

1971   1976   1981   1986   1991   1996   2001

1 State retirement pension age is 65 years for men and 60 years for women.

Source: Department of the Environment; The Scottish Office, Scottish Development Department

Whereas Chapter 1 considered individuals, this chapter examines the structure and characteristics of the households and families in which they live. The statistics contained in the tables and charts in this chapter generally exclude the population living in institutions, ie those living in boarding schools, hospitals, halls of residence, old people's homes, prisons, and other communal establishments.

One-parent families as a proportion of all families with dependent children increased from 8 per cent in 1971 to 19 per cent in 1990 (Chart 2.1), reflecting the rise in both divorce and births outside marriage.

One of the most notable features since the Second World War has been the increase in the number of people living alone; in 1990 more than a quarter of households in Great Britain were single person households, compared with about one-eighth in 1961 (Chart 2.2 and Table 2.3). Between 1961 and 1990 the proportion of larger households which contained five or more people fell from 16 to only 7 per cent. These changes have resulted in a reduction in the average household size, from 3.09 people in 1961 to an average of around 2.5 people in 1990.

Chapter 1 shows that the proportion of elderly people in the United Kingdom is increasing. However, the increase in one-person households is not caused solely by an increase in the numbers of elderly people living alone. Chart 2.2 shows that not only those of pensionable age, but younger people too, increasingly tend to live alone.

2.3 Households[1]: by size

Great Britain			Percentages and numbers
	1961	1971	1981	1990 −91

	1961	1971	1981	1990 −91
Household size				
1 person	12	18	22	26
2 people	30	32	32	35
3 people	23	19	17	17
4 people	19	17	18	15
5 people	9	8	7	5
6 or more people	7	6	4	2
All households	100	100	100	100
Average household size (number of people)	3.09	2.89	2.71	2.46
Number of households (thousands)	16,189	18,317	19,492	9,623[2]

1 See Appendix, Part 2: Households.
2 Sample size (number).

Source: Office of Population Censuses and Surveys

Social Trends 22, © Crown copyright 1992

2.4 Households[1]: by type

Great Britain   Percentages and thousands

	1961	1971	1981	1990 −91
One person households				
Under pensionable age	*4*	*6*	*8*	*11*
Over pensionable age	*7*	*12*	*14*	*15*
Two or more unrelated adults	*5*	*4*	*5*	*3*
One family households				
Married couple[2] with				
No children	*26*	*27*	*26*	*28*
1 – 2 dependent children[3]	*30*	*26*	*25*	*20*
3 or more dependent children	*8*	*9*	*6*	*4*
Non-dependent children only	*10*	*8*	*8*	*8*
Lone parent[2] with				
Dependent children[3]	*2*	*3*	*5*	*6*
Non-dependent children only	*4*	*4*	*4*	*4*
Two or more families	*3*	*1*	*1*	*1*
All households	*100*	*100*	*100*	*100*
Number of households (thousands)	16,189	18,317	19,492	9,604[4]

1 See Appendix, Part 2: Households.
2 Other individuals who were not family members may also have been included.
3 These family types may also include non-dependent children.
4 Sample size (numbers).

Source: Office of Population Censuses and Surveys

2.5 Households[1]: by type, Northern Ireland

Percentages and numbers

	1983	1986	1989 −90
One person households			
Under pensionable age	*6*	*7*	*8*
Over pensionable age	*14*	*13*	*15*
Two or more unrelated adults	*4*	*4*	*3*
One family households			
Married couple[2] with			
No children	*19*	*18*	*18*
1 – 2 dependent children[3]	*25*	*24*	*22*
3 or more dependent children	*13*	*13*	*11*
Non-dependent children only	*8*	*9*	*10*
Lone parent[2] with			
Dependent children[3]	*4*	*6*	*7*
Non-dependent children only	*5*	*6*	*5*
Two or more families	*1*	*1*	*1*
Sample size (= 100%) (numbers)	2,940	2,759	3,017

1 See Appendix, Part 2: Households.
2 Other individuals who were not family members may also have been included.
3 These family types may also include non-dependent children.

Source: Continuous Household Survey

Table 2.4 also shows the growth in one-person households illustrated in Chart 2.2. Whilst the proportion of one-person households has been increasing, the proportion containing a married couple with dependent children has been decreasing, reflecting the falling birth rate from the mid-1960s. However, this rate started to rise again in the 1980s (see Table 1.13).

In recent years Northern Ireland has conducted the Continuous Household Survey (CHS), similar to the General Household Survey (GHS) in Great Britain. Equivalent estimates to those in Table 2.4 are presented for the Province in Table 2.5. Household composition differs from that in Great Britain; there is a higher percentage of married couples with three or more children and a slightly higher percentage of one-parent families in Northern Ireland than in Great Britain.

Despite the increase in people living alone, Table 2.6 shows that around a third of all households contain a young person. Households headed by someone from the professional socio-economic group were most likely to include a youngster, and households from the unskilled manual group were least likely.

The proportion of one-parent households ranges from between one in a hundred and one in twenty headed by someone from the Chinese ethnic group to one in five headed by someone from the West Indian ethnic group. Over two-thirds of Pakistani and Bangladeshi households are couples with dependent children, compared to only one-fifth of West Indian households (Chart 2.7).

2.6 Households[1]: by socio-economic group of head of household[2] and type of household, 1989–90

Great Britain   Percentages and numbers

	Professional	Employers and Managers	Intermediate non-manual	Skilled manual	Semi-skilled manual	Unskilled manual	Total
One adult aged 16-59	*10*	*8*	*14*	*6*	*8*	*9*	*9*
Two adults aged 16-59	*20*	*18*	*16*	*17*	*11*	*9*	*16*
Youngest person aged 0-15	*36*	*33*	*25*	*33*	*26*	*23*	*30*
Three or more adults	*16*	*14*	*9*	*16*	*12*	*11*	*13*
Two adults, one or both aged 60 or over	*13*	*18*	*13*	*19*	*18*	*14*	*17*
One adult aged 60 or over	*4*	*9*	*24*	*9*	*27*	*34*	*16*
Sample size (= 100%)	594	1,909	2,044	2,982	1,653	558	9,790

1 See Appendix, Part 2: Households.
2 Excluding members of the Armed Forces, full-time students and those who have never worked.

Source: General Household Survey

2.7 Households: by type of household and ethnic group, 1987-89

Great Britain

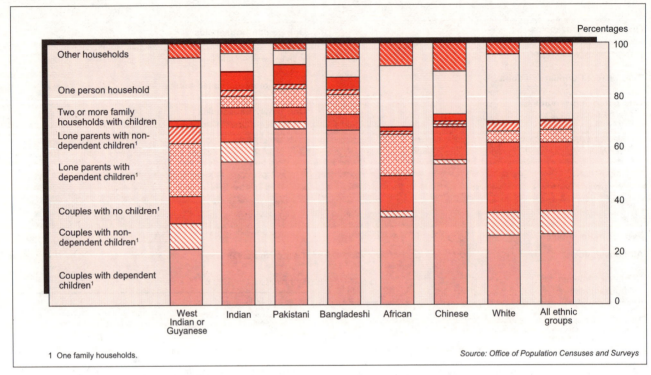

Legend:
- Other households
- One person household
- Two or more family households with children
- Lone parents with non-dependent children[1]
- Lone parents with dependent children[1]
- Couples with no children[1]
- Couples with non-dependent children[1]
- Couples with dependent children[1]

X-axis categories: West Indian or Guyanese, Indian, Pakistani, Bangladeshi, African, Chinese, White, All ethnic groups

Percentages (0–100)

1 One family households.

Source: Office of Population Censuses and Surveys

Families

Whereas a household is defined as a person or group of persons living together, a family comprises a married couple with or without children, or a lone parent. People living alone are not families. This section examines some of the characteristics of families. Three quarters of the population of Great Britain in 1990 lived in families headed by a married couple, a proportion which has fallen slightly since 1961 (Table 2.8). The proportion of people living in a 'traditional' family - that is, a married couple with dependent children - fell from 52 to 41 per cent between 1961 and 1990.

Although there has been a fall in the proportion of households containing a married couple with children, 85 per cent of dependent children still live in this type of family (Table 2.9). However, the percentage of all dependent children living in lone parent families almost doubled from 8 per cent in 1972 to 15 per cent in 1989.

2.8 People in households[1]: by type of household and family in which they live

Great Britain   Percentages

	1961	1971	1981	1990 −91
Type of household				
Living alone	3.9	6.3	8.0	10.6
Married couple, no children	17.8	19.3	19.5	23.6
Married couple with dependent children[2]	52.2	51.7	47.4	40.8
Married couple with non-dependent children only	11.6	10.0	10.3	10.3
Lone parent with dependent children[2]	2.5	3.5	5.8	6.5
Other households	12.0	9.2	9.0	8.1
All people in private households[3]	100	100	100	100

1 See Appendix, Part 2: Families.
2 These family types may also include non-dependent children.
3 The number of people in each census was 49,545 thousand in 1961, 52,347 thousand in 1971 and 52,760 thousand in 1981. The sample size of the General Household Survey in 1990-91 was 23,587.

Source: Office of Population Censuses and Surveys

2.9 Dependent children[1]: by type of family

Great Britain   Percentages and numbers

	1972	1975	1981	1989 −90
Married couple with				
1 dependent child	16	17	18	18
2 or more dependent children	76	74	70	67
Lone mother with				
1 dependent child	2	3	3	4
2 or more dependent children	5	6	7	9
Lone father with				
1 dependent child	—	—	1	1
2 or more dependent children	1	1	1	1
All dependent children (= 100%) (sample size)	9,474	9,293	8,216	5,827

1 Persons under 16, or aged 16-18 and in full-time education, in the family unit and living in the household.

Source: General Household Survey

2.10 Proportion of all families with dependent children headed by lone mothers: by marital status

Great Britain

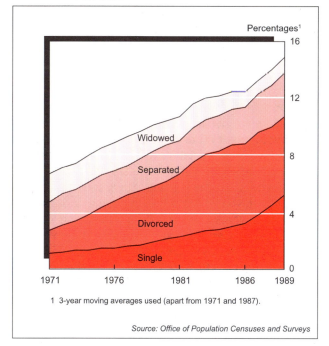

1 3-year moving averages used (apart from 1971 and 1987).

Source: Office of Population Censuses and Surveys

Chart 2.10 shows the marital status of lone mothers with dependent children. The proportions of those lone mothers who are single or divorced have increased steadily over the last 20 years. Following a decrease from 2.0 in 1971 to 1.8 by 1981 the average number of children in families containing dependent children has remained constant at the 1981 level. On average, lone parents tend to have fewer children on average than married or cohabiting couples, 1.6 compared with 1.8 in 1990.

Marriage and divorce

Table 2.12 gives a European Community comparison of marriage and divorce rates for 1981 and 1989. The United Kingdom had one of the highest marriage and divorce rates in both years. The divorce rate varies from country to country because of such factors as religious beliefs and legal requirements. In 1981 the lowest divorce rate of all the EC countries (excluding the Irish Republic) was in Italy, where divorce was introduced in 1975, at 0.9 per thousand existing marriages.

Whilst the number of marriages has slowly declined over the past two decades the number of divorces has steadily risen (Chart 2.13). There were 58 thousand fewer marriages in 1989 than 1971 and, over the same period, divorces more than doubled to reach over 150 thousand. There was a noticeable jump in the number of divorces between 1984 and 1985 following the *Matrimonial and Family Proceedings Act 1984* which was implemented in October of that year (see Table 2.16 and accompanying text).

2.11 Average number of children per woman: EC comparison

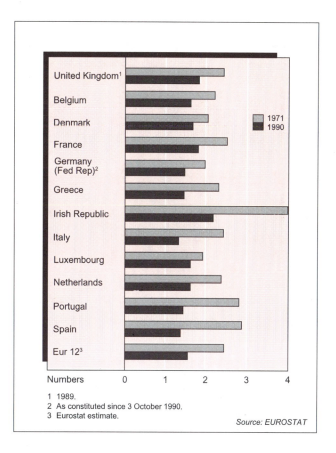

1 1989.
2 As constituted since 3 October 1990.
3 Eurostat estimate.

Source: EUROSTAT

The average number of children per woman has fallen in all EC countries between 1971 and 1990 (Chart 2.11). The Irish Republic, had the largest number of children per woman in both years. The country with the least number of children per woman in 1990 was Italy with 1.3.

2.12 Marriage and divorce: EC comparison, 1981 and 1989

Rates

	Marriages per 1,000 eligible population		Divorces per 1,000 existing marriages	
	1981	1989	1981	1989
United Kingdom	7.1	6.8	11.9	12.6[1]
Belgium	6.5	6.4	6.1	8.6
Denmark	5.0	6.0	12.1	13.6
France	5.8	5.0	6.8	8.4
Germany (Fed. Rep.)	5.8	6.4	7.2	8.7[2]
Greece	7.3	6.1	2.5	..
Irish Republic	6.0	5.0	0.0	0.0
Italy	5.6	5.4	0.9	2.1
Luxembourg	5.5	5.8	5.9	10.0
Netherlands	6.0	6.1	8.3	8.1
Portugal	7.7	7.1	2.8	..
Spain	5.4	5.6	1.1	..

1 1987.
2 1988.

Source: Statistical Office of the European Communities

2.13 Marriages and divorces

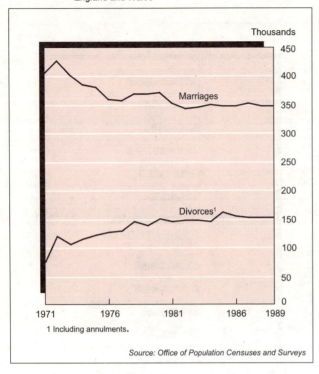

England and Wales

1 Including annulments.

Source: Office of Population Censuses and Surveys

The number of marriages in the United Kingdom has changed little in the last five years (Table 2.14). In 1989 marriages between bachelors and spinsters accounted for 64 per cent of all marriages compared with 86 per cent in 1961. Following the *Divorce Reform Act 1969*, after which the number of divorces doubled, there was a large increase between 1971 and 1973 in the numbers of marriages where one or both partners were remarrying after divorce.

More widowers and divorced men remarry than widows and divorced women (Chart 2.15). Despite the overall decrease in rates of marriage for both sexes there is still a consistently higher rate of remarriage for males than females. The rate for remarriages of widows and divorced women remains significantly below that of first (ie spinster) marriages. Marriage rates for both bachelors and spinsters have almost halved since the early 1970s.

Section 1 of the *Matrimonial and Family Proceedings Act 1984* which became law on 12 October 1984 had an immediate effect on divorce proceedings in England and Wales. This legislation allowed couples to petition for divorce after the first anniversary of their marriage, whereas under former legislation they could not usually petition for divorce unless their marriage had lasted at least three years. A record 191 thousand divorce petitions were filed in England and Wales in 1985, a 6 per cent increase over 1984 (Table 2.16). In 1986, the number of petitions fell back to the 1984 level, suggesting that a backlog effect had occurred in 1985, caused by a larger than usual number of couples who were first able to divorce that year. However the number of petitions had increased slightly by 1989. A total of 151 thousand decrees were made absolute in England and Wales in 1989, over twice the number in 1971 when the *Divorce Reform Act 1969* came into force in England and Wales. Between 1985 and 1989, the percentage of divorces where one or both partners had already been divorced before rose slightly; nearly a quarter of divorces in England and Wales in 1989 involved at least one partner who was divorcing for a second or subsequent time.

2.14 Marriages: by type

United Kingdom Thousands and percentages

	1961	1971	1976	1981	1986	1988	1989
Marriages (thousands)							
First marriage for both partners	340	369	282	263	254	253	252
First marriage for one partner only							
Bachelor/divorced woman	11	21	30	32	34	34	35
Bachelor/widow	5	4	4	3	2	2	2
Spinster/divorced man	12	24	32	36	38	39	38
Spinster/widower	8	5	4	3	2	2	2
Second (or subsequent) marriage for both partners							
Both divorced	5	17	34	44	48	50	50
Both widowed	10	10	10	7	6	5	5
Divorced man/widow	3	4	5	5	4	4	4
Divorced woman/widower	3	5	5	5	5	5	5
Total marriages	397	459	406	398	394	394	392
Remarriages[1] as a percentage of all marriages	*14*	*20*	*31*	*34*	*35*	*36*	*36*
Remarriages[1] of the divorced as a percentage of all marriages	*9*	*15*	*26*	*31*	*33*	*33*	*34*

1 Remarriage for one or both partners.

Source: Office of Population Censuses and Surveys; General Register Office (Scotland)

2.15 Marriage and remarriage: by sex

Great Britain

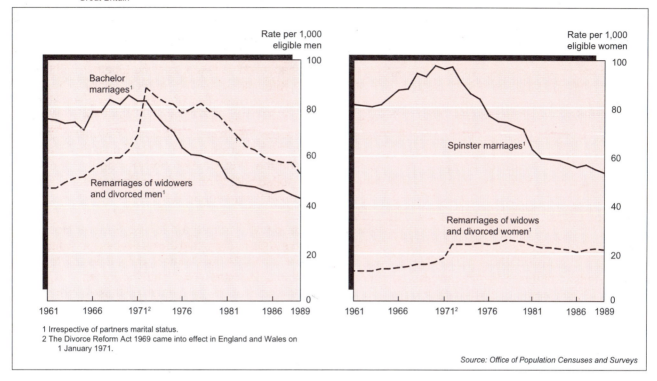

1 Irrespective of partners marital status.
2 The Divorce Reform Act 1969 came into effect in England and Wales on 1 January 1971.

Source: Office of Population Censuses and Surveys

2.16 Divorce[1]

	1961	1971	1976	1981	1984	1985	1986	1987	1988	1989
Petitions filed[2] (thousands)										
England & Wales										
By husband	14	44	43	47	49	52	50	50	49	50
By wife	18	67	101	123	131	139	131	133	134	135
Total	32	111	145	170	180	191	180	183	183	185
Decrees nisi granted (thousands)										
England & Wales	27	89	132	148	148	162	153	150	155	152
Decrees absolute granted (thousands)										
England & Wales	25	74	127	146	145	160	154	151	153	151
Scotland	2	5	9	10	12	13	13	12	11	12
Northern Ireland	—	—	1	1	2	2	2	2	2	2
United Kingdom	27	80	136	157	158	175	168	165	166	164
Persons divorcing per thousand married people										
England & Wales	2.1	6.0	10.1	11.9	12.0	13.4	12.9	12.7	12.8	12.7
Percentage of divorces where one or both partners had been divorced in an immediately previous marriage										
England & Wales	9.3	8.8	11.6	17.1	21.0	23.0	23.2	23.5	24.0	24.7
Estimated numbers of divorced people who had not remarried (thousands)										
Great Britain										
Men	101	200	405	653	847	918	990	1,047	..	..
Women	184	317	564	890	1,105	1,178	1,258	1,327	..	..
Total	285	517	969	1,543	1,952	2,096	2,248	2,374	..	..

1 This table includes annulment throughout. See Appendix, Part 2: Divorce.
2 Estimates based on 100 per cent of petitions at the Principal Registry together with a 2 month sample of county court petitions (March and September).

Source: Office of Population Censuses and Surveys;
Lord Chancellor's Department;
General Register Office (Scotland)

2.17 Divorce: by duration of marriage

Great Britain Percentages and thousands

	Year of divorce			
	1961	1971	1981	1990
Duration of marriage				
(percentages)				
0 – 2 years	1.2	1.2	1.5	9.5
3 – 4 years	10.1	12.2	19.0	13.7
5 – 9 years	30.6	30.5	29.1	27.5
10 – 14 years	22.9	19.4	19.6	17.9
15 – 19 years	13.9	12.6	12.8	12.9
20 – 24 years		9.5	8.6	9.3
25 – 29 years	21.2	5.8	4.9	4.9
30 years and over		8.9	4.5	4.1
All durations				
(= 100%) (thousands)	27.0	79.2	155.6	165.7

Source: Office of Population Censuses and Surveys;
General Register Office (Scotland)

Another impact of the 1984 Act can also be seen in Table 2.17. Whereas in 1981 only 1.5 per cent of divorces in Great Britain occurred within 2 years of marriage, this rose to almost 10 per cent by 1990. In each of the years shown most divorces occurred in marriages of between 5 to 9 years duration. These accounted for over a quarter of total divorces in 1990. Whereas only four in every ten divorces in 1961 affected marriages which had lasted less than ten years, this proportion had risen to five in every ten by 1990.

2.18 Divorce: by sex and age

England & Wales Rates[1]

	1961	1971	1981	1990
Males				
Aged 16 and over	2.1	5.9	11.9	12.2
16—24	1.4	5.0	17.7	21.6
25—29	3.9	12.5	27.6	29.0
30—34	4.1	11.8	22.8	25.1
35—44	3.1	7.9	17.0	17.9
45 and over	1.1	3.1	4.8	5.0
Females				
Aged 16 and over	2.1	5.9	11.9	12.1
16—24	2.4	7.5	22.3	23.4
25—29	4.5	13.0	26.7	27.3
30—34	3.8	10.5	20.2	22.7
35—44	2.7	6.7	14.9	15.6
45 and over	0.9	2.8	3.9	3.9

1 Per 1,000 married population.

Source: Office of Population Censuses and Surveys

There has been an increase in the incidence of divorce in England and Wales at all age groups since 1961, but for both sexes divorce is most likely to occur between the ages 25 and 29 (Table 2.18). Most divorce petitions are filed by women; in 1989 nearly three times as many petitions were filed by women than by men.

'Cohabitation' is taken as living together as husband and wife without having married legally. Chart 2.19 shows the proportion of women who cohabited with their future husband before marriage. In 1972 16 per cent of women who married had previously cohabited with their future husband. For women who married during the 1980s the proportion who had previously cohabited prior to marriage rose quite steeply to reach around 50 per cent by 1987.

Data derived from the 1987-88 General Household Survey (GHS) show that the peak ages for cohabitation were 20 to 24 for women and 20 to 29 for men. Cohabitation rates were higher for women who married at the age of 25 or over than those who married younger.

2.19 Proportion of women who cohabited with their future husband before marriage: by year of marriage

Great Britain

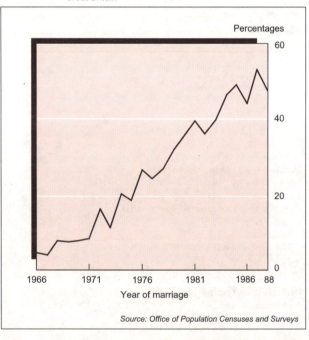

Source: Office of Population Censuses and Surveys

Family building

Estimates and projections of the number of children per woman and of the future numbers of births are important elements underlying the population projections discussed in Chapter 1; the assumptions used for England and Wales are illustrated in Chart 2.20. Women born in the earlier years shown will have already completed their families, but for the younger women examination of recent trends and evidence from the General Household Survey, where women are asked about their future child-bearing expectations, are taken into account.

Most women have children, though families are on average becoming smaller. Chart 2.20 shows that the percentage of women who had any children increased steadily from about 80 per cent of those born in 1920 up to a peak of 90 per cent of women born in 1945. For women born more recently the likelihood of remaining childless has increased and it is estimated that 17 per cent of women born in 1955 will not have any children. Corresponding to this upward trend in the proportion of women remaining childless, the proportion of women projected to have two or more children now looks likely to fall.

2.20 Estimated and projected[1] total number of children per woman: by woman's year of birth

England & Wales

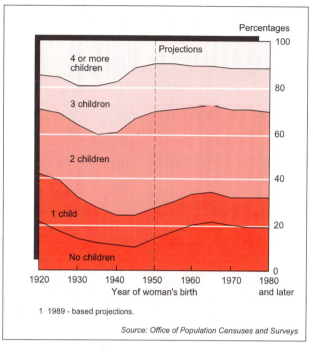

1 1989 - based projections.

Source: Office of Population Censuses and Surveys

2.21 Live births: by age of mother

Great Britain						Percentages and thousands
	1941	1951	1961	1971	1981	1990
Age of mother (years)						
15 – 19	4.3	4.3	7.2	10.6	9.0	7.9
20 – 24	25.4	27.6	30.8	36.5	30.9	25.5
25 – 29	31.1	32.2	30.7	31.4	34.0	35.9
30 – 34	22.1	20.7	18.8	14.1	19.7	22.1
35 – 39	12.7	11.5	9.6	5.8	5.3	7.3
40 – 44	4.2	3.4	2.7	1.5	1.0	1.3
45 – 49	0.3	0.2	0.2	0.1	0.1	0.1
All births (= 100%) (thousands)	669	768	912	870	704	772

Source: Office of Population Censuses and Surveys;
General Register Office (Scotland)

In 1941, 17 per cent of live births in Great Britain were to women over 35 years of age, but by 1981 the proportion had fallen to 6 per cent. By 1990 it had risen again to 9 per cent (Table 2.21). On the other hand, in 1941, 30 per cent of all births were to women under the age of 25 and this increased to 47 per cent in 1971 before decreasing to 33 per cent in 1990.

2.22 Live births outside marriage as a percentage of all births

United Kingdom

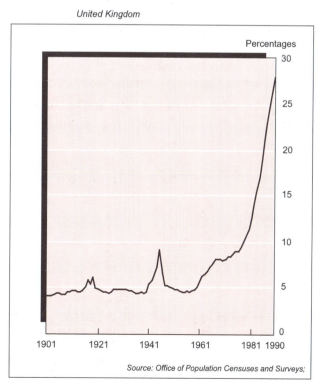

Source: Office of Population Censuses and Surveys;

During the first half of this century, the percentage of births in England and Wales which were outside marriage remained at around 4 to 5 per cent, with the exception of the period around both World Wars. The figure fell again after each war so that in the early 1950s the percentage of births outside marriage in the United Kingdom was still only slightly higher than it had been 50 years earlier (Chart 2.22). During the past 30 years the percentage of births outside marriage has risen from 5 per cent in 1960 to 11 per cent in 1979, when it started to rise steeply, so that by 1990 it had reached 28 per cent of all births.

2.23 Live births outside marriage as a percentage of all births: by registration

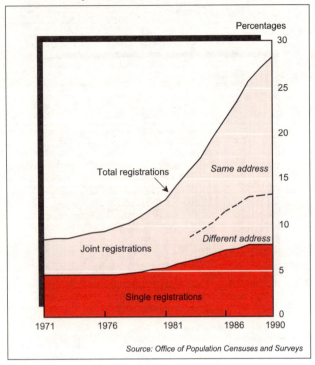

England & Wales

Source: Office of Population Censuses and Surveys

The trend towards more live births outside marriage has been accompanied in recent years by a trend towards joint registration - ie by both parents - of births outside marriage, possibly reflecting that the births are in a stable relationship even though they are outside marriage. Chart 2.23 shows that between 1971 and 1990 the percentage of births outside marriage with joint registrations rose quite sharply. In 1971 the proportion of live births outside marriage registered by both parents was 3.8 per cent, by 1984 one in ten births were outside marriage and registered jointly. By 1990 the percentage of births outside marriage and registered by both parents had reached one in five of all births.

2.24 Percentage of live births outside marriage: by age of mother and region, 1990

	Under 20	20 – 39	40 and over	Percentages All ages
United Kingdom	80.2	23.5	19.6	27.9
North	85.9	26.6	22.1	32.8
Yorkshire & Humberside	80.1	25.0	22.9	30.6
East Midlands	81.6	23.0	21.6	28.0
East Anglia	74.5	19.0	16.7	22.8
South East	76.8	23.0	20.2	25.9
South West	79.7	20.5	22.2	24.3
West Midlands	77.7	24.3	18.6	29.1
North West	85.3	28.8	19.5	34.4
England	80.2	24.0	20.4	28.3
Wales	81.2	23.7	21.7	29.3
Scotland	80.3	22.2	18.7	27.1
Northern Ireland	76.1	14.6	4.8	18.7

Source: Office of Population Censuses and Surveys;
General Register Office (Scotland)

Table 2.24 shows regional variations of live births outside marriage in 1990. Births outside marriage to women under the age of 20 in the United Kingdom accounted for 80 per cent of all births to women in that age group. Regionally, this ranged from 74 per cent in East Anglia to 86 per cent in the North.

2.25 Live births outside marriage as a percentage of all births: international comparison

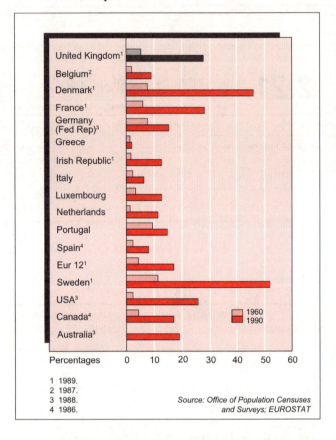

1 1989.
2 1987.
3 1988.
4 1986.

Source: Office of Population Censuses
and Surveys; EUROSTAT

Just over half of all live births in Sweden in 1989 were outside marriage (Chart 2.25). This is the largest proportion of all the countries shown. All countries show an increase in births outside marriage in the years between 1960 and 1990. Greece had the lowest proportion in both years, only 2 per cent in 1990.

Patterns of family building are changing, most people now wait longer to start a family (Table 2.26). In England and Wales in 1990 wives of those in the professional and managerial and technical social classes (as defined by occupation) tended to have waited longest between marriage and the birth of their first child, an average 34 months. Wives of semi-skilled and unskilled manual workers, however, show the most consistent increase over the period with the median interval between marriage and first birth 8 months longer in 1990 than in 1971. The median interval between first and subsequent births in Great Britain have remained fairly constant.

2.26 Birth intervals: by social class

England & Wales, and Great Britain   Months

	England & Wales[1]					Great Britain[2]	
	Median interval between marriage and first birth					Median interval between	
	Social class of father[3]					First and second birth	Second and third birth
	Professional and intermediate	Skilled non-manual	Skilled manual	Semi-skilled and unskilled manual	All socio-economic groups		
1971	29	26	19	13	20	.	.
1976	39	35	26	19	29	33	42
1981	39	34	26	19	28	31	40
1986	36	32	25	19	27	32	39
1987	35	31	25	18	27	32	38
1988	34	32	25	18	27	32	38
1989	32	32	25	20	27	32	38
1990	34	30	25	21	27	33	37

1 To women married once only.
2 All women.
3 As defined by Classification of Occupations. See Appendix, Part 2.

Source: Office of Population Censuses and Surveys

Conceptions can take place inside or outside marriage and can end in live births, stillbirths or legal abortions. The pattern of conceptions changed considerably between 1971 and 1989 (Table 2.27). Whereas in 1971, 86 per cent of conceptions were either inside marriage or marriage took place between conception and birth, this proportion had fallen to 62 per cent by 1989. The proportion of conceptions which were terminated by legal abortion rose from 12 per cent in 1971 to 20 per cent in 1989 (Table 2.30 gives more details on abortions).

2.27 Conceptions: by marital status and outcome

England & Wales   Percentages and thousands

	1971	1976	1981	1986	1988	1989
All conceptions[1]						
Inside marriage						
Maternities	72.6	70.7	65.9	58.1	54.1	53.3
Legal abortions[2]	5.2	6.1	5.6	4.7	4.5	4.4
Stillbirths	0.8	0.6	0.4	0.3	0.2	0.2
Outside marriage						
Maternities inside marriage	8.1	5.8	5.5	5.1	4.7	4.4
Maternities outside marriage[3]						
— joint registration	3.5	4.2	6.8	12.6	15.2	16.2
— sole registration	4.1	3.8	4.8	6.1	6.3	6.3
Still births	0.2	0.2	0.1	0.1	0.1	0.1
Legal abortions[2]	6.7	9.4	11.4	13.4	15.2	15.4
All conceptions (= 100%) (thousands)	835.5	671.6	752.3	818.9	849.5	864.7

1 Figures do not sum to 100% due to the stillbirths already being included in the maternity total and because of rounding.
2 Legal terminations under the *1967 Abortion Act*.
3 Births outside marriage can be registered by the mother only (sole registrations) or by both parents (joint registrations).

Source: Office of Population Censuses and Surveys

2.28 Conceptions to girls aged 16 or under: by outcome, 1989

Great Britain   Numbers

| | Number of conceptions | Outcome of conceptions | | | Legal abortions |
| | | Maternities | | | |
		Live	Still	Total	
Age at conception					
12 and under	24	11	0	11	13
13	226	108	0	108	118
14	1,765	779	4	783	982
15	6,367	3,113	11	3,124	3,243
All aged under 16	8,382	4,011	15	4,026	4,356
Aged 16	15,176	8,692	49	8,741	6,435

Source: Office of Population Censuses and Surveys

2.29 Contraception: by method used[1]

Great Britain   Percentages

	1976[2]	1983[3]	1986[3]	1989 –90[3]
Non-surgical				
Pill	29	28	26	25
IUD	6	6	8	6
Condom	14	13	13	16
Cap/Diaphragm	2	1	2	1
Withdrawal	5	4	4	4
Safe period	1	1	2	2
Other	1	1	1	1
Surgical				
Female sterilisation	7	11	11	11
Male sterilisation	6	10	12	12
Total using at least one method	68	75	75	72

1 Women aged 18-44.
2 Family Formation Survey, 1976.
3 General Household Survey, 1983, 1986 and 1989–90.
Source: Family Formation Survey, General Household Survey

2.30 Abortions: by marital status and age

England & Wales   Percentages and thousands

	1971	1976	1981	1986	1990
Single women					
Under 16	5.2	6.7	5.0	4.2	2.9
16-19	39.2	44.7	42.7	35.2	29.5
20-34	52.3	45.5	50.2	58.6	65.0
35-44	1.5	1.5	1.7	1.9	2.5
45 and over	0.0	0.0	0.0	0.0	0.0
Age not known	1.7	1.5	0.4	0.0	0.0
Total (= 100%) (thousands)	44.3	50.9	70.0	93.0	116.2
Married women					
Under 16	.	.	.	.	.
16-19	1.4	2.3	2.0	1.5	1.4
20-34	63.5	65.7	66.5	67.8	70.4
35-44	32.1	29.1	30.0	29.8	27.5
45 and over	0.9	1.0	1.0	0.8	0.7
Age not known	2.0	1.9	0.5	0.0	0.0
Total (= 100%) (thousands)	41.5	40.3	42.4	38.2	38.2

Source: Office of Population Censuses and Surveys

In Great Britain in 1989 there were over 23 thousand conceptions to girls aged 16 or under. Over one third of these were to girls aged under 16 (Table 2.28). Half of all conceptions to girls in the younger age groups (that is those aged under 16) ended in a legal abortion.

There has been a slight decline in the use of contraceptives in Great Britain since 1983 (Table 2.29). This is despite an increase in the use of condoms between 1986 and 1989. Use of the contraceptive pill has dropped slightly since 1976 although this is still the most popular method used.

More abortions are performed on single women than married women. In England and Wales in 1990 three times as many pregnancies to single women were terminated than those of married women (Table 2.30). The total number of abortions for single women has increased steadily since 1971, reaching 116 thousand in 1990. The number for married women, however, has remained relatively steady. The majority of abortions in both groups were in the age range 20 to 34 (two thirds or more).

BIBLIOGRAPHY

The following list contains selected publications relevant to Chapter 2: Households and Families. Those published by HMSO are available from the addresses shown on the back cover of Social Trends.

Annual Report of the Registrar General for Northern Ireland, HMSO
Annual Report of the Registrar General for Scotland, General Register Office (Scotland)
Birth Statistics (Series FM1), HMSO
Demographic Statistics, EUROSTAT
Family Expenditure Survey Report, HMSO
General Household Survey, HMSO
Household Projections, England, 1989-2011, HMSO

Key Population and Vital Statistics (Series VS/PP1), HMSO
Labour Force Survey, HMSO
Marriage and Divorce Statistics (Series FM2), HMSO
Population Trends, HMSO
Regional Trends, HMSO
Scottish Household Projections 1987 based (Statistical Bulletin HSG/1991/3), The Scottish Office

Chapter 3: Education

Education and day care of children under five

● A higher proportion of under fives attend school than ever before - over 50 per cent in 1990 compared with only 15 per cent in 1966. *(Table 3.2)*

Schools and their pupils

● As the number of pupils falls, so does the number of very large comprehensive schools. In 1979/80 43 per cent of schools had over one thousand pupils, by 1989/90 this proportion had fallen to 22 per cent. *(Table 3.7)*

● The percentage of pupils in independent schools continues to increase - to 7 per cent in 1990. *(Table 3.12)*

Qualifications and activities after age 16

● Girls are more likely to leave school with a qualification than boys. In 1988/89 67 per cent of girls and only 60 per cent of boys left school with at least one GCSE at grades A-C (or equivalent). *(Table 3.13)*

● For individual GCSE subjects, the greatest differences between the sexes are in Physics (where boys predominate) and in English (with girls outperforming boys). *(Chart 3.15)*

Further and higher education

● Housewives and the unemployed are now much more likely to enrol on Open University courses than they were when it first opened. *(Table 3.23)*

Educational standards of adults

● More men than women of working age hold a qualification - in 1990 72 per cent of men and 65 per cent of women held a qualification. *(Chart 3.29)*

Resources

● A higher proportion of teachers are graduates now than at the beginning of the 1980s. In 1988/89, 50 per cent of teachers were graduates compared with only 39 per cent in 1980/81. *(Table 3.32)*

3.1 School pupils: by type of school

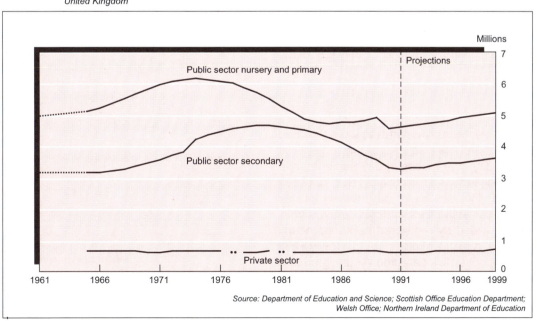

United Kingdom

Source: Department of Education and Science; Scottish Office Education Department; Welsh Office; Northern Ireland Department of Education

Education and childcare for children under five

3.2 Education and day care of children under five

United Kingdom   Thousands and percentages

		1966	1971	1976	1981	1986[1]	1988	1989	1990
Children under 5 in schools[2] (thousands)									
Public sector schools									
Nursery schools	— full-time	26	20	20	22	19	18	17	17
	— part-time	9	29	54	67	77	80	65	67
Primary schools	— full-time	220	263	350	281	306	314	317	346
	— part-time	—	38	117	167	228	243	273	286
Non-maintained schools	— full-time	21	19	19	19	20	23	26	27
	— part-time	2	14	12	12	15	17	18	19
Special schools	— full-time	2	2	4	4	4	4	4	4
	— part-time	—	—	1	1	2	2	2	2
Total		280	384	576	573	671	700	722	769
As a percentage of all children aged 3 or 4		*15.0*	*20.5*	*34.5*	*44.3*	*46.7*	*48.4*	*49.1*	*51.2*
Day care places[3] (thousands)									
Local authority day nurseries		21	23[2]	35	32	33	34	34	33
Local authority playgroups					5	5	6	4	3
Registered day nurseries		75	296	401	23	29	40[6]	49[6]	64[6]
Registered playgroups					433	473	479	480	491
Registered child minders[4]		32	90	86	110[5]	157	189	216	238
Total		128	409	522	603[5]	698	747	783	830

1 Data for 1985 have been used for Scotland for children under 5 in schools.
2 Pupils aged under 5 at December/January of academic year.
3 Figures for 1966 and 1971 cover England and Wales at end-December 1966 and end-March 1972 respectively. From 1976 data are at end-March except for the Northern Ireland component which is at end-December of the preceding year up to 1988.

4 Includes child minders provided by local authorities.
5 Because of a different method of collection of data between 1978 and 1981, these figures are less reliable.
6 No figures are available for registered nurseries in Scotland. An estimate has been made for the purposes of obtaining a United Kingdom total.

Source: Department of Health; Education Statistics for the United Kingdom, Department of Education and Science; The Scottish Office Social Work Services Group; Welsh Office; Department of Health and Social Services, Northern Ireland

The number of children under five who went to private or public sector schools in the United Kingdom rose from 280 thousand in 1966 to 769 thousand in 1990 (Table 3.2). The number of young children attending school is clearly affected by the number of children in the population. So, provision for the under fives can be better expressed as the number attending school as a percentage of the total population aged 3 to 4. This proportion rose from 15 per cent in 1966 to 51 per cent in 1990. Much of this increase occurred between 1966 and 1981 and was accounted for largely by an increase in the number of children attending for only part of the day.

As well as the increase in provision in schools, between 1966 and 1990 there was also a significant increase in the number of day care places in day nurseries and playgroups and with registered childminders. Between 1981 and 1990 the number of day nursery places provided by local authorities changed only slightly whilst those provided by registered nurseries nearly trebled. The vast majority of playgroup places were in registered (as opposed to local authority) playgroups in both 1981 and 1990.

3.3 Education and day care of children under five: by age and region, 1989[1]

Percentages and thousands

	Under fives in maintained schools[2]			
	As percentage of population in age group			Total
	Aged 2	Aged 3	Aged 4[3]	(thousands)
North	*8.7*	*62.0*	*96.1*	*53.9*
Yorkshire & Humberside	*4.5*	*50.6*	*89.4*	*73.0*
East Midlands	*4.1*	*36.4*	*80.3*	*47.3*
East Anglia	*0.8*	*15.2*	*78.6*	*16.9*
South East	*2.5*	*24.9*	*58.8*	*148.3*
South West	*1.2*	*12.6*	*80.4*	*36.2*
West Midlands	*4.9*	*42.7*	*83.8*	*71.2*
North West	*8.1*	*46.5*	*94.3*	*100.8*
England	*4.1*	*34.0*	*76.8*	*547.6*
Wales	*0.4*	*46.4*	*92.9*	*50.4*
Scotland	*0.3*	*18.2*	*60.1*	*49.8*
Northern Ireland	*—*	*15.0*	*75.3*	*30.1*

1 At January, except Scotland — at September 1988.
2 Ages at 31 August 1988 for England and 31 December 1988 for Scotland, Wales and Northern Ireland.
3 Excludes pupils aged 4 at 31 August 1988 who attained the age of 5 by 31 December 1988.

Source: Department of Education and Science

Social Trends 22, © Crown copyright 1992

Table 3.3 gives a regional comparison of education and day care of children under five for 1989. Best provision is in the North, which has the highest percentages at all ages, with over 96 per cent of 4 year olds attending maintained schools. In all regions over half of all children aged four attended maintained schools in 1989.

Chart 3.4 is an international comparison of the participation in education of children aged between three and five years. Such comparisons are not straight forward and are complicated by the different kinds of provision in each country and the different definitions of education. For most of the countries shown, compulsory schooling starts when children are six years old. The exceptions are in the United Kingdom and the Netherlands, where it begins earlier at age five years, and the Scandinavian countries, where it begins later at age seven. In the United States the age at which compulsory schooling starts varies from state to state and ranges from six to eight years old. In Belgium and France, nearly all three to five year olds participated in education in 1988, despite compulsory schooling not starting until the age of six. In the same year, nearly two thirds of three to five year olds in the United Kingdom participated in education.

3.4 Participation of 3-5 year olds in education[1]: international comparison, 1988[2]

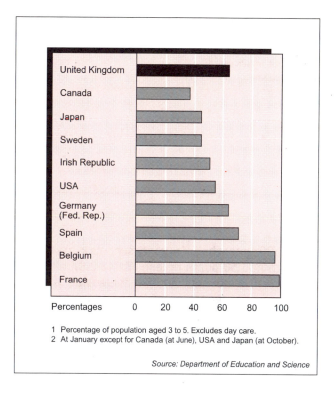

Percentages   0   20   40   60   80   100

1 Percentage of population aged 3 to 5. Excludes day care.
2 At January except for Canada (at June), USA and Japan (at October).

Source: Department of Education and Science

Schools and their pupils

3.5 School pupils[1]: by type of school[2]

United Kingdom				Thousands
	1961	1971	1981[3]	1990[3]
Public sector schools				
(full and part-time)				
Nursery schools	31	50	89	103
Primary schools				
Under fives	4,906	301	459	814
Other primary[4]		5,601	4,712	4,072
Secondary schools				
Under school leaving age	. .	. .	4,202	3,069
Over school leaving age	. .	. .	404	418
All secondary schools	3,165	3,555	4,606	3,848
Total public sector	8,102	9,507	9,866	8,477
Independent schools	680	621	619	613
Special schools				
(full-time equivalent)	77	103	147	109
All schools	8,859	10,230	10,632	9,199

1 Part-time pupils are counted as one (except for special schools).
2 See Appendix, Part 3: Main categories of educational establishments and Stages of education.
3 Figures for Scottish components are at previous September.
4 In Scotland, 11 year olds are customarily in primary schools.

Source: Department of Education and Science;
The Scottish Office Education Department; Welsh Office;
Northern Ireland Department of Education

This section covers all pupils in public sector schools, assisted and independent schools and special schools for the handicapped. An increase in the birth rate in the United Kingdom in the late 1940s and more recently in the mid-1960s led to increases in the number of pupils in public sector primary and secondary schools between 1961 and the late 1970s (Chart 3.1 and Table 3.5). The raising of the minimum school-leaving age from 15 to 16 years of age in 1972/73 also increased the number of secondary school pupils.

The number of pupils in public sector nursery and primary schools fell by 22 per cent between 1976 and 1986, reflecting falling birth rates in the late 1960s and 1970s. However, the number of pupils increased slightly in each year between 1986 and 1989 and projections to the turn of the century show a slight fall, followed by a steady increase. The number of pupils at public sector secondary schools fell between 1981 and 1990, but is projected to increase from 1992 till at least the year 1999.

3.6 Public sector nursery and primary schools: by size, 1979/80 and 1989/90

United Kingdom		Percentages and numbers		
	Nursery		Primary	
	1979/80	1989/90	1979/80	1989/90
Number of pupils on school register				
(percentages)				
50 and under	*52.4*	*45.9*	*11.0*	*9.6*
51 – 100	*39.0*	*42.9*	*13.6*	*13.6*
101 – 200	*8.6*	*11.2*	*31.5*	*33.6*
201 and over	*—*	*—*	*43.9*	*43.2*
Total schools (= 100%) (numbers)	1,236	1,337	26,764	24,268

Source: Education Statistics for the United Kingdom, Department of Education and Science

In 1989/90 almost half of nursery schools in the United Kingdom had 50 pupils or less (Table 3.6), although between 1979/80 and 1989/90 there was a small increase in the proportion of larger nursery schools (with over 100 pupils).

Between 1979/80 and 1989/90, the proportion of comprehensive schools in the United Kingdom with over one thousand pupils fell from 43 per cent to 22 per cent (Table 3.7). This reflected the fall over the period of the total number of pupils (see Table 3.5).

Table 3.8 shows the change in the structure of maintained secondary education in Great Britain between 1971 and 1990, with a shift from selective to comprehensive education (see Appendix: Part 3). In 1971, 36 per cent of pupils in maintained secondary schools in England attended comprehensive or middle deemed secondary schools compared to 59 per cent in both Wales and Scotland. However, by 1990 these proportions had increased to 92 per cent in England, 99 per cent in Wales and 100 per cent in Scotland.

3.7 Public sector secondary schools: by type and size, 1979/80 and 1989/90

United Kingdom		Percentages and numbers		
	Comprehensive		Other[1]	
	1979/80	1989/90	1979/80	1989/90
Number of pupils on school register[2]				
(percentages)				
400 and under	*5.5*	*9.0*	*31.7*	*44.9*
401 – 800	*30.0*	*46.0*	*55.3*	*46.4*
801 – 1,000	*21.6*	*22.7*	*7.9*	*5.9*
1,001 and over	*42.9*	*22.3*	*5.2*	*2.8*
Total schools (= 100%) (numbers)	3,982	3,890	1,589	986

1 Includes middle schools deemed secondary, secondary modern, grammar schools, technical and other schools.
2 The split between Comprehensive and Other secondary schools includes estimated data for Northern Ireland.

Source: Department of Education and Science; The Scottish Office Education Department; Welsh Office; Northern Ireland Department of Education

3.8 Pupils in public sector secondary education [1,2]: by type of school

England, Wales, Scotland and Northern Ireland	Percentages and thousands		
	1971	1981	1990
England *(percentages)*			
Maintained secondary schools			
Middle deemed secondary	*1.9*	*7.0*	*6.5*
Modern	*38.0*	*6.0*	*3.8*
Grammar	*18.4*	*3.4*	*3.4*
Technical	*1.3*	*0.3*	*0.1*
Comprehensive	*34.4*	*82.5*	*85.9*
Other	*6.0*	*0.9*	*0.3*
Total pupils (= 100%) (thousands)	2,953	3,840	2,863
Wales *(percentages)*			
Maintained secondary schools			
Middle deemed secondary	*0.1*	*0.1*	*—*
Modern	*22.3*	*1.8*	*—*
Grammar	*15.4*	*1.3*	*—*
Comprehensive	*58.5*	*96.6*	*99.2*
Other	*3.7*	*0.3*	*0.8*
Total pupils (= 100%) (thousands)	191	240	186
Scotland *(percentages)*			
Public sector secondary schools			
Selective	*28.3*	*0.1*	*—*
Comprehensive	*58.7*	*96.0*	*100.0*
Part comprehensive/part selective	*13.0*	*3.8*	*—*
Total pupils (= 100%) (thousands)	314	408	299
Northern Ireland *(percentages)*			
All Grant-aided secondary schools			
Secondary intermediate	*87.7*	*88.6*	*62.3*
Grammar[3]	*11.8*	*11.4*	*37.7*
Technical intermediate	*0 5*	*—*	*—*
Total pupils (= 100%) (thousands)	96	119	141

1 See Appendix, Part 3: Main categories of educational establishments and Stages of education.
2 Counts at January except 1981 data for Scotland which are at the preceding September.
3 Includes Voluntary Grammar Schools from 1989/90 — formerly independent sector.

Source: Education Statistics for the United Kingdom, Department of Education and Science

The large increase between 1970/71 and 1980/81 in the number of pupils at special schools was due mainly to the *Education (Handicapped Children) Act 1970*, under which local authorities in England and Wales assumed responsibility from April 1971 for all establishments catering for mentally handicapped children (Table 3.9). Previously, the most severely mentally handicapped children had been the responsibility of the health authorities. The *Education (Mentally Handicapped Children) (Scotland) Act 1974* made similar provisions in Scotland. The *Education Act 1981* abolished the ten statutory handicap groups into which pupils had previously fallen. Instead local education authorities assess a child's education needs, providing a statement of these needs where necessary. In 1989/90 there were some 400 full-time teachers teaching around four times as many full-time pupils in 60 hospital schools in England, Wales and Northern Ireland. Between 1985/86 and 1989/90 the number of pupils in public sector schools with statements of special needs increased by 69 per cent to reach over 64 thousand.

3.9 Pupils with special needs in public sector schools

England, Wales and Northern Ireland, United Kingdom   Numbers and thousands

	1970/71	1975/76	1980/81	1985/86	1988/89	1989/90
Hospital schools						
(England, Wales and Northern Ireland)						
Schools (numbers)	91	166	145	100	69	60
Full-time pupils (thousands)	3.8	9.7	7.3	4.6	2.8	1.6
Full-time teachers[1] (thousands)	0.5	1.2	1.2	0.7	0.5	0.4
Other special schools or departments[2]						
(United Kingdom)[3]						
Schools (numbers)	1,113	1,747	1,875	1,821	1,812	1,801
Full-time pupils (thousands)[2]	99.5	139.5	139.2	126.0	114.1	112.1
Full-time (or equivalent)						
teachers (thousands)[2]	9.3	15.8	18.4	18.5	18.7	19.0
Pupils with statements of special						
needs in other public sector schools						
(thousands) (United Kingdom)				38.2	57.4	64.4

1 Excluding part-time teachers, full-time equivalent in 1989/90 was 33.
2 Includes all Scottish special schools. 1984/85 data for Scotland have been used for 1985/86.

3 Figures from 1987 onwards include schools and pupils which were previously the responsibility of the Northern Ireland Department of Health and Social Security, and were formerly excluded.

Source: Education Statistics for the United Kingdom, Department of Education and Science

The average class size in public sector primary schools in England fell slightly between 1977 and 1981 and was still at the 1981 level in 1990 (Table 3.10). In secondary schools, the average class size was 21 in 1990, a slight fall from 22 in 1981. The proportion of large classes in secondary schools (ie with 31 or more pupils) halved between 1981 and 1990, when they represented only 4 per cent of all secondary school classes. In Scotland there were 437 thousand pupils attending 18 thousand primary school classes in September 1989 - an average class size of 24.7, slightly lower than in England.

The proportion of school pupils claiming free school meals rose from 11 per cent in 1971 to 15 per cent in 1978. The proportion then fell slightly before again increasing to reach a peak of 20 per cent in 1986. By 1990 it had dropped back to 12 per cent (Chart 3.11). During the 1970s schools changed the types of meals offered from the traditional style to simpler meals with greater choice. The *Education Act 1980* let local education authorities decide the kind of meal service that they wanted to provide. Net expenditure on school meals and milk fell in real terms by almost a half between 1979/80 and 1988/89.

3.10 Class sizes as taught[1]: by type of school

England

	1977	1981	1986	1990
Primary schools				
Percentage of classes taught by:				
One teacher in classes with				
1—20 pupils	*16*	*20*	*17*	*13*
21—30 pupils	*46*	*55*	*58*	*62*
31 or more pupils	*34*	*22*	*19*	*18*
Two or more teachers	*4*	*3*	*6*	*7*
Average size of class (numbers)	28	26	26	26
Number of classes (thousands)	171	161	142	146
Secondary schools				
Percentage of classes taught by:				
One teacher in classes with				
1—20 pupils	*42*	*44*	*46*	*46*
21—30 pupils	*42*	*45*	*45*	*45*
31 or more pupils	*12*	*8*	*6*	*4*
Two or more teachers	*4*	*2*	*3*	*5*
Average size of class (numbers)	22	22	21	21
Number of classes (thousands)	165	174	155	132

1 Class size related to one selected period in each public sector school on the day of the count in January. Middle schools are either primary or secondary for this table - see Appendix, Part 3: Stages of education.

Source: Department of Education and Science

3.11 School meals

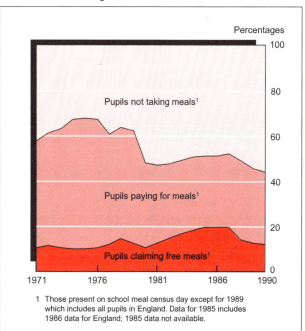

United Kingdom

Percentages

Pupils not taking meals[1]

Pupils paying for meals[1]

Pupils claiming free meals[1]

1971   1976   1981   1986   1990

1 Those present on school meal census day except for 1989 which includes all pupils in England. Data for 1985 includes 1986 data for England; 1985 data not available.

Source: Department of Education and Science; Welsh Office; Scottish Office Education Department; Northern Ireland Department of Education

3.12 Pupils in independent schools as a proportion of all pupils[1]: by sex and age[2]

Great Britain					Percentages
	1976	1981	1986[3]	1989	1990
Boys aged:					
Under 11	4	4	5	5	5
11—15	7	6	7	8	8
16 and over	16	17	19	19	20
All ages	6	6	6	7	7
Girls aged:					
Under 11	4	4	5	5	5
11—15	6	6	6	7	8
16 and over	13	12	14	15	16
All ages	5	5	6	6	7
All pupils	5	5	6	7	7

1 At January.
2 Ages are as at December of the previous year for 1976 and 1981. Thereafter ages are as at previous August for England and Wales and December for Scotland.
3 Includes estimates for Scotland.

Source: Department of Education and Science

In 1990, 7 per cent of all pupils in Great Britain attended independent schools - an increase from 5 per cent in 1976 (Table 3.12). The percentage increases with age - 20 per cent of boys and 16 per cent of girls aged 16 and over went to independent schools.

Implementation of a National Curriculum for all 5 to 16 year olds in public sector schools began in Autumn 1989. The National Curriculum covers 10 foundation subjects with the study of English, mathematics and science at its core. Welsh is also specified as either a core subject or a foundation subject in Wales. Individual pupils' performance is formally assessed at the end of four 'Key Stages' - at ages 7, 11, 14 and 16. The first assessments were for 7 year olds in English, mathematics and science in 1991 and combined teachers' judgements with performance during nationally designed tests. Schools were required to report the results of these assessments to pupils' parents in 1991, but were not required to publish them in aggregate form. In Scotland, there is no statutory National Curriculum, but The Scottish Office has introduced a programme that will have broadly the same effect.

In 1992 there will be a national pilot of the testing arrangements in mathematics and science for 14 year olds. All schools will be encouraged to take part in the pilot and to report the results of pupils to their parents. The first statutory assessments in these subjects plus English and technology (plus Welsh where appropriate) will take place in 1993. Schools will then be required to publish the results of the national assessments in aggregate form.

The Technical and Vocational Education Initiative (TVEI) is designed so that 14 to 18 year olds in maintained schools and colleges can develop the knowledge, skills and qualities required in the labour force. More practical and active learning methods are being introduced to help develop more enterprising and capable young people. Under TVEI every young person has the opportunity to undertake a period of work experience and receive a Record of Achievement. Guidance is given on appropriate career opportunities including further education and training. The government has allocated £900 million over the ten year period 1987-1997 to extend the opportunity to participate in TVEI to all 14 to 18 year olds in maintained schools and colleges.

Launched in 1988 as part of the government's Action for Cities programme, the Compact inner city initiative brings together young people, employers and schools and colleges. In 1991, the network of 61 inner city compacts was complete. Plans were announced in May 1991 for the Compact approach, adapted to local needs, to spread to other areas of the country. By 1991, 9 thousand employers and training organisations and over 500 schools were involved in their local Compact, working with 92 thousand young people.

Under the *Education Reform Act 1988* the Secretary of State for Education and Science can enter into agreement with any person to establish and maintain a City Technology College (CTC) or a City College for the Technology of the Arts. These non-fee paying colleges, located in urban areas, are intended for pupils aged between 11 and 18 years. CTCs have a broad curriculum with the emphasis on science and technology. The first CTC opened in Kingshurst in September 1988, followed by Nottingham and Teeside in September 1989, and Bradford, Dartford, Gateshead and Croydon in September 1990. In 1991, new CTCs were opened in Corby, Docklands, New Cross, Telford and Wandsworth and the first City College for the Technology of the Arts opened in Croydon.

Under the *Education Reform Act 1988*, all maintained primary and secondary schools are being given responsibility for the management of their own budget, and associated staffing powers. Local education authorities are organising the implementation for their own schools and the process will be complete by April 1994. Local management of schools is also about getting an open system for funding schools. The local education authorities' local management schemes each contain a formula for distributing funds to schools - principally based on the number and ages of pupils. In England, 87 schemes were approved for operation in April 1990; a further 10 were approved for operation from April 1991; and the remaining 12 authorities (in inner London) are due to have approved schemes in place for April 1992.

The *Education (No 2) Act 1986* changed the statutory composition of county and voluntary controlled school governing bodies. This created a new balance between elected parent and teacher governors, LEA appointed governors, and governors co-opted from the local business community. The intention was to give parents and the local community more say in how their schools are run. In the Act, school governors were also given more responsibilities in directing the conduct of schools. These responsibilities were further enhanced by the *Education Reform Act 1988*.

Since 1988, all local education authority maintained secondary, middle and primary schools have been able to apply for grant maintained status and receive grants direct from the Department of Education and Science. The governing body of any school applying becomes responsible for all aspects of school management, including the deployment of funds, employment of staff and the provision of most of the educational and support services for staff and pupils. In January 1991, there were 50 grant maintained schools in England and Wales.

Qualifications and activities after age 16

3.13 Highest qualification[1] attained by school leavers as a percentage of the relevant population: by sex

United Kingdom										Percentages and thousands
	Boys					Girls				
	1970/71	1975/76	1980/81[2]	1985/86	1988/89	1970/71	1975/76	1980/81[2]	1985/86	1988/89
Percentage with:										
2 or more 'A' levels/3 or more 'H' grades	15	14	15	15	18	13	12	13	14	19
1 'A' level/1 or 2 'H' grades	4	4	3	4	4	4	4	4	4	4
5 or more GCSE/'O' levels grades A – C[3] (no 'A'-levels)	7	7	8	10	12	9	9	10	12	15
1-4 GCSE/'O' levels grades A-C[3]	17	24	25	24	26	18	27	28	29	29
1 or more GCSE/'O' levels grades D – G[4]	57	30	34	34	30	56	28	32	31	26
No GCSE/GCE/SCE or CSE grades		21	15	13	10		19	12	10	7
Total school leavers (=100%) (thousands)	368	423	442	444	387	349	400	423	427	366

1 See Appendix, Part 3: School-leaving qualification.
2 Great Britain only.
3 Includes GCSE/'O' level grades A – C, CSE grade 1.

4 Includes GCSE grades D – G, 'O' level grades D – E, CSE grades 2 – 5.

Source: Department of Education and Science

Pupils in all parts of the United Kingdom have the option of leaving school at 16. However, school leaving dates in Scotland allow a large number of Scottish pupils to leave at 15. The proportion of school pupils who stay on for one extra year is much higher in Scotland than in England and Wales, as is the proportion staying on for two extra years. This is partly because staying on at school is the normal choice in Scotland for pupils who wish to gain entrance qualifications for higher education. In England and Wales many pupils attend further education colleges as an alternative to school. The higher proportions staying on at school in Scotland may also be partly due to the different structure of examinations.

In England, Wales and Northern Ireland a single examination system was introduced for those aged 16 and over in 1988. The General Certificate of Secondary Education (GCSE) replaced GCE 'O' levels and Certificates of Secondary Education (CSEs), and the first examinations were held in the summer of 1988. The GCSE examination is open to all pupils and the aim of the new system is to encourage pupils of all abilities to follow suitable courses and have these recognised with certificates which show their levels of achievement. The GCSE examinations are intended to give a clearer and more precise definition of the levels of attainment of 16 year olds in relation to their knowledge, understanding, skills and competence which the examination courses are designed to develop. The GCSE will be the principal means of assessing 16 year olds within the National Curriculum framework. (Further details can be found in the Government White Paper *Better Schools Cmnd 9469*).

The Advanced Supplementary ('AS') examination, introduced in 1989, runs alongside GCE 'A' levels to offer greater breadth in the curriculum for students in the sixth form (or equivalent). An 'AS' course takes about half the teaching and study time of an 'A' level course. Around 30 thousand students sat an 'AS' examination in at least one subject in 1990. Amongst the most popular subjects were mathematics, general studies, English, computing, and French.

Between 1975/76 and 1988/89 the proportion of boys leaving school with at least one GCE 'O' level (grades A-C) or equivalent rose from 49 per cent to 60 per cent, while among girls this percentage rose to an even greater extent from 52 per cent to 67 per cent (Table 3.13). It must be remembered that these figures are for school leavers only and it should be borne in mind that some pupils gain qualifications from further education colleges.

3.14 School leavers' examination achievements[1]: by sex and region, 1988/89

Percentages and thousands

	1 or more 'A' levels[2] (or SCE highers)	GCSEs[3] or SCE O/standard (no 'A' levels or SCE highers)	No graded results[4]	All leavers (= 100%) (thousands)
Males				
North	17.4	72.2	10.4	20.9
Yorkshire & Humberside	17.1	72.6	10.4	35.1
East Midlands	18.8	73.1	8.1	26.9
East Anglia	20.1	71.3	8.5	14.1
South East	23.8	67.9	8.3	104.4
South West	20.7	73.4	5.9	31.6
West Midlands	18.7	71.4	10.0	39.5
North West	18.7	69.7	11.6	44.6
England	20.4	70.6	9.1	317.0
Wales	19.0	65.0	16.0	20.2
Scotland	33.4	52.9	13.7	37.2
Northern Ireland	24.4	51.9	23.7	13.0
Females				
North	18.8	74.0	7.2	20.5
Yorkshire & Humberside	18.1	73.9	8.1	33.2
East Midlands	18.6	76.8	4.6	24.6
East Anglia	19.9	73.7	6.3	13.1
South East	23.6	70.3	6.2	101.8
South West	23.5	72.7	3.9	28.8
West Midlands	19.1	72.9	7.9	36.9
North West	18.6	72.7	8.6	41.8
England	20.8	72.5	6.7	300.7
Wales	21.0	68.0	11.0	18.9
Scotland	42.8	47.3	9.9	35.5
Northern Ireland	31.6	54.7	13.8	12.1

1 Excludes results in further education.
2 Two 'AS' levels are counted as equivalent to one 'A' level.
3 And equivalent grades at GCE and CSE.
4 Includes those pupils with no graded results in GCSE, SCE or A/AS

levels. Leavers sitting other examinations (eg Certificate of Education etc) are excluded.

Source: Department of Education and Science;
The Scottish Office Education Department;
Welsh Office; Department of Education Northern Ireland

Girls are less likely than boys to leave school with no graded examination results (Table 3.14). In England, 9 per cent of male school leavers and 7 per cent of female school leavers failed to achieve at least 1 GCSE grade G result in 1988/89. Among the English regions, the South West had the best performance -only 6 per cent of boys and 4 per cent of girls leaving without a

qualification. School leavers in Wales, Scotland and Northern Ireland were more likely to have no graded results in 1988/89 than their English counterparts. However, both boys and girls in Northern Ireland and Scotland were more likely than those in England to leave with at least one 'A' level pass (or equivalent).

DES Education Statistics Publications

Education Statistics for the United Kingdom 1990 £11.50

Available from HMSO Bookshops and Agents (see yellow pages) or through any good bookshop

ISBN 011 270703 3

Chart 3.15 shows the proportion of boys and girls leaving school in Great Britain who gained grade A-C results at GCSE or the Scottish equivalent qualification in selected subjects. Girls were more likely than boys to have gained results in English, Biology, French, and History, whilst boys were more likely than girls to have results in Mathematics, Physics, Geography, and Chemistry. The greatest differences between the sexes were for Physics (boys outperforming girls) and English (girls outperforming boys).

For many pupils, their achievements at GCSE are a stepping stone to further studies. Table 3.16 shows what 16 year old pupils in England and Wales intended to do the following year. Of the 619 thousand 16 year old pupils in 1989/90, 38 per cent intended to stay on at school and 17 per cent to continue in full-time further or higher education. The proportion continuing their education in one form or another ranged from 10 per cent of those with no graded results to 90 per cent of those with 5 or more GCSE grades A to C.

The actual destinations of Scottish school leavers who left school in the academic year 1987/88 are shown in Table 3.17. The majority of school leavers without qualifications went to either full-time employment or to a place on a Youth Training Scheme (YTS). Those with qualifications were almost equally as likely as those without qualifications to enter full-time employment but were much more likely to continue in full-time education.

3.15 Percentage of school leavers with grades A - C at GCSE[1]: by subject and sex, 1988/89

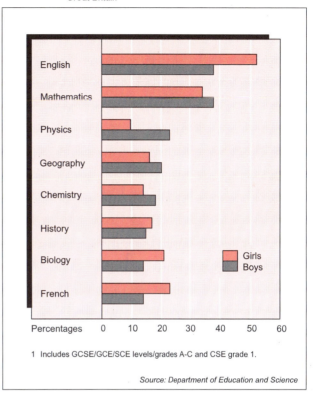

Great Britain

1 Includes GCSE/GCE/SCE levels/grades A-C and CSE grade 1.

Source: Department of Education and Science

3.16 Intended destinations of 16 year old pupils: by attainments at GCSE, 1989/90

England & Wales — Percentages and thousands

	5 or more grades A-C	1-4 grades A-C	Grades D-G only	No graded results	Total
Intended destination					
Staying on at school	72.3	30.4	14.1	7.4	38.4
Full-time further and					
* higher education*	17.4	24.9	13.4	2.6	17.4
of which:					
* A level/AS courses*	8.3	2.8	0.4	0.1	3.8
* GCSE courses*	0.1	2.1	1.4	0.3	1.1
* Other courses*	9.0	20.0	11.6	2.2	12.5
Total	89.7	55.3	27.4	10.1	55.7
Youth training scheme	1.5	10.5	18.7	13.7	10.0
Available for employment[1]	5.4	21.7	35.8	34.8	21.1
Other and not known	3.4	12.5	18.1	41.5	13.2
Total (= 100%)(thousands)	211.7	184.7	174.7	47.6	618.6

1 Including those going to temporary employment pending entry into full-time further/ higher education.

Source: Department of Education and Science

3.17 Actual destination of pupils leaving school[1]: by destination and qualification, 1989

Scotland — Percentages and thousands

	Full-time education	Full-time employment	YTS	Unemployed	Other/ destination unknown	All leavers (= 100%) (thousands)
Leavers with qualifications	32.3	31.7	26.8	5.2	4.0	63.1
Leavers without qualifications[2]	4.3	30.2	37.5	12.8	15.2	11.8
All leavers	27.9	31.5	28.5	6.4	5.8	74.8

1 Leavers from 1987/88.
2 With no SCE O grades 4-5 or equivalent.

Source: The Scottish Office Education Department

Further and higher education

3.18 Percentage of 16–18 year olds in education and training[1]: by age and type of study, international comparison, 1987[2]

Years and percentages

	Minimum leaving age (years)	16 years			16 to 18 years		
		Full-time	Part-time	All	Full-time	Part-time	All[3]
United Kingdom[4] 1987	16	50	41	91	35	34	69
1989	16	53	40	93	37	33	70
Belgium	14	92	4	96	82	4	87
Denmark	16	89	2	91	73	6	79
France	16	80	8	88	69	8	77
Germany (Fed. Rep.)[5]	15	71	29	100	49	43	92
Italy[2]	14	54	15	69	47	18	65
Netherlands[2,5]	16	92	6	98	77	9	86
Spain[6]	16[11]	65	—	65	50	—	50
Australia[2]	15[12]	71	11	82	50	16	66
Canada[7]	16/17	92	—	92	75	—	75
Japan[8,9]	15	92	3	96	77	3	79
Sweden[10]	16	91	1	92	76	2	78
USA[8]	16–18[13]	95	—	95	80	1	81

1 Includes apprenticeships, YTS and similar schemes.
2 1985 for Sweden; 1982 for Italy, 1986 for Netherlands and Australia.
3 Includes higher education for some 18 year olds.
4 Includes estimates for those studying only in the evening; also includes estimates of private sector further and higher education.
5 Includes compulsory part-time education for 16 and 17 year olds.
6 Excludes 18 year olds in universities.
7 Excludes certain part-time students, 10% at 16-18.

8 Includes private sector higher education.
9 Estimated for special training and miscellaneous schools providing vocational training.
10 Includes estimates for part-time.
11 By 1988–89; formerly 14.
12 16 in Tasmania.
13 Varies between states.

Source: Department of Education and Science

The proportion of 16 to 18 year olds participating in education and training varies between the different countries shown in Table 3.18. In Spain only 50 per cent of 16 to 18 years olds are in education and training, the proportion rises to 92 per cent in the Federal Republic of Germany. The United Kingdom participation rate was lower than in most of the countries shown. Looking solely at 16 year olds, the United Kingdom had the lowest full-time participation rate in 1988.

The number of students who enroled on further education courses in the United Kingdom fell by 61 thousand between 1970/71 and 1980/81 but rose by 398 thousand between 1980/81 and 1989/90 (Chart 3.19). Female students accounted for over 80 per cent of this increase. Full-time students accounted for slightly over one-fifth of all further education students in 1989/90, the same proportion as in 1980/81.

The Enterprise in Higher Education (EHE) initiative is designed to encourage the development of qualities of enterprise in those taking higher qualifications so that they are better prepared for the world of work. It enables universities, polytechnics and colleges of higher education to build on existing work to develop the curriculum, introduce new teaching methods, train and develop staff, and build new and closer partnerships with employers. EHE works through offering contracts valued at up to £1 million over 5 years. Since the programme started in 1988, 56 contracts (with a total of 60 institutions) have been agreed for participation in EHE.

3.19 Students in further education: by sex and whether full-time or part-time

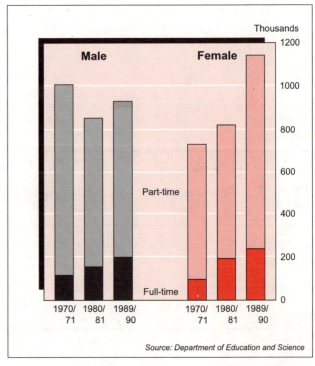

United Kingdom

Source: Department of Education and Science

3.20 Higher education[1] – full-time students: by sex, origin and age

United Kingdom   Thousands and percentages

	Males					Females				
	1970 /71	1975 /76	1980 /81	1985 /86	1989 /90	1970 /71	1975 /76	1980 /81	1985 /86	1989 /90
Full-time students by origin (thousands)										
From the United Kingdom										
Universities[2] — post-graduate	23.9	23.2	20.7	21.0	21.2	8.0	10.2	11.3	12.6	15.0
— first degree	} 128.3	130.1	145.1	{ 134.3	143.1	} 57.0	73.6	96.2	{ 99.9	115.3
— other[3]				1.5	1.4				1.2	1.4
Polytechnics and colleges	102.0	109.3	111.9	143.5	157.4	113.1	120.1	96.4	132.2	161.4
Total full-time UK students	254.2	262.6	277.7	300.4	323.1	178.2	203.8	203.9	245.9	293.2
From abroad	20.0	38.6	40.7	38.4	46.1	4.4	9.9	12.6	15.3	26.6
Total full-time students	274.2	301.2	318.4	338.7	369.2	182.6	213.7	216.5	261.3	319.8
Full-time students by age (percentages)										
18 years and under	10	11	[4] 16	15	15	17	14	[4] 19	17	17
19–20 years	36	35	37	38	36	45	42	41	42	38
21–24 years	38	36	30	29	30	24	28	25	26	27
25 years and over	15	19	17	18	18	14	16	15	15	19

1 See Appendix, Part 3: Stages of education.
2 From 1984 origin is based on students' usual places of domicile. Prior to 1984 origin is on fee-paying status except for EC students domiciled outside the United Kingdom, who from 1980/81 are charged home rates but are included with students from abroad.

3 University first diplomas and certificates.
4 In 1980 measurement by age changed from 31 December to 31 August.

Source: Education Statistics for the United Kingdom,
Department of Education and Science

The number of students on full-time higher education courses in the United Kingdom rose by nearly 30 per cent between 1980/81 and 1989/90 to stand at 689 thousand (Table 3.20). This increase was mainly confined to polytechnics and colleges as university numbers rose only slightly over the period. In 1989/90, 73 thousand students from abroad attended full-time higher education courses in the United Kingdom, - 10.5 per cent of all students on such courses.

Female students made up 47 per cent of all students on full-time first degree courses in 1989/90 compared to only 41 per cent in 1979/80 (Chart 3.21). The proportion of women studying the individual selected subjects in 1989/90 ranged from 78 per cent of all students on Education degree courses to only 12 per cent on Engineering and Technology courses. In all cases ,the proportion of women studying each subject increased between the two years shown.

3.21 Female students as a percentage of all students: by selected full-time first degree courses, 1979/80 and 1989/90

United Kingdom

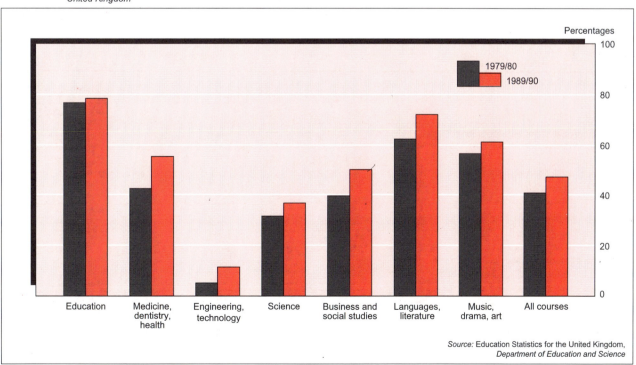

Percentages

Legend: ■ 1979/80 ■ 1989/90

Categories: Education, Medicine dentistry health, Engineering technology, Science, Business and social studies, Languages literature, Music drama art, All courses

Source: Education Statistics for the United Kingdom,
Department of Education and Science

3.22 Universities—mean 'A' level 'score'[1] of home undergraduate new entrants: by selected subject, 1989/90

Great Britain

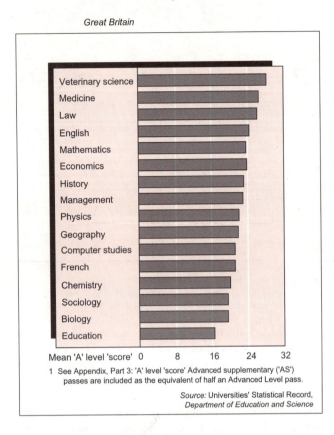

Subject (Mean 'A' level 'score' 0 to 32)
Veterinary science
Medicine
Law
English
Mathematics
Economics
History
Management
Physics
Geography
Computer studies
French
Chemistry
Sociology
Biology
Education

Mean 'A' level 'score'   0   8   16   24   32

1 See Appendix, Part 3: 'A' level 'score' Advanced supplementary ('AS') passes are included as the equivalent of half an Advanced Level pass.

Source: Universities' Statistical Record, Department of Education and Science

As a convenient way of measuring overall 'A' level performance, the Universities Central Council on Admissions (UCCA) translate 'A' level grades into a score (see Appendix: Part 3). The mean 'A' level score of new undergraduate university entrants varied considerably between subjects in 1989/90 from 28.3 for Veterinary Science students to 16.7 for Education

3.23 Open University students: by occupation of new undergraduates[1]

United Kingdom   Percentages and thousands

	1971	1981	1989
Occupation *(percentages)*			
Housewives	10	18	17
Teachers and lecturers	40	20	7
Technical personnel	12	12	14
Clerical and office staff	6	11	12
The professions and the arts	8	11	12
Shopkeepers, sales and services	3	5	7
Administrators and managers	5	3	4
Armed forces	2	3	4
Qualified scientists and engineers	6	3	3
In other employment	3	9	10
Not in employment	2	4	10
No information	2	—	—
Total new students (= 100%) (thousands)	20	14	17

1 Finally registered new students at commencement of studies.

Source: Open University Statistics; Department of Education and Science

students (Chart 3.22). Medicine, Law, English and Mathematics were among the subjects whose students had higher 'A' level scores and Biology, Sociology, and Chemistry among those whose students had lower scores.

The shift in the occupations of people studying at the Open University can be clearly seen in Table 3.23. In 1971, 40 per cent of new undergraduate students at the Open University were teachers, compared with only 7 per cent in 1989. Whilst the proportion of teachers fell over this period, there were large increases in the proportion of unemployed (from 2 per cent to 10 per cent) and housewives (from 10 per cent to 17 per cent).

3.24 Higher education[1] — part-time students[2]: by sex, type of establishment and age

United Kingdom   Thousands and percentages

	Males					Females				
	1970 /71	1975 /76	1980 /81	1985 /86	1989 /90	1970 /71	1975 /76	1980 /81	1985 /86	1989 /90
Part-time students by establishment										
(thousands)										
Universities	18.1	19.3	22.6	26.3	30.6	5.7	7.0	10.7	16.0	23.2
Open University[3]	14.3	33.6	37.6	41.7	46.7	5.3	22.0	30.1	36.0	42.3
Polytechnics and colleges										
— part-time day courses	69.8	80.2	110.5	112.2	118.1	6.7	15.4	30.8	49.9	73.5
— evening only courses	39.8	35.0	35.1	34.4	35.8	5.0	5.8	15.2	20.3	27.1
Total part-time students	142.0	168.1	205.7	214.6	231.2	22.7	50.2	86.8	122.2	166.1
Part-time students by age *(percentages)*										
18 years and under	..	..	6	4	4	..	..	4	2	2
19 – 20 years	..	..	16	14	12	..	..	9	7	7
21 – 24 years	..	..	23	22	19	..	..	18	17	16
25 years and over	..	..	54	60	65	..	..	69	73	75

1 See Appendix, Part 3: Stages of education.
2 Excludes students enrolled on nursing and paramedic courses at Department of Health establishments.

3 Calendar years beginning in second year shown. Excludes short course students up to 1982/83.

Source: Education Statistics for the United Kingdom, Department of Education and Science

3.25 First year mature home students[1]: by sex and establishment

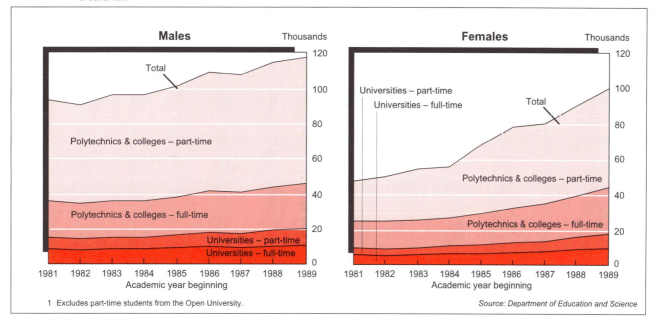

Great Britain

1 Excludes part-time students from the Open University.

Source: Department of Education and Science

The Open University is one way in which people can study part-time. Between 1970/71 and 1989/90 the number of students in part-time higher education in the United Kingdom more than doubled to stand at 397 thousand (Table 3.24). The Open University accounted for 12 per cent of part-time students when it opened in 1970/71, but by 1989/90 this proportion had risen to 22 per cent. Women accounted for 42 per cent of part-time students in 1989/90 compared to only 14 per cent in 1970/71.

The number of mature students starting higher education courses increased by 55 per cent between 1981 and 1989 to stand at 216 thousand (Chart 3.25) (this figure excludes those studying at the Open University). Mature students are those aged 21 and over when starting an undergraduate course and 25 and over when starting a postgraduate course.

The number of higher education qualifications awarded in the United Kingdom rose by a quarter between 1981 and 1988 to stand at 279 thousand (Table 3.26). Over this period, the number of postgraduate degrees (35 per cent) and qualifications below degree level (34 per cent) rose by most. The number of first degree awards rose more modestly by 18 per cent.

3.26 Higher education qualifications obtained[1]: by type of qualification and sex

United Kingdom — Thousands

	1981	1986	1988
Type of qualification			
Below degree level[2]			
Males	45	54	50
Females	17	26	33
Total	62	80	83
First degree[3]			
Males	76	78	80
Females	48	61	66
Total	124	139	146
Post-graduate[4]			
Males	24	27	30
Females	13	16	19
Total	37	42	50
All higher education qualifications			
Males	144	158	160
Females	78	103	118
Total	222	262	279

1 Includes estimates of successful completions of public sector professional courses (44 thousand in 1988-89). Excludes successful completions of nursing and paramedic courses at Department of Health establishments (31 thousand in 1988-89) and the private sector.
2 First university diplomas and certificates; CNAA diplomas and certificates below degree level; BTEC/SCOTVEC higher diplomas and certificates.
3 University degrees, estimates of CNAA degrees (and equivalent) university validated degrees (Great Britain only) and Open University (honours and ordinary) degrees (from 1988).
4 Universities, CNAA, PGCEs and Open University (higher degrees) (from 1988).

Source: Education Statistics for the United Kingdom, Department of Education and Science

3.27 Destination of first degree graduates, 1982/83 and 1989/90

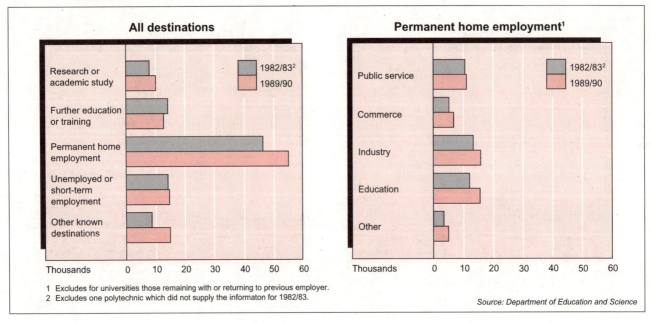

Great Britain

All destinations

Permanent home employment[1]

1982/83[2]
1989/90

Research or academic study

Further education or training

Permanent home employment

Unemployed or short-term employment

Other known destinations

Public service

Commerce

Industry

Education

Other

Thousands 0 10 20 30 40 50 60

Thousands 0 10 20 30 40 50 60

1 Excludes for universities those remaining with or returning to previous employer.
2 Excludes one polytechnic which did not supply the informaton for 1982/83.

Source: Department of Education and Science

Unfortunately, it is not always possible to record exactly what a student does after graduation. However, in 1989/90 the destinations of 107.4 thousand first degree graduates were known. Of these first degree graduates, just over half started a job which was expected to last for more than 3 months, a similar proportion to 1982/83 (Chart 3.27). Of those who started such a job in 1989/90, 29 per cent were in commerce and a further 29 per cent in industry.

Table 3.28 shows the value of the standard maintenance grant in England and Wales, excluding those studying in London and those studying elsewhere who were living with their parents. In real terms, the value of the standard maintenance grant has fallen over time. Most parents are required to contribute to the standard maintenance grant, depending on their level of income. The percentage share of this parental contribution has increased to reach nearly a third by 1989/90.

In Scotland, the proportion of the maintenance grant contributed by parents rose from 21 per cent to 41 per cent between 1980/81 and 1989/90. Parental contribution was higher in Scotland than in England and Wales for two main reasons. Firstly, fewer Scottish students studied in London and more lived at home. Secondly, mortgage interest payments are off-set

against income when determining parental contribution - the larger public housing sector in Scotland and lower house prices meant that parental contribution was generally higher.

3.28 Student awards — real value and parental contributions

England & Wales

| | Standard maintenance grant[1] (£) | Index of the real value of the grant deflated by | | Average assessed contribution by parents[4] (percentages) |
		Retail prices index[2]	Average earnings index[3]	
1979/80	1,245	100	100	13
1980/81	1,430	97	99	13
1981/82	1,535	96	95	14
1982/83	1,595	93	91	19
1983/84	1,660	90	89	20
1984/85	1,775	89	89	25
1985/86	1,830	91	87	30
1986/87	1,901	88	82	30
1987/88	1,972	89	78	31
1988/89	2,050	87	74	31
1989/90	2,155	85	72	31
1990/91	2,265	81	..	..

1 Excludes those studying in London and those studying elsewhere living in the parental home. Prior to 1982/83 Oxford and Cambridge were also excluded. Since 1984/85 has included an additional travel allowance of £50.
2 September 1979 = 100.
3 Great Britain average earnings for the whole economy has been used as the deflator. February 1980 = 100.
4 Assuming full payment of parental and other contributions including a notional assessment in respect of students for whom fees only were paid by LEAs. Of the students assessed for parental contributions in 1989/90 there were 107.4 thousand mandatory award holders (27 per cent) who were receiving the maximum grant because their parents' assessed contribution was nil.

Source: Department of Education and Science; Employment Department

Educational standards of adults

In 1990, 81 per cent of men and 79 per cent of women aged between 25 and 29 had some sort of qualification compared with 59 per cent of men aged between 50 and 64 and 43 per cent of women aged between 50 and 59 (Chart 3.29). At the higher qualification levels, 12 per cent of men and 9 per cent of women aged between 25 and 29 had a degree or equivalent qualification.

Table 3.30 uses combined data from the 1988, 1989 and 1990 Labour Force Surveys (LFS) to compare the level of qualifications held by people aged between 16 and retirement age for different ethnic groups in Great Britain. It shows that both males and females from the Pakistani/Bangladeshi ethnic group were not as well qualified as those from other groups; over two thirds of women from the Pakistani/Bangladeshi ethnic group held no qualifications.

Men from the Indian ethnic group were more likely than White men to hold higher qualifications, although the difference partly reflects the fact that the Indian ethnic groups has a younger age structure than the White ethnic group (see Chapter 1).

3.29 **Percentage of the population[1] with a qualification[2]: by sex and age, 1990**

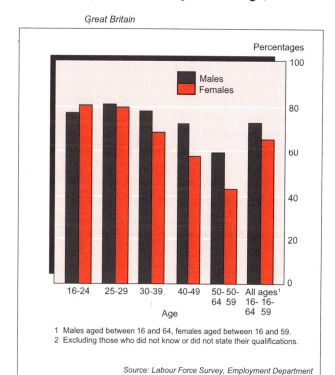

1 Males aged between 16 and 64, females aged between 16 and 59.
2 Excluding those who did not know or did not state their qualifications.

Source: Labour Force Survey, Employment Department

There are also differences between socio-economic groups. Table 3.31 shows the highest qualification level of those aged between 25 and 49 in 1989-90, analysed by the socio-economic group of their father.

Those with fathers in the unskilled manual group were most likely to have no qualifications whilst those with fathers who were professionals were most likely to have degrees.

3.30 Highest qualification level of the population[1]: by ethnic origin and sex, 1988-1990[2]

Great Britain   Percentages

	Ethnic origin					
	White	West Indian/ Guyanese	Indian	Pakistani/ Bangladeshi	Other[3]	All[4]
Highest qualification held[5]						
(percentages)						
Males						
Higher	15	. .	19	8	22	15
Other	57	58	51	40	56	57
None	29	36	30	52	21	29
Females						
Higher	13	16	13	. .	20	13
Other	51	52	46	28	52	51
None	36	32	41	68	28	36
All persons						
Higher	14	11	16	6	21	14
Other	54	55	49	34	54	54
None	32	34	36	60	25	32

1 Aged 16 to retirement age (64 for males and 59 for females).
2 Combined data using the 1988, 1989 and 1990 (preliminary) Labour Force Surveys.
3 Includes African, Arab, Chinese, other stated and Mixed origin.

4 Includes those who did not know or did not state their ethnic origin.
5 See Appendix, Part 3: Qualification level. Excludes those who did not know or did not state their qualifications.

Source: Labour Force Survey, Employment Department

3.31 Highest qualification level attained[1]: by socio-economic group of father, 1989

Great Britain   Percentages and numbers

	Professional	Employers and managers	Intermediate and junior non-manual	Skilled manual and own account non-profess-ional	Semi-skilled manual and personal service	Unskilled manual	All persons
Highest qualification level attained							
Degree	38	17	18	5	4	3	11
Higher education	18	16	16	12	7	6	13
'A' level	10	14	13	9	8	6	10
'O' level	20	24	27	22	20	14	22
CSE	4	8	9	13	13	13	11
Foreign	5	5	3	3	2	3	3
No qualifications	6	17	14	37	47	54	31
Sample size (=100%) (numbers)	440	1,656	835	3,383	1,059	438	7,811

1 Persons aged 25-49 not in full time education. See Appendix, Part 3: Education.   *Source: General Household Survey*

Resources

The financial and manpower resources required by the education system are closely linked to the size of the population of school age. The peak in births in the mid-sixties led to a peak in the number of school children from the early 1970s to the early 1980s (see Chart 3.1). By the end of the 1980s these people would have passed through the education system unless they were in higher education or were mature students.

The number of full-time school teachers employed in the United Kingdom fell by 8 per cent between 1980/81 and 1988/89 to 518 thousand (Table 3.32) reflecting the falling school population. As the fall in the number of full-time teachers was less than the decline in pupil numbers, both class sizes (see Table 3.10) and pupil/teacher ratios (Table 3.34) also fell. Over the same period the percentage of teachers who were graduates rose from 39 to 50 per cent. Between 1980/81 and 1988/89, the number of full-time lecturers in United Kingdom universities fell by 3 thousand to 31 thousand, while the number of full-time lecturers in further and higher education establishments rose by 5 thousand to 94 thousand.

3.32 Selected statistics of manpower employed in education: by type of establishment

United Kingdom   Thousands and percentages

	1970/71	1975/76	1980/81	1985/86[1]	1988/89[2]	Percentage who were graduates 1980/81	Percentage who were graduates 1988/89
Full-time teachers and lecturers							
Schools							
Public sector							
Primary schools[3]	203	240	222	201	209	16	31
Secondary schools	199	259	281	266	244	54	64
Non-maintained schools[4]	36	39	43	43	45	63	71
Special schools	10	17	19	19	19	22	35
Total	448	555	565	529	518	39	50
Establishments of further and higher education[5]	69	86	89	93	94	43	47
Universities[6]	29	32	34	31	31	99	99
Total educational establishments[7]	546	677	693	657	643	42	52

1 Data for 1984/85 have been used for manpower in schools in Scotland.
2 Data for maintained schools in England and Wales are estimated.
3 Includes nursery schools.
4 Excludes independent schools in Scotland and Northern Ireland.
5 Includes former colleges of education.
6 Excludes Open University. There were 671 professors and lecturers

and 5,282 part-time tutorial and counselling staff employed by the Open University at January 1989. Also excludes the independent University College of Buckingham.
7 Includes miscellaneous teachers in England and Wales (3.8 thousand in 1988/89) not shown elsewhere above.

Source: Education Statistics for the United Kingdom, Department of Education and Science

3.33 Teacher vacancies[1] in maintained secondary schools[2]: by main teaching subject

England & Wales   Numbers and percentages

	1981		1990		1991	
	Numbers	As a percent-age of filled teaching posts	Numbers	As a percent-age of filled teaching posts	Numbers	As a percent-age of filled teaching posts
Main teaching subject[3]						
Science	396	1.1	417	1.5	290	1.1
Mathematics	383	1.3	279	1.2	190	0.9
English	195	0.6	317	1.4	247	1.1
Languages	215	1.1	366	2.4	344	2.3
Craft, design & technology	177	1.2	137	1.1	90	0.8
Physical education	110	0.6	223	1.6	139	1.0
Home economics or needlework	94	0.8	80	0.8	45	0.5
Music	91	1.3	131	2.7	115	2.4
Geography	57	0.4	90	1.0	75	0.8
Commercial and business studies	45	1.1	72	1.8	28	0.7
Religious education	58	0.8	102	2.2	60	1.3
Art or light craft	55	0.5	77	0.9	58	0.7
History	53	0.4	89	1.0	62	0.7
Other	258	1.1	557[4]	1.5	393	1.1
Total vacancies	2,187	0.9	2,937	1.5	2,136	1.1

1 Vacancies for full-time teachers as at January.
2 Includes middle deemed secondary schools.
3 The breakdown of teachers in post by main teaching subjects has been estimated from the 1984 and 1988 secondary school staffing surveys.
4 Includes heads and deputy heads who had been allocated by subject in 1981. The percentages however, are comparable between years.

Source: Department of Education and Science

In 1991, the number of teaching vacancies in maintained secondary schools in England and Wales was 2,136 (1 per cent of filled teaching posts) (Table 3.33). In 1991, the highest vacancy rates were in music (2.4 per cent) and languages (2.3 per cent). The lowest were in home economics and needlework (0.5 per cent). In Scotland, the number of advertised full-time teaching vacancies was 121, (0.5 per cent of filled teaching posts). The highest proportions of vacancies were in religious education (2.9 per cent) and music (1.2 per cent). The lowest were in mathematics and physical education (0.1 per cent).

Table 3.34 shows the average number of pupils per teacher for schools in the United Kingdom, usually

3.34 Pupil/teacher ratios[1]: by type of school

United Kingdom   Ratio[1]

	1971	1981	1990
Public sector schools			
Nursery	26.6	21.5	21.8
Primary	27.1	22.3	21.8
Secondary[2]	17.8	16.4	14.9
All public sector schools	23.2	19.0	18.3
Non-maintained schools	14.0[3]	13.1[4]	10.9
Special schools	10.5[3]	7.4	5.9
All schools	22.0[3]	18.2[4]	17.1

1 See Appendix, Part 3: Pupil/teacher ratios.
2 Includes voluntary grammar schools in Northern Ireland from 1989/90, (formerly in the non-maintained sector.)
3 Excludes independent schools in Scotland.
4 Excludes independent schools in Northern Ireland.

Source: Education Statistics for the United Kingdom,
Department of Education and Science

3.35 Government expenditure on education: by type

United Kingdom   £ million and percentages

	1970 −71	1980 −81	1989 −90
Current expenditure (£ million)			
Schools			
Nursery	7	52	5,889
Primary	546	2,840	
Secondary	619	3,695	6,835
Special	50	443	1,009
Higher, further and adult education[1]	265	1,591	2,730[4]
Training of teachers: tuition	60	78	
Universities[1]	246	1,264	2,358
Other education expenditure	95	516	1,206
Related education expenditure	350	1,510	2,225
Total current expenditure	2,242	11,989	22,251
Capital expenditure (£ million)			
Schools	245	480	769
Other education expenditure	161	283	459
Total capital expenditure	406	763	1,228
VAT[2]	92	189	477
Total government expenditure[3] (£ million)	2,740	12,941	23,956
Of which, expenditure by local authorities	2,318	11,162	20,456
Expenditure as a percentage of GDP	5.2	5.4	4.6

1 Includes tuition fees.
2 Vat refunds to local authorities.
3 Excludes additional adjustments to allow for capital consumption made for National Accounts purposes amounting to £1,040 million in 1989/90.
4 Includes training of teachers.

Source: Department of Education and Science;
Central Statistical Office

referred to as the pupil/teacher ratio. Averaged over types of school this ratio has fallen from 22.0 in 1971 to 17.1 in 1990. Of the public sector schools, secondary schools had the lowest pupil/teacher ratio whilst nursery and primary schools had higher ratios.

In 1989-90 government expenditure on education was £24 billion (Table 3.35). Capital expenditure accounted for 5 per cent of total education expenditure in 1989-90 compared to 15 per cent in 1970-71. It is not easy to express these figures in real terms, but the contribution that education expenditure made to GDP has fallen during the 1980s.

Table 3.36 shows expenditure on education in real terms in both 1980-81 and 1989-90. The general GDP deflator has been used to convert all the figures to constant prices. Expenditure per pupil (in real terms) in English secondary schools increased from £1,297 per pupil in 1980-81 to £1,853 per pupil in 1989-90 (Table 3.36). Over the same period, expenditure per pupil in nursery and primary schools rose by a quarter in real terms. Expenditure per pupil in Scottish secondary schools rose from £1,726 in 1980-81 to £2,498 in 1989-90 in real terms.

3.36 Expenditure per pupil[1]: by type of expenditure, 1980-81 and 1989-90

England £ per pupil at 1989–90 prices

	Nursery and primary school		Secondary school	
	1980–81	1989–90	1980–81	1989–90
Expenditure on:				
Staff				
Teaching	653	830	920	1,290
Educational support	34	59	32	46
Premises-related	60	52	71	65
Administrative, clerical, and other	21	66	30	81
Premises	125	145	177	232
Books and equipment	27	38	50	79
Other supplies[2]	3	0	16	22
Other expenditure[2]	11	31	20	64
Net unit cost[3]	927	1,210	1,297	1,853

1 Recurrent institutional expenditure per full-time equivalent pupil. This includes costs of providing tuition but excludes certain costs such as central administration and school meals. Figures are rounded to the nearest £1 but they do not necessarily have that degree of accuracy.
2 Changes in these expenditure categories mean these data are not comparable between 1980–81 and 1989–90.
3 The net unit cost is the sum of expenditure on items shown in the table less certain charges.

Source: Department of Education and Science

BIBLIOGRAPHY

The following list contains selected publications relevant to Chapter 3: Education. Those published by HMSO are available from the addresses shown on the back cover of Social Trends.

Committee of Directors of Polytechnics: First Destination of Students, A Statistical Report
Training Statistics, Employment Department
Education Statistics Actual, CIPFA
Education Statistics Estimates, CIPFA
Education Statistics for the United Kingdom, HMSO
Employment Gazette, HMSO
Northern Ireland Education Department Statistical Bulletins, HMSO
Regional Trends, HMSO
Scottish Education Department Statistical Bulletins, HMSO
The Scottish Office Social Work Services Group Statistical Bulletins, HMSO
Statistical Bulletins, Department of Education and Science

Statistics of Education, Finance and Awards England and Wales, HMSO
Statistics of Education, Further Education, HMSO
Statistics of Education, Schools, Department of Education and Science
Statistics of Education, Schools Examination Survey, HMSO
Statistics of Education, Teachers in Service, HMSO
Statistics of Education in Wales, Welsh Office
Statistics of Finance and Awards, Department of Education and Science
The Handbook of Education Unit Costs, CIPFA
UK National Accounts ('CSO Blue Book'), HMSO
Universities Statistics Series, Universities' Statistical Record
Youth Cohort Study, Social and Community Planning Research

Chapter 4: Employment

The labour force

● Many more women than men have entered the labour force in recent years. Between 1971 and 1990, the number of women in the labour force rose by 3 million while the number of men rose by only 300 thousand.
(Chart 4.1)

● The number of young people in the labour force is falling and is projected to continue to fall by a further 800 thousand by the year 2001.
(Table 4.4)

Type of employment

● Self-employment has increased dramatically over the last decade. After changing little during the 1970s, the number of self-employed increased by 57 per cent between 1981 and 1990.
(Table 4.11)

● In 1990, two thirds of part-time workers said that they did not want a full-time job.
(Table 4.15)

Time at work

● Workers in the United Kingdom are among the most likely to take sick leave from work - only the Netherlands had a higher rate in the EC.
(Chart 4.22)

Unemployment

● Unemployment rates are highest among the young. In 1990, the unemployment rate for men aged under 20 was almost double the average male unemployment rate.
(Table 4.29)

● Unemployment rates are still higher among ethnic minorities, although falls in unemployment rates have been greater for the ethnic minority groups than for the white population.
(Table 4.30)

Employment and training measures

● Those on YTS schemes are increasingly likely to leave with a qualification - the proportion gaining a qualification doubled between 1986-87 and 1989-90.
(Table 4.35)

4.1 Civilian labour force[1]: by sex

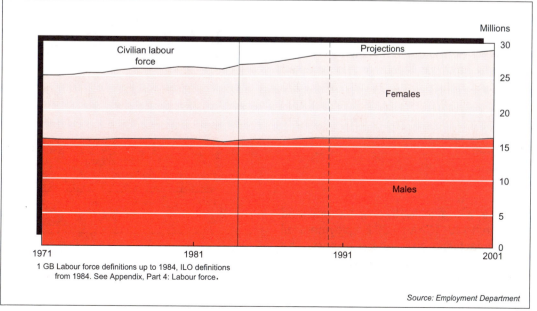

Great Britain

Millions

Civilian labour force

Projections

Females

Males

1971   1981   1991   2001

1 GB Labour force definitions up to 1984, ILO definitions from 1984. See Appendix, Part 4: Labour force.

Source: Employment Department

Glossary of terms

The economically active - people in employment plus the unemployed as measured by household surveys and censuses.

The economically inactive - people who are not economically active, eg full-time students who neither have, nor are seeking, paid work and those who are keeping house, have retired or are permanently unable to work.

The total labour force - the economically active.

The civilian labour force - The total labour force less the armed forces.

Employees in employment - a count of civilians in jobs, both main and secondary, paid by an employer who runs a PAYE tax scheme.

Self-employed persons - those who, in their main employment, work on their own account, whether or not they have any employees.

Work related government training programmes - in which the participants in the course of their participation receive training in the context of a workplace but are not employees, self-employed or in the armed forces.

The workforce in employment - employees in employment, self-employed, HM Forces and participants on work related government training programmes.

The workforce - the workforce in employment plus people claiming unemployment-related benefits at Unemployment Benefit Offices.

The population of working age - males aged 16 to 64 years and females aged 16 to 59 years.

Civilian economic activity rate - the percentage of the population in a given age group which is in the civilian labour force.

Unemployment - there are two main measures according to the source of the statistics. Firstly, there is the International Labour Organisation (ILO) measure used in household surveys such as the Labour Force Survey. By this measure the unemployed are those aged 16 and over who are available to start work in the next two weeks and who have been seeking a job in the last four weeks. Secondly, there is the measure derived from administrative sources. This measure counts as unemployed people claiming unemployment related benefits at Unemployment Benefit Offices. Both measures are used in Social Trends.

The labour force

The civilian labour force grew at an average rate of 130 thousand a year during the 1970s to reach 26.2 million by 1981, before falling by over 300 thousand between 1981 and 1983 (Chart 4.1, on the previous page) . The upward trend then resumed and in 1990 the civilian labour force had reached 28.1 million. Some 90 per cent of the overall increase of 3.1 million between 1971 and 1990 was attributable to an increase in the number of women in the civilian labour force (around 0.2 million of the increase is due to a change of definition in 1984 - see Appendix: Part 4). This trend is projected to continue. Between now and the turn of the century the number of males in the civilian labour force is expected to remain static at around 15.9 million, whilst the number of women is projected to increase by 600 thousand to reach 12.8 million. At the turn of the century women will make up 45 per cent of the total civilian labour force.

The workforce in employment fell by over 400 thousand in the year to March 1991 (Chart 4.2). Employment fell in both the manufacturing and service sectors. The number of unemployed (using the claimant count) rose above 2 million for the first time since the final quarter of 1988.

4.2 **Workforce and workforce in employment**

United Kingdom

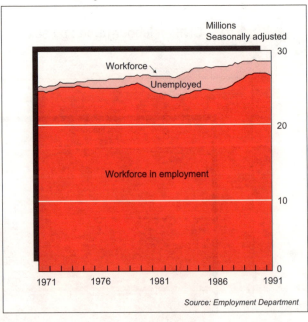

Source: Employment Department

4.3 Population of working age: by sex and economic status[1]

Great Britain

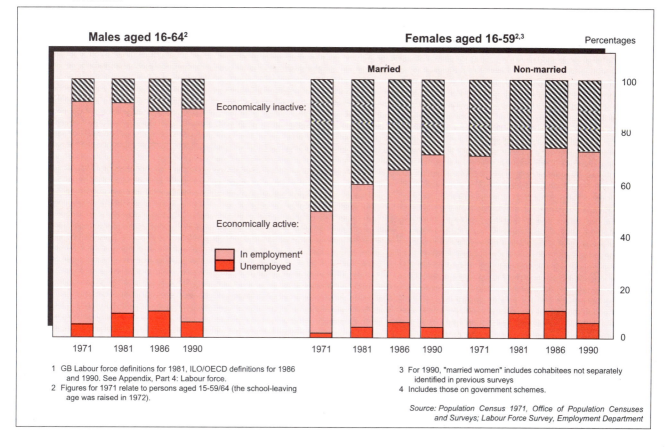

Males aged 16-64[2]   **Females aged 16-59[2,3]**   Percentages

Married   Non-married

Economically inactive:

Economically active:

In employment[4]
Unemployed

1971   1981   1986   1990   1971   1981   1986   1990   1971   1981   1986   1990

1 GB Labour force definitions for 1981, ILO/OECD definitions for 1986 and 1990. See Appendix, Part 4: Labour force.
2 Figures for 1971 relate to persons aged 15-59/64 (the school-leaving age was raised in 1972).

3 For 1990, "married women" includes cohabitees not separately identified in previous surveys
4 Includes those on government schemes.

Source: Population Census 1971, Office of Population Censuses and Surveys; Labour Force Survey, Employment Department

Chart 4.3 shows the population of working age and whether or not they are economically active. Between 1971 and 1990 the proportion of males of working age in Great Britain who were economically inactive increased from 9 per cent to 11.5 per cent. Conversely, the proportion of married females who were economically inactive decreased sharply from 51 per cent to 29 per cent. In 1990 there were 12 million economically active women in Great Britain.

4.4 Civilian labour force[1]: by age

Great Britain   Millions

	16 – 24	25 – 54	55 and over	All aged 16 and over
Estimates				
1971	5.1	15.0	4.9	24.9
1976	5.1	16.1	4.5	25.7
1979	5.6	16.3	4.2	26.0
1983	5.9	16.4	3.7	25.9
1984	6.0	16.7	3.6	26.4
1984	6.1	16.8	3.7	26.6
1986	6.2	17.3	3.4	26.9
1990	5.8	18.8	3.5	28.2
Projections				
1996	4.9	20.2	3.4	28.6
2001	5.0	20.3	3.6	28.9

1 Estimates for 1971 are based on the Census of Population. Those for 1976-1984 are based on the GB Labour Force definitions, and from 1984 on the ILO definitions. See Appendix, Part 4: Labour force.

Source: Employment Department

Table 4.4 shows a simple age distribution of the civilian labour force, which is obviously affected by the age structure of the general population. The relatively high birth rates in the 1960s had the effect of increasing the number of 16 year old entrants to the civilian labour force in the second half of the 1970s. However, this effect reached its peak in 1981 after which the number of 16 year old entrants fell.

In 1990, 16-24 year olds made up 21 per cent of the civilian labour force, by 2001 this is projected to fall to 17 per cent, whilst the proportion of those aged 55 and over is expected to remain static at around 12 per cent.

The proportion of the resident population above the minimum school leaving age who are in the civilian labour force is usually referred to as the economic activity rate. In 1990, the economic activity rate for males was 74.2 per cent and is projected to fall slightly to 72.5 per cent by 2001 (Table 4.5). The economic activity rate for females was 52.8 per cent in 1990 and the generally increasing trend since 1971 is projected to continue. The increase in female activity rates has been partly due to an increase in the availability of part-time jobs and other social and economic changes

4.5 Civilian labour force economic activity rates[1,2] : by age and sex

Great Britain   Percentages

	16—19 years	20—24 years	25—44 years	Females 45—54 Males 45—59 years	Females 55—59 Males 60—64 years	Females 60 Males 65 and over	All aged 16 and over
Males							
Estimates							
1971	69.4	87.7	95.4	94.8	82.9	19.3	80.5
1976	70.5	85.9	95.7	94.9	80.4	14.5	78.9
1979	73.0	86.7	95.7	93.8	73.0	10.3	77.5
1981	72.4	85.1	95.7	93.0	69.3	10.3	76.5
1983	69.6	84.1	94.5	90.2	59.4	8.1	74.2
1984[2]	72.9	84.7	94.4	89.1	56.7	8.2	74.3
1984[2]	73.5	85.0	94.5	89.6	57.3	8.4	74.5
1986	73.2	86.2	94.2	88.3	53.8	7.7	73.8
1989	74.3	87.3	94.4	88.0	54.6	9.0	74.2
1990	74.2	86.3	94.5	88.2	54.4	8.6	74.2
Projections							
1996	73.1	83.9	94.1	88.0	52.5	6.6	73.2
2001	74.6	82.6	93.9	87.5	51.5	5.4	72.5
Females							
Estimates							
1971	65.0	60.2	52.4	62.0	50.9	12.4	43.9
1976	68.2	64.8	60.0	66.5	54.3	10.3	46.8
1979	72.0	67.7	61.7	67.0	53.8	7.4	47.4
1981	70.4	68.8	61.7	68.0	53.4	8.2	47.6
1983	66.8	68.2	62.2	68.1	50.6	7.5	47.0
1984[2]	68.8	69.2	65.2	69.2	51.1	7.6	48.4
1984[2]	69.4	70.2	65.9	69.5	51.8	7.8	49.0
1986	70.3	70.7	67.8	70.5	51.8	6.5	49.6
1989	72.9	75.2	72.0	72.2	54.3	7.6	52.5
1990	70.7	74.8	73.1	72.8	54.9	7.5	52.8
Projections							
1996	69.6	75.7	76.2	73.5	54.9	6.7	53.9
2001	70.4	77.4	79.4	73.4	54.9	6.6	55.1

1 The percentage of the resident population, or any sub-group of the population, who are in the civilian labour force.

2 Labour force definitions up to 1984, ILO from 1984. See Appendix, Part 4: Labour force.

Source: Employment Department

encouraging women into the labour force. Certain demographic factors are related to female economic activity rates. Comparatively low birth rates in the 1970s and a rise in the average age at which women have children have been associated with increased activity rates among younger women.

The changing age structure of the labour force presents recruitment problems for employers. Those employers who rely on young people as a significant source of their recruits face declining numbers until the mid 1990s. Better use must therefore be made of alternative recruitment sources, such as the unemployed, women returners to the labour market and older workers. The policies followed, and decisions made, by employers in response to labour market indicators, will affect the accuracy of the projections in Table 4.5. If employers are particularly successful in attracting women back to work, through measures such as flexible hours packages or subsidised child care, then activity rates for women will rise even faster.

Data on ethnic origin are obtainable from the Labour Force Survey, but to obtain reliable estimates from a large enough sample it is necessary to combine data

4.6 Economic activity rates: by age, sex and ethnic origin, 1988-1990

Great Britain   Percentages

	Age			All of working age[1]	
	16-24	25-44	Females 45—59 Males 45-64	Male	Female
Ethnic origin					
White	80	85	74	89	71
West Indian or Guyanese	72	83	82	84	76
Indian	58	82	71	85	60
Pakistani or Bangladeshi	45	53	55	76	24
Other[2]	56	72	78	76	60
All[3]	79	84	74	88	71

1 Males aged 16-64, females aged 16-59.
2 Includes African, Arab, Chinese, Mixed origin and other stated.
3 Includes ethnic origin not stated.

Source: Labour Force Survey, Employment Department

4.7 Economic activity rates[1]: by sex, EC comparison, 1989

Percentages

	Males	Females	All
United Kingdom	75.8	52.9	63.9
Belgium	61.9	36.7	48.9
Denmark	75.1	60.8	67.8
France	66.6	47.3	56.5
Germany (Fed. Rep.)	70.8	42.4	55.9
Greece	68.0	36.3	51.4
Irish Republic	72.1	35.3	53.4
Italy	65.8	35.5	50.1
Luxembourg	69.5	34.9	51.7
Netherlands	70.4	42.6	56.4
Portugal	72.2	47.6	59.2
Spain	66.3	32.7	49.0

1 The civilian labour force aged 16 years and over as a percentage of the population aged 16 years and over.

Source: Statistical Office of the European Communities

from surveys in different years. Table 4.6 combines data from the 1988, 1989 and 1990 surveys to show economic activity rates by ethnic origin. The table shows that the economic activity rate for males was highest in the White population (89 per cent) followed by the Indian group (85 per cent). Amongst women, economic activity rates varied considerably between ethnic groups. The average rate for all groups was 71 per cent, but this varied between 76 per cent for the West Indian/Guyanese group and only 24 per cent for the Pakistani/Bangladeshi group.

The latest year for which economic activity rates are available for the European Community (EC) is 1989. Among EC countries the United Kingdom had the second highest economic activity rate behind Denmark (Table 4.7). While United Kingdom men had the highest rate, women had the second highest rate. Men had higher activity rates than women in all 12 countries, but the difference between the sexes ranged from 14 percentage points in Denmark to 37 percentage points in the Irish Republic.

Whether or not women have young dependent children is a major factor in whether or not they are economically active. Table 4.8 shows the proportion of women working according to the age group of their youngest child and their own socio-economic group.

In all socio-economic groups women were most likely to be in full-time work if they had no dependent children, although the proportions varied considerably between socio-economic groups. Only 9 per cent of unskilled manual women without dependent children worked full-time compared to 77 per cent of professional or managerial women. However, 56 per cent did work part-time compared to only 9 per cent of professional or managerial women. A higher proportion of professional women worked full-time than any other socio-economic group, irrespective of whether they had children, or the age of their children.

4.8 Economic activity of women: by own socio-economic group and age of youngest child, 1987-1989[1]

Great Britain   Percentages

	Professional or employer/ manager	Intermediate and junior non-manual	Skilled manual	Semi-skilled manual	Unskilled manual	All women[2] aged 16-59
Youngest child aged 0-4						
Working full-time	30	12	16	7	1	11
Working part-time	27	27	34	22	46	26
Unemployed	3	6	5	6	6	6
Economically inactive	39	54	45	64	47	57
Youngest child aged 5-9						
Working full-time	37	19	27	11	1	17
Working part-time	39	48	43	48	76	48
Unemployed	2	4	3	5	4	4
Economically inactive	21	29	26	36	20	31
Youngest child aged 10 and over						
Working full-time	61	32	36	21	7	30
Working part-time	26	45	39	47	65	44
Unemployed	2	2	2	5	3	3
Economically inactive	11	21	22	27	25	23
No dependent children						
Working full-time	77	62	52	40	9	50
Working part-time	9	18	19	26	56	22
Unemployed	2	3	4	7	4	5
Economically inactive	11	15	24	25	31	22
All women aged 16-59						
Working full-time	65	44	39	27	7	36
Working part-time	16	27	28	31	59	28
Unemployed	2	4	4	6	4	5
Economically inactive	16	24	28	34	31	30

1 Combined data.
2 Includes women in the Armed forces, inadequately described occupations and those who have never worked.

Source: General Household Survey

A recent report by the Policy Studies Institute showed that mothers are now more likely to go back to full-time work, and to the same job, working for the same employer, than they were in 1981. In the early 1980s mothers returning to work mostly sought part-time work, or less challenging positions. This often resulted in a waste of their previous skills and a reduction in their hourly rates of pay. Women who leave full-time work when they become pregnant are now just as likely to return to full-time employment as part-time following the birth of their child. This is particularly so in the public sector and for higher paid jobs rather than lower.

Table 4.8 also shows the increase in women's economic activity as their children get older. This was most evident among intermediate and junior non-manual women.

Type of employment

Chart 4.9, using estimates from the spring 1990 Labour Force Survey shows that just under half of men and two-thirds of women in employment were in non-manual occupations. The main difference between the sexes was between those employed in clerical and craft occupations. In 1990, 31 per cent of women were in clerical and related occupations compared with only 6 per cent of men and 25 per cent of men were in craft or similar occupations compared with only 4 per cent of women. These percentages have changed little since 1981.

On 9 March 1990, the Secretary of State for Employment announced the development of the Labour Force Survey in Great Britain to deliver results on a quarterly rather than annual basis. The introduction of the quarterly survey is expected to reduce the scale and frequency of revisions to both the employees in employment and the self-employed series. When the enhanced survey is fully operational, it is expected that the first results will be available 12 weeks after the end of the quarter to which they relate. It is anticipated that the full scale enhanced survey will be launched in Spring 1992.

Table 4.10 shows the number of employees in various industries. Since 1971 there has been a significant fall in the number of employees in manufacturing industries (which fell by over a third between 1971 and 1990) and a corresponding increase in the number of employees in service industries (up by a third over the same period). In June 1990 employment in manufacturing accounted for 23 per cent of all employees. Later figures show that in March 1991 employment in manufacturing fell below five million for the first time since 1959, when records were first kept on this basis. Within the service sector, numbers employed in banking, finance and insurance doubled since 1971.

4.9   **Employees and self-employed: by sex and occupation[1], 1990[2]**

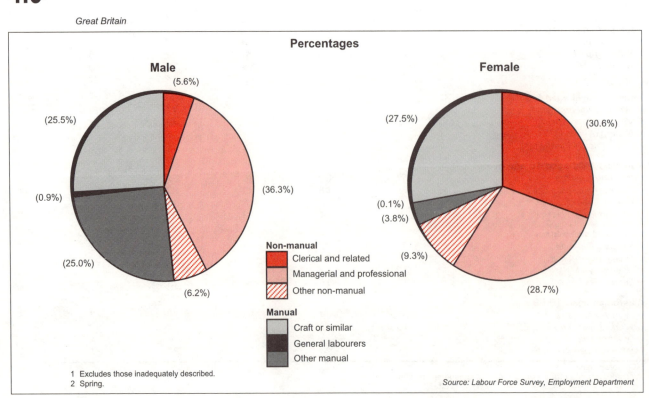

Great Britain

Percentages

Male
(5.6%)
(25.5%)
(0.9%)
(25.0%)
(6.2%)
(36.3%)

Female
(27.5%)
(30.6%)
(0.1%)
(3.8%)
(9.3%)
(28.7%)

Non-manual
Clerical and related
Managerial and professional
Other non-manual

Manual
Craft or similar
General labourers
Other manual

1 Excludes those inadequately described.
2 Spring.

Source: Labour Force Survey, Employment Department

4.10 Employees in employment: by sex and industry[1]

United Kingdom   Thousands

	Standard Industrial Classification (1980)	1971	1979	1981	1983	1986	1989	1990
All industries	0—9	22,139	23,173	21,892	21,067	21,387	22,661	22,855
of which								
Males		13,726	13,487	12,562	11,940	11,744	11,992	12,050
Females		8,413	9,686	9,331	9,127	9,644	10,668	10,806
Manufacturing	2—4	8,065	7,253	6,222	5,525	5,227	5,187	5,151
Services	6—9	11,627	13,580	13,468	13,501	14,297	15,627	15,868
Other	0,1,5	2,447	2,340	2,203	2,042	1,863	1,847	1,836
Employees in employment by SIC division								
Agriculture, forestry and fishing	0	450	380	363	350	329	300	298
Energy and water supply	1	798	722	710	648	545	465	451
Other minerals and ore extraction, etc	2	1,282	1,147	939	817	729	711	728
Metal goods, engineering and vehicles	3	3,709	3,374	2,923	2,548	2,372	2,351	2,316
Other manufacturing industries	4	3,074	2,732	2,360	2,159	2,126	2,125	2,106
Construction	5	1,198	1,239	1,130	1,044	989	1,082	1,087
Distribution, catering and repairs	6	3,686	4,257	4,172	4,118	4,298	4,730	4,824
Transport and communication	7	1,556	1,479	1,425	1,345	1,298	1,362	1,374
Banking, finance, insurance, etc	8	1,336	1,647	1,739	1,875	2,166	2,627	2,734
Other services	9	5,049	6,197	6,132	6,163	6,536	6,908	6,936

1 As at June each year.   Source: Employment Department

Partly as a result of government policies in the 1980s to encourage people to start up their own business, the number of self-employed people in Great Britain increased by 57 per cent between 1981 and 1990. By 1990, almost 3.25 million people were self-employed (Table 4.11). Between 1981 and 1990, the number of self-employed increased for each industry grouping except agriculture, forestry and fishing. Almost half of all the self-employed work in either the construction sector or the distribution, catering and repairs sector of the economy.

4.11 Self-employed: by sex and industry[1]

Great Britain   Thousands

	Standard Industrial Classification (1980)	1971	1979	1981	1983	1986	1989	1990
All industries	0—9	1,953	1,842	2,058	2,160	2,567	3,182	3,222
of which								
Males		1,556	1,494	1,641	1,652	1,937	2,428	2,449
Females		397	348	417	508	630	754	773
Manufacturing	2—4	129	140	146	150	209	280	272
Services	6—9	1,199	1,102	1,274	1,355	1,622	1,934	1,981
Other	0,1,5	625	601	638	656	736	967	969
Employees in employment by SIC division								
Agriculture, forestry and fishing	0	282	257	250	246	248	243	247
Energy and water supply	1	0	1	1	1	1	2	3
Other minerals and ore extraction, etc	2	4	6	7	9	11	13	18
Metal goods, engineering and vehicles	3	35	42	46	46	62	83	85
Other manufacturing industries	4	90	92	93	95	136	185	168
Construction	5	342	343	388	409	487	722	718
Distribution, catering and repairs	6	726	636	698	701	782	824	809
Transport and communication	7	65	87	99	92	111	162	172
Banking, finance, insurance, etc	8	148	145	188	214	275	372	409
Other services	9	261	234	288	348	454	576	591

1 As at June each year.   Source: Employment Department

Whereas Tables 4.10 and 4.11 show employment and self-employment by industry, Table 4.12 is analysed by sector - that is by public or private sector. The workforce in employment has risen steadily since 1983 to reach 27.3 million by mid-1990. In 1961, around 24 per cent of the workforce in employment were in the public sector. By 1981 this proportion had risen to 30 per cent, but it had fallen back to 22 per cent by 1990.

Most of the decrease in public sector employment since 1981 has been accounted for by a fall in employment in public corporations, partly due to privatisation. Over 200 thousand employees were re-classified to the private sector following the privatisation of British Telecom in November 1984, a further 100 thousand British Gas employees were re-classified in December 1986, a further 53 thousand British Steel employees were re-classified in December 1988 and 60 thousand polytechnic staff were re-classified in April 1989.

4.13 Full-time employees as a percentage of all employees: by industry, 1984 and 1990

	Great Britain	Percentages
	1984	1990
Industry division (SIC 1980)		
0 Agriculture, forestry and fishing	81.7	80.2
1 Energy and water supply	97.3	96.3
2 Other minerals and ore extraction, etc.	95.7	95.6
3 Metal goods engineering and vehicles	95.8	95.5
4 Other manufacturing industries	88.5	88.7
5 Construction	93.7	93.4
6 Distribution, catering and repairs	62.7	60.0
7 Transport and communication	93.8	91.3
8 Banking, finance, insurance, etc.	84.3	85.4
9 Other services	64.4	60.7
All industries	77.7	75.1

Source: Employment Department

In 1990, three quarters of employees worked full-time (Table 4.13). Within individual industries, this ranged from 60 per cent in the distribution, hotels and catering, repairs and other services categories to 96 per cent in energy and water supply. These percentages have not changed significantly since 1984.

The number of part-time and temporary jobs in the whole of the European Community (EC) has grown rapidly in the last decade. There are now 14 million part-time employees, and 10 million temporary workers throughout the EC.

4.12 Workforce in employment[1]: by sector[2]

United Kingdom Millions

	Public sector			Private sector	Work related government training programmes	Workforce in employment
	General government	Public corporations	Total			
1961	3.7	2.2	5.9	18.6	.	24.5
1971	4.6	2.0	6.6	17.9	.	24.5
1976	5.3	2.0	7.3	17.5	.	24.8
1979	5.4	2.1	7.4	18.0	.	25.4
1981	5.3	1.9	7.2	17.1	.	24.3
1986	5.3	1.2	6.5	17.9	0.2	24.6
1987	5.4	1.0	6.4	18.4	0.3	25.1
1988	5.4	0.9	6.3	19.3	0.3	25.9
1989	5.2	0.8	6.1	20.2	0.5	26.7
1990	5.3	0.8	6.0	20.9	0.4	26.9
Males	2.1	0.7	2.8	12.3	0.3	15.0
Females	3.2	0.1	3.2	8.6	0.2	11.8

1 See Appendix, Part 4: Workforce.
2 As at mid-year. See Appendix, Part 4: Sector classification.

Source: Central Statistical Office; Employment Department

Labour markets differ greatly between countries. Whilst part-time work is unusual in Italy, Portugal and Greece, more than one in five jobs are part-time in Denmark and the Netherlands and the United Kingdom. Temporary work is popular in Spain, Portugal and Greece, where about one in five are employed in this way.

4.14 People with a second job[1]: by sex

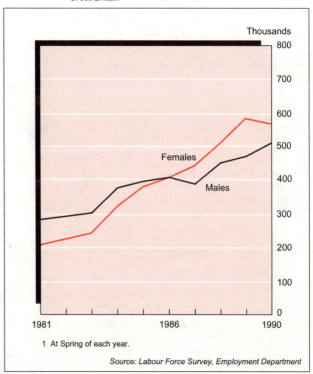

Great Britain

1 At Spring of each year.

Source: Labour Force Survey, Employment Department

It is estimated from Labour Force Surveys, that from Spring 1981 to Spring 1985, more men had second jobs than women (Chart 4.14). In Spring 1986, the levels were about the same for both men and women, but in the period from Spring 1987 to Spring 1990 more women had second jobs than men. In 1990, over one million people had a second job, more than double the number in 1981. Of those with second jobs in 1990, two-thirds of those jobs were as employees and one-third were self employed.

Of those who worked part-time in 1990, 86 per cent were women. Many people who work part-time do so because they want to. Only 6 per cent worked part-time because they could not find a full-time job (Table 4.15), indeed two thirds of those working part-time did not want a full-time job.

4.15 Reasons for taking a part-time job: by sex and, for women, marital status, 1990

Great Britain				Percentages and thousands
		Females		
			Non-	All	All
	Males	Married	married	females	persons
Reasons for taking part-time job *(percentages)*					
Student/still at school	33	—	32	6	10
Ill or disabled	4	1	2	1	2
Could not find a full-time job	14	4	11	5	6
Did not want a full-time job	33	79	40	71	66
Other reason	16	16	15	16	16
Part-time workers (thousands) (= 100%)	775	3,904	934	4,837	5,612

Source: Labour Force Survey, Employment Department

Time at work

It is estimated from the Spring 1990 Labour Force Survey that four out of five male employees had basic usual weekly hours (ie excluding meal breaks and overtime) of between 35 and 45 (Table 4.16). Half of all female employees worked for less than 35 hours per week and two fifths for between 35 and 40 hours. Very few self-employed people worked short hours. For both sexes, the self-employed worked longer hours than employees, a quarter of all self-employed women worked for more than 45 hours per week and a quarter of all self-employed men worked for more than 60 hours per week.

The latest year for which hours worked data are available for the whole of the European Community is 1989 (Table 4.17) and it should be noted that these data include overtime (unlike Table 4.16). Men in the United Kingdom (along with Portugal) worked longer hours than their European counterparts, whereas women in the United Kingdom worked fewer hours than elsewhere in the EC apart from The Netherlands.

4.16 Basic[1] usual hours worked: by sex and type of employment, 1990

Great Britain				Percentages
	Males		Females	
	Employees	Self-employed	Employees	Self-employed
Hours per week				
Less than 5	0.5	0.9	1.8	6.6
5 but less than 10	1.2	0.9	6.4	6.7
10 but less than 15	1.0	1.1	7.6	7.9
15 but less than 20	0.8	1.0	9.3	7.1
20 but less than 25	0.9	2.4	11.3	8.9
25 but less than 30	1.0	1.0	5.9	5.7
30 but less than 35	2.9	2.9	7.1	7.8
35 but less than 40	51.3	10.1	39.3	9.8
40 but less than 45	27.5	25.2	9.0	13.4
45 but less than 50	5.2	12.7	1.0	6.6
50 but less than 55	3.0	12.9	0.5	4.7
55 but less than 60	1.2	4.8	0.2	2.2
60 and over	3.3	23.8	0.6	12.3

1 Excluding paid and unpaid overtime and meal breaks.

Source: Labour Force Survey, Employment Department

4.17 Average hours usually worked[1] per week[2]: by sex, EC comparison, 1989

			Hours
	Males	Females	All persons
United Kingdom	44.0	30.3	37.7
Belgium	38.3	32.2	36.0
Denmark	37.3	31.7	34.6
France	40.0	34.9	37.7
Germany (Fed. Rep.)	40.2	34.0	38.7
Greece	40.4	37.3	39.3
Irish Republic	41.0	35.4	38.8
Italy	39.5	35.2	37.9
Luxembourg	40.3	35.7	38.7
Netherlands	36.0	25.8	32.2
Portugal	43.2	38.5	41.2
Spain	40.9	37.3	39.8
EUR 12	40.6	33.3	37.7

1 Employees aged 16 and over only.
2 Excludes meal breaks but includes paid and unpaid overtime.

Source: Statistical Office of the European Communities

4.18 Employment[1]: by sex and hours of work

Great Britain				Millions
	Males		Females	
	Full-time	Part-time	Full-time	Part-time
1986	12.7	1.1	5.7	4.5
1987	12.7	1.3	5.8	4.7
1988	13.1	1.3	6.1	4.8
1989	13.3	1.4	6.4	5.0
1990	13.3	1.5	6.3	5.2

1 Includes employees in employment, self-employed, HM Forces (treated as full-time) and work related government training programmes (treated as part-time)

Source: Employment Department

Table 4.18 shows that women are much more likely to work part-time than men. In 1990, only one in ten men, and more than four in ten women in employment, were part-time workers.

Table 4.19, derived from Labour Force Survey estimates, shows people who were working 'unsociable' hours during 1990, that is people working at weekends, on night shifts or on other shift work. It is estimated that almost half of all those in employment at that time did some weekend work, slightly higher than in 1985. As

4.20 Industrial disputes[1]: working days lost and number of stoppages

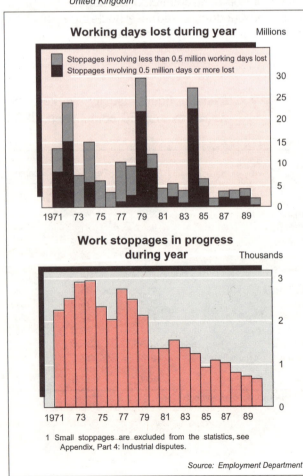

United Kingdom

Working days lost during year — Millions

Stoppages involving less than 0.5 million working days lost
Stoppages involving 0.5 million days or more lost

Work stoppages in progress during year — Thousands

1971 73 75 77 79 81 83 85 87 89

1 Small stoppages are excluded from the statistics, see Appendix, Part 4: Industrial disputes.

Source: Employment Department

4.19 People engaged in weekend working, shift work and night work, 1985 and 1990

Great Britain			Thousands and percentages	
	1985		1990	
	Total (thousands)	As a percentage of all in employment	Total (thousands)	As a percentage of all in employment
Weekend working[1]	10,523	*44.3*	12,701	*48.5*
Shift work[2]	2,926	*12.3*	3,454	*13.2*
Night work[3]	394	*1.7*	486	*1.9*

1 Persons who worked on a Saturday or Sunday or both in the four week period prior to interview (includes weekend shifts).
2 Includes weekend and night shifts.
3 Persons who usually work at night or do night shifts (including at weekends), only.

Source: Labour Force Survey, Employment Department

one person may work at the weekend, in shifts and during the night, it is not possible to add together the figures in the table to calculate exactly how many were working 'unsociable' hours.

There were 1.9 million working days lost through industrial disputes during 1990 (Chart 4.20), the lowest annual figure since 1963. There were 630 stoppages in progress in 1990, 71 fewer than in 1989 - the number of stoppages in progress was actually the lowest for more than half a century. Comparisons of the number of stoppages must be made with caution because of the exclusion of some of the smallest stoppages from the statistics (see Appendix: Part 4).

Using data from the Labour Force Survey, it is possible to estimate the percentage of employees who were absent from work (for at least one day) in the week before interview. It should be remembered that the surveys were conducted at a particular time of year (spring), sickness absences will clearly be different at different times of the year. From Table 4.21, it can be seen that females were marginally more likely to have taken sickness absence in both Spring 1984 and 1990. In 1990, amongst women, those aged 16-19 years were the most likely to be absent, whereas for men the likeliest age group was 60-64 years.

The latest year for which absence data is available for the whole of the European Community (EC) is 1989 (Chart 4.22). As with the previous table, the data reflect absences in Spring. During the reference week, over 3 million people were absent from work because of illness or injury in the EC, equivalent to more than the entire population of Wales. It is estimated that 2 per cent of the usual working week in the EC was lost to injury or illness. The rate was lowest in Greece (at half of one per cent) and highest in the Netherlands (at 4 per cent). The United Kingdom was next highest at 2.7 per cent.

4.21 Employees absent from work owing to sickness: by sex and age, 1984 and 1990

Great Britain	Males		Females	Percentages
	1984	1990	1984	1990
Percentage of each age group absent from work because of sickness[1]				
16-19	4.5	5.1	4.9	6.6
20-24	4.2	5.0	5.1	5.4
25-44	4.2	3.8	4.9	5.2
Females 45-54/Males 45-59	4.6	4.4	5.5	5.4
Females 55-59/Males 60-64	7.1	6.2	5.6	5.8
Females 60/Males 65 and over	3.1	2.9	3.8	5.3
All aged 16 and over	4.5	4.3	5.1	5.4

1 At least one day away from work during the week before interview.

Source: Labour Force Survey, Employment Department

4.22 Percentage of working week lost due to illness, Spring 1989

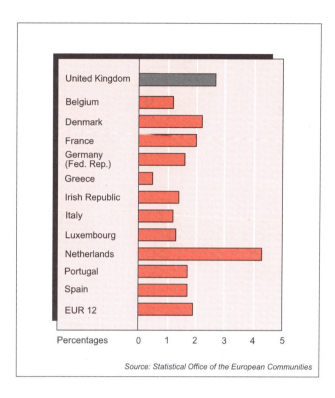

Source: Statistical Office of the European Communities

Unemployment

Unemployment is used as both an economic and a social indicator and can be defined in two different ways. There are two basic methods. The first, the claimant count, exploits administrative systems to count those people recorded at government offices as unemployed. Figures from this source are available quickly, frequently and relatively cheaply, providing a regular indicator of the trend in unemployment. This measure can be quoted simply as recorded. However, in order to provide a series free from the influence and distortions due to changes in the coverage of the administrative systems, the Employment Department publish a consistent seasonally adjusted series. This is recalculated back to 1971 each time there is a significant change in coverage and is the series given most prominence in the media. Its disadvantage is that when rules for entitlement to benefit change then the series has to be recalculated in order to avoid inconsistency over time.

The second measure is by a survey of individuals who are asked whether they have a job and, if not, whether they would like work and what steps they have taken to find it. Surveys, such as the Labour Force Survey, can not only collect information on whether a person is in work or seeking work, but can also record information on the characteristics of the unemployed. In estimating unemployment the Labour Force Survey uses the International Labour Organisation definition (see Glossary of Terms). The process of collecting, verifying and analysing the information means that estimates

are not available as quickly or as frequently as claimant count estimates but has the advantage of not being affected by legislative measures. The Employment Department uses both methods by publishing the

4.23 Comparisons of alternative measures of unemployment

Great Britain

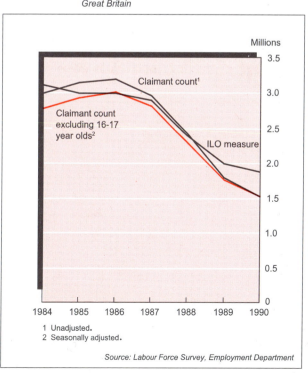

1 Unadjusted.
2 Seasonally adjusted.

Source: Labour Force Survey, Employment Department

4.25 Unemployment rate[1]: annual averages by sex

United Kingdom

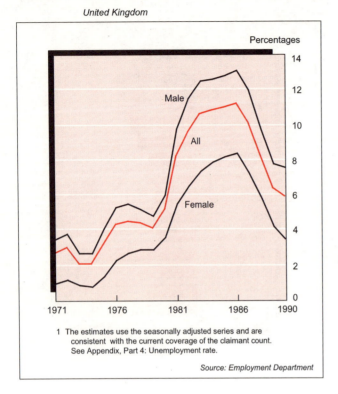

1 The estimates use the seasonally adjusted series and are consistent with the current coverage of the claimant count. See Appendix, Part 4: Unemployment rate.

Source: Employment Department

4.24 Unemployment and vacancies

United Kingdom

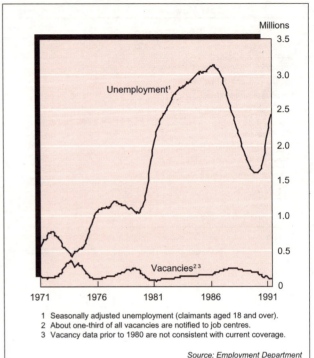

1 Seasonally adjusted unemployment (claimants aged 18 and over).
2 About one-third of all vacancies are notified to job centres.
3 Vacancy data prior to 1980 are not consistent with current coverage.

Source: Employment Department

monthly claimant count and by sponsoring the Labour Force Survey. Chart 4.23 compares the two measures; Labour Force Survey estimates of unemployment with the claimant count (both the adjusted and unadjusted series). The three measures show broadly similar trends, a general decline in the number of unemployed between 1984 and 1990. However, by 1990, the Labour Force estimate of unemployment was nearly a quarter higher than the claimant count.

Chart 4.24 shows the number of unemployed consistent with the current coverage of the claimant count and the number of vacancies remaining unfilled at job centres

since 1971. The number unemployed rose above one million in December 1975, above two million in March 1981 and above three million in February 1985 to reach a peak at 3.12 million in July 1986. Since then, the number unemployed fell for 44 successive months to reach 1.6 million by March 1990, but has risen each successive month to reach almost 2.5 million in October 1991.

An additional way of expressing unemployment figures is as a rate, that is expressed as a percentage of the

4.26 Unemployment rates adjusted to OECD concepts[1]: international comparison

Percentages

	Annual averages													
	1976	1979	1980	1981	1982	1983	1984	1985	1986	1987	1988	1989	1990
United Kingdom	5.6	5.0	6.4	9.8	11.3	12.4	11.7	11.2	11.2	10.2	8.5	7.1	6.9
Belgium	6.4	8.2	8.8	10.8	12.6	12.1	12.1	11.3	11.2	11.0	9.7	8.1	7.9
France	4.4	5.9	6.3	7.4	8.1	8.3	9.7	10.2	10.4	10.5	10.0	9.4	9.0
Germany (Fed. Rep.)	3.7	3.2	3.0	4.4	6.1	8.0	7.1	7.2	6.4	6.2	6.2	5.6	5.1
Italy	6.6	7.6	7.5	7.8	8.4	8.8	9.4	9.6	10.5	10.9	11.0	10.9	9.9
Netherlands	5.5	5.4	6.0	8.5	11.4	12.0	11.8	10.6	9.9	9.6	9.2	8.3	7.5
Portugal	..	..	..	..	..	7.9	8.4	8.5	8.4	7.0	5.7	5.0	4.6
Spain	4.6	8.5	11.2	13.9	15.8	17.2	20.0	21.4	21.0	20.1	19.1	16.9	15.9
Australia	4.7	6.2	6.0	5.7	7.1	9.9	8.9	8.2	8.0	8.1	7.2	6.1	6.9
Canada	7.1	7.4	7.4	7.5	10.9	11.8	11.2	10.4	9.5	8.8	7.7	7.5	8.1
Finland	3.8	5.9	4.6	4.8	5.3	5.4	5.2	5.0	5.3	5.0	4.5	3.4	3.4
Japan	2.0	2.1	2.0	2.2	2.4	2.6	2.7	2.6	2.8	2.8	2.5	2.3	2.1
Sweden	1.6	2.1	2.0	2.5	3.2	3.5	3.1	2.8	2.7	1.9	1.6	1.4	1.5
United States	7.6	5.8	7.0	7.5	9.5	9.5	7.4	7.1	6.9	6.1	5.4	5.2	5.4

1 See Appendix, Part 4: Definitions of unemployment-OECD concepts.

Source: Main Economic Indicators and Quarterly Labour Force Statistics, OECD

4.27 Unemployment : by region

United Kingdom

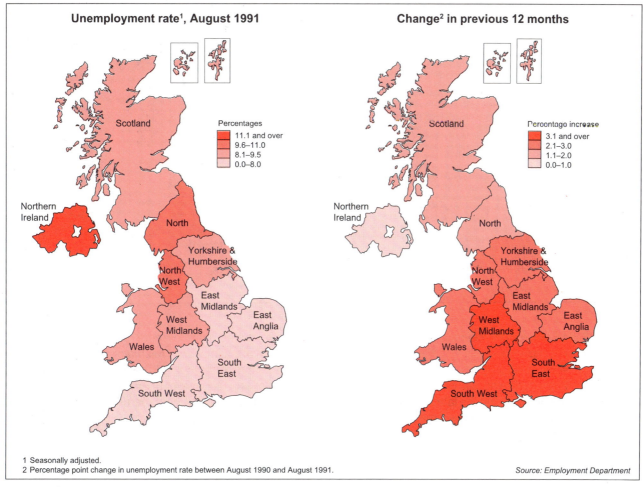

Unemployment rate[1], August 1991

Percentages
- 11.1 and over
- 9.6–11.0
- 8.1–9.5
- 0.0–8.0

Change[2] in previous 12 months

Percentage increase
- 3.1 and over
- 2.1–3.0
- 1.1–2.0
- 0.0–1.0

1 Seasonally adjusted.
2 Percentage point change in unemployment rate between August 1990 and August 1991.

Source: Employment Department

workforce (see Appendix, Part 4: Unemployment rate). Chart 4.25 shows unemployment rates for both men and women. Unemployment rose very sharply in 1980 and 1981 and this upward trend continued, although the rate of increase slowed down, until 1986. It then fell and in 1990 it stood at 5.8 per cent. The male and female rates have followed a similar pattern, with the male rate consistently higher than the female rate.

As previously stated, unemployment is measured differently in different countries. The Organisation for Economic Co-operation and Development (OECD) use a standard set of concepts to compare unemployment between countries. These rates are estimated by OECD to conform, as far as possible, to International Labour Organisation guidelines and they are calculated as percentages of the total labour force.

Table 4.26 shows that unemployment rates rose between 1981 and 1982 for all the countries shown and stand at more than 10 per cent in the United Kingdom,

Belgium, The Netherlands, Spain and Canada. More recently, between 1989 and 1990 the only countries where rates rose were Australia, Canada, Sweden and the United States. In every country in the table, unemployment rates were lower in 1990 than they had been in 1986.

As well as differing between countries, unemployment rates differ within regions. Chart 4.27 shows unemployment rates (using the claimant count definition) in the standard regions of the United Kingdom and the change during the previous twelve months. In August 1991, the lowest unemployment rates were in East Anglia (6.2 per cent) and the South East (7.4 per cent), the highest was in Northern Ireland (14.1 per cent). Generally however, those regions with the lowest unemployment rates experienced the highest rises in unemployment rates during the previous year (3.4 percentage points in the South East) while areas of high unemployment experienced the lowest rises (less than one percentage point in Northern Ireland).

4.28 Unemployed claimants: by duration, sex and age, 1991[1]

United Kingdom   Percentages and thousands

| | Duration of unemployment (percentages) | | | | | | |
	Up to 13 weeks	Over 13 up to 26 weeks	Over 26 up to 52 weeks	Over 52 up to 104 weeks	Over 104 up to 156 weeks	Over 156 weeks	Total (= 100%) (thousands)
Males aged:							
18-19	48.2	24.3	20.7	6.8	.	.	119.6
20-24	38.4	22.1	20.9	11.9	3.8	2.8	345.4
25-34	34.4	20.1	19.6	13.5	4.8	7.6	502.8
35-49	32.6	18.7	17.5	12.9	4.7	13.5	417.9
50-59	25.4	14.8	14.5	11.6	5.8	28.0	240.7
60 and over	38.8	23.0	23.5	8.5	1.4	4.9	40.2
All males aged 18 and over	34.6	19.8	18.8	12.2	4.3	10.4	1,666.6
Females aged:							
18-19	51.3	23.1	19.9	5.6	.	.	65.8
20-24	45.2	21.6	19.1	9.0	2.6	2.6	128.3
25-34	43.2	20.8	20.5	8.9	2.5	4.2	136.4
35-49	40.7	18.4	17.8	11.6	3.9	7.6	120.0
50-59	25.1	13.3	15.1	12.4	6.5	27.6	77.8
60 and over	5.6	4.7	4.6	6.1	8.1	71.0	0.6
All females aged 18 and over	41.4	19.6	18.6	9.6	3.1	7.6	528.8

1 At April.   *Source: Employment Department*

Table 4.28, derived from the claimant count, shows the duration of uncompleted spells of unemployment for those who were unemployed in April 1991. The proportions of claimants who had been unemployed for over one year declined during the late 1980s. However, in 1991, one quarter of unemployed males and one in five unemployed females had been out of work for more than one year.

4.29 Unemployment rates[1]: by sex and age

United Kingdom   Percentages

	1984	1986	1988	1989	1990
Males					
16-19	23	22	15	12	13
20-29	16	16	11	9	9
30-39	9	9	7	6	6
40-49	8	8	6	5	4
50-59	9	9	9	7	7
60 and over	10	10	9	9	8
All males aged 16 and over	12	12	9	7	7
Females					
16-19	21	20	12	9	10
20-29	16	14	11	9	8
30-39	11	10	9	7	6
40-49	7	7	5	5	5
50-59	7	6	6	6	5
60 and over	7	5	5	5	4
All females aged 16 and over	12	11	8	7	6

1 Using the ILO definition of unemployment. See Appendix, Part 4: Definition of unemployment - OECD concepts.

Source: Labour Force Survey, Employment Department

In 1990, the unemployment rate was highest among the young (Table 4.29). Although male unemployment rates have declined for all age groups since 1984, rates for those aged under 20 remain almost double the average male unemployment rate.

Factors contributing to more prolonged periods of unemployment include a mismatch between the skills (and location) of unemployed people and those required by employers, the level of unemployment benefits, low economic activity and how the unemployed go about looking for a job.

The table shows that the length of unemployment increases with age. In 1991, only 18 per cent of unemployed males aged 20-24 had been out of work

4.30 Unemployment rates: by sex and ethnic origin

Great Britain   Percentages

	1984	1986	1988	1989	1990
Males					
White	11	11	9	7	7
West Indian or Guyanese	30	26	18	15	13
Indian	13	16	11	10	8
Pakistani/Bangladeshi	33	27	24	18	15
Other[1]	19	17	9	8	12
All males[2]	12	11	9	7	7
Females					
White	11	10	8	7	6
West Indian or Guyanese	18	19	11	14	..
Indian	20	19	13	9	11
Pakistani/Bangladeshi	..	..	..	..	..
Other[1]	19	17	10	8	9
All females[2]	12	11	8	7	7
All persons					
White	11	11	9	7	7
West Indian or Guyanese	24	23	15	14	11
Indian	16	17	12	9	9
Pakistani/Bangladeshi	34	28	24	22	17
Other[1]	19	17	10	8	11
All persons[2]	12	11	9	7	7

1 Includes those of mixed origins.
2 Includes those who did not state their ethnic origin.

Source: Employment Department

4.31 The unemployed[1]: by sex and previous occupation group[2], 1984 and 1990

Great Britain   Percentages and thousands

	Males		Females		All	
	1984	1990	1984	1990	1984	1990
Percentage of the unemployed aged 16 and over in each previous occupation group						
Managerial and professional	8.4	11.1	8.0	9.9	8.2	10.6
Clerical and related	1.7	3.5	14.7	15.8	7.0	8.6
Other non-manual	3.6	4.2	7.3	8.1	5.1	5.8
All non-manual previous occupations	13.7	18.8	30.0	33.7	20.3	25.0
Craft and similar	18.8	17.9	3.7	4.3	12.6	12.2
General labourers	4.0	2.6	—	—	2.5	1.6
Other manual	27.8	28.9	21.7	24.8	25.3	27.2
All manual previous occupations	50.6	49.4	25.6	29.3	40.4	41.0
All those with previous occupation stated	64.2	68.3	55.7	63.1	60.8	66.1
No previous occupation stated[3]	35.8	31.7	44.3	36.9	39.2	33.9
Total unemployed[4] (= 100%) (thousands)	1,838	1,089	1,256	780	3,094	1,869

1 Using the ILO definition of unemployment. See Appendix, Part 4:
  Definitions of unemployment — OECD concepts.
2 Previous occupation of those who had left their last job within the
  last 3 years.

3 Includes a small number of people who did not know or who
  inadequately described their previous occupation.
4 Includes those who have never been in employment and those who
  have been unemployed for 3 years or more.

Source: Labour Force Survey, Employment Department

for more than a year, compared to over 45 per cent of unemployed males aged between 50 and 59, with 28 per cent having been unemployed for more than 3 years.

Similar trends emerge for women, but the figures are affected by women's entitlement to benefit; for example many married women stop signing on at an Unemployment Benefit Office after one year because they exhaust their entitlement to unemployment benefit and are often not subsequently entitled to income support in their own right, for example if their husband is working or claiming benefits himself.

As well as age and sex, studies suggest that other factors also influence unemployment durations, for example race, disability or previous occupation.

Unemployment rates are higher among ethnic minorities than among Whites (Table 4.30). Between 1984 and 1986 unemployment rates changed little among ethnic groups (with the exception of the Pakistani/Bangladeshi group where unemployment fell by 6 percentage points), Since 1986, the fall in unemployment rates has been greater among ethnic minority groups than among the White group. In particular, unemployment among West Indian or Guyanese males fell from 26 per cent in 1986 to 13 per cent in 1990.

Table 4.31, derived from the Labour Force Survey, shows the previous occupation of the unemployed. In 1990, of the unemployed who had stated a previous occupation, 28 per cent of men but more than half of women had been non-manual workers. This was a similar pattern to 1984. Care should be taken in

TRAINING STATISTICS 1991

Training Statistics 1991 is the second in an annual series. The 1990 edition brought together a wide range of training-related data which had previously been scattered amongst many different reports, journals and other sources. Training Statistics 1991 builds on its predecessor and extends its coverage to include more regional data and information on particular groups of individuals such as the self employed, those with health problems and people from ethnic minorities.

Training Statistics 1991 is published by HMSO for the Department of Employment
Paperback £11.25 ISBN 011 361 3237

4.32 Job search methods of the unemployed: by age, 1990

Great Britain — Percentages

	Age						All unemployed aged 16 and over
	16–19	20–24	25–34	35–49	50–59	60 and over	
Percentage[1] of each age group using the following as their main method of job search							
Visiting a jobcentre[2]	41	37	28	24	30	23	30
Study situations vacant columns in newspapers	23	28	35	36	35	45	33
Answering advertisements in newspapers or journals[3]	8	9	10	12	9	11	10
Personal contacts	8	10	11	13	11	12	11
Direct approach to firms/employers	13	10	10	7	9	4	9
Name on private agency books	3	2	2	4	2	1	2
Other[4]	4	3	4	5	4	5	4

1 Percentages are based on data excluding those who did not know or preferred not to state their job search methods and those temporarily not looking for work because they were either waiting to start a new job, temporarily sick or on holiday. The unemployed are based on the ILO definition of unemployment. See Appendix, Part 4: Definition of unemployment

2 Includes job clubs, career offices and government employment offices.

3 Includes notices outside factories or in shop windows.

4 Includes advertising in newspapers/journals and awaiting job application results.

Source: Labour Force Survey, Employment Department

interpreting the figures as a third of the unemployed did not state their previous occupation, either because they had never had a job or because they had been unemployed for more than three years.

There are a number of ways in which the unemployed can attempt to find a job, these are detailed in Table 4.32. Those aged under 24 years were most likely to use a jobcentre as their main method of job search, while those aged over 35 favoured the situations vacant columns in newspapers.

Jobsearch methods also varied between occupations. Unemployed people who had previously been in non-manual occupations were less likely than manual workers to visit a jobcentre, and more likely to use newspapers or private employment agencies.

In 1986, the government introduced the Restart Programme, aimed at the long-term unemployed. Initially, all those who had been unemployed for at least 12 months were invited to an interview and offered help towards employment. In 1987, the programme was extended to cover those unemployed for 6 months or over.

Opportunities offered include an interview for a job, a place on Employment Training, a place on a Restart Course, a Jobstart Allowance, a place on an Enterprise Allowance Scheme or a place on a Jobclub. Jobclubs aim to help people who have been unemployed for 6 months or more by providing help in finding jobs and free facilities such as telephones and stationery. In 1989-90, around 2 million people were interviewed under the Restart Programme. Developments in 1990 included issuing a personal back to work plan for clients, help for some after only 13 weeks of unemployment and more intensive help for those unemployed for 2 years.

The frequency with which people search for jobs is related to the duration of their unemployment. A recent study of people attending Restart interviews found that

4.33 Economic inactivity: by sex and reason for inactivity, 1990

Great Britain

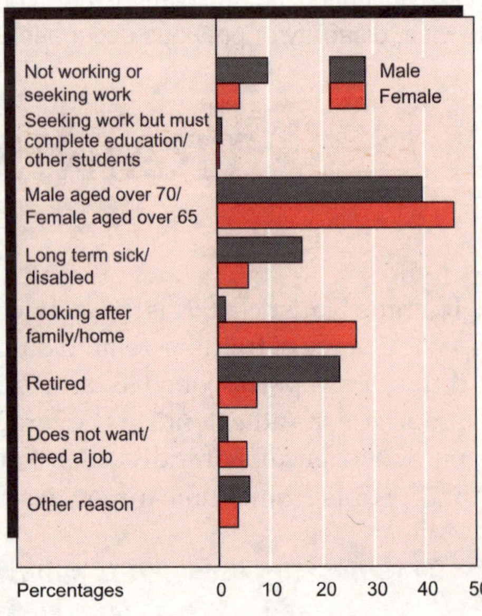
Not working or seeking work
Seeking work but must complete education/ other students
Male aged over 70/ Female aged over 65
Long term sick/ disabled
Looking after family/home
Retired
Does not want/ need a job
Other reason
Male
Female
Percentages
0
10
20
30
40
50

Source: Labour Force Survey, Employment Department.

Social Trends 22, © Crown copyright 1992

those who had short spells of unemployment were more likely to search actively for work. Overall, only half of the people interviewed had applied for a job in the previous four weeks. Of those who had, half had made only one application.Some people do not want, or need, work. People who are not in employment or training and who are not seeking work or waiting to start a new job are classified not as unemployed, but as economically inactive. Over half of both the male and female economically inactive were either five years older than the state retirement age, or were younger but said they were retired (Chart 4.33). A further quarter of economically active females looked after the family or home. The number of discouraged workers, that is people who said that they would like work but were not seeking it because they believed there were no jobs available, represented less than one per cent of the economically inactive.

Employment and training measures

A number of employment and training measures have been developed in response to the rise in unemployment during the 1970s and 1980s these are described in the Appendix: Part 4.

The government announced in December 1989 its intention to restructure the training and enterprise system and to set up a network of Training and Enterprise Councils (TECs) in England and Wales (and Local Enterprise Companies (LECs) in Scotland). These aim to establish a partnership which encourages growth in local economies through strengthening the skill base and helping local enterprise expand and compete. A network of 82 TECs is now complete. The role of TECs is to address local issues in order to: promote more effective training, provide practical help to employers wishing to improve their training efforts, deliver and develop Youth Training, develop Employment Training, stimulate enterprise and economic growth through the Enterprise Allowance Scheme, enterprise training and counselling programmes for small firms and stimulate business education partnerships.

TECs are business-led local companies which contract with the Secretary of State for Employment to take charge of training and enterprise in their area. At least two thirds of a TEC Board of Directors must be top private sector business leaders. The balance is drawn from local authorities, trade unions, the voluntary sector, education and others.

Employment Training (ET) was launched on 5 September 1988, replacing a range of employment and training programmes for the unemployed. The aim is to provide training for the longer-term unemployed to help them get and keep jobs. Training is offered at all levels, from basic literacy and numeracy to postgraduate training in high technology skills. Those participating have their training needs assessed and agree an individual training plan, training is then organised on projects or with employers.

4.34 Youth Training Scheme[1]: number of starts

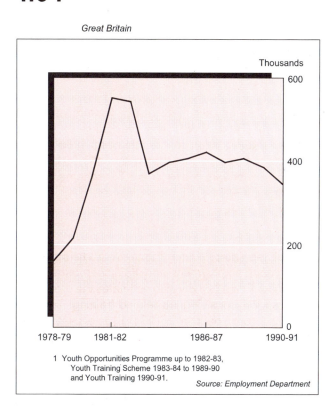

Great Britain

1 Youth Opportunities Programme up to 1982-83, Youth Training Scheme 1983-84 to 1989-90 and Youth Training 1990-91.

Source: Employment Department

The Youth Training Scheme (YTS) was introduced in April 1983 to provide up to one year of training and work experience. It was extended in April 1986 to a two year scheme aimed at providing broad-based vocational training in a variety of occupations mainly for 16 and 17 year old school leavers. In May 1990, YTS was replaced by Youth Training, with greater emphasis on participants gaining vocational qualifications. This is administered at local level by TECs in England and Wales and by LECs in Scotland. Almost 350 thousand young people started Youth Training in 1990-91 (Chart 4.34).

4.35 Youth Training Scheme leavers

Great Britain   Percentages and thousands

	1983–84	1984–85	1985–86	1986–87[1]	1987–88	1988–89	1989–90
Leavers							
Percentage of leavers who:							
Gained a qualification	..	27[4]	21	21	29	41	43
Destination							
Full-time work							
Same employer	12[3]	23	28[5]	28	23	32	34
Different employer [2]	37	32	25	29	34	31	30
Part-time work	..	1	4	4	4	4	3
Full-time course at college/training							
centre	1	3	3	3	4	3	4
Different YTS Scheme	12	6	7	11	12	12	11
Other	3	2	4	3	3	3	4
Unemployed	34	32	28	23	21	14	14
All leavers (thousands)	128	368	418	428	326	414	406

1 The information on leavers in 1986-87 is not representative of two year YTS, as there are very few two year completers before April 1988.
2 Includes self-employed.
3 These figures are based on a sample of YTS trainees used in a survey of nine area offices.

4 Based on an early sample follow-up survey in the period June 1984 to March 1985.
5 These figures include YTS1 leavers in the period April 1986 to September 1986.

Source: YTS Management Information System; YTS Follow-up Survey

In 1989-90, nearly two thirds of YTS leavers left for full time work (Table 4.35). The proportion of leavers gaining a qualification doubled between 1986-87 and 1989-90, but was still less than half of all YTS leavers. One in ten leavers leave one YTS scheme to join another.

As well as interviewing those in participation in government employment and training programmes, the Labour Force Survey also estimates the proportion of employees receiving job-related training. This has increased from 9 per cent in 1984 to 15 per cent in 1990 (Table 4.36). Of these, over 70 per cent had received at least some of their training away from their job. The proportion receiving job-related training decreases with age, 25 per cent of those aged 16 to 19 had received training in 1990, but only 8 per cent of those aged 50 to 59 years.

Chart 4.37 shows data from the Confederation of British Industry (CBI) Quarterly Industrial Trends Survey. The data are the percentage of respondents in the manufacturing industry who expected skill shortages to limit output over the following four months. In October 1973, over half the respondents expected skill shortages to limit output, this fell to between only 2 and 4 per cent in 1981 and 1982, before gradually increasing to reach 28 per cent by October 1988. Since then, the trend has been downwards and in July 1991, only 5 per cent expected skill shortages to limit output. The Skills Monitoring Survey (SMS) collects information about the extent of employers' recruitment difficulties, the occupations involved and employers' responses. The second SMS, *Skill Needs in Britain 1991*, was published in October 1991. Overall, only 7 per cent of employers reported recruitment difficulties at the time of the survey while nearly a quarter had experienced difficulties.

4.36 Percentage of employees[1] receiving job-related training during the last four weeks[2]: by age

Great Britain   Percentages

	1984	1985	1986	1987	1988	1989	1990
Percentage in each age group receiving training							
16–19	20	24	22	21	23	23	25
20–24	14	16	16	17	19	19	21
25–29	11	13	14	14	16	17	18
30–39	9	10	11	13	14	15	16
40–49	6	7	7	9	11	12	13
50–59	2	4	4	5	6	8	8
60–64 (males only)	2	2	2	2	3	3	4
All of working age	9	10	11	12	13	14	15

1 Those in employment, excluding the self-employed and people on government schemes.
2 Includes both on-the-job and off-the-job training.

Source: Employment Department

4.37 Expectations of skill shortages[1,2]

United Kingdom

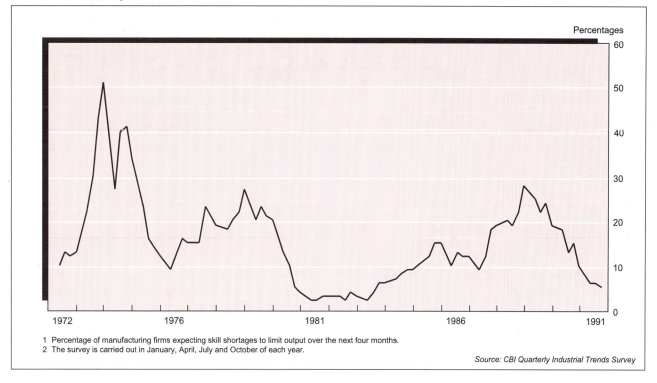

1 Percentage of manufacturing firms expecting skill shortages to limit output over the next four months.
2 The survey is carried out in January, April, July and October of each year.

Source: CBI Quarterly Industrial Trends Survey

BIBLIOGRAPHY

The following list contains selected publications relevant to Chapter 4: Employment. Those published by HMSO are available from the addresses shown on the back cover of Social Trends.

A New Look at Skill Shortages (a Summary of Key Finding of Skill Needs in Britain), Training Agency
British Social Attitudes, Gower
CBI Quarterly Industrial Trends Survey, CBI
Employment Gazette, HMSO
General Household Survey, HMSO
Labour Force Survey, HMSO
Labour Market and Skill Trends, Employment Department
Labour Market Quarterly Report, Employment Department

Main Economic Indicators, OECD
Regional Trends, HMSO
Scottish Economic Bulletin, HMSO
Skills Bulletin, Employment Department
Time Rates and Hours of Work, Employment Department
Training Statistics, HMSO
Youth Cohort Study, Social and Community Planning Research

1991

NEW EARNINGS SURVEY

The results of the New Earnings Survey 1990 have been published in six parts, forming a comprehensive report on the survey. They are available from HMSO, price **£11.00** each net.

Subscriptions for the set of six, including postage, **£63.00**

The contents of the **six parts** are:

Part A ISBN 011 728952 3
Streamlined analyses giving selected results for full-time employees in particular wage negotiation groups, industries, occupations, age groups, regions and sub-regions; Summary analyses for broad categories of employees; Description of survey, glossary of terms and definitions, questionnaire, grouped list of occupations, and region and sub-region classifications.

Part B ISBN 011 728953 1
Analyses of earning and hours for particular wage negotiation groups.

Part C ISBN 011 728954 X
Analyses of earnings and hours for particular industries.

Part D ISBN 011 728955 8
Analyses of earnings and hours for particular occupations.

Part E ISBN 011 728956 6
Analyses of earnings and hours by region and county and by age group.

Part F ISBN 011 728957 4
Distribution of hours;
Joint distribution of earnings and hours;
Analyses of earnings and hours of part-time women employees.

HMSO
PO Box 276
London SW8 5DT
or
HMSO Bookshops

Chapter 5: Income and Wealth

Household income

● Disposable household income continues to grow. Between 1971 and 1990, average real disposable household income per head increased by nearly three quarters. *(Chart 5.1)*

● The gap between the top ten per cent of wage earners and the bottom ten per cent is widening, particularly for manual employees. *(Table 5.6)*

● The real income of pensioners grew by two thirds between 1971 and 1988. *(Chart 5.7)*

Taxes

● The share of total income tax paid by the top taxpayers has increased during the 1980s and early 1990s. In 1981-82, the top ten per cent of income taxpayers paid 35 per cent of total tax, by 1991-92 this had risen to 42 per cent. *(Table 5.12)*

Income distribution

● The share of income going to the top fifth of households has increased. In 1977, the top fifth received 37 per cent of total household post-tax income, by 1988 this had risen to 44 per cent. *(Table 5.19)*

Wealth

● An increasing share of personal wealth is in dwellings, 37 per cent in 1989 compared with only 23 per cent in 1971. *(Table 5.20)*

● The most wealthy 10 per cent of the population own more than half of total wealth. *(Table 5.21)*

● Despite wider share ownership, the proportion of shares in private hands has decreased over time. The proportion of total share value held by individuals halved between 1963 and 1990. *(Chart 5.25)*

5.1   **Real household disposable income per head**

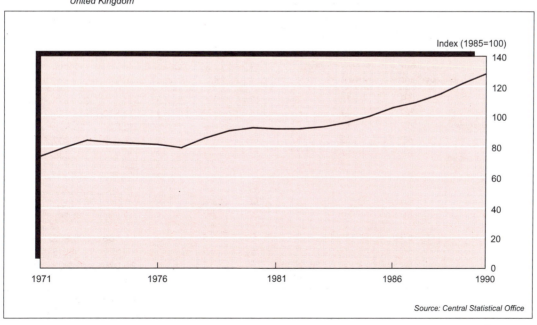

United Kingdom

Index (1985=100)

Source: Central Statistical Office

Household income

5.2 Household income[1]

United Kingdom

	1971	1976	1981	1984	1985	1986	1987	1988	1989	1990
Source of income *(percentages)*										
Wages and salaries[2]	67	67	63	61	60	59	60	60	60	59
Income from self-employment[3]	9	9	8	9	9	10	10	10	10	10
Rent, dividends, interest	6	6	7	6	7	7	7	7	8	9
Private pensions, annuities, etc	5	5	6	7	8	8	8	8	8	9
Social security benefits	9	11	13	13	13	13	12	12	11	11
Other current transfers[4]	2	2	2	3	3	3	3	3	2	2
Total household income										
(= 100%) (£ billion)	44.7	100.4	202.1	256.7	282.6	310.0	336.0	370.9	415.0	464.4
Direct taxes etc *(percentages of total household income)*										
Taxes on income	14	17	14	15	15	14	14	14	14	15
National insurance contributions[5]	3	3	3	4	4	4	4	4	4	3
Contributions to pension schemes	1	2	2	2	2	2	2	2	2	2
Total household disposable income (£ billion)	36.4	78.3	162.4	203.6	224.5	248.1	269.8	297.3	333.3	372.6
Real household disposable income per head										
(index numbers — 1985 = 100)	73	81	92	96	100	106	110	115	122	128
Annual change on previous year (percentages)	0.3	-1.0	-1.1	2.8	4.2	5.6	3.9	4.7	5.8	5.2

1 See Appendix, Part 5: The household sector.
2 Includes Forces' pay and income in kind.
3 After deducting interest payments, depreciation, and stock appreciation.

4 Mostly other government grants, but including transfers from abroad and from non-profit-making bodies.
5 By employees and the self-employed.

Source: Central Statistical Office

Disposable income measures the amount of money households have to spend or invest - it is made up of income from all sources less taxes on income, national insurance contributions and contributions to pension schemes. When expressed in real terms, the series shows how household income has changed over time after allowing for inflation.

Between 1971 and 1990, real disposable income per head increased by nearly three quarters. Chart 5.1 shows that over this period, real disposable income fell in each year between 1973 and 1977 and again between 1980 and 1981 but otherwise rose every year in the last two decades.

5.3 Household income[1]: by source and region, 1989

United Kingdom

	Income from employment	Income from self-employment	Income from invest-ment	Occupat-ional & state pensions	Social security benefits	Other income	Total house-hold income (= 100%) (£ million)	Total (£ million)	£ per head index (UK=100)	£ per household index (UK=100)
	Percentage of income from each source							Household disposable income		
United Kingdom	59	11	8	13	6	3	420,011	337,814	100.0	100.0
North	60	9	6	15	8	4	19,530	16,239	89.5	89.1
Yorkshire & Humberside	58	10	8	14	6	3	32,524	26,578	91.2	90.2
East Midlands	59	10	9	13	5	3	28,002	22,417	95.0	94.7
East Anglia	55	14	11	13	4	2	15,277	12,165	100.8	100.6
South East	62	11	9	12	4	2	149,553	117,300	114.3	112.5
South West	54	13	12	15	5	2	35,266	28,685	104.5	103.1
West Midlands	60	9	8	14	6	3	35,020	28,126	91.4	92.2
North West	60	9	7	13	7	3	42,297	34,391	91.3	92.1
England	60	11	9	13	5	3	357,469	285,902	101.6	100.9
Wales	56	10	8	15	8	3	17,812	14,916	88.0	91.4
Scotland	60	10	6	13	7	4	35,075	28,802	95.9	95.9
Northern Ireland	54	13	5	13	11	3	9,654	8,194	87.7	101.8

1 See Appendix, Part 5: The household sector.

Source: Regional Accounts, Central Statistical Office

5.4 Average weekly household disposable income per head : by region, 1989

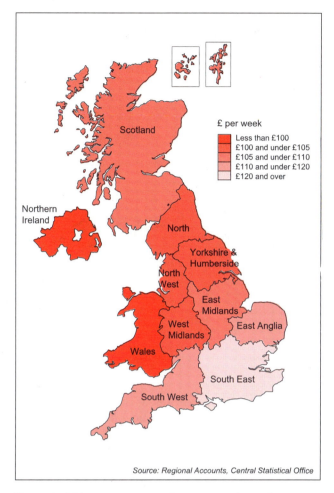

£ per week
- Less than £100
- £100 and under £105
- £105 and under £110
- £110 and under £120
- £120 and over

Source: Regional Accounts, Central Statistical Office

Although national household income figures are available for 1990, regional statistics are only available up to 1989 (Table 5.3 and Chart 5.4). In 1989 disposable income per head was highest in the South East and lowest in Northern Ireland and Wales. Differences between regions arise because of both demographic and economic factors. For example, the higher proportions of income from state and occupational pensions in the South West are a reflection of the large number of retired people in the region. Self-employment income is more important in East Anglia partly due to the importance of agriculture to the region's economy.

Households are made up of people. The more people there are in a household, the more disposable income they will need to cover their expenditure and (depending on the number of adults) the higher their earning power. It is interesting to compare the two measures of income per head and income per household - both of which are in Table 5.3. In 1989, Northern Ireland had the lowest disposable income per head but the third highest per household. This apparent paradox is because households in the province are larger than elsewhere in the United Kingdom.

As Tables 5.2 and 5.3 show, earnings from employment are the main source of household income. One measure of changes in the level of earnings is the average earnings index and Chart 5.5 shows the annual percentage change in this index and the underlying rate of change. Most people's earnings change as a result of annual pay increases.

Household income comes from a number of sources and the share of each source is shown in Table 5.2. Wages and salaries are the most important source of household income although their importance has declined since 1971. In that year, wages and salaries accounted for 68 per cent of household income but this figure fell to 59 per cent in 1990. The share of income from social security benefits increased from 10 per cent in 1971 to 13 per cent in 1981, before falling back to 11 per cent in 1989 and 1990. Some of the changes are attributable to large increases in the number of unemployed during the early 1980s and an increase in self-employment; see Chapter 4. The United Kingdom has a growing number of elderly people. This coupled with the increases in the number of the people entitled to occupational pensions has resulted in an increasing proportion of household income from private pensions and annuities (9 per cent in 1990).

The proportion of total household income paid in income tax increased from 14 per cent in 1971 to 17 per cent in 1976. Between 1981 and 1990 this proportion remained fairly steady at between 14 and 15 per cent. The proportion paid in national insurance contributions was around 3 per cent in the 1970s and around 4 per cent in the 1980s. Chapter 6 gives details of how people spend their disposable incomes.

The annual rate of increase in average earnings rose from about 10 per cent in early 1978 to above 20 per cent during 1980. The rate then fell to below 6 per cent between February and August 1984, largely because the figures were affected by the dispute in the coal industry. The underlying rate takes account of such fluctuations to present a less volatile picture. Even during the period when the main index was affected by the coal dispute, the underlying rate of increase remained between 7.5 and 8 per cent. Between August 1984 and the end of 1987 the underlying rate of earnings growth remained at about 7.5 to 7.75 per cent but then rose steadily to reach 9.5 per cent in March 1989. The underlying rate edged down slightly in the Summer of 1989, but then continued to rise to reach a peak of 10.25 per cent in July 1990. Subsequently, the rate of growth of earnings has declined and the 7.5 per cent figure reached in July 1991 was the lowest for over 4 years.

For many people earnings vary according to such factors as the amount of overtime they work and entitlement to bonuses, shift allowances, grade increments and other productivity and incentive payments. In addition most employees also have an annual pay settlement or review. Any increases may

5.5 Average earnings index[1]

Great Britain

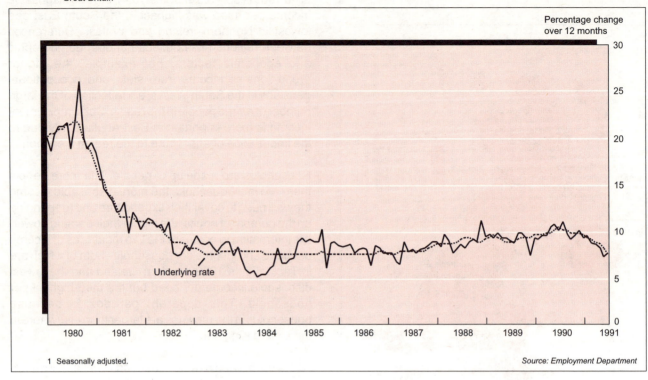

1 Seasonally adjusted.

Source: Employment Department

be influenced by the profitability of the employer, inflation, productivity, recruitment and retention, comparability with others and the economic climate.

The rates of earnings growth shown by the average earnings index in Chart 5.5 and the New Earnings Survey figures used in Table 5.6 are not directly comparable. While the average earnings index covers

all employees, the New Earnings Survey figures shown relate to only full-time adult employees whose earnings during the survey period were unaffected by absence.

The New Earnings Survey figures allow us to look at the spread or distribution of earnings around the average over time. The highest decile is the minimum amount earned by the top ten per cent of employees, the lowest

5.6 Gross weekly earnings of full-time employees[1]: by sex and type of employment

Great Britain

£ and percentages

	Males					Females				
	1971	1981	1986	1989	1990	1971	1981	1986	1989	1990
Manual employees										
Mean (£)	29.0	120.2	174.4	217.8	237.2	15.3	74.7	107.5	134.9	148.0
Median (£)	27.7	112.8	163.4	203.9	221.3	14.6	71.6	101.1	125.9	137.3
As percentage of median										
Highest decile	*147*	*151*	*155*	*158*	*159*	*143*	*143*	*150*	*156*	*157*
Lowest decile	*68*	*69*	*65*	*63*	*63*	*71*	*70*	*69*	*69*	*68*
Non-manual employees										
Mean (£)	38.5	160.5	244.9	323.6	354.9	20.0	97.5	145.7	195.0	215.5
Median (£)	34.0	147.0	219.4	285.7	312.1	18.2	87.7	131.5	173.5	191.8
As percentage of median										
Highest decile	*175*	*167*	*175*	*181*	*182*	*169*	*172*	*167*	*174*	*173*
Lowest decile	*60*	*60*	*57*	*54*	*55*	*65*	*68*	*65*	*62*	*62*
All employees										
Mean (£)	32.4	138.2	207.5	269.5	295.6	18.4	92.0	137.2	182.3	201.5
Median (£)	29.4	124.6	185.1	235.5	258.2	16.7	82.8	123.4	160.1	177.5
As percentage of median										
Highest decile	*162*	*168*	*173*	*180*	*181*	*165*	*172*	*170*	*181*	*179*
Lowest decile	*65*	*64*	*60*	*59*	*58*	*66*	*68*	*65*	*63*	*63*

1 Figures relate to April each year and to full-time employees on adult
rates whose pay for the survey pay period was not affected by absence.

Source: New Earnings Survey, Employment Department

Social Trends 22, © Crown copyright 1992

5.7 Income of pensioners[1]: by source

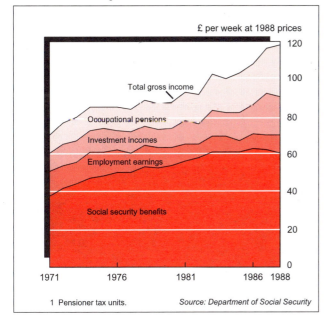

United Kingdom

£ per week at 1988 prices

Total gross income
Oooupational pensions
Investment incomes
Employment earnings
Social security benefits

1971　1976　1981　1986 1988

1 Pensioner tax units.　　*Source: Department of Social Security*

decile is the maximum amount earned by the bottom ten per cent of employees. By comparing these decile points with the mid-point of the earnings range (the median), it is possible to see the widening gap between the highest and lowest earners in recent years.

The difference between the highest and lowest decile points as a percentage of the median is a common measure of the spread of earnings. The gap has widened especially for manual employees: by 17 percentage points between 1971 and 1990. Some of

this was the result of falls in employment in manufacturing, where pay is concentrated around the middle of the earnings distribution. The table also shows differences between male and female earnings. However, the table only shows weekly earnings; full-time women work fewer hours per week than full-time men, and so a better comparison would be hourly earnings excluding overtime.

As Chapter 1 shows, the number of people of pensionable age has increased over the past forty years and this trend is projected to continue. The income of pensioners will therefore remain an important issue. Chart 5.7 shows that between 1971 and 1988, gross incomes of pensioners grew by two thirds in real terms (using the all items index of the Retail Prices Index). Social security benefits have tended to be fairly stable in real terms in recent years because they are now uprated in line with prices rather than whichever is the higher of wages or prices. Between 1981 and 1988, the proportion of gross income which came from retirement pension and other social security benefits (fell from 61 to 51 per cent) as income from investments and occupational pensions increased in importance. In 1988, 23 per cent of pensioner income came from occupational pensions compared with 16 per cent in 1981 and 14 per cent in 1971.

For households as a whole, social security benefits (including state retirement pensions) are the second most important source of income after income from employment (Tables 5.8 and 5.9). Social security remains by far the largest single public expenditure programme, accounting for more than one quarter of all General Government expenditure in 1990 (see Chapter

5.8 Contributory benefits expenditure and recipients: by type of benefit

Great Britain　　　　　　　　　　　　　　　　　　　　　　　　£ million and thousands

	Expenditure (£ million)				Recipients[1] (thousands)			
	1976−77	1981−82	1986−87	1989−90	1976−77	1981−82	1986−87	1989−90
National insurance benefits								
Pension benefits								
Retirement pensions	5,662	12,126	17,779	20,697	8,250	9,015	9,575	9,795
Widows benefit and industrial death benefit	466	738	886	911	490	460	430	405
Industrial disablement benefit	167	315	440	470	200	260	285	295
Invalidity benefit	585	1,370	2,673	3,837	510	660	935	1,190
Lump sum payments to contributory pensioners	.	101	107	112	.	10,100	10,700	11,200
Other benefits								
Unemployment benefit	559	1,702	1,734	733	625	1,220	1,005	375
Sickness benefit	552	680	179	204	520	445	100	105
Statutory sick pay[2]	.	.	757	949	.	.	320	360
Maternity allowance	60	158	168	30	80	125	110	20
Statutory maternity pay[3]	.	.	.	286	.	.	.	90
Death grant[4]	15	17	18	.	.	.	.	.
Administration and miscellaneous services[5]	571	733	733	856				

1 Estimated average number receiving benefit on any one day, except for lump sum payments and death grants, which because they are single payments are the total number paid in each year.
2 Introduced in April 1983 and extended to 28 weeks from April 1986.

3 Introduced in April 1987.
4 Replaced in April 1987 by payments from the Social Fund.
5 Figure for 1976-77 represents administration cost of both contributory and non-contributory benefits.

Source: Department of Social Security

5.9 Non-contributory social security expenditure and recipients: by type of benefit

Great Britain   £ million and thousands

	Expenditure (£ million)				Recipients[1] (thousands)			
	1976–77	1981–82	1986–87	1989–90	1976–77	1981–82	1986–87	1989–90
Non-contributory benefits								
Pension benefits								
Non-contributory retirement pension	36	39	37	35	80	50	40	35
War pension	283	479	590	641	415	345	280	265
Attendance allowance	114	330	779	1,159	230	350	605	795
Invalid care allowance[2]	2	6	104	184	5	5	25	115
Severe disablement allowance[3]	34	130	285	346	105	180	265	280
Mobility allowance	8	173	514	769	30	210	460	585
Lump sum payments to non-contributory pensioners	.	. 6	8	9	.	600	800	900
Other benefits								
Supplementary pension[4,5]	573	1,418	1,178	.	1,675	1,740	1,810	.
Supplementary allowance[4]	1,140	3,422	6,784	.	1,305	1,985	3,285	.
Income support	.	.	.	7,675	.	.	.	4,155
Child benefit[6]	544	3,372	4,513	4,537	6,915	13,145	12,175	12,000
Family income supplement	18	66	161	.	70	125	215	.
Family credit	.	.	.	425	.	.	.	305
One-parent benefit	.	76	148	199	.	470	615	735
Maternity grant[7]	15	16	14	.	. .	. .	. .	.
Housing benefit[5] — rent rebates and allowance[8]	201	562	3,235	3,804	. .	1,840	4,900	3,905
Social Fund[9]	.	.	.	130	.	.	.	1,525
Administration and miscellaneous service[10]	571	498	1,020	1,584				

1 Estimated average number receiving benefit on any one day, except for lump sum payments, maternity grant and social fund payments which, because they are single payments are the total number paid in each year.
2 Extension of invalid care allowance to married women announced in June 1986, 1986-87 expenditure includes substantial arrears.
3 Non-contributory invalidity benefit before November 1984.
4 In 1986-87, the number of recipients includes those receiving housing benefit supplement who are also included in the housing benefit recipients.
5 Up to 1982, housing costs of supplementary benefit recipients were

paid as part of that benefit, since then they have been paid as housing benefit.
6 Child benefit recipients relate to the number of qualifying children except for 1976-77 which relates to the number of qualifying families.
7 Maternity grant was abolished in April 1987 and replaced by payments from the Social Fund.
8 Expenditure represents central government grants to local authorities.
9 Net expenditure after repayment of loans.
10 1976-77 figure represents administration cost of both contributory and non-contributory benefits.

Source: Department of Social Security

6). Of all social security benefits, total expenditure on retirement pensions is by far the largest. The number of recipients of retirement pensions has grown steadily over the period covered by the tables, to reach 9.8 million by 1989-90. When interpreting the recipient figures in Tables 5.8 and 5.9 it should be remembered that individuals can receive more than one type of benefit. Most benefits are uprated from year to year,

5.10 Social security benefits[1] for the unemployed[2]: by sex

Great Britain   Percentages and thousands

	1961	1971	1976	1981	1986	1989	1990
Unemployed male claimants receiving each benefit							
(percentages)							
Unemployment benefit only	47.2	40.9	30.0	28.2	20.2	11.6	16.2
Unemployment and supplementary benefit/income support	9.4	13.6	10.9	11.4	7.5	6.4	4.7
Supplementary benefit/income support only	21.9	27.1	42.4	46.0	59.3	67.5	65.1
No benefit	21.6	18.4	16.6	14.4	13.0	14.5	13.9
Total unemployed male claimants (=100%) (thousands)	283	721	1,076	1,994	2,086	1,062	1,174
Unemployed female claimants receiving each benefit							
(percentages)							
Unemployment benefit only	39.7	41.0	29.1	38.9	33.5	22.3	23.9
Unemployment and supplementary benefit/income support	2.5	6.7	3.9	3.8	2.7	2.8	1.3
Supplementary benefit/income support only	12.2	20.5	44.6	37.4	40.8	51.7	53.2
No benefit	45.5	31.8	22.4	20.0	23.0	23.2	21.5
Total unemployed female claimants (=100%) (thousands)	101	138	380	709	955	391	384

1 At November each year except for 1976 when figures relate to August and 1981 when figures for 1982 are used. From April 1988 supplementary benefit was replaced by income support.
2 Prior to 1981 count of registered unemployed; for 1981 count of registered unemployed claimants, after then, count of unemployed claimants.

Source: Department of Social Security

but Child Benefit remained at the same level of £7.25 per child from 1986 to April 1991. The rate for the eldest eligible child in each family was then increased to £8.25. It was further increased in October 1991 to £9.25 for the eldest eligible child and to £7.50 for subsequent children.

The social security reforms introduced in the *Social Security Act 1986* took effect in April 1988, with income support replacing supplementary benefit, family credit replacing family income supplement and the social fund replacing some ad hoc payments.

Between 1961 and 1990 there was a marked fall in the percentage of the unemployed claimants receiving only unemployment benefit and a big increase in the percentage receiving only supplementary benefit and income support. A more recent comparison between 1981 and 1990 shows that the proportion of male unemployed claimants receiving only unemployment benefit fell from 28 to 16 per cent while the proportion receiving only supplementary benefit and income support rose from 46 to 65 per cent (Table 5.10). In 1990, 14 per cent received no benefits at all because, for example, they had exhausted their right to unemployment benefit but their savings were too high to be eligible for income support.

Taxes

Until the end of tax year 1989-90 a wife's income was treated for tax purposes as if it belonged to her husband. The husband was responsible for completing tax returns of both his own and his wife's income and for paying the tax due. Tax was offset by a wife's earned income allowance. This was changed with the introduction of Independent Taxation on 6 April 1990. Since this date, all taxpayers are taxed separately on their own incomes and take responsibility for their own tax affairs.

During the year 1991-92 it is estimated that just over 25 million taxpayers will have a total income tax bill of just over £62 billion (Table 5.11). The average amount of

tax payable ranges from £190 per year (around 4 per cent of income) for those with an annual income of between £3 thousand and £5 thousand to £21,100 (around 30 per cent of income) for those with an annual income of over £40 thousand.

Tax rates have been reduced considerably since 1978-79. The basic rate has been cut from 33 per cent to 25 per cent, the higher rates of tax which rose to a maximum of 83 per cent have been replaced by one 40 per cent rate, and the surcharge of up to 15 per cent on investment income has been abolished. The top ten per cent of taxpayers are currently paying a larger

5.11 Income tax payable: by income[1] range, 1991-92[2]

United Kingdom

Annual income	Total annual income (£ million)	Tax payable at basic rate		Tax payable at excess over basic rate		Total tax payable (£ million)	Average rate of tax payable (%)	Average amount of tax payable (£)
		Number of taxpaying individuals (millions)	Amount[3] (£ million)	Number of taxpaying individuals (millions)	Amount (£ million)			
Annual income								
£3,000 but under £5,000	9,120	2.2	400	0	0	400	4	190
£5,000 but under £7,500	24,190	3.8	2,060	0	0	2,060	8	530
£7,500 but under £10,000	36,730	4.2	4,350	0	0	4,350	12	1,030
£10,000 but under £15,000	79,980	6.5	11,000	0	0	11,000	14	1,700
£15,000 but under £20,000	68,760	4.0	10,800	0	0	10,800	16	2,710
£20,000 but under £30,000	69,310	2.9	12,260	0.1	20	12,280	18	4,230
£30,000 but under £40,000	27,080	0.8	5,220	0.8	540	5,760	21	7,260
£40,000 and over	52,580	0.7	11,340	0.7	4,350	15,690	30	21,100
All ranges	367,750	25.1	57,430	1.6	4,910	62,340	17	2,480

1 Total income of the individual for income tax purposes including earned and investment income. All figures in the table relate to taxpayers only.

2 Based on a projection from the 1989-90 Survey of Personal Incomes.

3 Including the basic rate component of tax payable at higher rate.

Source: Inland Revenue

5.12 Shares of total income tax liability[1]

United Kingdom   Percentages and £ billion

	1976 −77	1981 −82	1986 −87	1990 −91[2]	1991 −92[2]
Quantile groups of taxpayers					
Top 1 per cent	11	11	14	16	15
Top 5 per cent	25	25	29	32	32
Top 10 per cent	35	35	39	43	42
Next 40 per cent	45	46	43	42	43
Lower 50 per cent	20	19	16	15	15
All taxpayers (= 100%) (£ billion)	18.3	30.5	42.8	59.4	62.3

1 Independent taxation was introduced from 6 April 1990. For years up to and including 1986−87, married couples are counted as one taxpayer and their incomes are combined. For 1990−91 and 1991−92, husbands and wives are counted separately.
2 Estimates are based on a projection of the 1989−90 Survey of Personal Incomes.

Source: Inland Revenue

proportion of income tax than they did in 1976-77 (Table 5.12). In 1976-77 they paid 35 per cent of total income tax, but in 1991-92 it is estimated that they will pay 42 per cent.

The percentage of income paid in income tax has fallen at all levels of income since 1981-82 (Table 5.13). Employee's contributions to national insurance have also decreased since 1981-82 - although there was some increase in the early part of this period.

The combined effect of changes in gross earnings, income tax, NI contributions and child benefit are illustrated in Table 5.14. This table also shows the introduction in 1988 of family credit in place of family income supplement. A single man earning the minimum amount earned by the top ten per cent (ie at the highest decile point) saw his real weekly net earnings increase the most between 1981 and 1990 (by 42 per cent).

Conversely, a married man with two children not claiming family credit earning the maximum amount earned by the bottom ten per cent (ie at the lowest decile point) saw his real net earnings increase the least (by 15 per cent). However, if family credit was claimed then a married man with two children saw his real weekly net earnings increase by almost 20 per cent.

However, it should be noted that changes in the distribution of earnings do not necessarily indicate the movements in earnings of individuals or groups of individuals. They are caused by several factors including the change in the structure of employment. Over time, people themselves move within the distribution.

5.13 Percentage of income paid in income tax and national insurance contributions[1]: by marital status and level of earnings[2]

United Kingdom   Percentages

	1981−82	1984−85	1985−86	1986−87	1987−88	1988−89	1989−90	1990−91	1991−92[3]
Single person									
Half average earnings									
Tax	17.5	15.3	14.9	14.4	13.9	13.0	13.1	13.3	13.1
NIC	7.7	9.0	7.0	7.0	7.0	7.0	6.7	6.4	6.3
Average earnings									
Tax	23.7	22.7	22.4	21.7	20.4	19.0	19.1	19.1	19.1
NIC	7.7	9.0	9.0	9.0	9.0	9.0	8.3	7.7	7.6
Twice average earnings									
Tax	27.3	26.3	26.2	25.4	23.7	22.0	22.0	23.3	22.4
NIC	6.1	7.1	7.1	7.2	6.9	6.6	6.2	5.7	5.9
Married man[4]									
Half average earnings									
Tax	10.5	6.9	6.3	6.2	6.5	6.1	6.4	6.6	6.9
NIC	7.7	9.0	7.0	7.0	7.0	7.0	6.7	6.4	6.3
Average earnings									
Tax	20.2	18.5	18.1	17.6	16.7	15.5	15.7	15.8	16.0
NIC	7.7	9.0	9.0	9.0	9.0	9.0	8.3	7.7	7.6
Twice average earnings									
Tax	25.1	24.2	24.1	23.3	21.9	20.3	20.3	20.5	20.5
NIC	6.1	7.1	7.1	7.2	6.9	6.6	6.2	5.7	5.9

1 Employees' contributions. Assumes contributions at Class 1, contracted in, standard rate.
2 Average earnings for full-time adult male manual employees working a full week on adult rates.

3 1990-91 based projections.
4 Assuming wife not in paid employment.

Source: Inland Revenue

5.14 Real[1] weekly earnings[2] after income tax, national insurance contributions, child benefit and family credit: by selected family type

Great Britain   £ and percentages

	1971	1981	1986	1988	1989	1990	Percentage change 1971–1981	Percentage change 1981–1990
Single man								
Lowest decile point	89.2	97.4	105.1	114.0	114.2	117.0	9.2	20.2
Median	131.9	144.4	163.6	183.0	184.8	188.1	9.5	30.2
Highest decile point	208.6	235.3	275.5	323.1	330.4	335.1	12.8	42.4
Single woman								
Lowest decile point	57.2	72.7	82.5	88.9	89.8	90.9	27.1	25.0
Median	79.8	100.4	114.6	128.2	130.3	134.8	25.8	34.3
Highest decile point	124.5	162.8	183.2	216.1	223.3	227.0	30.8	39.4
Married man[3], no children								
Lowest decile point	95.6	104.9	114.5	122.5	122.6	125.3	9.6	19.5
Median	138.3	151.9	173.1	191.5	193.1	196.4	9.8	29.2
Highest decile point	215.0	242.8	284.9	331.5	338.8	345.1	12.9	42.1
Married man[3], 2 children[4]								
Lowest decile point[5]								
Family credit claimed	112.0	121.5	132.6	148.7	147.4	145.3	8.5	19.6
Family credit not claimed[6]	112.0	121.5	132.6	139.6	138.4	139.8	8.5	15.1
Median	154.6	168.6	191.2	208.6	209.0	210.9	9.0	25.1
Highest decile point	231.4	259.4	303.0	348.7	354.7	359.6	12.1	38.6

1 At April 1990 prices.
2 Figures relate to April each year and to full-time employees on adult rates whose pay for the survey pay-period was not affected by absence.
3 Assuming no wife's earnings.
4 Aged under 11.

5 In years up to 1987, there was no entitlement to Family Income Supplement for this category.
6 Families with capital of more than £3,000 would only be eligible to receive reduced amounts of family credit, or may not be eligible at all.

Source: Inland Revenue; Department of Social Security

Chart 5.15 shows the net income after rent and community charge of three different family types earning between £50 and £250 per week in October 1991. These data are not estimated from surveys of real families but are modeled according to a set of assumptions and the application of current rates of tax. In order to model net income, it is assumed that there is no income other than the earnings of the head of household and social security benefits, for which full entitlement is claimed, that they have only their personal tax allowances, that they live in local authority rented accommodation and that they are not contracted out of the state pension scheme. Average local authority rent and Community Charge are deducted from their net incomes to arrive at net weekly spending power.

Entitlement to certain benefits changes as earnings change. The poverty trap occurs when an increase in earnings causes a reduction in benefit such that net income falls or remains static. The poverty trap has been virtually removed by social security reforms and in general, net income after rent and Community Charge increases with gross income. There are a very small number of particular points at which net income can fall as earnings increase. However, since the revisions to National Insurance contributions in October 1989, this only occurs where a rise in earnings reduces theoretical benefit entitlements to below the de minimis 50p award for family credit or housing benefit.

5.15 Net income after rent and community charge[1]: by level of gross earnings and type of family, 1991[2]

Great Britain

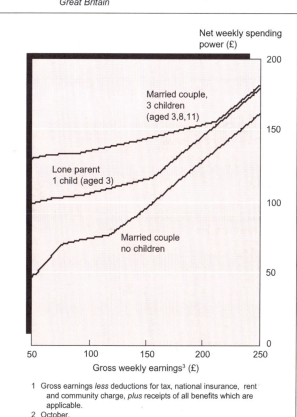

1 Gross earnings *less* deductions for tax, national insurance, rent and community charge, *plus* receipts of all benefits which are applicable.
2 October.
3 Gross earnings from full-time work where head of household only is in employment.

Source: Department of Social Security

Income distribution

This section details some of the distributive effects on household income of the government's tax-benefit system. Directly or indirectly most government revenue is raised from households, and its expenditure benefits households. One of the consequences of this is a tendency to even out the distribution of income. Initially, households receive income from various sources: from their employment; from occupational pensions; from investments; and from other households. Total income from these sources is defined as original income. The addition to original income of cash benefits by the state (eg retirement pensions and income support) gives gross income. Income tax payments, NI contributions and domestic rates (now replaced by Community Charge) are deducted to produce disposable income. Deducting indirect taxes such as Value Added Tax (VAT) yields post-tax income. Final income is obtained by adding the imputed benefits from government expenditure on certain services such as education and health. Where a household gets more money and services from the government than it pays in taxes and other contributions, the tax-benefit system has redistributed income in the household's favour.

The methodology for calculating the effects of taxes and benefits on household income was reviewed in 1989 and it was decided to move to an equivalised basis - this has been used in this section when dividing households up into five equal sized groups (quintile groups). Equivalisation means adjusting household income to take account of household size and composition in order to recognise different needs. For example, to achieve the same standard of living, a household of five people would need a higher income than a single person and this is reflected in the equivalisation. Distributions based on equivalised income put all households on an equal footing regardless

5.16 Redistribution of income through taxes and benefits[1], 1988

United Kingdom   £ per year and numbers

	Quintile groups of households ranked by equivalised disposable income[2]					All house-holds
	Bottom fifth	Next fifth	Middle fifth	Next fifth	Top fifth	
Average per household (£ per year[3])						
Earnings of main earner	740	3,090	7,400	10,830	19,500	8,310
Earnings of others in the household	90	470	1,940	3,830	6,200	2,500
Occupational pensions, annuities	160	500	790	830	1,300	720
Investment income	160	260	480	590	1,950	690
Other income	70	120	140	170	220	140
Total original income	1,210	4,440	10,750	16,260	29,170	12,360
+ Benefits in cash						
Contributory	1,640	1,640	960	640	430	1,060
Non-contributory	1,580	1,150	800	440	280	850
Gross income	4,430	7,240	12,500	17,340	29,880	14,280
—Income tax[4] and NIC[5]	200	740	1,920	3,220	5,990	2,420
—Domestic rates (gross)	470	480	530	570	700	550
Disposable income	3,760	6,020	10,050	13,540	23,190	11,310
Equivalised disposable income[2]	3,840	5,740	8,230	11,420	21,320	10,110
—Indirect taxes	1,080	1,470	2,410	2,900	3,710	2,320
Post-tax income	2,680	4,540	7,650	10,640	19,480	9,000
+ Benefits in kind						
Education	790	790	960	810	420	760
National Health Service	1,120	1,060	980	820	720	940
Housing subsidy	100	100	50	30	10	60
Travel subsidies	40	50	50	50	70	50
School meals and welfare milk	60	20	20	10	10	30
Final income	4,800	6,570	9,700	12,360	20,700	10,830
Number of households in sample	1,453	1,453	1,453	1,453	1,453	7,265

1 See Appendix, Part 5: Redistribution of income for definitions of the income measures. The 1987 figures published in Social Trends 21 and these 1988 figures incorporate major changes to the methodology, and are not comparable with figures prior to 1987 published in earlier editions of Social Trends.

2 Equivalised disposable income has been used for ranking to construct the quintile groups. The average equivalised disposable income for each group is shown below disposable income, but all other income values are unequivalised.

3 Rounded to the nearest £10.

4 After tax relief at source on mortgage interest and life assurance premiums.

5 Employees' national insurance contributions.

Source: Central Statistical Office, from the Family Expenditure Survey

5.17 Composition of quintile groups of household income: by economic status of head of household, 1988

United Kingdom   Percentages

Economic status of head of household	Quintile groups of households ranked by equivalised disposable income[1]					All house- holds
	Bottom fifth	Next fifth	Middle fifth	Next fifth	Top fifth	
Employed	9	30	59	74	74	49
Self-employed or employer	5	7	11	10	16	10
Unemployed but seeking work	14	5	3	2	1	5
Unemployed because of sickness or injury, but seeking work	1	1	—	—	—	1
Unemployed because of sickness or injury, but not seeking work	6	6	2	1	1	3
Retired [2]	43	41	21	11	7	24
Other economically inactive	23	11	4	2	1	8

1 Equivalised disposable income has been used to construct the quintile groups.

2 Including Job Release Scheme.

Source: Central Statistical Office from the Family Expenditure Survey

of size or composition and therefore provide a more meaningful way of comparing the incomes of households.

In 1988, total original income ranged from an average of £1,210 per household for the bottom quintile group to £29,170 for the top quintile group (Table 5.16). After adding in cash benefits, subtracting taxation and other contributions and adding in benefits in kind, final income ranged from £4,800 to £20,700 - that is, the income gap between the two groups narrowed.

Table 5.17 shows which households appear in each of the five quintile groups. Households headed by someone who is retired, unemployed or economically inactive tend to have the lower incomes and are therefore concentrated in the lower quintiles. On the other hand, the employed and self-employed are concentrated in the middle and higher quintile groups.

The composition of these groups has an obvious connection with the way in which household income is redistributed through taxes and benefits. The lower two

5.18 Sources of gross income: by income grouping, 1988[1]

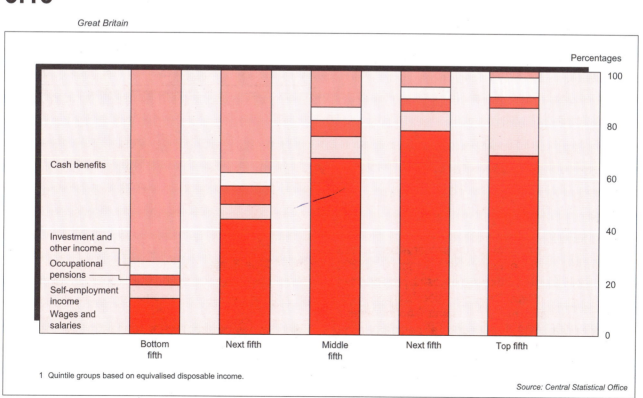

Great Britain

Percentages

Cash benefits

Investment and other income

Occupational pensions

Self-employment income

Wages and salaries

Bottom fifth   Next fifth   Middle fifth   Next fifth   Top fifth

1 Quintile groups based on equivalised disposable income.

Source: Central Statistical Office

quintile groups have the lowest earnings and the highest proportions of retired people and therefore those groups receive most of their income in the form of cash benefits (Table 5.16 and Chart 5.18). The top two quintile groups have the higher incomes and therefore tend to pay the most taxes - direct and indirect.

Table 5.19 shows how total household income is shared between households. In 1988, the top twenty per cent of households (top quintile) received half of all the original income (Table 5.19). Even after allowing for cash benefits, rates and taxes, they still received 44 per cent of total post-tax income. Over the period covered by the table, the share of income going to the top 20 per cent of households has increased over time - at each stage of the tax-benefit system. Although the redistributive effects of the system meant that the share of income going to the bottom 20 per cent increased from 2 per cent of original income to 7 per cent of post-tax income, this 7 per cent was lower than in earlier years. Trends in final income are not shown in this table because equivalisation is not appropriate for this income measure.

Some care must be exercised in interpreting these figures. Unlike Chart 5.1, Table 5.2, Chart 5.7 and Table 5.14, this table does not show trends in the division of household income without indicating how the total income has changed over the same period. It should also be borne in mind that any quintile group is different from year to year as some households and individuals move from one quintile group to another.

5.19 Shares of household income

United Kingdom   Percentages

| | Quintile groups of households ranked by equivalised disposable income | | | | | |
	Bottom fifth	Next fifth	Middle fifth	Next fifth	Top fifth	Total
Equivalised original income						
1977	4	10	18	26	43	100
1979	2	10	18	27	43	100
1981	3	9	17	26	46	100
1983	3	8	17	26	47	100
1985	2	7	17	27	47	100
1987	2	7	16	25	50	100
1988	2	7	16	25	50	100
Equivalised gross income						
1977	9	13	18	24	37	100
1979	8	13	18	24	37	100
1981	8	12	17	23	39	100
1983	8	12	17	23	39	100
1985	8	12	17	24	40	100
1987	8	11	16	23	43	100
1988	7	11	16	23	43	100
Equivalised disposable income						
1977	10	14	18	23	36	100
1979	9	13	18	23	36	100
1981	9	13	17	23	38	100
1983	10	13	17	23	38	100
1985	9	13	17	23	38	100
1987	8	12	16	23	41	100
1988	8	11	16	23	42	100
Equivalised post-tax income						
1977	9	14	17	23	37	100
1979	10	13	18	23	37	100
1981	9	13	17	22	39	100
1983	9	13	17	22	39	100
1985	9	13	17	23	39	100
1987	8	12	16	22	43	100
1988	7	11	16	22	44	100

Source: Central Statistical Office, from Family Expenditure Survey

Wealth

The value of net wealth held by the personal sector rose from just over £800 billion in 1981 to nearly £2,300 billion in 1989 (Table 5.20). An increasing proportion of this personal sector wealth has been tied up in dwellings, reflecting increasing home ownership and increasing house prices. In 1989, 37 per cent of all personal sector wealth was in dwellings. A substantial fall in share prices during the early 1970s caused the proportion of wealth invested in stocks and shares to fall from 20 per cent in 1971 to only 6 per cent in 1981. However, during the 1980s firmer market prices and wider share ownership have increased the proportion invested to over 8 per cent of all personal sector wealth in 1989.

Inland Revenue have recently reviewed their estimates of the distribution of personal wealth, the methods used are described in the October 1990 and November 1991 editions of Economic Trends. The value of pension rights depends on future changes in pension payments and

5.20 Composition of the net wealth[1] of the personal sector

United Kingdom		Percentages and £ billion		
	1971	1981[2]	1986	1989
Net wealth *(percentages)*				
Dwellings				
(net of mortgage debt)	23.0	31.9	31.8	36.6
Other fixed assets	9.3	9.8	6.6	6.0
Non-marketable				
tenancy rights	10.3	11.4	8.0	7.3
Consumer durables	9.2	9.6	7.9	7.0
Building society shares	6.3	7.0	7.9	6.1
National Savings, bank				
deposits, notes				
and coin	11.9	9.3	7.9	8.3
Stocks and shares	19.9	5.5	8.1	8.1
Other financial assets				
net of liabilities	10.1	15.5	21.8	20.6
Total (= 100%)				
(£ billion)	191.7	806.7	1,462.0	2,296.9

1 See Appendix, Part 5: Net wealth of the personal sector.
2 Data have been revised from 1981 onwards to include certain public sector pensions.

Source: Central Statistical Office

investment returns. When looking at wealth in a past year, it is possible to use the value of pension rights based on legislation and expectations of investment returns made at that time (the historic valuation). Additionally, it is possible to value pension rights in a past year on the basis of legislation and expectations at the time the valuation is made (the latest valuation). Both valuations are shown in Table 5.21.

There has been little change in the overall distribution of marketable wealth between 1976 and 1989. The share of the richest one per cent has fallen slightly, while that of the remainder of the richest 25 per cent has risen. In 1989, the wealthiest 10 per cent of the adult population owned more than half of the marketable wealth of the United Kingdom.

As an increasing amount of wealth is tied up in dwellings, the table also looks at the distribution of marketable wealth after the value of dwellings (net of mortgage debt) has been removed.

For many adults, their non-marketable rights in pension schemes have represented an increasingly important component of personal wealth over and above their holdings of marketable wealth. There were substantial changes to the type of pensions available in the United Kingdom during the late 1970s and 1980s. The State Earnings-Related Pension Scheme (SERPS) was introduced in 1978 although employers could contract out of SERPS if they provided their own salary-related

5.21 Distribution of wealth[1]

United Kingdom		Percentages and £ billion		
	1976	1981	1986	1989
Marketable wealth				
Percentage of wealth				
owned by[2]:				
Most wealthy 1%	21	18	18	18
Most wealthy 5%	38	36	36	38
Most wealthy 10%	50	50	50	53
Most wealthy 25%	71	73	73	75
Most wealthy 50%	92	92	90	94
Total marketable				
wealth (£ billion)	280	565	955	1,578
Marketable wealth less				
value of dwellings				
Percentage of wealth				
owned by[2]:				
Most wealthy 1%	29	26	25	28
Most wealthy 5%	47	45	46	53
Most wealthy 10%	57	56	58	66
Most wealthy 25%	73	74	75	81
Most wealthy 50%	88	87	89	94
Marketable wealth plus				
occupational and				
state pension rights				
(historic valuation)				
Percentage of wealth				
owned by[2]:				
Most wealthy 1%	12	10	10	11
Most wealthy 5%	24	23	23	26
Most wealthy 10%	34	33	34	38
Most wealthy 25%	54	55	57	62
Most wealthy 50%	78	78	81	83
Marketable wealth plus				
occupational and				
state pension rights				
(latest valuation)				
Percentage of wealth				
owned by[2]:				
Most wealthy 1%	13	11	10	11
Most wealthy 5%	26	24	24	26
Most wealthy 10%	36	34	35	38
Most wealthy 25%	57	56	58	62
Most wealthy 50%	80	79	82	83

1 Estimates for 1976, 1981 and 1986 are based on the estates of persons dying in those years. Estimates for 1989 are based on estates notified for probate in 1989 – 90. Estimates are not strictly comparable between 1989 and earlier years.
2 Percentages and total marketable wealth are of population aged 18 and over.

Source: Inland Revenue

pension scheme. Since July 1988, employees have also been entitled to contract out of SERPS individually or to leave their employer's scheme in favour of a personal pension scheme. Such schemes give tax relief on contributions up to a specified maximum percentage of earnings. Employers cannot now make their own schemes compulsory to their employees nor can they insist that employees remain in their schemes once they have joined.

5.22 Membership of current employer's pension scheme[1]: by socio-economic group, 1989-90

Great Britain

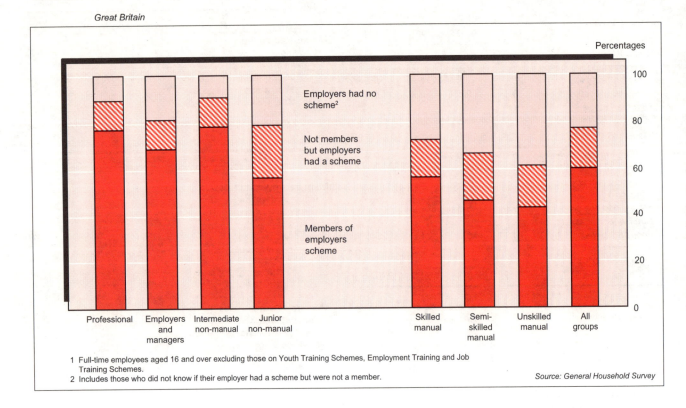

Percentages

Employers had no scheme[2]

Not members but employers had a scheme

Members of employers scheme

Professional | Employers and managers | Intermediate non-manual | Junior non-manual | Skilled manual | Semi-skilled manual | Unskilled manual | All groups

1 Full-time employees aged 16 and over excluding those on Youth Training Schemes, Employment Training and Job Training Schemes.
2 Includes those who did not know if their employer had a scheme but were not a member.

Source: General Household Survey

In 1989-90, 61 per cent of employees were members of their employer's pension scheme and 19 per cent were or had been contributors to a personal pension scheme. Membership of an employer's scheme varies considerably between different socio-economic groups and between different sizes of employer (Chart 5.22 and Table 5.23). Those in the intermediate non-manual group were the most likely to be members of an employer's scheme in 1989-90 (78 per cent) and those in the unskilled manual group were the least likely (43 per cent). Much of the difference between the groups was due to the availability of an employer's scheme. Where an employer had a scheme, the proportions who were members were 86 per cent for the intermediate non-manual group and 70 per cent for the unskilled manual group.

There are similar variations in membership between those employed by small and large employers. Table 5.23 shows that the more people employed by a firm, the more likely that employees are members of the

5.23 Membership of current employer's pension scheme and personal pension schemes[1]: by size of employer

Great Britain — Percentages

	Percentage of employees who were members of current employer's pension scheme		Percentage of employees who have ever contributed to a personal pension scheme	
	1988	1989	1988	1989
Number employed by current employer				
Under 3	33	28	18	29
3 and under 25	41	40	18	28
25 and under 100	57	59	14	22
100 and under 1000	72	71	9	13
1000 and over	83	84	7	11
All employers	61	61	12	19

1 Full-time employees aged 16 and over, excluding those in Youth Training Schemes, Employment Training, and Job Training Schemes.

Source: General Household Survey

5.24 Shareholders as a percentage of the adult population

Great Britain

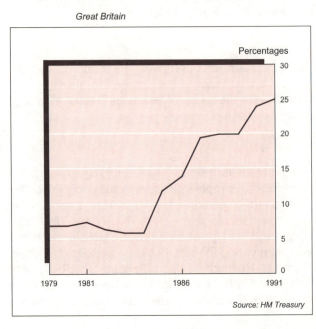

Percentages

1979 1981 1986 1991

Source: HM Treasury

5.25 Shares held in United Kingdom companies[1]: by sector

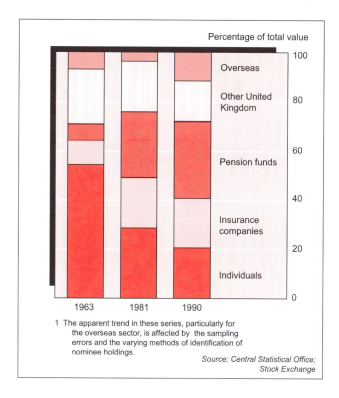

Percentage of total value

Overseas

Other United Kingdom

Pension funds

Insurance companies

Individuals

1963   1981   1990

1 The apparent trend in these series, particularly for the overseas sector, is affected by the sampling errors and the varying methods of identification of nominee holdings.

Source: Central Statistical Office; Stock Exchange

During the 1980s, share ownership became an increasingly important component of wealth (see Table 5.20). Chart 5.24 shows the wider ownership of shares. In 1990, one quarter of the adult population in Great Britain were shareholders. This compares with only one in 13 people in 1981. These figures are calculated from a Treasury/Stock Exchange survey. The survey found that 14 per cent of adults owned shares in privatised companies, over half of all shareholders only have shares in one company.

Despite this wider share ownership, the proportion of shares in private hands has decreased over time. Chart 5.25 includes figures from three of the seven surveys on shareholdings in United Kingdom companies carried out between the late-1950s and 1990. The 1963 figures are taken from a survey by the Department of Applied Economics at Cambridge University, the 1981 figures are taken from a Stock Exchange survey, and the 1990 figures from a survey carried out on behalf of the Central Statistical Office.

employer's pension scheme. This is not surprising as it is generally the case that the larger the firm the more likely they are to operate a scheme. Instead, employees of smaller firms turn to private pension schemes with 29 per cent of people employed by firms with less than 3 employees contributing (or had contributed) to a private scheme in 1989-90.

Although the value of shares held by individuals increased between 1963 and 1990, their proportion of the total value of all shares in United Kingdom companies more than halved. Over the same period, the proportion held by pension funds increased from 6 per cent to 31 per cent and the proportion held by insurance companies more than doubled.

BIBLIOGRAPHY

The following list contains selected publications relevant to Chapter 5: Income and Wealth. Those published by HMSO are available from the addresses shown on the back cover of Social Trends.

Economic Trends, HMSO
Employment Gazette, HMSO
Family Expenditure Survey, HMSO
Fiscal Studies, Institute for Fiscal Studies
General Household Survey, HMSO
Households Below Average Income, A Statistical Analysis, Department of Social Security
Inland Revenue Statistics, HMSO
New Earnings Survey, HMSO

Regional Trends, HMSO
Social Security Statistics, HMSO
Tax/Benefit Model Tables, Department of Social Security
The Personal Income Tax Base: A Comparative Study, OECD
The Tax/benefit Position of Production Workers, OECD
UK National Accounts ('CSO Blue Book'), HMSO

The CSO Blue Book
1991 Edition

United Kingdom National Accounts

This publication is the essential data source for everyone concerned with macro-economic policies and studies.

The principal annual publication for national accounts statistics, the *CSO Blue Book,* provides detailed estimates of national product, income and expenditure for the United Kingdom.

The Blue Book covers value added by industry, personal sector, companies, public corporations, central and local government, capital formation and financial accounts. Tables contain up to 22 years' data. There are definitions and detailed notes.

HMSO £13.95 net   ISBN 0 11 620452 4

Central Statistical Office publications are published by HMSO.
They are obtainable from HMSO bookshops and through booksellers.

Chapter 6: Expenditure and Resources

Household expenditure

- Consumers' expenditure continues to rise in real terms - by nearly 70 per cent between 1971 and 1990, although the rate of growth slowed down considerably between 1989 and 1990.

  (Chart 6.1)

- Households at the lower end of the income scale spend higher proportions on essentials such as food, housing and fuel and light - half of their total expenditure.

  (Table 6.3)

- Foreign holidaymakers coming to the United Kingdom outspend United Kingdom holidaymakers both at home and abroad.

  (Chart 6.7)

Prices

- In 1990, the 1951 "pound in our pocket" was worth just 8 pence.

  (Chart 6.10)

- In 1971, it would have taken about a week's work (40 hours and 31 minutes) for a married man on average earnings to earn enough to pay for a motor car licence. In 1989, it would have taken less than half those hours.

  (Table 6.13)

Consumer credit and household saving

- Outstanding consumer credit continues to grow. The amount of outstanding debt doubled in real terms between 1981 and 1990.

  (Chart 6.14)

Public income and expenditure

- Expenditure on social security accounts for nearly 30 per cent of total general government expenditure.

  (Table 6.20)

National resources

- The 1,374 million tonnes of oil and 752 billion cubic metres of gas already recovered may be only one-fifth of total reserves in United Kingdom fields.

  (Table 6.23)

6.1 Consumers' expenditure at constant prices: by selected item

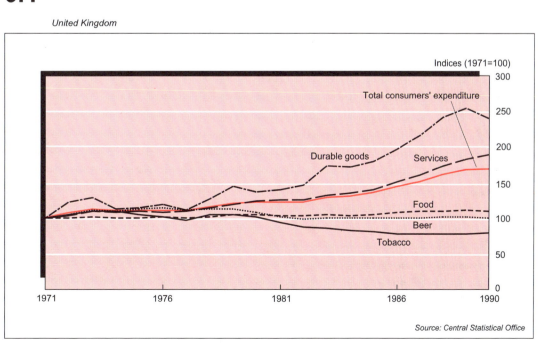

United Kingdom

Indices (1971=100)

Total consumers' expenditure

Durable goods

Services

Food

Beer

Tobacco

Source: Central Statistical Office

Household expenditure

Whereas Chapter 5 discusses people's income, this section looks at how they spend it and how much of it they manage to save. The chapter also includes statistics on consumer credit.

Chart 6.1 shows changing patterns of consumers' expenditure on selected items between 1971 and 1990. The chart is fixed to an index of 1971=100, making real terms comparisons easy. Total consumers' expenditure rose by almost 70 per cent in real terms between 1971 and 1990. Over this period however it is noticeable that expenditure on tobacco decreased by over one-fifth and expenditure on beer changed very little. The most significant increase during the period covered by the chart was in expenditure on consumer durables, which rose by 140 per cent.

Over the more recent period 1989 to 1990, total consumers' expenditure changed very little (an increase of less than one per cent), following more substantial

6.2 Household expenditure[1]

United Kingdom

	1976	1981	1985	1986	1989	1990 Indices/ per- centages	1990 £ million (current prices)
Indices at constant 1985 prices							
Food	96	99	100	103	105	104	41,885
Alcoholic drink	93	95	100	100	105	104	21,730
Tobacco	126	117	100	97	97	98	8,835
Clothing and footwear	68	79	100	109	116	115	20,301
Housing	83	91	100	104	113	117	47,818
Fuel and power	93	97	100	103	99	100	12,269
Household goods and services							
Household durables	83	86	100	107	126	120	10,296
Other	89	89	100	110	130	133	11,712
Transport and communication							
Purchase of vehicles	65	78	100	109	145	132	18,805
Running of vehicles	81	90	100	107	127	134	24,405
Other travel	82	92	100	107	131	131	11,494
Post and telecommunications	62	85	100	108	127	134	6,194
Recreation, entertainment and education							
TV, video, etc	50	67	100	113	141	142	7,685
Books, newspapers, etc	111	112	100	103	104	105	4,434
Other	82	94	100	105	123	125	18,794
Other goods and services							
Catering (meals, etc)	90	89	100	108	146	150	29,242
Other goods	89	88	100	107	139	141	12,601
Other services	56	73	100	114	146	152	22,260
Less expenditure by foreign tourists, etc	87	74	100	96	97	98	−8,785
Household expenditure abroad	47	94	100	112	157	149	8,902
Total household expenditure	82	90	100	106	122	123	330,877
Percentage of total household expenditure at current prices							
Food	*19.2*	*16.3*	*14.4*	*14.0*	*12.5*	*12.7*	41,885
Alcoholic drink	*7.6*	*7.3*	*7.4*	*6.9*	*6.3*	*6.6*	21,730
Tobacco	*4.1*	*3.6*	*3.3*	*3.2*	*2.6*	*2.7*	8,835
Clothing and footwear	*7.7*	*6.7*	*7.0*	*7.1*	*6.2*	*6.1*	20,301
Housing	*13.6*	*14.9*	*15.4*	*15.5*	*15.8*	*14.5*	47,818
Fuel and power	*4.7*	*5.1*	*4.9*	*4.6*	*3.6*	*3.7*	12,269
Household goods and services	*7.6*	*6.9*	*6.7*	*6.7*	*6.7*	*6.7*	22,008
Transport and communication	*15.4*	*17.2*	*17.4*	*17.1*	*18.2*	*18.4*	60,898
Recreation, entertainment and education	*9.2*	*9.4*	*9.4*	*9.4*	*9.2*	*9.3*	30,913
Other goods, services and adjustments	*10.8*	*12.5*	*14.1*	*15.5*	*18.7*	*19.4*	64,220
Total	*100.0*	*100.0*	*100.0*	*100.0*	*100.0*	*100.0*	330,877

1 See Appendix, Part 6: Household expenditure.

Source: United Kingdom National Accounts, *Central Statistical Office*

6.3 Pattern of household expenditure: by household income, 1989

United Kingdom

	Food	Housing	Fuel, light and power	Alcohol	Tobacco	Clothing and footwear	House-hold goods and services	Trans-port and vehicles	Other goods, services, miscel-laneous	Average total expendi-ture (£ per week) (=100%)	Number of house-holds in sample
Average household weekly income											
Under £60	27.3	14.1	13.0	3.7	4.3	5.2	12.5	6.8	13.1	58.46	682
£60 and under £100	25.4	21.6	9.6	2.8	3.5	5.4	11.2	8.4	12.0	91.02	866
£100 and under £150	23.0	22.2	7.2	3.7	3.3	6.6	10.5	9.3	14.2	127.77	815
£150 and under £200	20.1	20.1	5.9	3.4	2.8	5.6	9.8	14.6	17.7	171.88	674
£200 and under £250	20.5	19.5	5.6	4.7	2.8	6.2	10.9	14.8	15.0	186.10	632
£250 and under £300	19.2	17.1	4.6	4.3	2.4	6.6	13.6	16.7	15.4	223.19	608
£300 and under £350	19.3	17.1	4.8	4.8	2.4	6.8	11.5	17.0	16.3	235.03	634
£350 and under £400	18.7	16.0	3.9	4.6	2.0	6.5	11.5	17.5	19.3	268.19	485
£400 and under £525	17.7	15.6	3.9	4.6	1.9	7.1	11.8	18.4	19.0	321.48	961
£525 and over	15.8	16.4	3.1	4.5	1.2	7.9	12.1	18.3	20.7	436.51	1,053
All households	18.8	17.4	4.8	4.3	2.2	6.9	11.7	16.2	17.8	221.28	7,410

Source: Family Expenditure Survey, Central Statistical Office

year-on-year increases in the previous few years. Indeed there were real terms falls in a number of categories which had previously seen steady increases over a number of years. For example, consumers' expenditure on durable goods fell by nearly 6 per cent between 1989 and 1990.

Table 6.2 gives a more detailed breakdown of household expenditure, fixed to constant 1985 prices. Again, this highlights the real terms falls in expenditure in a number of categories between 1989 and 1990, against the recent trend of year-on-year increases. The most notable change was in expenditure on vehicles. Between 1988 and 1989, expenditure on the purchase of vehicles increased by 11 per cent. However, between 1989 and 1990, this expenditure fell back to the 1988 level. The fastest growing category between 1976 and 1990 was household expenditure abroad, which more than trebled.

The bottom half of Table 6.2 shows changes in the pattern of household expenditure. Over the period covered by the chart there is a general trend of expenditure switching from food to transport, communication and other goods and services. The proportion of total expenditure spent on food fell by 6.5 percentage points between 1976 and 1990, from 19.2 per cent to 12.7 per cent. Table 6.3 shows the expenditure patterns of households at various income levels, using data from the 1989 Family Expenditure Survey (FES). The table shows that households at the lower end of the income scale spend a higher proportion of their expenditure on such necessities as food, housing and fuel and light than those households with higher incomes. In 1989, these three items accounted for over half of total expenditure of households with an average weekly income of less than £150. Households at the higher end of the income scale spend a much higher proportion on motoring and fares than low income households. The proportion of household expenditure on tobacco falls as income rises.

Population Trends

Population Trends is the journal of the Office of Population Censuses and Surveys (OPCS). It is published four times a year in March, June, September and December.

Annual Subscription **£28** Single Issues **£7.25**

Published by HMSO, it can be obtained from Government bookshops and through good booksellers

6.4 Households with durable goods: by socio-economic group of head, 1989–90

Great Britain　　　　　　　　　　　　　　　　　　　　　　　　　　　Percentages and numbers

	Economically active					All econo-mically active heads of households	Econo-mically inactive heads of households	All heads of households
	Profess-ional	Employers and managers	Other non-manual	Skilled manual[1]	Un-skilled manual			
Percentage of households with:								
Deep-freezers[2]	91	92	84	87	72	87	67	80
Washing machine	95	96	90	92	81	92	75	86
Tumble drier	61	66	52	52	43	56	26	45
Microwave oven	60	69	56	57	38	59	26	47
Dishwasher	33	34	14	8	2	17	4	12
Telephone	98	98	93	85	62	90	82	87
Television	97	99	98	99	97	99	98	98
Colour	95	97	95	95	88	95	90	93
Black and white only	2	2	3	4	9	3	8	5
Video	77	82	72	79	61	78	30	60
Home computer	44	34	26	24	10	28	5	19
CD player	29	27	21	18	10	21	6	16
Sample size (= 100%) (numbers)	499	1,416	1,217	2,832	240	6,204	3,536	9,740

1 Includes semi-skilled manual.
2 Includes fridge-freezers.

Source: *General Household Survey*

Table 6.4 shows that, with the exception of televisions (which at 98 per cent have almost reached saturation coverage), the professional or employers and managerial groups have the highest ownership of every consumer durable shown.

As well as varying between income groups, the pattern of household expenditure also varies from one part of the country to another. The regional analyses shown in Table 6.5 are based on the average of two years survey data, 1988 and 1989, (to give a larger sample size and hence more reliable estimates). For the two-year period shown the highest average weekly household expenditure was in the South East (£250). At the other end of the scale, the lowest weekly expenditure was in Yorkshire and Humberside (£188), slightly below expenditure in the North. Spending on food accounted for the largest proportion of expenditure in every region except the South East (where a higher proportion was spent on housing). However, the proportions spent on food varied from 17.7 per cent in the South East to 21 per cent in Northern Ireland. Expenditure on housing varied from just 11.9 per cent of average weekly household expenditure in Northern Ireland to 18.6 per cent in the South East.

6.5 Household expenditure: by commodity and service and region, 1988-1989[1]

United Kingdom　　　　　　　　　　　　　　　　　　　　　　　　　Percentages and £ per week

	Average weekly household expenditure as a percentage of total									Average expend-iture per household (£ per week)
	Housing	Fuel, light and power	Food	Alcohol and tobacco	Clothing and footwear	Household goods and services	Motoring and fares	Leisure goods and services	Miscella-neous and personal goods and services	
United Kingdom	17.2	4.9	18.5	6.5	6.9	13.2	15.3	13.4	4.2	216.05
North	15.7	5.4	19.5	7.7	7.0	12.7	15.9	12.4	3.6	191.68
Yorkshire and Humberside	15.0	5.5	19.5	7.4	7.7	12.5	15.8	12.5	4.3	188.80
East Midlands	17.2	5.2	18.8	6.8	6.2	12.7	16.1	12.6	4.5	199.39
East Anglia	17.6	4.7	18.2	5.4	6.2	13.0	15.1	15.6	4.2	219.30
South East	18.6	4.1	17.7	5.5	6.8	13.8	14.8	14.3	4.5	250.98
South West	17.0	4.9	18.1	5.9	6.0	13.9	15.8	14.5	3.9	220.11
West Midlands	17.9	5.1	19.1	6.6	6.8	13.0	16.2	11.4	4.0	200.72
North West	16.8	5.1	18.3	7.7	6.7	12.2	14.6	14.2	4.4	205.26
England	17.5	4.7	18.3	6.3	6.7	13.2	15.3	13.6	4.3	219.57
Wales	15.4	5.7	19.2	7.0	7.6	13.1	15.8	11.8	4.2	197.10
Scotland	16.3	5.4	19.6	7.9	8.1	12.4	14.2	12.1	4.0	196.27
Northern Ireland	11.9	7.4	21.0	5.7	9.2	13.9	17.6	9.7	3.7	200.99

1 Averages for the two calendar years taken together.

Source: *Family Expenditure Survey, Central Statistical Office*

Social Trends 22, © Crown copyright 1992

6.6 Household expenditure: EC comparison, 1989

Percentages

	Food, beverages, tobacco[1]	Clothing and footwear	Rent, fuel and power	Furniture, furnishings, house-hold equipment	Medical care and health expenses	Transport and comm-unication	Recreation, enter-tainment, education, culture	Miscell-aneous goods and services	Total
United Kingdom	21.1	6.2	19.5	6.9	1.3	17.7	9.5	17.8	100.0
Belgium	19.1	7.6	16.7	10.9	11.0	12.9	6.5	15.5	100.0
Denmark	21.4	5.5	27.4	6.5	1.9	16.4	10.0	11.1	100.0
France	19.4	6.9	18.9	8.1	9.2	16.8	7.3	13.9	100.0
Germany (Fed. Rep.)	16.6	7.7	18.4	8.8	14.3	15.1	9.0	10.2	100.0
Greece	37.9	9.3	11.5	8.4	3.4	13.4	6.0	10.1	100.0
Irish Republic[2]	39.0	6.9	10.9	7.0	3.5	12.6	11.1	9.1	100.0
Italy	21.7	9.6	14.3	8.9	6.3	12.9	9.1	17.3	100.0
Luxembourg	19.8	6.4	20.0	10.3	7.6	17.9	4.1	13.7	100.0
Netherlands	18.4	6.8	18.6	8.2	12.5	11.3	9.9	14.2	100.0
Portugal[3]	37.2	10.3	5.0	8.6	4.5	15.4	5.7	13.4	100.0
Spain	22.0	9.1	12.6	6.6	3.6	15.7	6.5	24.0	100.0

1 Includes for the UK, Ireland and Greece expenditure on food (Ireland and Greece only) alcoholic and non-alcoholic drinks and tobacco in restaurants, cafes and hotels. For other countries these are classified as miscellaneous goods and services.

2 Data are for 1988.
3 Data for 1986.

Source: Statistical Office of the European Communities

Table 6.6 shows, for each country in the European Community, the pattern of household expenditure on various goods and services. Care should be taken in comparing expenditure patterns of the countries shown, mainly because of differences in provision of certain free services. Medical care and health expenses are the most important examples of such differences. In countries such as the United Kingdom and Denmark where health care is provided, in the main, free at the time of use the proportion of household expenditure on this item is naturally very low. Where health care is paid for directly by households, who are subsequently reimbursed by the social security administration, such as in France, Germany and the Netherlands, the proportions are naturally much higher.

In all countries except Denmark, the Federal Republic of Germany, Luxembourg and the Netherlands expenditure on food, beverages and tobacco made up the highest proportion of household expenditure. However, there are large differences between the countries. In the Irish Republic 39 per cent of total household expenditure was on food, beverages and tobacco, in the Netherlands the proportion was less than 19 per cent.

The earlier Table 6.2 illustrated the increase in United Kingdom household expenditure abroad. Chart 6.7 compares the holiday expenditure of United Kingdom

residents (spent both here and abroad) with money spent by foreign holidaymakers in this country. United Kingdom holidaymakers spend less per day on holidays abroad than they do on short (1 to 3 nights) holidays here in the United Kingdom - £24 per day abroad compared to £28 per day on short domestic holidays. However, foreign holidaymakers outspend United Kingdom residents, spending an average of £39 per day when they are on holiday in the United Kingdom.

6.7 Holiday expenditure: by visitor, destination and length of stay, 1989

United Kingdom

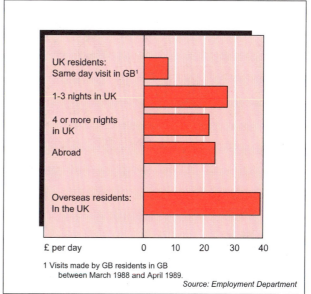

1 Visits made by GB residents in GB between March 1988 and April 1989.

Source: Employment Department

Prices

6.8 Retail prices index and tax and price index

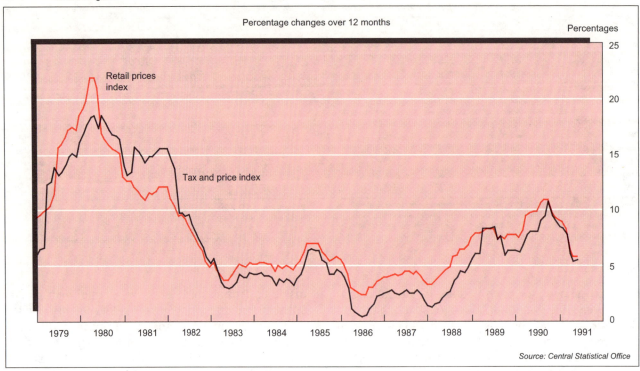

United Kingdom

Source: Central Statistical Office

The rate of growth in retail prices in the United Kingdom, often referred to as the rate of inflation, is measured by changes in the Retail Prices Index (RPI). This index monitors the change from month to month in the cost of a representative 'basket' of goods and services of the sort bought by a typical household. It is an important macroeconomic indicator which is used widely in pay negotiations, contractual arrangements, and the up-rating of benefits, savings and securities. An error in the index of just one tenth of one per cent would directly affect government expenditure and receipts by around £80 million in total in a year.

6.9 Index of retail prices: rates of change

United Kingdom   Percentages and weights

	Average annual percentage change						Weights	
	1961-1971	1971-1976	1976-1981	1981-1986	1986-1989	1989-1990	1961	1991
General index								
All items	4.6	14.5	13.4	5.5	5.6	9.5	1,000	1,000
All items, except housing	..	..	12.8	5.0	4.3	6.9	913	808
Food	4.7	17.4	11.7	4.6	4.0	8.1	350	151
Catering[1]	4.5[3]	17.0	15.1	6.7	6.4	8.5	.	47
Alcoholic drink	4.9	11.6	14.0	7.1	4.9	9.7	71	77
Tobacco	3.8	12.0	15.9	10.3	3.1	6.8	80	32
Housing	5.8	13.3	17.3	8.5	12.4	21.0	87	192
Fuel and light	5.4	16.4	15.8	5.9	2.4	8.0	55	46
Clothing and footwear	2.9	11.9	8.4	1.9	3.4	4.6	106	63
Pensioner indices[2]								
All items, except housing								
One-person households	4.8[4]	15.5	12.8	5.4	3.8	7.5	.	
Two-person households	4.8[4]	15.5	12.8	5.3	4.0	7.4	.	

1 Described as "Meals bought and consumed outside the home" prior to 1987.
2 Pensioner indices relate to households in which at least 75 per cent of total income is derived from state pensions and benefits.

3 Not separately identified until 1968; the figure relates to 1968 – 1971.
4 Figure relates to 1962 – 1971.

Source: Central Statistical Office

The index is compiled using a large and representative selection of more than 600 separate goods and services for which price movements are regularly measured in about 180 towns throughout the country. Well over 120 thousand separate price quotations are used each month in compiling the index.

Following the high levels of inflation recorded between 1979 and 1981 (Chart 6.8) the rate remained below 5 per cent for much of the period between 1983 and 1988, but went above that level in mid-1988 and then continued to rise for most of the next twelve months. The rate changed little between late 1989 and early 1990, but then rose again, reaching a peak in double figures in Autumn 1990, before falling during the first half of 1991.

The RPI can also be regarded as a measure of changes in the purchasing power of net income. It is affected by changes in indirect taxes, such as VAT and petrol duty, but not by changes in national insurance contributions or in income tax, other than through changes in tax relief on mortgage interest payments. Thus, for example, if there is a cut in income tax the RPI will remain unchanged, though people's purchasing power will increase. The Tax and Price Index (TPI), also shown in Chart 6.8, was developed as a supplement to the RPI, to take account of changes in households' purchasing power arising not only from changes in prices but also from changes in income tax and national insurance (NI) contributions. It therefore indicates the extent by which the gross income - ie before tax and NI contributions - of most taxpayers would need to change to maintain the purchasing power of their net income. For non-taxpayers, the RPI remains the appropriate measure of changes in purchasing power.

Between April 1983 and March 1989 the 12-month percentage increase in the TPI was less than in the RPI, indicating that changes in income tax had increased the purchasing power of taxpayers. Between April and August 1989 the TPI 12-month change rose marginally above the RPI figure.

The composition of the 'basket' of goods and services on which the RPI is based - that is, the relative importance or 'weight' attached to each of the various goods and services it contains is revised every year using the latest available information on household spending patterns from the Family Expenditure Survey. Thus, for example out of a total weight of 1,000, food accounted for 350 in 1961 but only 151 in 1991 (Table 6.9), reflecting the fall in the proportion of expenditure on food.

6.10 Purchasing power of a 1951 pound

United Kingdom

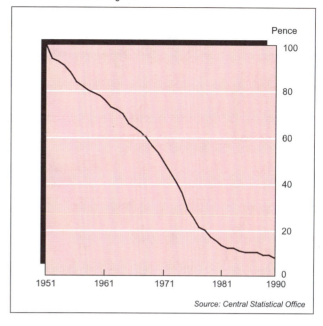

Source: Central Statistical Office

Although Table 6.9 does not show all the categories covered in the RPI, it is possible to see how price changes for the more important goods and services within the 'basket' have changed within the overall RPI. Between 1989 and 1990, the RPI increased by 9.5 per cent: however, within this increase, housing costs rose the most, by 21 per cent, and clothing and footwear prices rose the least, by only 4.6 per cent.

The RPI does not cover households with very high incomes, that is those in the top 4 per cent, nor those households with retired people mainly dependent on state pensions and benefits. These restrictions are designed to make the RPI more representative of typical households. For many years special price indices for one and two person pensioner households have been calculated separately. For technical reasons these pensioner price indices exclude housing costs. Between 1989 and 1990 the indices for one and two-person pensioner households increased by 7.5 and 7.4 per cent respectively, higher than the rise of 6.9 per cent in the general RPI excluding housing.

As the RPI increases, so the amount of goods and services which can be purchased with a given sum of money, ie purchasing power, decreases. Chart 6.10 illustrates the erosion of the purchasing power of the pound since 1951. Between 1951 and 1971 its purchasing power halved. Within 5 years (1971-1976) it halved again. The relatively high inflation during the late 1970s and early 1980s fuelled a further erosion in the purchasing power of the 1951 pound from 41 pence in 1973 to just 12 pence in 1982. In 1990, the 1951 pound was worth just 8 pence (ie one pound in 1990 could only purchase just under one-tenth of the goods it could have purchased in 1951).

6.11 Purchasing power of the pound in the European Community[1], 1981 and 1991

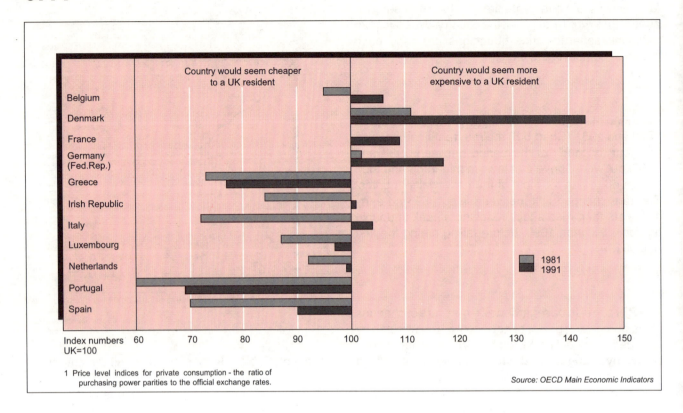

Index numbers UK=100

1 Price level indices for private consumption - the ratio of purchasing power parities to the official exchange rates.

Source: OECD Main Economic Indicators

Purchasing power varies not only over time, as shown in Chart 6.10 but also between countries. Chart 6.11 shows the purchasing power of the pound in the European Community (EC). This allows a quick and simple comparison of those countries which would appear more expensive to a United Kingdom resident and those which would appear cheaper. The purchasing power parity between the United Kingdom and another country is the amount of that country's currency required to buy the equivalent of consumer goods and services costing one pound in the United Kingdom - in other words, to give the consumer the same purchasing power in that country as in the United Kingdom. If this is greater than the official exchange rate the country would seem more expensive to a United Kingdom resident. Conversely if the index is less than 100 the country would seem cheaper.

Thus, in both 1981 and 1991 Greece, Luxembourg, the Netherlands, Portugal and Spain would have seemed cheaper to someone coming from the United Kingdom. However, Denmark would seem particularly expensive to a United Kingdom resident. Movements in these indices are affected by changes both in price levels in these countries and in exchange rates.

Chart 6.12 shows the annual average percentage change in consumer prices between 1981 and 1990 in each country of the EC. The highest rates of price inflation over this period were in Greece and Portugal which, at 18.4 and 16.8 per cent respectively. The rate in Greece was over three times the rate of 6.0 per cent in the United Kingdom.

Most people pay for goods and services out of their earnings, so when looking at expenditure and prices it is useful to consider earnings as well. A particularly interesting way to analyse price levels and changes over time is to calculate how long someone would have to work to earn enough to pay for certain goods and services. This is done in Table 6.13, which takes as its base the net income of a married man on average earnings with two children aged under 11 and whose wife was not earning. Between 1971 and 1990 the length of time the husband would have needed to work to pay for all the items shown fell in each case. This is also true over the more recent 1986 to 1990 period. The most noticeable difference between the lengths of time needed to work to pay for the commodities shown between 1971 and 1990 was for a motor car licence. In 1971 it would have required 40 hours and 31 minutes work - in 1989 it would have required less than half this length of time to pay for a motor car licence.

6.12 Change in consumer prices: EC comparison, 1981-1990

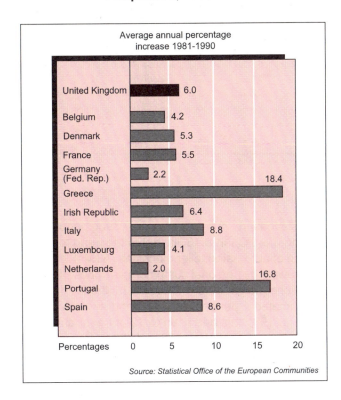

Average annual percentage increase 1981-1990

	Percentages
United Kingdom	6.0
Belgium	4.2
Denmark	5.3
France	5.5
Germany (Fed. Rep.)	2.2
Greece	18.4
Irish Republic	6.4
Italy	8.8
Luxembourg	4.1
Netherlands	2.0
Portugal	16.8
Spain	8.6

Percentages 0 5 10 15 20

Source: Statistical Office of the European Communities

6.13 Length of time necessary to work to pay for selected commodities and services

Great Britain   Hours and minutes

	Married couple with husband only working[1]			
	1971[2]	1981[2]	1986[2]	1990[2]
	Hrs mins	Hrs mins	Hrs mins	Hrs mins
1 large loaf (white sliced)	9	8	6	5
1lb of rump steak	56	60	46	40
500g of butter (home produced)	19	20	16	13
1 pint of fresh milk	5	4	4	3
1 dozen eggs (55-60g)	22	17	15	12
100g of coffee (instant)	22	20	21	14
1 pint of beer (draught bitter)	14	13	13	11
20 cigarettes (king size filter)	22	20	21	17
Motor car licence	40 31	27 11	25 39	17 55
Colour television licence	19 27	13 12	14 37	12 32
1 litre of petrol (4 star)	8	8	6	5

1 Length of time necessary for married man on average hourly male adult earnings for all industries and services, with non-earning wife and two children under 11, to work so that his net income pays for the various goods.
2 At April.

Source: Central Statistical Office

Consumer credit and household saving

Consumer credit in the United Kingdom has increased very substantially since 1975; in cash terms the amount of outstanding debt more than trebled between 1981 and 1990 (Chart 6.14). Even after adjusting for the effect of inflation as measured by the RPI, the amount of outstanding debt still more than doubled between 1981 and 1990. This credit outstanding excludes borrowing for house purchase; for information on mortgage debt see Chapter 8. The growth in consumer credit has been accompanied by a corresponding growth in retail sales.

The bulk of consumer credit in the United Kingdom is financed by banks and other institutions authorised to take deposits under the *Banking Act 1987* (Table 6.15). In 1990 credit from these institutions represented just under two thirds of all credit outstanding. The importance of retailers as a source of credit has declined steadily during the 1980s and in 1990 this form of credit represented less than 5 per cent of all credit outstanding. Lending through bank credit cards and by credit companies increased in importance during the early 1980s, to peak in 1986. In 1988 and 1989, the percentage fell, but by 1990 had recovered to the 1986 level. It should be noted that lending by credit companies

includes much of the traditional hire purchase lending as well as credit extended through retailers' credit cards where the schemes are financed by credit companies.

6.14 Consumer credit: amount outstanding

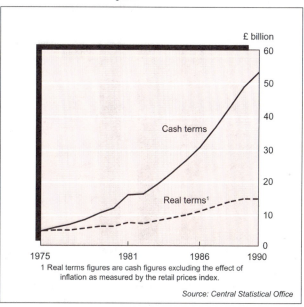

United Kingdom

£ billion

Cash terms

Real terms[1]

1975   1981   1986   1990

1 Real terms figures are cash figures excluding the effect of inflation as measured by the retail prices index.

Source: Central Statistical Office

6.15 Composition of consumer credit

United Kingdom   Percentages and £ billion

	1981	1984	1985	1986	1987	1988	1989	1990
Bank credit card lending	11.7	14.8	15.8	17.3	16.6	15.8	14.9	17.0
Bank loans[1]	65.0	63.2	62.3	61.7	62.7	64.8	65.9	64.2
Finance houses[2]	8.8	9.9	10.8	11.8	12.1	11.5	12.1	11.9
Insurance companies	2.2	3.1	2.8	2.7	2.5	2.3	2.1	2.2
Retailers	12.2	9.0	8.4	6.4	6.1	5.6	4.9	4.7
Credit outstanding at the end of year (= 100%) (£ billion)	15.5	22.2	26.0	30.1	36.2	42.5	48.4	52.6

1 Banks and all other institutions authorised to take deposits under the Banking Act 1987.

2 Finance houses and other credit companies.

Source: Central Statistical Office

The percentage of men and women holding credit/charge and store cards has increased dramatically in recent years. In 1989 a survey sponsored by the Association for Payment Clearing Services (APACS) showed that 43 per cent of men and 33 per cent of women held credit and/or charge cards. APACS also reported that, in 1989, fewer than 12 million adults did not have a current account at a bank or building society. These were largely the younger adults, those on social benefits (especially the elderly) and housewives, although most of the latter will have access to a current account within their household.

Two thirds of all adults and four-fifths of all current account holders now possess some kind of plastic money card. In 1989, 40 per cent of adults made use of cash dispensers, prime users were young people and working men. Chart 6.16 illustrates the trend towards the use of automated teller machines (ATMs) for cash withdrawals by personal customers as opposed to the use of cheques or other withdrawal methods. In 1976 an estimated 1 per cent of cash withdrawals were by ATM. In 1981 this had risen to 12 per cent and then climbed to 48 per cent in 1986 and 62 per cent in 1989. These figures are, however, estimates of the actual number of withdrawals and not on the amounts withdrawn. In 1988 the average value of a bank operated ATM cash withdrawal was about £37 - less than two-thirds the value of an average cheque encashment. The development of ATM networks and the increase in the number of cards which operate the machines are obvious factors in the growth in card usage. In 1976 there were less than a million cards in circulation compared to 7 million in 1981 and 28 million

6.16 Personal customers cash withdrawals: by type of withdrawal

United Kingdom

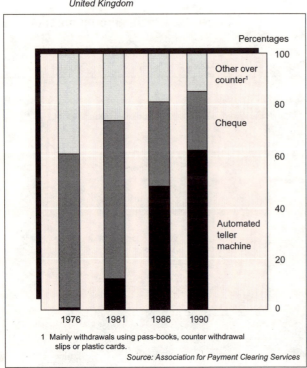

Other over counter[1]

Cheque

Automated teller machine

1 Mainly withdrawals using pass-books, counter withdrawal slips or plastic cards.

Source: Association for Payment Clearing Services

6.17 Household saving[1] as a percentage of household disposable income

United Kingdom

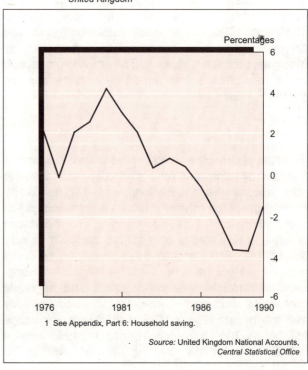

1 See Appendix, Part 6: Household saving.

Source: United Kingdom National Accounts, Central Statistical Office

in 1988. Additionally, it should be remembered that an increasing number of people have their wages and salaries paid directly into a bank or building society rather than in cash, and therefore must use some form of withdrawal service simply to get at their salaries.

Chart 6.17 shows household saving as a percentage of household disposable income. Since 1986 this percentage has been negative, indicating that the total of all households' current expenditure exceeded their disposable income (sometimes called dissaving) and underlining the effect of the growth in credit outstanding.

The latest 1990 figure, although still negative, shows an improvement over the 1989 figure. Because household savings are measured as the difference between two much larger figures (disposable income and current expenditure), the estimates are necessarily subject to a wide margin of error. Nevertheless the available evidence appears to confirm this mid 1980s turning point in the savings ratio. However, at the same time life assurance premiums paid (which form part of household expenditure but which are in effect a form of savings) have grown strongly and, if they were taken into account, the savings ratio would have declined but remain positive.

Public income and expenditure

6.18　General government expenditure as a percentage of GDP[1]

United Kingdom

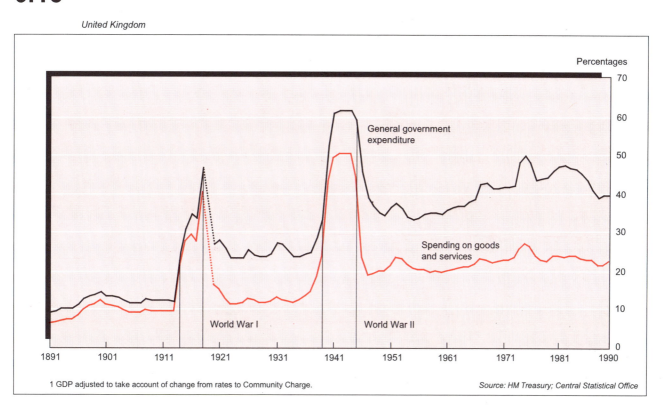

1 GDP adjusted to take account of change from rates to Community Charge.

Source: HM Treasury; Central Statistical Office

So far in this chapter, attention has been focused on spending by individuals and households. This section examines expenditure by general government (central government plus local authorities). The government's own consumption is measured by its spending on goods and services. However, the government also has to make interest payments and transfer payments such as grants, loans and pensions and these also contribute to the amount which the government has to raise by taxation and borrowing. This wider measure is known as general government expenditure (GGE) and is used for analysing overall trends in public spending. Growth in GGE may be compared to growth in the

economy as a whole by expressing it as a percentage of gross domestic product (GDP). Chart 6.18 shows that the peaks in this percentage coincide with periods of war. A peak of around 60 per cent was reached during World War II. Although GGE fell back as a percentage of GDP at the end of each World War, in both cases it never dropped as far as its pre-war levels. During the early 1950s the percentage rose a little at the time of the Korean War (1951 to 1952) and there was a small peak in 1968 and a larger one in the mid 1970s. In 1982 the percentage reached its highest level since the mid 1970s but since then has fallen to reach 39.5 cent in 1990.

6.19 Central government and local authority income: by source

United Kingdom   Percentages and £ million

	1961	1971	1981	1986	1989	1990	1990 (£ million)
Central government *(percentages)*							
Taxes on income							
Paid by persons[1]	27.9	31.9	26.1	25.5	27.2	28.1	55,791
Paid by corporations[2]	10.7	7.4	8.1	9.8	12.5	10.8	21,471
Taxes on expenditure							
Customs and Excise duties (including VAT)	32.0	25.9	24.4	28.8	31.1	29.7	59,045
Other indirect taxes[3]	3.2	6.2	6.1	3.5	3.4	7.5	14,896
Social security contributions							
Paid by employees	7.2	6.6	6.5	8.4	8.4	7.3	14,512
Paid by employers[4]	6.3	7.1	8.3	9.2	10.1	10.1	20,091
Transfer payments[5]	—	0.1	0.2	0.2	0.1	0.1	172
Rent, interest, dividends, royalties and other current income	6.7	8.0	7.5	7.0	6.9	6.1	12,039
Taxes on capital [6]	3.3	3.3	1.4	1.9	2.4	2.1	4,082
Borrowing requirement	2.9	3.1	9.8	5.7	−2.9	−2.3	−4,611
Other financial receipts	−0.2	0.4	1.6	0.3	1.0	1.0	1,939
Total (= 100%) (£ million)	7,941	20,413	105,773	147,764	176,993	198,587	198,587
Local authorities *(percentages)*							
Current grants from central government							
Rate support grants and other non-specific grants	23.3	33.3	38.4	32.5	26.5	26.4	16,423
Special grants	7.3	3.7	9.1	16.0	17.4	18.1	11,255
National non-domestic rates[3]	.	.	.	.	.	16.7	10,410
Total current grants from central government	30.6	37.0	47.5	48.5	43.9	61.2	38,088
Rates[3]	30.8	27.0	31.8	34.0	36.3	8.2	5,126
Community charge[7]	.	.	.	.	1.1	14.1	8,811
Rent	9.3	9.1	10.3	6.8	5.9	5.5	3,406
Interest, dividends and other current income	7.2	6.3	6.8	6.2	7.3	6.6	4,098
Capital grants and other capital receipts	1.7	2.3	1.1	2.2	4.3	3.4	2,111
Borrowing requirement	17.6	17.8	0.8	1.5	1.1	6.3	3,915
Other financial receipts	2.8	0.6	1.7	0.8	0.1	−5.3	−3,277
Total (= 100%) (£ million)	2,702	7,725	32,020	44,933	54,811	62,278	62,278
Total general government income[8] (£ million)	9,725	23,673	120,994	160,882	198,215	217,170	217,170

1 Includes surtax.
2 Includes profits tax and overspill relief.
3 National non-domestic rates (a central government tax) replaced local authority non-domestic rates in Great Britain from April 1990.
4 Includes employers' contributions to the redundancy fund.
5 Payments in lieu of graduated contributions/state scheme premiums.

6 Death duties, capital transfer tax, capital gains tax and development land tax. Also includes other capital receipts.
7 Community Charge replaced domestic rates in Scotland from April 1989 and in England and Wales from April 1990.
8 Some intra-sector transactions are included in the lines on borrowing requirements and on interest, dividends and other current income.

Source: United Kingdom National Accounts, *Central Statistical Office*

Government spending solely on goods and services as a percentage of GDP has followed the same pattern as GGE; in the early years of the century the two were virtually identical indicating the relative unimportance of transfer payments in those times.

In order to finance its expenditure, government has to raise revenue by taxation and borrowing and Table 6.19 shows the sources of income for both central and local government. The proportion of central government income raised through personal income tax rose from 28 per cent to 32 per cent between 1961 and 1971 but then fell back to 26 per cent by 1981. Since then, the proportion of central government income raised through personal income tax has increased slightly to reach 28 per cent by 1990. The other major source of revenue is taxes on expenditure; these fell from 35 per cent of central government income in 1961 to 32 per cent in 1971 and 30 per cent in 1981. However the proportion had risen again to 37 per cent (including national non-domestic rates) by 1990. The central government borrowing requirement has fallen from a peak of over 13 per cent of income in 1979 to become a debt repayment in 1988, 1989 and 1990.

Table 6.20 summarises general government expenditure by broad function. Expenditure totalled £214.3 billion in 1990, an increase of 9 per cent on 1989. The figures in the table are not comparable with government expenditure figures published in some earlier editions of Social Trends, which came from HM Treasury's public expenditure data rather than data produced by the Central Statistical Office. The current table is compiled on the same basis as the *CSO National Accounts 'Blue Book'*. One of the important differences is that privatisation proceeds are treated as an offset to expenditure on each function. It is therefore possible, as in the case of fuel and energy, to have a net expenditure figure which is negative

Social security expenditure accounted for 29 per cent of total general government expenditure, the largest proportion of any function. There have been some significant variations in the proportions of total expenditure incurred on particular functions since 1981. Expenditure on housing and community amenities in 1981 represented just 6 per cent of total expenditure compared to less than 4 per cent in 1990.

6.20 General Government expenditure[1]: by function

United Kingdom | | | | £ billion

Function	1981	1986	1989	1990
Defence	12.6	19.1	21.0	22.9
Public order and safety	4.3	6.8	9.4	11.0
Education	14.3	19.3	24.8	26.8
Health	13.4	19.2	25.1	27.7
Social security	31.1	49.9	57.3	62.8
Housing and community amenities	7.1	8.1	8.0	7.9
Recreational and cultural affairs	1.6	2.4	3.2	3.6
Fuel and energy	0.3	−1.2	−1.9	−3.8
Agriculture, forestry and fishing	1.7	2.1	2.0	2.6
Mining, mineral resources, manufacturing and construction	3.6	1.9	1.6	1.3
Transport and communication	4.2	3.7	7.1	9.2
General public services	4.6	6.3	9.5	10.9
Other economic affairs and services	2.9	4.1	4.9	6.4
Other expenditure	15.4	20.5	24.8	25.0
Total expenditure	117.1	162.2	196.8	214.3

1 Includes privatisation proceeds.   Source: Central Statistical Office

---

National Resources

One of our most important national resources is our national income. Chart 6.21 shows United Kingdom gross domestic product (GDP) since the late 1940s. The chart shows GDP in real terms as each year's production has been revalued at the price levels which prevailed in 1985. The picture is very much one of general growth over the period - there were slight contractions in the mid 1970s (as a result of sharp increases in the price of oil) and the early 1980s (during the world-wide recession).

6.21 Gross domestic product

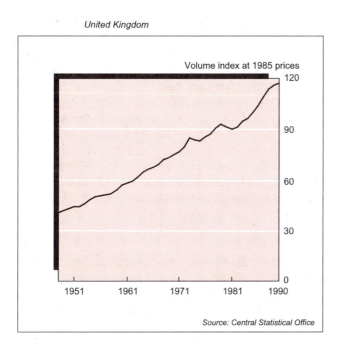

United Kingdom

Volume index at 1985 prices

Source: Central Statistical Office

6.22 Gross domestic product at factor cost and current prices: by region

United Kingdom | | Index per head (UK=100) | |

	1976	1981	1986	1989
United Kingdom[1]	100.0	100.0	100.0	100.0
North	95.6	93.5	87.4	86.6
Yorkshire & Humberside	94.0	92.0	93.2	88.3
East Midlands	96.7	96.9	96.5	94.6
East Anglia	95.9	96.4	100.8	99.0
South East	112.2	117.1	117.6	120.6
Greater London	125.2	127.7	125.7	129.5
Rest of South East	102.9	110.0	112.3	115.0
South West	91.1	93.3	94.3	95.4
West Midlands	98.4	90.6	91.2	91.6
North West	96.2	94.3	93.6	91.6
England	101.6	102.1	102.3	102.4
Wales	87.2	83.6	83.2	84.6
Scotland	98.3	96.3	95.0	93.2
Northern Ireland	80.7	78.8	78.7	76.4

1 United Kingdom less continental shelf.

Source: UK Regional Accounts, Central Statistical Office

6.23 Oil and gas reserves, 1990

United Kingdom continental shelf	Oil (million tonnes)	Gas (billion cubic metres)
Fields already discovered		
Proven reserves	1,910	1,295
Probable reserves	660	655
Possible reserves	620	580
Total initial reserves in present discoveries of which:	1,910-3,190	1,295-2,535
Already recovered	1,374	752
Estimates in potential future discoveries	500-3,130	280-1,260
Total recoverable reserves	2,409-6,319	1,575-3,795

Department of Energy

Each year, the Central Statistical Office produces a breakdown of GDP for the regions of the United Kingdom. Levels of GDP and GDP growth over time vary between different parts of the country. Table 6.22 shows GDP per head of population for regions compared with the national average. GDP per head remains highest in the South East and lowest in Northern Ireland. Although the principal differences between the regions are long-standing, there have been changes to the relative positions of the regions since the early 1970s. East Anglia and the South East outside Greater London have had above average increases and the West Midlands and the North West have had above average decreases.

In comparing GDP per head between regions, it is important to bear in mind the differing population structures. The South West for example has a relatively high proportion of economically inactive retired people, so GDP per head is slightly lower. Changes in GDP per head reflect population changes as well as GDP growth. In East Anglia for example, growth in total GDP has been much greater than growth in GDP per head because the population has grown.

The oil and gas reserves in the United Kingdom and on the continental shelf are an extremely important national resource. By 1990, 1,374 million tonnes of oil and 752 billion cubic metres of gas had already been recovered from the United Kingdom reserves (Table 6.23). Estimating total reserves is very difficult as some of them lie in fields which have yet to be discovered. However, the oil already recovered represents over 70 per cent of proven reserves, but it is estimated that it could be only 20 per cent of total recoverable reserves. Similarly, the amount of gas already recovered, while representing nearly 60 per cent of proven reserves may be only 20 per cent of total reserves.

6.24 Production of primary fuels

United Kingdom

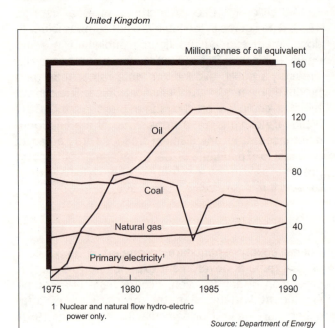

1 Nuclear and natural flow hydro-electric power only.

Source: Department of Energy

In 1975 the United Kingdom produced only 1.6 million tonnes of oil. By 1981 annual output had risen to 89.5 million tonnes and production continued to rise until 1985 when it reached a peak of 127.6 million tonnes (Chart 6.24). Production fell slightly during the following two years and then more substantially to stand at 91.6 million tonnes by 1990. There were 49 offshore and 16 onshore fields in production at the end of 1989. Seven new offshore fields and five new onshore fields came onstream in 1990. Production in 1990 was significantly restricted by scheduled maintenance programmes to install platform level emergency shutdown valves and for general refurbishment. The Forties field in particular suffered an 11 per cent drop in production due to valve installation.

Other fuels are also included in Chart 6.24. Production of natural gas has risen fairly steadily since 1975 and the production of primary electricity (that is nuclear and natural flow hydro-electric power only, rather than electricity produced by burning one of the other fuels) doubled over the period. The chart quotes all fuels in million tonnes of oil equivalent so that it is possible to make direct comparisons between the different fuel types. The production of coal was affected by the industrial dispute in the coal industry in 1984.

A similar picture emerges when looking at consumption of fuel. In 1990, 43 per cent of fuel consumed in the United Kingdom was petroleum, with a further 32 per cent being natural gas (Chart 6.25). Industry, road transport and domestic use each make up around one quarter of total final energy consumption.

6.25 Energy consumption: by fuel and consumer, 1990

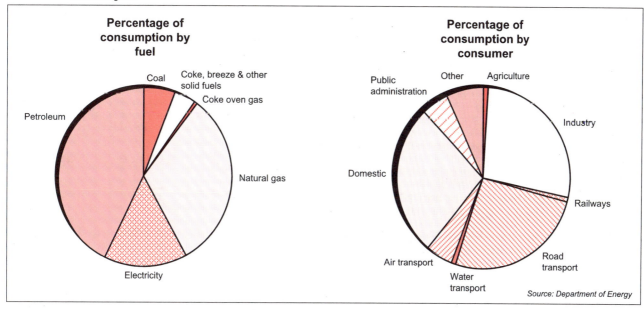

United Kingdom

Percentage of consumption by fuel

Coal

Coke, breeze & other solid fuels

Coke oven gas

Petroleum

Natural gas

Electricity

Percentage of consumption by consumer

Public administration

Other

Agriculture

Industry

Domestic

Railways

Air transport

Road transport

Water transport

Source: Department of Energy

BIBLIOGRAPHY

The following list contains selected publications relevant to Chapter 6: Expenditure and Resources. Those published by HMSO are available from the addresses shown on the back cover of Social Trends.

British Tourism Survey, Monthly, British Tourist Authority

Development of the Oil and Gas Resources of the United Kingdom, HMSO

Digest of the United Kingdom Energy Statistics, HMSO

Economic Trends, HMSO

Employment Gazette, HMSO

Energy Trends, HMSO

Family Expenditure Survey, HMSO

Financial Statistics, HMSO

General Household Survey, HMSO

International Passenger Survey, Employment Department

Local Government Financial Statistics England, HMSO

Regional Trends, HMSO

Retail Prices Index, HMSO

Scottish Economic Bulletin, HMSO

The Government's Expenditure Plans, HMSO

Welsh Economic Trends, HMSO

UK National Accounts ('CSO Blue Book'), HMSO

STATISTICAL BULLETIN

DEPARTMENT OF HEALTH

In the series of Statistical Bulletins publications by DH the following bulletins have been produced since January 1990.

NUMBER	TITLE	DATE OF ISSUE	
2(1)90	NHS hospital activity statistics for England 1979 - 1988/89	JAN	1990
2(2)90	Personal social services provision for mentally handicapped people in England 1978-88.	JAN	1990
4(4)90	Prescriptions dispensed by pharmacists and appliance contractors, England 1978-88.	FEB	1990
2(5)90	Statistics of elective admissions and patients waiting: England six months ending 30 September 1989.	APR	1990
4(6)990	Statistics for general medical practitioners in England and Wales: 1978 to 1988.	JULY	1990
4(7)90	A survey of GP practise computing March/April 1990	JULY	1990
2(8)90	Statistics of blood service activity: 1982-89.	SEPT	1990
2(9)90	Statistics of elective admissions and patients waiting: England six months ending 31 March 1990	OCT	1990
2(10)90	NHS hospital activity statistics for England 1979 - 1989/90.	DEC	1990
2(11)90	Hospital medical staff, England 1980 to 1989.	DEC	1990
2(1)91	Legal status of formally detained patients 1984 - 1988/89.	FEB	1991
3(2)91	Personal social services for elderly people and younger physically handicapped people England 1979-1989.	MAR	1991
2(3)91	Statistics of elective admissions and patients waiting: England six months ending 31 September 1990.	APR	1991
4(4)91	Statistics for general medical practitioners in England and Wales 1979-1989	MAY	1991
3(5)91	Causes of blindness and partial sight among young children aged under 16, newly registered as blind or partially sighted between April 87 and March 1990.	JUNE	1991
4(6)91	Prescriptions dispensed by pharmacists and appliance contractors England 1979-89.	JUNE	1991

Each bulletin contains information on trends, usually over a decade, with tables, graphs and commentary. Further bulletins are planned, which will widen the range of topics covered. For the most part, they will be annual publications. Copies of the bulletins listed above may be obtained, price £2.00 each. From:

Department of Health

Information Division
Government Buildings
Honeypot Lane
Stanmore
Middlesex HA7 1AY

Chapter 7: Health and Personal Social Services

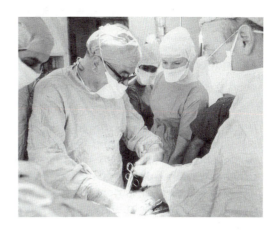

The nation's health

● Despite improvements in infant mortality, differences remain between the social classes. Mortality rates are higher for those whose fathers are in the unskilled or semi-skilled groups.

(Chart 7.2)

Diet

● Some aspects of the household diet have changed considerably over the past 30 years. Consumption of eggs has halved since 1961 and consumption of butter has fallen by three quarters. *(Table 7.12)*

Social habits and health

● The young are the heaviest drinkers, though they now drink less than they used to. Men aged 18-24 years consumed an average of 20 units of alcohol (equivalent to 10 pints of beer) per week during the late 1980s, compared to 26 units per week in 1978. *(Chart 7.18)*

Accidents

● Accidental deaths are on the decline - there were 13 thousand accidental deaths in 1990, a third fewer than in 1971. *(Table 7.23)*

Blood and organ donation

● Organ transplants have been one of the great medical advances in recent years. In 1990, there were 95 combined heart and lung transplants compared with just one in 1983. *(Table 7.30)*

Health services

● More patients are being treated in fewer hospital beds - between 1971 and 1989-90 the number of in-patients increased by 27 per cent, while the average number of beds available fell by more than one fifth. *(Table 7.31)*

Personal social services

● The number of children in care is falling - by one third since 1980. *(Chart 7.38)*

7.1 Infant mortality

United Kingdom[1]

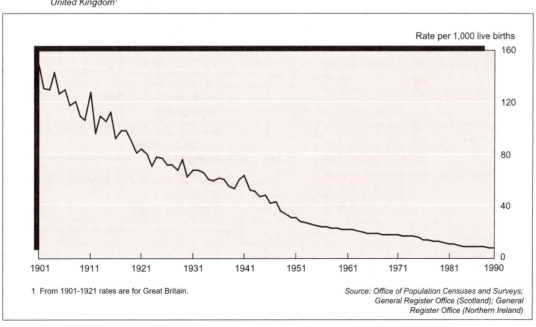

Rate per 1,000 live births

1 From 1901-1921 rates are for Great Britain.

Source: Office of Population Censuses and Surveys; General Register Office (Scotland); General Register Office (Northern Ireland)

The nation's health

In the United Kingdom, as in many countries in Europe, diseases such as cholera and typhoid are virtually non-existent because of improvements in public health and sanitation. Other diseases such as poliomyelitis and diphtheria have been largely controlled by vaccination over the last twenty to thirty years. The reduction in notifications of infectious diseases are shown later in this chapter in Table 7.7. The effect of improvements since the turn of the century, not only in health care, but in health education, housing, and nutrition is also reflected in improved infant mortality (Chart 7.1).

The general downward trend is clear, between 1950 and 1990 there were only two occasions when infant mortality actually increased from one year to the next. There was a marked fall of almost 50 per cent in the 1940s from 61 deaths per 1,000 live births in 1940 to only 31 by 1950. Recently, as very low levels of infant

7.2 Infant mortality [1,2]: by social class of father, 1989

England & Wales

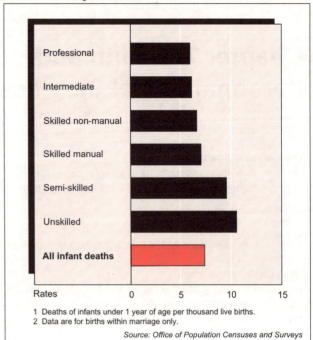

Rates

1 Deaths of infants under 1 year of age per thousand live births.
2 Data are for births within marriage only.

Source: Office of Population Censuses and Surveys

7.3 Infant mortality[1] and maternal mortality[2]: international comparison 1986-1988[3]

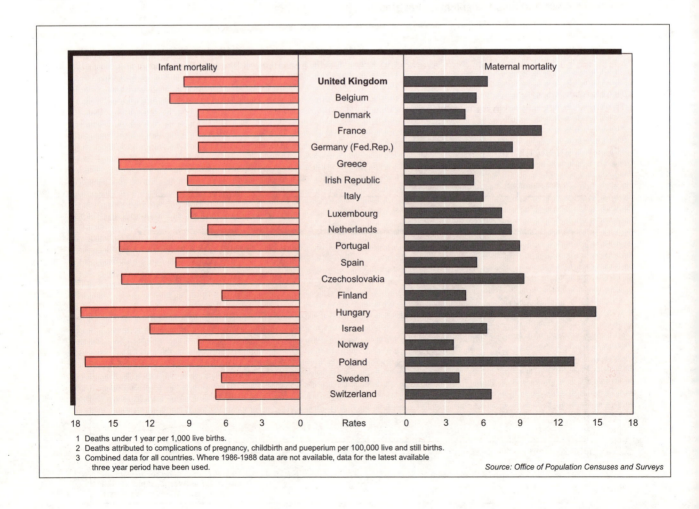

1 Deaths under 1 year per 1,000 live births.
2 Deaths attributed to complications of pregnancy, childbirth and pueperium per 100,000 live and still births.
3 Combined data for all countries. Where 1986-1988 data are not available, data for the latest available three year period have been used.

Source: Office of Population Censuses and Surveys

Social Trends 22, © Crown copyright 1992

mortality have been reached, there have been less pronounced improvements. Despite this, in 1990 the infant mortality rate fell to 7.9 per thousand live births, representing a fall of one third compared with 1981.

Despite these improvements in infant mortality, differences between the social classes remain. Rates are higher for those whose fathers are in the unskilled or semi-skilled groups (Chart 7.2). Indeed, infant mortality rates were over three quarters higher among babies whose fathers were unskilled than those whose father had a professional occupation.

There are a number of European countries which have lower infant mortality rates than the United Kingdom (Chart 7.3). The chart shows comparisons of infant (death under one year) and maternal (deaths of mothers from complications during pregnancy and childbirth) mortality rates for twenty countries.

7.4 Expectation of life: by sex and age

United Kingdom   Years

	1901	1931	1961	1981	1991	2001
Expectation of life[1]						
Males						
At birth	45.5	58.4	67.9	70.8	73.2	74.5
At age:						
1 year	53.6	62.1	68.6	70.7	72.8	74.0
10 years	50.4	55.6	60.0	62.0	64.0	65.2
20 years	41.7	46.7	50.4	52.3	54.2	55.4
40 years	20.1	29.5	31.5	33.2	35.1	36.2
60 years	13.3	14.4	15.0	16.3	17.6	18.7
80 years	4.9	4.9	5.2	5.7	6.3	7.0
Females						
At birth	49.0	62.4	73.8	76.8	78.8	79.9
At age:						
1 year	55.8	65.1	74.2	76.6	78.3	79.3
10 years	52.7	58.6	65.6	67.8	69.5	70.5
20 years	44.1	49.6	55.7	57.9	59.6	60.6
40 years	28.3	32.4	36.5	38.5	40.0	41.0
60 years	14.6	16.4	19.0	20.8	21.9	22.7
80 years	5.3	5.4	6.3	7.5	8.3	8.8

1 Further number of years which a person might expect to live. See Appendix, Part 7: Expectation of life.

Source: Government Actuary's Department

Generally newborn babies are more likely to die in the poorer areas of Europe. Hungary and Poland have the highest rates of those countries shown for both infant and maternal mortality, three times higher than those nations with the lowest rates. Such differences may be due to general standards of living such as housing and diet as well as the differing standards of medical service offered throughout Europe.

Improvements in the expectation of life are shown in Table 7.4. The expectation of life is the further number of years that a man or woman might expect to live when he or she has reached a certain age, on the assumption that the death rates prevailing at the time continue unchanged into the future. For example, a female who had reached the age of 40 in 1991 could expect to live for another 40 years.

Until 1979, the expectation of life had been lower at birth than at age 1, reflecting higher infant mortality rates in earlier years. However, the decline in infant mortality to its current level means that there is now little room for substantial improvement in the expectation of life at birth relative to that at age 1.

Overall improvements in life expectancy are expected to continue in the foreseeable future; for example it is assumed that the expectation of life at birth will rise to 75 years for a male and 80 years for a female by the year 2001. In 1931 their life expectancies were just 58 and 62 years respectively.

Some causes of death can be classified as potentially avoidable. Although the number of "avoidable" deaths has fallen since the 1970s, it is estimated that some 15 per cent of deaths in the European Community each year are avoidable. Timely and appropriate medical help or public health action can significantly reduce premature deaths from (among others) tuberculosis, cervical cancer, heart disease, appendicitis, asthma, high blood pressure and stroke.

Smoking (see Tables 7.15-7.17) is the largest single preventable cause of disease and premature death. It contributes towards a high proportion of deaths from lung cancer and coronary heart disease and is linked with other diseases such as bronchitis and emphysema. Many people also still eat and drink in ways which, over time, can contribute to the risk of developing serious ill-health and premature death (see Diet).

7.5 Selected causes of death[1]: by sex, 1951 and 1990

United Kingdom

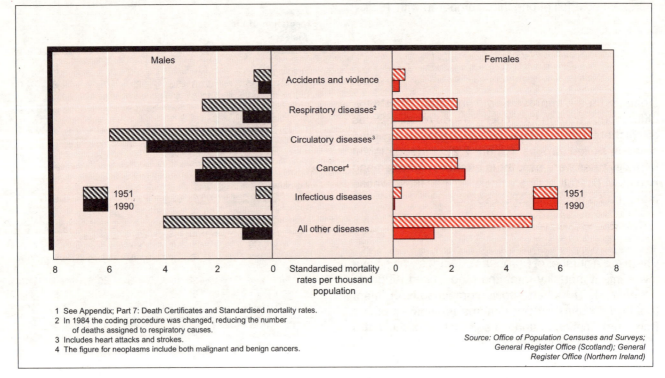

1 See Appendix; Part 7: Death Certificates and Standardised mortality rates.
2 In 1984 the coding procedure was changed, reducing the number
   of deaths assigned to respiratory causes.
3 Includes heart attacks and strokes.
4 The figure for neoplasms include both malignant and benign cancers.

*Source: Office of Population Censuses and Surveys;
General Register Office (Scotland); General
Register Office (Northern Ireland)*

Chart 7.5 shows mortality rates for selected causes of death for 1951 and 1990. The data, which are standardised for age, show that rates (expressed here as numbers per 1,000 population) for all causes have fallen for both males and females with the exception of cancer. Rates for circulatory diseases, including all types of heart disease, fell by almost a quarter for males and a third for females.

While female mortality rates from lung cancer have increased since 1971, the rates for males have dropped by 16 per cent, after remaining fairly static until the early 1980s. This is thought to be in response to the beneficial effects of early anti-smoking campaigns targeted mainly at young and middle-aged males.

The rise in death rates from cancer highlighted in Chart 7.5 can be broken down further into separate mortality rates for different types of cancer (Chart 7.6). Cancer is not necessarily a fatal disease. Today, about half of all people with cancer have a good chance of survival. In addition, as highlighted in the chart, significant reductions have occurred in certain types of cancer, most notably stomach cancer, perhaps due to improved eating habits.

Cases of infectious diseases identified by doctors are notified to the proper officer for each local authority area. Table 7.7 looks at these notifications between 1951 and 1990. Figures for some infectious diseases are liable to large year on year fluctuations, due to the cyclical nature of epidemics. An upsurge of whooping cough generally occurs every four years. Notifications of whooping cough fell gradually between 1951 and 1974, when there were 18,259 notifications.

Female death rates from cancers of the cervix uteri have remained relatively unchanged over time. However, those from lung cancer increased rapidly over the period covered by the chart and by 1990 had almost doubled compared with 1971. Despite this large increase, lung cancer remained only the second largest cancer killer of women behind cancer of the breast.

Following the fall in the rate of immunisation in the mid-1970s peaks of 70 thousand notifications were received in 1978 and 1982. After a gradual increase in immunisation rates since the early 1980s, the annual number of notifications reached a four-yearly peak of under 40 thousand in 1986. In the four years after this, the number of notifications dropped back in 1987 and 1988 before rising again in 1989 and 1990, although the 1990 figures were still well below the 1986 peak.

7.6 Standardised mortality rates[1] from cancers: by sex and selected sites

United Kingdom

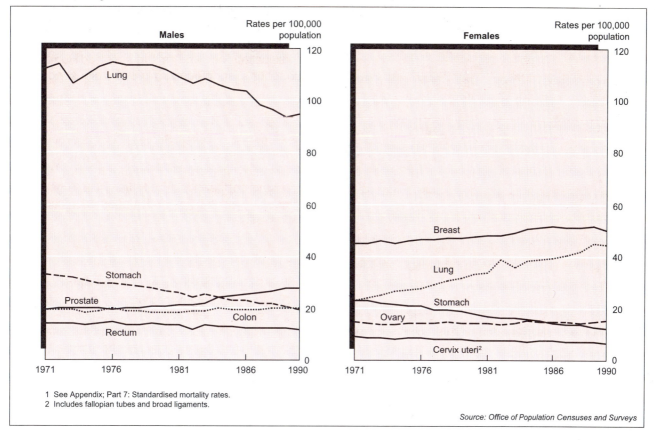

1 See Appendix; Part 7: Standardised mortality rates.
2 Includes fallopian tubes and broad ligaments.

Source: Office of Population Censuses and Surveys

In 1990, for the first time, the number of whooping cough notifications exceeded those for measles. Before 1970, measles epidemics occurred every two years. However since the introduction of immunisation against measles in 1968, the pattern has become less regular with a general decrease in the total number of cases. Upsurges since 1972 have lasted for 18-24 months with a peak every three years, the latest being in 1987. Large scale immunisation during the measles epidemic in the summer of 1988, and the introduction of the new combined measles, mumps and rubella vaccine from October 1988 helped reduce the incidence still further, to under 16 thousand in 1990.

7.7 Notifications of selected infectious diseases

United Kingdom

Thousands and numbers

	1951	1961	1971	1976	1981	1984	1986	1987	1988	1989	1990
Notifications (thousands)											
Infective jaundice[1]	..	..	17.9	7.6	11.0	7.0	4.3	4.4	6.4	8.3	9.8
Whooping cough	194.9	27.3	19.4	4.4	21.5	6.2	39.9	17.4	5.9	13.6	16.9
Measles	636.2	788.8	155.2	68.4	61.7	67.6	90.2	46.1	90.6	31.0	15.6
Tuberculosis											
Respiratory[2]	..	22.9	10.8	9.1	6.8	5.6	5.4	4.5	4.5	4.6	4.5
Other[2]	..	3.4	3.0	2.6	2.5	1.4	1.5	1.2	1.3	1.4	1.5
Meningococcal meningitis[3]	..	..	0.6	0.7	0.5	0.4	0.9	1.1	1.3	1.3	1.1
Notifications (numbers)											
Malaria[4]	217	107	268	1,243	1,328	1,480	1,744	1,264	1,333	1,538	1,566
Typhoid fever[5]	214	105	136	216	195	160	167	148	181	173	190
Paratyphoid fever[5]	1,218	347	109	78	82	75	93	67	188	100	103

1 Viral hepatitis for Scotland, and for England and Wales from 1989.
2 From 1984, categories overlap, therefore some cases will be included in respiratory and other tuberculosis.
3 England and Wales only.
4 Great Britain only until 1989. United Kingdom from 1990.

5 Great Britain only for 1951 and 1961.

Source: Office of Population Censuses and Surveys;
Scottish Health Service, Common Services Agency;
Department of Health and Social Services,
Northern Ireland

7.8 Food poisoning[1]:by region

United Kingdom Rates per 1,000,000 population

	1971	1976	1981	1986	1990
United Kingdom	149	200	231	338	663
North	104	79	260	283	937
Yorkshire & Humberside	107	386	209	292	1,010
East Midlands	81	162	177	274	779
East Anglia	111	109	114	272	565
South East	131	159	203	362	706
South West	199	220	164	356	703
West Midlands	122	144	190	264	542
North West	175	186	234	331	596
England	133	184	201	323	720
Wales	211	192	188	437	877
Scotland	289	384	571	476	593
Northern Ireland	70	133	88	174	515

1 Formal notifications in England and Wales; formal notifications and cases ascertained by other means in Scotland and Northern Ireland.

Source: Office of Population Censuses and Surveys;
Scottish Health Service, Common Services Agency;
Department of Health and Social Services, Northern Ireland

Recorded cases of food poisoning increased in every region of the United Kingdom in 1990 compared with 1981 (Chart 7.8). Reports of notifications of food poisoning to the Office of Population Censuses and Surveys (covering England and Wales only), are based on a clinical diagnosis by a doctor rather than on a microbiological examination of either the patient or food. There is inevitably a degree of subjectiveness in such reporting. Increased awareness of food poisoning by the public and the medical profession towards the end of 1988 may have made some contribution to the increase in reporting during the late 1980s. Although notifications did increase between 1981 and 1990, there was not a significant rise between 1989 and 1990 and figures from the early part of 1991 are lower than in 1990. In Scotland and Northern Ireland no distinction is made centrally between formal notifications and cases identified by other means.

The smallest increase in notifications since 1981 was in Scotland (4 per cent) where notifications have been generally higher than elsewhere in the United Kingdom. The highest increase was in Northern Ireland (up six-fold), although the rate of notification in 1990 was lower than for any other part of the country. The highest rates of notifications occurred in Yorkshire and Humberside, with reports for one person in every thousand.

The General Household Survey (GHS) collects data on long-standing illness, disability or infirmity. This measure of chronic sickness is based on people's own assessment of their health and differences in individuals' attitudes, expectations and judgements can affect responses.

Table 7.9 shows the prevalence of selected conditions among the different socio-economic groups. In 1989-90, there was a clear difference between the groups, with prevalence rates lowest among the professional group and highest among those in the unskilled manual group for most of the illnesses and disabilities shown in the table. Similar questions have been asked in the GHS regularly since 1972. Throughout the period the prevalence of chronic sickness in the manual groups has been higher than in the non- manual groups.

Chart 7.10 and Table 7.11 provide data on Acquired Immune Deficiency Syndrome (AIDS). The first chart shows AIDS cases reported by end-March 1991 per million population in European Community (EC) countries. The EC average was 135 cases per million population. At 78 cases per million population the United Kingdom rate was well below this average. Only

7.9 Reported long-standing illness or disability: by socio-economic group and condition group, 1989-90

Great Britain Rates[1] and numbers

	Professional	Employers and Managers	Intermediate	Skilled manual	Semi-skilled manual	Unskilled manual	Total[2]
Condition group							
Musculoskeletal system	100	126	130	155	171	201	145
Heart and circulatory system	64	81	80	94	118	121	91
Respiratory system	52	52	68	64	72	96	64
Digestive system	21	33	40	39	48	50	38
Nervous system	25	21	31	27	29	44	28
Eye complaints	15	22	29	20	30	32	24
Ear complaints	·19	14	19	27	25	31	22
All long-standing illness	291	325	349	370	416	478	365
Sample size (persons aged 16 and over)	1,164	3,557	4,065	5,987	3,190	981	19,562

1 Rate per 1,000 people.
2 Members of the Armed Forces, persons in inadequately described occupations and all persons who have never worked are not shown as separate categories but are included in the total.

Source: General Household Survey

7.10 Reported AIDS cases: EC comparison, 1991[1]

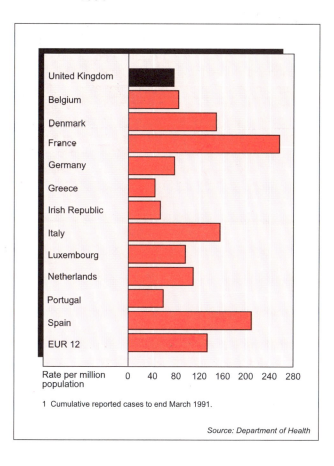

Rate per million population

0 40 80 120 160 200 240 280

1 Cumulative reported cases to end March 1991.

Source: Department of Health

estimated that Africa currently has five-sixths of the world's HIV-positive women. The World Health Organisation (WHO) estimate that more than ten thousand people a month globally are developing AIDS. By the end of the decade WHO estimate that ten million children around the world will have been infected by their mothers. Finally, WHO predict that the populations of some African countries will actually decline because of the virus.

In the absence of a cure for AIDS or a vaccine against HIV, preventing the spread of HIV depends crucially on people changing behaviour that puts them at risk. There are three main routes of transmission of the Human Immunodeficiency Virus (HIV), which is the cause of AIDS: through penetrative sexual intercourse, via infected blood (including in the process of injecting drugs), and from an infected mother to her unborn child. Ten years after infection approximately half of those infected will have developed AIDS and a further substantial number will have signs or symptoms associated with immunodeficiency. There has been some progression in the development and use of drugs which may extend the lifespan and improve the quality of life of infected people, but, at the moment, AIDS still has no known cure.

Portugal, the Irish Republic and Greece had lower rates than the United Kingdom. Within the European Community, France has the most serious AIDS problem with 257 cases per million population. However, the rates in Europe are overshadowed by the rapid spread of HIV across sub-Saharan Africa and Asia. It is

Table 7.11 covers AIDS cases and related deaths, and newly identified HIV antibody positive persons. At the end of March 1991, over 15 thousand HIV antibody positive reports had been received in the United Kingdom although the actual number of people who are HIV positive is thought to be significantly higher. Over half of these HIV antibody positive reports were for

7.11 AIDS cases and related deaths and HIV antibody positive reports: by exposure category, to end March 1991

United Kingdom Numbers

	AIDS				HIV antibody positive reports		
	Cases		Related deaths				
	Males	Females	Males	Females	Males	Females	Not Known
Exposure category							
Sexual intercourse							
between men	3,489	.	2,017	.	8,796	.	.
between men and women	195	113	96	49	635	728	10
Injecting drug use (IDU)	206	45	99	23	1,537	640	30
Blood							
blood factor (eg haemophilia)	242	4	165	2	1,243	7	1
blood/tissue transfer							
(eg transfusion)	30	39	22	25	77	64	2
Mother to child	16	23	6	11	91	91	35
Other/Undetermined	48	4	32	2	1,078	184	88
Total	4,226	228	2,437	112	13,457	1,714	166

Source: Public Health Laboratory Service, Communicable Disease Surveillance Centre; Communicable Diseases (Scotland) Unit

homosexual or bisexual males. 4,454 people had been reported as having AIDS in the United Kingdom, of which over 2,500 had died. Cases of AIDS in heterosexuals are increasing faster than any other transmission category. In the year to June 1991, there was a 63 per cent increase in reports of AIDS acquired by heterosexual intercourse. There was also a similar increase in those infected by using contaminated injecting equipment.

Injecting drug users (IDUs) comprised 14 per cent of HIV reports. This group, and the group of heterosexual contact reports, are of particular importance as together they form a group of infected people who, however they themselves acquired the infection, may transmit the virus to any heterosexual partner by heterosexual intercourse.

Under present circumstances, public health measures, for instance the screening of donated blood, health education and other preventive activities to secure changes in sexual and drug using behaviour, offer the only effective way to limit the spread of the disease. The government has made action against AIDS a high priority and has developed a comprehensive strategy to limit the further spread of HIV infection and to provide diagnostic and treatment facilities, and counselling and support services for those infected or at risk.

Diet

The nutritional value of a person's diet depends upon the overall mix of foods that is eaten during the course of weeks, months or years and upon the needs of the individual eating them. No single food can be good or bad in isolation. Thus it is consistent overeating and not the occasional over indulgence that results in obesity; conversely, it takes a consistent reduction in energy intake or increase in energy expenditure and not sporadic bouts of intensive dieting to effect permanent weight loss. Similarly, eating large amounts of fat at a single meal is unlikely to increase risk of a heart attack.

The main sources of fat in household food purchases are meat and meat products, fats and oils, dairy products and some cereal products. These may be purchased in a wide variety of forms including pies, sausages, butter, margarine, cheese spreads, cakes and biscuits.

7.12 Purchases[1] of selected foods for home consumption

Great Britain	\multicolumn{5}{c}{Indices[2] (1986 = 100)}
	1961	1971	1981	1986	1990
Type of food					
Milk and cream	125	124	107	100	92
Cheese	74	87	94	100	96
Eggs	155	151	122	100	73
Beef and veal	138	121	106	100	80
Mutton and lamb	224	180	141	100	97
Pork	54	84	105	100	82
Poultry	33	67	100	100	109
All other meat and meat products	100	107	103	100	91
Fish and fish products	110	100	95	100	98
Butter	273	244	163	100	71
Margarine	80	77	100	100	78
All other fats	62	71	79	100	102
Fresh potatoes	146	127	108	100	91
Other fresh vegetables	103	100	99	100	93
Other vegetables and vegetable products	51	65	87	100	95
Fresh fruit	85	99	98	100	105
Other fruit and fruit products	61	64	76	100	98
Bread, standard white loaves	218	181	132	100	89
All other bread	64	41	66	100	94
Cakes, biscuits, etc	130	125	102	100	99
Sugar	225	197	138	100	75
Tea	163	137	114	100	87
Instant coffee	29	80	95	100	87

1 Also includes the household consumption of 'free' foods, eg garden and allotment produce, etc.
2 Indices of average quantities per person per week.

Source: National Food Survey, Ministry of Agriculture, Fisheries and Food

7.13 Nutritional value of household food as a percentage of Reference Nutrient Intake, 1990

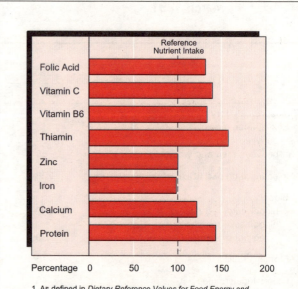

Great Britain

1 As defined in *Dietary Reference Values for Food Energy and Nutrients for the United Kingdom* published by Department of Health in 1991.

Source: Ministry of Agriculture, Fisheries and Food

Social Trends 22, © Crown copyright 1992

7.14 Percentage of food energy contributed by fat and fatty acids

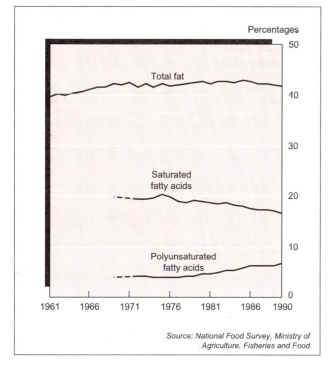

Great Britain

Source: National Food Survey, Ministry of Agriculture, Fisheries and Food

Table 7.12 shows that there were marked changes in domestic food consumption between 1961 and 1990. The consumption of milk and cream declined by one-quarter over this period and the consumption of eggs more than halved. The consumption of butter declined by nearly three quarters between 1961 and 1990. However, the consumption of margarine rose in the late 1970s and early 1980s as soft margarine became popular, and has only declined again in recent years. At least part of this decline in the consumption of traditional yellow fats has been offset by the increase in purchases of other fats, including low fat and dairy spreads. The rise in consumption of fruit products, is largely due to the increased popularity of fruit juices. Expenditure on fruit juice is now equivalent to over one quarter of the average fresh fruit expenditure.

Chart 7.13 compares the nutritional value of the nation's food purchases with some of the Department of Health Dietary Reference Values, published in 1991. Where intake is under 100 this is considered to be below recommended levels. Current intake of dietary fibre (not shown in the chart) is around three quarters of reference value.

High concentrations of cholesterol in the blood are associated with an increased risk of coronary heart disease, and high intakes of saturated fatty acids can increase this cholesterol. It is clearly good practice to develop basic eating patterns that are as conducive to good health as possible. This involves eating a balanced diet providing sufficient but not excessive energy from a variety of foods chosen from among the cereals, vegetables, fruit, meat, poultry or fish, dairy products and oils and fats. For example, the diet is much more likely to contain enough Vitamin C if fruit, fruit juice or vegetables are eaten every day than if they are eaten only infrequently. Diet may be particularly important for people whose needs are relatively high but whose appetites may be small, such as young children, pregnant women and elderly people.

Chart 7.14 shows the contribution to energy made by fat and fatty acids in the British domestic diet. Although total fat intake has fallen by approximately a quarter between 1961 and 1990, total energy intake has also fallen by a similar proportion. These effects will be partly offset by increases in the consumption of confectionery and of food eaten outside the home but may also be associated with lower physical activity. Fat intake still represents about 42 per cent of total energy compared with a target of 35 per cent.

Whilst the average proportion of energy derived from saturated fatty acids has decreased to 17 per cent of total energy, this is still above recommended levels. The Department of Health has advised that saturated fatty acids should provide 11 per cent of energy.

Social habits and health

The effects of smoking are now incontrovertible. It is the greatest cause of preventable death in the United Kingdom, responsible for more than 100,000 premature deaths each year. Of every one thousand young male adults currently smoking, on average only six will die on the roads but 250 will die before their time from smoking. Most of these will die from lung cancer, respiratory disease or heart disease. Many will die in middle age.

Progress has been made in controlling smoking in public places and the workplace. All government departments have signed to the "Look After Your Heart" workplace programme and are introducing controls on smoking in offices. Many United Kingdom employers, including the Ford Motor Company and the Metropolitan Police, have introduced written policies on smoking. Public transport in London is, with the exception of black-cabs, smoke free.

7.15 Percentage of pupils who were regular smokers[1]: by sex and parental smoking behaviour, 1990

England			Percentages
	Boys	Girls	Total
Parental smoking behaviour			
Neither parent smokes	5	6	6
Only father smokes	8	9	9
Only mother smokes	14	11	13
Both parents smoke	13	17	15
Not living with both parents	12	16	14
No answer on parental smoking	13	15	14

1 Pupils smoking at least one cigarette a week.

Source: Survey of Smoking Among Secondary Schoolchildren,
Office of Population Censuses and Surveys

7.16 Smoking behaviour of children[1]: by sex

England & Wales		Percentages and numbers		
	1982	1986	1988[2]	1990[2]
Smoking behaviour				
(percentages)				
Boys				
Regular smokers	11	7	7	9
Occasional smokers	7	5	5	6
Used to smoke	11	10	8	7
Tried smoking once	26	23	23	22
Never smoked	45	55	58	56
Sample size (= 100%)				
(numbers)	1,460	1,676	1,489	1,643
Girls				
Regular smokers	11	12	9	11
Occasional smokers	9	5	5	6
Used to smoke	10	10	9	7
Tried smoking once	22	19	19	18
Never smoked	49	53	59	58
Sample size (= 100%)				
(numbers)	1,514	1,508	1,529	1,478

1 Aged 11-15 years.
2 England only. *Source: Office of Population Censuses and Surveys*

As smoking is a major contributory factor to premature death, smoking habits, particularly those of children, are likely to play a crucial role in the future of the nation's health. Tables 7.15 and 7.16 show the smoking behaviour of children. Around a quarter of a million children are regular smokers. Girls are more likely to smoke than boys, but boys who smoke do so more heavily than girls.

The relationship between parental smoking and the smoking habits of their children is shown in Table 7.15. In cases where neither parent smoked both sexes were least likely to smoke themselves. Conversely, where both parents smoked, children were most likely to smoke themselves. A recent survey by the Office of Population Censuses and Surveys (OPCS) found that the overwhelming majority of pupils said that their families would try to stop them smoking or would try to persuade them not to smoke. However, over half of fourth-year secondary school pupils who smoked thought that their parents did not know that they smoked. They were also more likely to keep their smoking a secret if their parents did not smoke themselves.

In 1990, the proportion of children who smoked regularly was similar to that in the early 1980s (Table 7.16). The Health Education authority spends about £5 million a year on anti-smoking campaigns, most of which are targeted at teenagers and young adults.

The Health Education Authority also participates in No-Smoking Day, an annual event which has been held for the last five years. It helps as many as fifty thousand people a year to give up cigarettes, and, at an estimated cost of £350,000, costs just £7 for every smoker who gives up.

Table 7.17 looks at people who have given up smoking. Throughout the period covered, the proportion of people who had given up smoking cigarettes was greater among older people than younger. Up to age 24, there is little difference between men and women in the proportion of ex-regular smokers, but among those aged 25 and over the proportion was greater for men than for women. This difference increased through the age range. More than half of men but just over a quarter of women aged 60 and over were ex-regular cigarette smokers. However, it is worth remembering that, among older people, men are much more likely to have ever been smokers.

7.17 Ex-regular cigarette smokers: by sex and age

Great Britain					Percentages
	1972	1976	1980	1986	1989-90
Males aged					
16-19	4[1]	5	5	5	4
20-24	8	11	8	11	8
25-34	12	20	18	20	16
35-49	17	27	27	33	32
50-59	22	33	35	38	42
60 and over	28	43	45	52	52
All males aged 16 and over	23	27	28	32	32
Females aged					
16-19	4[1]	5	4	7	6
20-24	9	10	9	9	8
25-34	10	13	13	16	14
35-49	10	12	13	20	20
50-59	12	15	17	18	20
60 and over	9	14	19	23	27
All females aged 16 and over	10	12	14	18	19

1 Aged 15-19. *Source: General Household Survey*

7.18 Average number of units of alcohol consumed weekly: by age and sex, 1978 and 1987-9

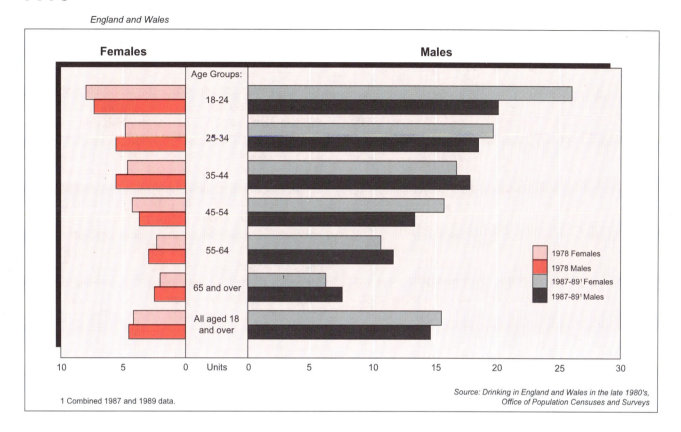

England and Wales

1 Combined 1987 and 1989 data.

Source: Drinking in England and Wales in the late 1980's,
Office of Population Censuses and Surveys

Alcohol and drug misuse are major social problems which place a massive burden on the National Health Service and cause ill-health, accidents and death. They are also major contributors to problems in law and order, family breakdown and industrial inefficiency.

Chart 7.18 uses data from surveys of alcohol consumption in England and Wales, carried out by the Office of Population Censuses and Surveys (OPCS) in 1978, 1987 and 1989.

7.19 Alcohol consumption[1]: by sex and social class[2], 1987 and 1989

England & Wales			Units of alcohol	
	Males		Females	
	1987	1989	1987	1989
Professional	11.4	10.2	4.3	5.3
Managerial and junior professional	15.4	15.0	6.1	5.3
Other non-manual	14.0	11.8	5.3	3.5
Skilled manual	15.4	13.1	4.6	4.1
Semi-skilled manual	12.5	16.3	3.4	3.2
Unskilled manual	17.3	14.8	3.7	4.1
All persons aged 16 and over	14.5	13.9	4.8	4.2

1 Average number of units consumed in the seven days before interview. See Appendix, Part 7: Drinking.
2 As defined by the occupation of the head of the household.

Source: Drinking in England and Wales in the late 1980s,
Office of Population Censuses and Surveys

The heaviest drinkers of alcohol are in the 18-24 age group, after which consumption generally declines with age. Average weekly consumption over the period fell for males by around one unit (see Appendix, Part 7) but increased slightly for females.

Consumption of alcohol is difficult to measure from social surveys, which consistently record less consumption than would be expected from Customs and Excise statistics of alcohol. The Customs' data support the evidence of little change in total consumption between 1978 and 1987-1989, but they indicate that consumption was not stable over this period; rather that alcohol consumption peaked in 1979, fell until 1982 and has risen slowly since then.

A central aim of the 1987 and 1989 OPCS surveys was to compare alcohol consumption and drinking behaviour before and after the implementation of the *1988 Licensing Act*. The surveys found little change in consumption between 1987 and 1989. It is clear that the extension to permitted opening hours (afternoon opening, and in many places later evening closing) has not lead to a marked increase in overall consumption.

Table 7.19 shows consumption for each socio-economic group. With only one exception (professionals), male consumption was more than double the equivalent female consumption. Consumption by semi-skilled

7.20 New addicts notified: by type of drug

United Kingdom						Numbers
	1973	1981	1986	1988	1989	1990
Type of drug						
Heroin	508	1,660	4,855	4,630	4,883	5,819
Methadone	328	431	659	576	682	1,469
Dipipanone	28	473	116	124	109	154
Cocaine	132	174	520	462	527	633
Morphine	226	355	343	203	259	296
Pethidine	27	45	33	44	36	39
Dextromoradine	28	59	97	80	75	78
Opium	0	0	23	18	15	14
Others	2	4	4	2	1	4
Total addicts notified[1]	806	2,248	5,325	5,212	5,639	6,923

1 As an addict can be reported as addicted to more than one notifiable drug, the figures for individual drugs cannot be added together to produce totals.

Source: Home Office

manual males increased by 30 per cent between 1987 and 1989 while consumption by all other male socio-economic groups fell.

In 1990 approximately two thirds of notified drug addicts were reported to be injecting drugs. The numbers of new addicts notified increased between 1973 and 1990 for each drug shown in Table 7.20. Between 1981 and 1990 the number of dipipanone notifications fell by over two thirds, possibly reflecting reduced availability of the drug after controls were placed on its prescription with effect from 1 April 1984.

The table shows that there were over eight times as many new drug addicts reported in 1990 as in 1973. The vast majority of new addicts are reported as addicted to heroin (over 8 out of 10 in 1990). These data relate to notifications under the *Misuse of Drugs (Notification of and Supply to Addicts) Regulations 1973*, which require doctors to send to the Chief Medical Officer at the Home Office particulars of persons whom they consider to be addicted to any of the fourteen controlled drugs to which the regulations apply (mainly opiates). Changes in the numbers of notified addicts reflect changes in both doctors' awareness of the requirement to notify and the proportion of addicts attracted into treatment as well as changes in the overall number of addicts.

The number of addicts who are formally notified is probably only a small proportion of the number misusing notifiable drugs. Many will not have sought medical treatment and will not therefore have been notified. It may also be that, for a variety of reasons, doctors do not notify all the addicts that they see. Researchers have demonstrated that there are considerable local variations in the extent to which the number of notified addicts underestimates the number of regular users of notifiable drugs. It also excludes the larger number of misusers of other controlled drugs such as cannabis, LSD, amphetamines, barbiturates and benzodiazepines.

Although attention often focuses on notified addicts, it is possible to be addicted to legally prescribed drugs. Benzodiazepines, launched in the 1960s and prescribed as an anti-depressant, and barbiturates, used as a sedative, are two examples. If only a tiny fraction of legal prescriptions for drugs used to calm or induce sleep, such as benzodiazepines and barbiturates, were to people addicted to or misusing these drugs, this would be a far greater problem than notified addicts. Following concern over their long term effects and addictive qualities doctors were given advice about the use of these drugs and made aware of the need to prescribe them carefully. Chart 7.21 shows that there were over 21 million prescriptions for benzodiazepines in 1989, down from a peak of over 30 million in 1978 and 1979. Prescriptions for barbiturates have fallen fairly steadily to less than 10 per cent of their 1972 level. However, this still represents over one million prescriptions a year.

There were 175 thousand new cases of sexually transmitted diseases (excluding HIV) seen at NHS genito-urinary medicine clinics in the United Kingdom in 1989 (Table 7.22). Among the diseases shown in the table, gonorrhoea was the only one to have shown a

7.21 Prescriptions for barbiturates and benzodiazepines

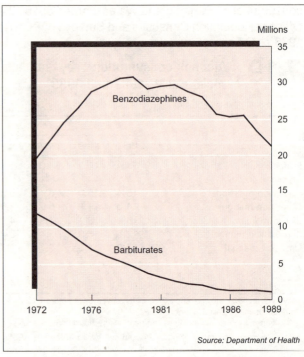

Great Britain

Source: Department of Health

large decline in the number of new cases between 1971 and 1989. The number of males with the disease decreased by almost three quarters over this period and the number of females with the disease fell by over half.

These figures cannot be taken as giving a complete picture of the incidence of sexually transmitted diseases as patients can also receive treatment outside the NHS. They do however provide a useful indication of trends as NHS genito-urinary medicine clinics are believed to cover about 90 per cent of all patients needing treatment.

7.22 Selected sexually transmitted diseases: by sex

United Kingdom — Thousands

	1971	1981	1986	1989
New cases seen				
Male				
Syphilis	2	3	2	1
Gonorrhoea	43	37	28	12
Herpes simplex	3[1]	7	11	11
Non-specific genital infection	65	99	119	82
Female				
Syphilis	1	1	1	1
Gonorrhoea	20	21	18	9
Herpes simplex	1[1]	5	9	10
Non-specific genital infection	14[2]	33	56	49

1 England and Wales only.
2 Excludes Scotland.

Source: Department of Health; Welsh Office; Scottish Health Service, Common Services Agency; Department of Health and Social Services, Northern Ireland

Accidents

The earlier Chart 7.5 showed the relative importance of deaths from accidents and violence. This section goes on to look into accidents in more detail.

7.23 Accidental deaths: by cause

Great Britain — Numbers

	1971	1981	1986[1]	1990[1]
Cause of death				
Railway accident	212	95	99	140
Road accident[2]	7,970	4,880	5,565	5,590
Other transport accident	219	143	235	236
Accident at home or in residential accommodation[3]	7,045	..[4]	5,522	4,714
Accident elsewhere[3]	3,807	..[4]	2,620	2,478
Total accidental deaths	19,246	15,097	14,024	13,145

1 See Appendix, Part 7: Death certificates.
2 These figures are not comparable with those issued by the Department of Transport: see Appendix, Part 7: Road accident deaths.
3 Late effects of accidental injury are included in the individual cause figures for Scotland, but are excluded from the total.
4 Data not available separately due to 1981 registration officers industrial dispute.

Source: Office of Population Censuses and Surveys; General Register Office (Scotland)

The first table in this section (7.23) summarises the main causes of accidental deaths in Great Britain since 1971. It excludes those deaths where it was not known whether the death was accidental or inflicted on purpose. The total number of accidental deaths in 1990, at just over 13 thousand, was 13 per cent lower than in 1981 and one-third lower than the 1971 total. Deaths from road accidents fell by 30 per cent between 1971 and 1990, but were higher than in 1981, and remained the biggest killer.

Further information on road traffic accidents is given in Chapter 13.

Chart 7.24 looks at deaths in four industries. Prior to 1981 fatal occupational injuries to employees were reported directly to enforcement authorities under various different pieces of legislation. However, some employees, notably in service industries such as water

7.24 Industrial fatalities[1]: by selected industry

Great Britain

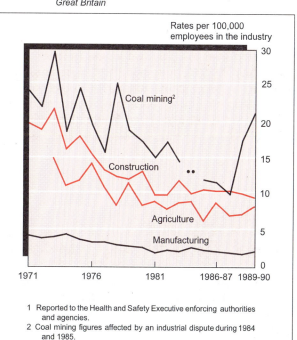

1 Reported to the Health and Safety Executive enforcing authorities and agencies.
2 Coal mining figures affected by an industrial dispute during 1984 and 1985.

Source: Health and Safety Executive

7.25 Fatal accidents in the home: by sex and age, 1989

England & Wales   Percentages and numbers

	Males					Females					All persons
	0-4	5-14	15-64	65-74	75 and over	0-4	5-14	15-64	65-74	75 and over	
Type of accident *(percentages)*											
Poisonings by drugs and biologicals	2	3	12	3	1	—	5	13	6	1	6
Other poisonings	—	3	8	3	2	1	—	6	3	1	4
Falls	4	13	18	55	69	7	5	15	51	75	44
Fire and flames	36	40	12	15	12	36	64	12	10	10	13
Natural and environmental factors	—	—	—	1	2	1	—	1	4	2	2
Submersion, suffocation and foreign bodies	38	27	10	5	5	28	9	8	9	4	8
Other accidents	8	3	3	2	3	10	—	2	2	2	3
Undetermined whether or not accident	11	10	37	16	6	17	18	43	15	3	21
Total (= 100%) (numbers)	99	30	1,079	246	536	72	22	601	299	1,093	4,077

Source: Department of Trade and Industry; Office of Population Censuses and Surveys

supply, education and health care were not covered by the legislation. From 1 January 1981, all fatal occupational injuries became reportable under the *Notification of Accidents and Dangerous Occurrences Regulations (1980)* (NADOR). NADOR was superseded by the introduction of the *Reporting of Injuries, Diseases and Dangerous Occurrences Regulations (1985)* (RIDDOR) on 1 April 1986. However, the reporting requirements for fatal injuries remained the same under NADOR and RIDDOR.

The chart shows that fatal injury incidence rates (fatal injuries per 100,000 employees in the industry) fell for each of the selected industries between the early 1970s and 1989-90, although the rate has increased in coalmining over the past two years. In recent years there have been similar numbers of deaths in the construction and manufacturing industries. However, in 1989-90 the injury incidence rate in construction (9.4) was over four times higher than in manufacturing (2.1), although neither were as high as in the mining sector in 1989-90.

There were over 4 thousand deaths caused by accidents in the home during 1989 (Table 7.25). Over two fifths of such accidents were from falls. Fatal accidents to females age 75 and over was the largest single group. Among these women accidental falls accounted for three quarters of fatal accidents. The chief cause of accident among children aged under 15 was fire and flames.

In 1989 fire brigades attended 456 thousand fires in the United Kingdom (Table 7.26), the highest since 1976 compared with an average of 370 thousand between 1979-1988. This was partly due to a large increase in the number of outdoor fires, especially the more weather dependent grassland and heathland fires, which increased by 63 thousand from 1988 to 1989 due to the hot, dry summer.

7.26 Fires[1] and resulting casualties: by location

United Kingdom   Thousands and numbers

	1971	1976	1981	1986	1989
Fires (thousands)					
Dwellings	46.0	51.1	56.0	63.5	64.5
Other buildings	43.3	44.7	38.8	42.1	45.7
Road vehicles	18.1	25.1	33.8	47.7	51.7
Other locations[2]	209.4	375.5	201.0	233.9	294.3
All fires	316.8	496.4	329.6	387.3	456.2
Fatal casualties (numbers)					
Dwellings	574	690	780	753	642
Other buildings	152	84	80	75	77
Road vehicles	54	60	63	82	136
Other locations[2]	42	61	52	47	46
All fatal casualties	822	895	975	957	901
Non-fatal casualties[3] (numbers)					
Dwellings	3,040	3,830	6,343	9,403	10,388
Other buildings	1,292	1,494	1,794	2,200	2,453
Road vehicles	187	261	286	485	484
Other locations[2]	498	809	569	680	834
All non-fatal casualties	5,017	6,394	8,992	12,768	14,159

1 Fires attended by local authority fire brigades.
2 Includes outdoor fires, fires in derelict buildings and chimney fires.
3 The reporting system changed in 1978, the level of reporting of non-fatal casualties is thought to have been lower under the old system.

Source: Home Office

 Social Trends 22, © Crown copyright 1992

Two thirds of people who died in fires in dwellings in 1989 had been trapped, often because they were unaware of the fire until too late. The commonest cause of death in dwelling fires was being overcome by gas or smoke. It is clear that an early warning that fire has started would prevent deaths - smoke alarms are one way of alerting people to the danger.

In 1989, 3 per cent of fires in dwellings attended by fire brigades were discovered by smoke alarms. These were discovered faster and associated with much lower death rates than dwelling fires not discovered by alarms.

The number of deliberate car fires, which in 1989 accounted for one third of all car fires more than doubled between 1979 and 1989, whereas the number of accidental fires increased by one third in the same period. The cause of 80 per cent of accidental car fires in 1989 was attributed to vehicle defects or possible defects.

The number of deaths from fires in cars rose from 58 in 1988 to a record 119 in 1989, mainly due to a doubling in deaths from car fires following crash or collision. Although such car fires represent only a small proportion (3 per cent) of the total number of car fires, they cause 70 per cent of the deaths.

Prevention

Table 7.27 shows the number of cervical cancer smear tests carried out in Great Britain between 1976 and 1988-89. Such tests are an important aspect of prevention and five-yearly screening can reduce deaths among women screened by 80 per cent.

In 1976 over 2.9 million smears were taken and by 1988-89 this had risen to over 5 million, an increase of over 70 per cent. These figures relate to the number of smears examined and not to numbers of women - some women have more than one smear test - an indication of the increased proportion of women having smear tests can be seen by relating the number of smears taken to the number of women aged 15 and over, this had risen from 13.3 per cent in 1976 to 21.5 per cent in 1988-89. There was a gradual decline in the number of deaths from cervical cancer between 1976 and 1981 but the numbers remained stable between 1981 and 1989. The cervical screening programme forms an important part of the government strategy to promote women's health. Within 3 years the cervical cancer programme, involving computerised call and recall systems, will have invited around 13 million women in England, for cervical smear tests, all women in the age range 20-64 years who are registered with a General Practitioner. Programmes for cervical cancer screening on similar lines are being implemented in Scotland, Wales and Northern Ireland. The United Kingdom is one of the first countries in the world to announce the implementation of such a nationwide programme. It should be noted that cervical cancer commonly has a long detectable pre-cancerous stage during which the condition is curable. Research studies have indicated an association between cervical cancer and the number of sexual partners both in the woman herself and her partner.

Breast cancer is the commonest cause of death among women aged 35-64. Around 1 in 12 women in the United Kingdom will develop it. Between 1987 and 1990, £70 million was provided to set up and run the nationwide breast screening programme. Women aged between 50 and 64 will be invited every three years for mammographic screening. Specialised screening centres are now operating and all eligible women should have been invited for screening by 1993. The national screening programme was launched with the target that at least 70 per cent of eligible women should be screened. Figures for those centres operational for the whole of 1988-89 indicated that around 70 per cent of women receiving invitations accepted them. Recent figures produced by the NHS breast screening programme suggest that in 1990-91 around the same proportion of women invited for screening accepted the invitations and were screened. A report by the Advisory Committee on Breast Cancer Screening concluded that it could reduce mortality in the eligible age group by around a quarter by the year 2000.

7.27 Cervical cancer: deaths and screening

Great Britain							Thousands and percentages	
	1976	1981	1983	1984	1985	1986	1987–88	1988–89
Deaths	2.4	2.2	2.2	2.1	2.2	2.2	2.1	2.1
Smears taken	2,923	3,442	3,669	3,911	4,455	4,468	4,754	5,032
Smears as a percentage of women aged 15 and over	*13.3*	*15.2*	*16.0*	*17.0*	*19.3*	*19.2*	*20.4*	*21.5*

Source: Department of Health; Welsh Office;
Scottish Health Service, Common Services Agency

7.28 Vaccination and immunisation of children

	1971[1]	1976	1981	1986	1989 −90[2]
United Kingdom					Percentages
Percentage vaccinated[3]					
Diptheria	80	73	82	85	89
Whooping cough	78	39	46	66	79
Poliomyelitis	80	73	82	85	89
Tetanus	80	73	82	85	89
Measles	46	45	54	71	85

1 England and Wales only.
2 England figures are for children born in 1987−88 and vaccinated before 2nd birthday during 1989−90.
3 Children born two years earlier and vaccinated by the end of the specified year.

Source: Department of Health; Welsh Office; Scottish Health Service, Common Services Agency; Department of Health and Social Services, Northern Ireland

Vaccinations very rarely result in harmful side effects. *The Vaccine Damage Payments Act 1979* provides for a specified lump sum payment to those children found to be severely disabled as a result of vaccination against specified diseases. Chart 7.28 shows that the proportion of infants vaccinated against diphtheria, poliomyelitis and tetanus rose from 73 per cent to 89 per cent between 1976 and 1989-90. There was a considerable drop in the proportion of babies being vaccinated against whooping cough during the mid-1970s. Following safety scares the proportion of children vaccinated in 1976 was half that of 1971. However, by 1989-90 the proportion had risen to a level slightly above that of 1971.

The World Health Organisation (WHO) immunisation target for its European region was 90 per cent coverage by 1990. More recent estimates than those in the table, produced by Cover of Vaccination Evaluated Rapidly (COVER) managed by the Communicable Diseases Surveillance Centre, show that in February 1991 the percentages for England had reached 90 per cent for diphtheria, 89 per cent for MMR (measles, mumps, rubella) and 85 per cent for whooping cough.

Blood and organ donations

The number of blood donations in the United Kingdom between 1981 and 1990 remained fairly constant (Chart 7.29). In 1990 there were over 2.5 million such donations, slightly lower than in 1989, but still 4 per cent higher than in 1981. These figures do not necessarily reflect the number of donors as each donor could donate blood more than once during the year.

Most healthy people aged between 18 and 60 are generally accepted as donors, and those who donate regularly can do so up to the age of 65. However, individuals at risk of AIDS or Hepatitis B, or any other disease transmissible by blood, are excluded. Visitors to those parts of the world where diseases such as malaria are endemic are deferred from donating for an appropriate period.

Plasmapheresis is a method of removing plasma from the donor and returning the red cells. It is normally performed using a machine and a single donation is

7.29 Blood donations

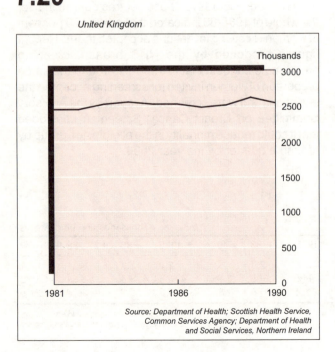

United Kingdom

Source: Department of Health; Scottish Health Service, Common Services Agency; Department of Health and Social Services, Northern Ireland

7.30 Organ transplants: by type

	United Kingdom			Numbers
	Organ transplanted			
	Heart and lung	Heart	Kidney	Liver
1981	0	24	905	11
1982	0	36	1,033	21
1983	1	53	1,144	20
1984	10	116	1,443	51
1985	37	137	1,336	88
1986	51	176	1,493	127
1987	72	243	1,485	172
1988	101	274	1,575	241
1989	94	295	1,732	295
1990	95	329	1,730	359

Source: Department of Health

approximately 500-600ml. In this manner about three times more plasma per donation can be extracted than could be received from a single donation of whole blood. The plasma can be donated as frequently as fortnightly, compared to whole blood which can only be donated every three months.

Although the number of blood donations has only increased slightly, the number of plasma donations through plasmapheresis rose sevenfold between 1982 and 1989. In 1989 there were over 31 thousand plasma donors.

Transplantation of organs has been one of the great medical advances of the last 25 years. Organs may be removed after a person's death if they have indicated in writing their willingness to be a donor, for example by signing an organ donor card, or if the surviving relatives have no objection. Hearts, livers and most kidneys for transplantation are removed from donors very soon after the diagnosis of brain-stem death while respiration is artificially maintained. Normally organs must be

transplanted quickly after removal from the donor or they cannot be used. Improving techniques have lengthened the time allowable between removal and transplantation giving a greater flexibility; for example organs can be transported greater distances, thus widening the pool of well-matched recipients.

Donor organs are usually matched with the recipient for blood group and tissue type as the risk of the organ being rejected and the transplant failing is significantly lessened if there is a good match between the donor organ and recipient. Donor organs transplanted into children also have to be matched for size and weight.

Heart and liver transplants save the lives of people suffering otherwise fatal conditions. Between 1986 and 1990 the number of heart transplants increased by 87 per cent and the number of liver transplants nearly trebled (Table 7.30). In 1990 heart/lung transplants accounted for over one-fifth of transplants performed involving the heart.

Health Services

More patients are being treated in fewer hospital beds; between 1971 and 1988-89 the number of in-patient cases increased by 27 per cent to over 8 million. The average number of beds available daily fell by more

than one fifth to 337 thousand and as a result the number of patients treated per available bed per year increased by over 60 per cent (Table 7.31).

7.31 National Health Service in-patient summary: by ward type, 1981 and 1989-90

England, Scotland and Northern Ireland

	Acute[1]	General patients elderly	Maternity	Mental Illness	Mental handicap[2]	Total
1981						
Discharges and deaths (thousands)	5,288	307	940	224	31	6,794
Average daily available beds (thousands)	172	68	22	107	55	427
In-patients per available bed (rate)	30.7	4.5	43.1	2.1	0.6	15.9
Average length of stay (days)						
England	8.6	66.1	5.5	. .	. .	. .
Scotland	3.0	160.9	6.2	197.7	1,021.8	22.4
Northern Ireland	9.4	255.3	6.1	168.3	828.0	19.8
1989-90						
Discharges and deaths[3] (thousands)	6,707	498	1,107	253	61	8,641
Average daily available beds (thousands)	146	63	18	77	33	337
In-patients per available bed (rate)	46.0	7.9	62.7	3.3	1.9	25.7
Average length of stay (days)						
England	6.4	36.2	3.9	218.2	922.7	19.3
Scotland	6.9	93.0	4.3	152.5	380.7	17.3
Northern Ireland	6.9	98.4	5.3	136.2	252.5	15.2

1 Wards for general patients, excluding elderly, younger physically
  disabled, neonate cots not in maternity units.
2 Excluding mental handicap community units.
3 Finished consultant episodes for England.

Source: Department of Health;
Scottish Health Service, Common Services Agency;
Department of Health and Social Services, Northern Ireland

7.32 National Health Service hospital activity: day cases and out-patients, all specialties

United Kingdom   •   Thousands and numbers

	1971	1976	1981	1986	1988–89	1989–90
Day case attendances (thousands)	..	565	863	1,288	1,259	1,484
New out-patient attendances (thousands)						
Accidents and emergency	9,358	10,463	11,342	12,682	13,201	13,570
Other out-patients	9,572	9,170	9,816	10,758	10,409	10,593
Average attendances per new out-patient (numbers)						
Accidents and emergency	1.6	1.6	1.4	1.3	1.3	1.3
Other out-patients	4.2	4.0	4.4	4.3	4.2	4.2

Source: Department of Health; Welsh Office;
Scottish Health Service, Common Services Agency;
Department of Health and Social Services, Northern Ireland

In 1989-90 National Health Service hospitals dealt with almost 1.5 million day case attendances (Table 7.32), an increase of over 70 per cent compared to 1981, and two and half times as many as in 1976.

A recent report by the Audit Commission found that 80 per cent of day patients found their type of treatment preferable to in-patient care. Although 16 per cent of day cases felt that their length of stay was too short, that was not significantly different from the 11 per cent of in-patients who felt the same.

Waiting lists have been a feature of the National Health Service since it's inception in 1948. They represent a mechanism for prioritising patients according to clinical priority. At 31 March 1991 there were 830 thousand people waiting for in-patient treatment in the United Kingdom, 13 per cent more than in 1981 (Table 7.33). However, between September 1990 and March 1991 there was a decrease of 11 thousand in the total number of people waiting for hospital admission. The most notable decrease was in people awaiting NHS treatment for plastic surgery where waiting list figures fell by 19 per cent.

The most relevant measure for individuals is the time they have to wait, not the size of the waiting list (Table 7.34). The financial cost of long waits for treatment is impossible to quantify. People waiting for admissions often represent a continuing cost to the health and social services; community nursing visits, prescription charges, sick pay, their General Practitioner's time might all continue while the person waits.

It is quite possible for the size of the waiting list to grow while waiting times fall as more patients are being treated. Furthermore, waiting list statistics are known to be inflated with the names of patients who no longer require treatment because, for example, they have recovered, moved to another part of the country or had an operation elsewhere. The length of time a patient is on the list depends to a large extent on the severity and urgency of their condition. If the need to treat some patients is, or becomes, urgent they are usually admitted to hospital very quickly. Half of all patients are admitted immediately, and are not put on to a waiting list. Of those admitted from waiting lists, half go into hospital within five weeks, and 80 per cent within six months.

Table 7.34 compares, for each Health Authority region, the median waiting time for various in-patient treatment during 1989-90. The median waiting time for all specialities in England was just under 5 weeks. Waiting

7.33 National Health Service hospital in-patient waiting lists[1]: by specialty

United Kingdom   Thousands

	1976	1981	1986	1990	1991
Specialty					
General surgery	200.5[2]	169.1[2]	180.3[2]	173.3	169.0
Orthopaedics	109.8	145.1	160.5	154.1	151.5
Ear, nose or throat	121.7	115.4	132.2	125.5	125.3
Gynaecology	91.8	105.6	106.6	98.7	97.8
Oral surgery	26.5	35.5	56.3	52.5	49.7
Plastic surgery	44.7	49.2	46.1	51.3	41.7
Ophthalmology	41.2	43.4	64.6	91.2	99.5
Urology	22.0[3]	29.1[3]	42.7[3]	47.3	46.7
Other	42.5	44.2	41.3	47.9	49.0
All specialties	700.8	736.6	830.6	841.2	830.1

1 At 30 September each year except 1991, at 31 March.
2 Includes the Northern Ireland figures for 'Urology'.
3 Great Britain only.

Source: Department of Health; Welsh Office;
Scottish Health Service, Common Services Agency;
Department of Health and Social Services, Northern Ireland

7.34 Median waiting time spent on National Health Service in-patient waiting lists[1]: by specialty and region, 1989-90

United Kingdom   Weeks

	General Surgery	Ortho-paedics	Ear nose and throat	Gynae-cology	Oral surgery	Plastic surgery	Ophthal-mology	Urology	All special-ties
Northern	4.3	8.0	6.3	4.1	7.8	3.4	9.6	7.3	4.3
Yorkshire	2.8	5.6	6.7	3.9	8.1	4.6	7.5	4.8	3.3
Trent	4.6	8.4	8.6	4.7	9.7	8.4	10.9	5.8	4.5
East Anglia	4.6	10.7	10.2	4.3	11.0	5.9	10.4	6.8	5.1
North West Thames	4.2	7.6	9.7	3.0	7.1	5.6	12.9	5.9	4.3
North East Thames	5.0	9.2	11.9	4.0	6.6	4.9	10.6	6.7	4.8
South East Thames	4.6	11.3	10.4	4.6	5.0	5.8	13.6	6.1	5.0
South West Thames	5.0	11.1	9.9	4.6	9.5	8.0	12.9	7.6	5.8
Wessex	5.8	12.2	8.7	6.5	6.5	9.1	19.5	6.5	7.0
Oxford	4.9	8.9	8.0	5.5	11.9	7.5	9.9	8.3	5.2
South Western	4.8	10.6	12.1	4.2	9.5	5.8	12.9	7.2	4.6
West Midlands	5.5	7.8	10.8	6.0	11.7	7.8	13.2	8.1	6.1
Mersey	5.3	6.7	9.4	5.9	8.8	6.4	10.6	7.8	5.2
North Western	4.9	7.5	12.1	6.3	6.9	4.8	9.4	6.4	5.1
Special Health Authorities	2.6	7.4	11.9	1.0	14.5	7.6	7.8	3.4	2.5
England	4.7	8.6	9.5	4.7	8.3	5.9	11.0	6.6	4.8
Scotland	4.0	7.6	8.4	4.0	7.4	7.4	9.0	5.0	4.4
Wales	6.0	11.3	8.9	5.4	. .	. .	13.0	. .[2]	5.9
Northern Ireland	4.1	4.1	9.8	5.5	11.1	6.4	24.7	17.7	6.4

1 Patients who have been treated.
2 Not separately available. Figures are included within General Surgery.

Source: Department of Health; Welsh Office; Scottish Health Service, Common Services Agency; Department of Health and Social Services, Northern Ireland

times are generally lower for gynaecological treatment, but the median was still 5 weeks. Longest median waiting times occurred for ear, nose and throat treatment (9 weeks) and ophthalmology (11 weeks). There were large regional variations in the table. The median waiting time for trauma and orthopaedics varied between 12 weeks in Wessex to 5 weeks in Yorkshire. In the West Midlands median waiting times were above the

England average in eight of the nine categories shown. Whereas in Yorkshire Health Authority waiting times were below the England average for all specialities in the table.

In England, in 1989-90 there were 59 thousand mental illness beds available in National Health Service hospitals, compared with 87 thousand in 1980. The number of mentally ill patients staying in hospital for long periods has been falling since the late 1970s.

7.35 Discharges from mental illness and mental handicap hospitals and units: stays of five or more years

Great Britain

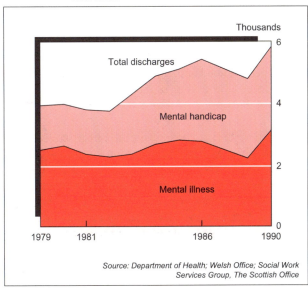

Thousands

Source: Department of Health; Welsh Office; Social Work Services Group, The Scottish Office

The majority of people with mental illness or a mental handicap have always been cared for in the community. With further improvements in health and social services, even less reliance is now placed on in-patient care of the mentally ill or handicapped, and more use is made of community care and day-patient treatment. Chart 7.35 shows the increase in the number of patients released from mental illness or mental handicap hospitals and units who had previously been resident in such units for five years or more. There has also been an associated rise in the number of community psychiatric nurses which trebled from 1,083 in 1981 to 3,380 in 1989.

7.36 Family practitioner and dental services

United Kingdom

	General medical and pharmaceutical services						General dental services	
	Number of doctors[1] in practice (thousands)	Average number of patients per doctor[1] (thousands)	Prescriptions dispensed[2] (millions)	Average total cost per prescription (£)	Average number of prescriptions per person	Average prescription cost[3] per person (£)	Number of dentists[4] in practice (thousands)	Average number of persons per dentist (thousands)
1961	23.6	2.25	233.2	0.41	4.7	1.9	11.9	4.4
1971	24.0	2.39	304.5	0.77	5.6	4.3	12.5	4.5
1981	27.5	2.15	370.0	3.46	6.6	23.0	15.2	3.7
1985	29.7	2.01	393.1	4.77	7.0	33.4	17.0	3.3
1986	30.2	1.99	397.5	5.11	7.0	36.0	17.3	3.3
1987	30.7	1.97	413.6	5.47	7.3	40.0	17.6	3.2
1988	31.2	1.94	427.7	5.91	7.5	44.1	18.0	3.2
1989	31.5	1.91	435.8	6.26	7.5	47.2	18.4	3.1
1990	31.6	1.89	446.6	6.68	7.8	52.1	18.6	3.2

1 Unrestricted principals only. See Appendix, Part 7:
  Unrestricted principals.
2 Prescriptions dispensed by general practitioners are excluded. The
  number of such prescriptions in the United Kingdom is not known

precisely, but in England during 1990 totalled some 27 million.
3 Total cost including dispensing fees and cost.
4 Principals plus assistants.

Source: Department of Health

The number of General Practitioners in the United Kingdom increased by 5 per cent between 1986 and 1990 to 31,600 - one-third more than in 1961 (Table 7.36). The average number of patients per doctor in the United Kingdom was 1,900 in 1990, a reduction of 15 per cent on the 1961 figure. The number of dentists providing general dental services increased by over a half between 1961 and 1990 while the average number of persons per dentist fell by one quarter over the same period. Nearly 447 million prescriptions were dispensed in 1990, an increase of 20 per cent since 1981. The average total cost of a prescription (as opposed to charges paid by patients) rose to £6.68 compared with £6.26 in 1989. Prescription charges rose from 20 pence per item in 1976 to £3.40 per item from 1 April 1991.

Whereas Table 7.36 shows that the number of available beds in NHS hospitals has fallen in recent years, Table 7.37 shows that the total number of beds available in private hospitals, homes and clinics registered under Section 23 of the *Registered Homes Act 1984* more than trebled between 1981 and 1989-90.

7.37 Private health services: number of beds

England — Thousands and percentages

	1971	1981	1986	1988 -89	1989 -90
NHS hospitals authorised beds for private in-patient care (thousands)	4.4	2.7	3.0	3.0	3.0
Registered private nursing homes, hospitals and clinics					
Total available beds (thousands)	25.3	33.5	62.1	94.5	113.3
Percentage of available beds in premises with an operating theatre	..	..	14.5	10.0	9.7

Source: Department of Health

Personal Social Services

The Children Act 1989, which was implemented on 14 October 1991, recasts the law on caring for, bringing up and protecting children in England and Wales. The Act has for example replaced the Place of Safety Order with the Emergency Protection Order and has simplified the legislation under which children can be looked after by local authorities.

Chart 7.38 shows trends in the numbers of children and young persons in care, admitted to care or removed to a place of safety in England and Wales. The total number of children in care has declined by one third

since 1980. Until 1985, there had generally been a reduction in the number of children admitted to care. Increases between 1985 and 1987 were followed by further falls. In 1990 there were just over 33 thousand children admitted to care. Over the period covered by the chart, children could be placed in the care of a local authority under a number of different statutes either by court order or by voluntary agreement. A child removed to a place of safety is not in care. The figures only include children where the local authority is responsible for removal to a place of safety or makes provision for the child to be accommodated.

7.38 Children in care: admissions to care and children removed to a place of safety

England, Wales and Northern Ireland

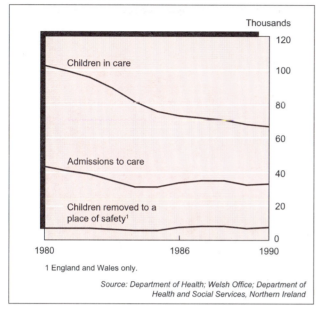

1 England and Wales only.

Source: Department of Health; Welsh Office; Department of Health and Social Services, Northern Ireland

7.39 Children in care

England, Wales and Northern Ireland

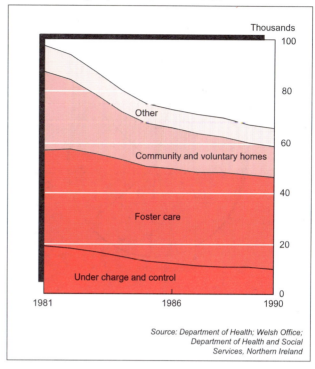

Source: Department of Health; Welsh Office; Department of Health and Social Services, Northern Ireland

Chart 7.39 shows the change in type of accommodation used for children in care. In particular, the proportion of children placed with foster parents increased from 37 per cent of all children in care in 1981 to 56 per cent in 1990.

Comprehensive statistics about the number of children on child protection registers have been collected by the Department of Health and the Welsh Office since 1989 following a pilot survey in 1988. Some of the results are given in Table 7.40 and Chart 7.41.

7.40 Children and young persons on the Child Protection Registers : by sex and age, 1990[1]

	England & Wales	Thousands and rates
	Boys	Girls
Children aged (thousands)		
Under 1	1.5	1.4
1 – 4	7.7	7.3
5 – 9	7.5	7.3
10 – 15	4.9	6.6
16 and over	0.5	1.1
All children	22.2	23.7
Children aged (rates[2])		
Under 1	4.2	4.2
1 – 4	5.7	5.6
5 – 9	4.6	4.7
10 – 15	2.7	3.8
16 and over	0.7	1.7
All children	3.8	4.2

1 At 31 March.
2 Rates per 1,000 population in each age group.

Source: Department of Health; Welsh Office

Table 7.40 shows that there were over 22 thousand boys and just under 24 thousand girls on Child Protection Registers in England and Wales at 31 March 1990 (the equivalent 1989 figures were 21 and 22 thousand respectively). These totals represented a rate of 4.2 girls per thousand population aged under 18, and 3.8 for boys.

The table also shows that younger children at least 1 year old were more likely to be on the register than children over 10 years old. The highest rates were found in the 1-4 age group for both boys and girls. Under the age of ten, boys and girls were equally likely to be on the register; from the age of ten onwards, girls were more likely to be on the register. This was especially true for girls aged 16 and over, who were more than twice as likely to be on the register as boys of the same age, largely due to the numbers of girls in this age group registered under sexual abuse.

Of the 46 thousand children on the Child Protection Registers in England and Wales at end-March 1990, two fifths were registered under the category 'grave concern' and one-quarter under 'physical abuse'. A further 13 per cent were on the registers due to neglect (Chart 7.41).

7.41 Children on child protection registers: by reason, 1990[1]

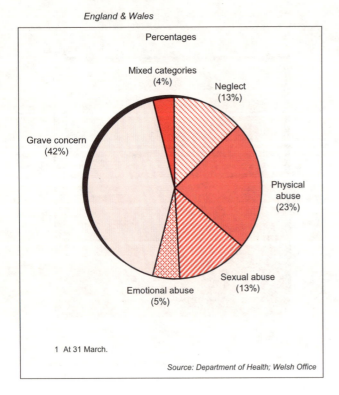

England & Wales

Percentages

Mixed categories (4%)
Neglect (13%)
Grave concern (42%)
Physical abuse (23%)
Emotional abuse (5%)
Sexual abuse (13%)

1 At 31 March.

Source: Department of Health; Welsh Office

7.42 Elderly people in residential accommodation[1]

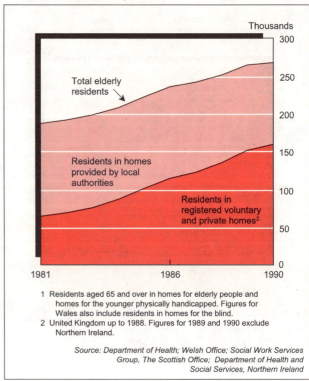

United Kingdom

Thousands

Total elderly residents

Residents in homes provided by local authorities

Residents in registered voluntary and private homes[2]

1981   1986   1990

1 Residents aged 65 and over in homes for elderly people and homes for the younger physically handicapped. Figures for Wales also include residents in homes for the blind.
2 United Kingdom up to 1988. Figures for 1989 and 1990 exclude Northern Ireland.

Source: Department of Health; Welsh Office; Social Work Services Group, The Scottish Office; Department of Health and Social Services, Northern Ireland

Under Section 21 of the *National Assistance Act 1948*, local authorities have a statutory duty to provide residential accommodation for people who by reason of age or infirmity are in need of care and attention not otherwise available. Local authorities may themselves provide the accommodation, either in their own homes or in joint user premises shared with other local authorities or district health authorities. They may also make arrangements with voluntary organisations, private homes or private individuals.

Between 1981 and 1990, there was a 13 per cent reduction in the number of elderly people resident in local authority homes while the number in private residential care homes more than doubled (Chart 7.42). Residents in homes for elderly people and for younger physically handicapped people may be financially self-supporting or supported either by the local authorities, by the State, or by charities. In 1988, a quarter of a million people aged 65 and over were resident in local authority or private homes in the United Kingdom, a rise of one third since 1981.

Health and Personal Social Services Statistics for England

1991 edition

The eighteenth in a series of annual publications in which information is presented on a wide variety of developments in NHS manpower and hospitals, family practitioner committee services, community health services and personal social services. There is a section covering the financial implications of providing these services and a supporting section on population trends.

HMSO PRICE £11.50 ISBN 0 11 321460 X

Resources

7.43 Manpower in the health and personal social services[1]

United Kingdom   Thousands

	1981	1984	1986	1987	1988	1989	1990
Regional and District Health Authorities							
Medical and dental (excluding locums)	49.7	51.4	52.4	52.0	53.7	55.0	56.1
Nursing and midwifery (excluding agency staff)	492.8	500.8	505.4	507.3	507.6	508.5	505.2
Professional and technical	80.2	89.2	93.4	96.8	98.0	99.6	103.0
Administrative and clerical	133.3	135.5	137.2	141.2	142.9	149.6	159.2
Ancillary	220.1	198.1	167.4	156.6	146.4	136.6	127.6
Other non-medical	56.2	55.4	55.3	54.4	52.4	50.8	48.4
Total health service staff	1,032.2	1,030.4	1,011.0	1,008.3	1,001.0	1,000.0	999.5
Family practitioner services	54.3	58.2	57.3	58.4	59.3	59.8	59.7
Personal social services							
Social work staff	28.4	30.1	32.2	33.4	34.6	35.4	..
Managerial, administrative and ancillary	27.7	29.1	30.4	32.0	32.9	34.6	..
Other[2]	194.8	207.1	217.7	222.7	226.3	239.4	..
Total personal social services staff	250.9	266.3	280.3	288.2	293.9	309.4	..

1 Figures for family practitioner services are numbers, all other figures
 are whole-time equivalents. See Appendix, Part 7: Manpower.
2 Includes home help service and other community support staff, day
 care, residential day care and other staff.

*Source: Department of Health; Welsh Office; Scottish Health Service,
Common Services Agency; Social Works Services Group,
The Scottish Office; Department of Health and Social
Services, Northern Ireland*

Table 7.43 analyses staffing levels in the various health and personal social services in the United Kingdom. Between 1981 and 1990 total National Health Service manpower fell by 3 per cent. There were increases in qualified staff. Medical and dental staff increased by 13 per cent and professional and technical staff by 28 per cent. At the other end of the scale, ancillary staff fell by 42 per cent as a result of Competitive Tendering mainly involving the laundry, catering and domestic areas of work.

United Kingdom figures for Local Authority personal social services staff are available to 1989. Between 1981 and 1989, staff numbers increased by 9 per cent to stand at 273 thousand. It is not possible to give a complete functional breakdown for these figures, but, during this period the number of social work staff increased by 11 per cent and managerial, administrative, and ancillary staff increased by 9 per cent.

Chart 7.44 shows expenditure per head of the population on health and personal social services during 1990-91. Not surprisingly, expenditure was highest among the very young and the very old. Within the hospital and community health service alone, expenditure per birth averaged almost £1,500. The cost of care for the elderly was highest with expenditure on those aged 75

and over averaging over £1,300 per head. For this group, personal social services expenditure also averaged over £500 per head and Family Health Service expenditure £270 per head.

7.44 Expenditure on Health and Personal Social Services per head: by age, 1990-91

England

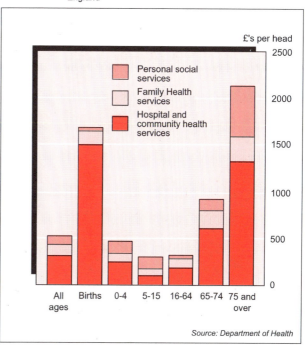

Source: Department of Health

BIBLIOGRAPHY

The following list contains selected publications relevant to Chapter 7: Health and Personal Social Services. Those published by HMSO are available from the addresses shown on the back cover of Social Trends.

Activities of Social Service Departments, Welsh Office

Annual Report of the Registrar General for Northern Ireland, HMSO

Annual Report of the Registrar General for Scotland, General Register Office (Scotland)

Cancer Statistics Registrations (Series MB1), HMSO

Children in Care in England and Wales, Department of Health

Communicable Disease Statistics (Series MB2), HMSO

Drinking in England and Wales in 1987, HMSO

Fire Statistics, United Kingdom, Home Office

General Household Survey, HMSO

Health and Personal Social Services Statistics for England, HMSO

Health and Personal Social Services Statistics for Northern Ireland, DHSS Northern Ireland

Health and Personal Social Services Statistics for Wales, Welsh Office

Health and Safety Statistics, HMSO

Health Service Costing Returns, HMSO

Hospital and Health Service Yearbook, Health and Safety Executive

Household Food Consumption and Expenditure 1989: Annual Report of the National Food Survey Committee, HMSO

Mortality Statistics for England and Wales (Series DH1, 2, 3, 4), HMSO

NHS Hospital Activity Statistics for England 1974-1989/90, Department of Health

Personal Social Services Statistics, CIPFA

Population Trends, HMSO

Regional Trends, HMSO

Residential Accommodation for the Elderly and for Younger Physically Handicapped People: All Residents, HMSO

Residential Accommodation for the Elderly and for Younger Physically Handicapped People: Local Authority Supported Residents, Department of Health

Scottish Health Service Costs, The Scottish Office

Scottish Health Statistics, Common Services Agency, Scottish Health Service

Smoking among Secondary School Children, HMSO

Social Work Services group of The Scottish Office, Statistical Bulletins

Statistics of Elective Admissions and Patients Waiting, Department of Health

Statistics of the Misuse of Drugs: Addicts Notified to the Home Office, United Kingdom, Home Office

Statistical Publications on aspects of Health and Personal Social Services activity in England, Department of Health

Survey of Children and Young Persons on Child Protection Registers, Department of Health

Chapter 8: Housing

Housing supply

●   More people own their homes. Over two-thirds of dwellings are now owner-occupied.   *(Chart 8.1)*

●   The number of new specialised homes being built for the elderly is falling - by a third between 1981 and 1990.

(Table 8.7)

Housing standards

●   The standard of houses in England has improved - between 1971 and 1986, the number of houses lacking basic amenities fell by 80 per cent.   *(Chart 8.8)*

Homelessness

●   Local authorities are increasingly having to use bed and breakfast, hostel or other temporary accommodation for homeless households. At the end of 1990, 48 thousand households were in such temporary accommodation - more than double the number in 1986.   *(Table 8.15)*

●   The Census found more than 2,700 people sleeping rough in England and Wales in April 1991 - nearly half of these were in London.   *(Page 151)*

Housing costs and expenditure

●   Repossessions because of non-payment of mortgages increased to 43 thousand in 1990, a further 36 thousand were reported in the first half of 1991.   *(Table 8.22)*

●   The cost to the Exchequer of mortgage interest tax relief has increased dramatically over the last 30 years - more than ten-fold even in real terms between 1961-62 and 1990-91.   *(Chart 8.26)*

Characteristics of occupants

●   Employers, managers and people in the professions are more likely than others to own their own homes.

(Chart 8.27)

8.1   Stock of dwellings: by tenure[1]

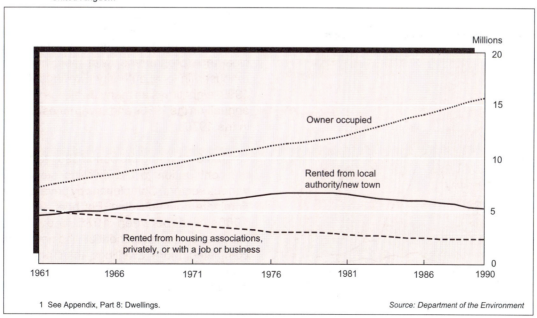

United Kingdom

Owner occupied

Rented from local authority/new town

Rented from housing associations, privately, or with a job or business

1961   1966   1971   1976   1981   1986   1990

Millions — 20, 15, 10, 5, 0

1 See Appendix, Part 8: Dwellings.

Source: Department of the Environment

Housing supply

8.2   Average annual change in dwelling stock

United Kingdom   Thousands

	1961–1970	1971–1980	1981	1983	1984	1985	1986	1987	1988	1989	1990
New construction											
Private enterprise	198	161	119	153	165	163	177	190	205	185	160
Housing associations	4	16	19	17	17	14	13	13	13	14	17
Local authorities	152	111	58	37	35	29	24	21	21	18	17
New town corporations	9	12	10	2	2	1	1	1	—	—	1
Government departments	5	2	1	—	—	—	—	1	—	1	—
Total new construction	368	302	207	209	220	208	216	225	239	218	195
Other changes											
Slum clearance	– 65	– 55	– 30	– 17	– 14	– 11	– 11	– 10	– 9	– 8	– 8
Other[1]	– 44	– 19	– 9	2	– 2	2	3	2	– 1	2	2
Total other changes	– 109	– 74	– 39	– 15	– 16	– 9	– 8	– 8	– 10	– 6	– 6
Total net gain	258	228	168	194	204	199	208	217	229	212	189

1 Comprises net gains from conversions and other causes, and losses other than by slum clearance. Excludes figures for Wales.

Source: Department of the Environment; Welsh Office; The Scottish Office; Department of the Environment, Northern Ireland

The number of dwellings in the United Kingdom totalled 23 million at December 1990, an increase of more than one-third since 1961 (Chart 8.1 on previous page). More people own their own homes; between 1961 and 1990 the number of owner occupied dwellings more than doubled to 15.7 million, while the number of dwellings rented from housing associations, rented privately or with a job or business more than halved to 2.4 million despite steady growth in the housing association stock.

The stock of local authority or new town dwellings rose by 47 per cent between 1961 and 1981 but fell back during the 1980s when almost 1.5 million such dwellings

8.3   Housebuilding completions: by sector

United Kingdom

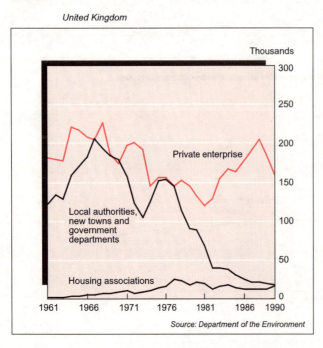

Source: Department of the Environment

were sold to occupiers in Great Britain (see Chart 8.4). Despite these sales, the total number of local authority and new town dwellings in 1990 was 5.3 million, similar to 20 years ago. The proportion of dwellings which were owner-occupied rose from 43 per cent of all dwelling stock in 1961 to 67 per cent in 1990.

Table 8.2 shows average annual changes in the stock of dwellings. The annual change fell from a net gain of 258 thousand during the 1960s to 228 thousand during the 1970s. During the first half of the 1980s the annual net gain was below 200 thousand although by 1988 it had recovered to 225 thousand. Between 1988 and 1989 the annual net gain fell back to 205 thousand, due mainly to a fall in new constructions by private enterprises.

Increases to the number of dwellings are made by building new homes and by converting existing properties. These are offset by slum clearance and other demolitions. Since the second world war about 2 million dwellings have been demolished under the slum clearance programme, with most households being rehoused in local authority dwellings. Compared with 1990, eight times as many dwellings were demolished annually in the 1960s and seven times as many annually in the 1970s.

Chart 8.3, covering the period 1961 to 1990, illustrates the contribution to the dwelling stock made by the various sectors. Completions by private enterprise now dominate housebuilding. For brief periods in the late 1960s and between 1975 and 1977, housing associations, local authorities and new towns together completed more dwellings than private enterprise. However, in the 1980s private enterprise built the majority of new houses and reached 82 per cent of all dwellings in 1990.

       Social Trends 22, © Crown copyright 1992

The *Housing Act 1980* and its Scottish equivalent gave local authority tenants and tenants of other public bodies the right to buy their own homes with discounts if they had been tenants for more than three years. This was subsequently reduced to two years by the *Housing and Building Control Act 1984*, which also increased the maximum available discount, from 50 to 60 per cent. The maximum available discount for flats was further increased in January 1987 to 70 per cent.

As a result of this legislation, almost 1.5 million local authority and new town tenants bought their homes during the 1980s. Annual sales peaked at 226 thousand in 1982, but fell to less than half this level in 1985 and 1986 (Chart 8.4). Between 1986 and 1989 sales increased in each year before again falling in 1990 when only 140 thousand dwellings were sold (nearly a third fewer than in 1989). It is expected that this fall will continue into 1991, when sales are likely to be below even the 1986 level.

The changing size (number of bedrooms) of houses built in England and Wales is illustrated in Table 8.5. Between 1976 and 1990 the trend was away from 3 bedroom dwellings which predominated in earlier years and towards both smaller and larger properties. In 1976, 58 per cent of houses and flats built for local authorities and new towns had only 1 or 2 bedrooms, by 1990 this figure had risen to 76 per cent. There was a similar trend for privately built homes. The changes in house sizes can be linked to the changing structure of households and in particular to the growth in one-person households (see Chapter 2). Many of the

8.4 Sales of dwellings owned by local authorities and new towns[1]

United Kingdom

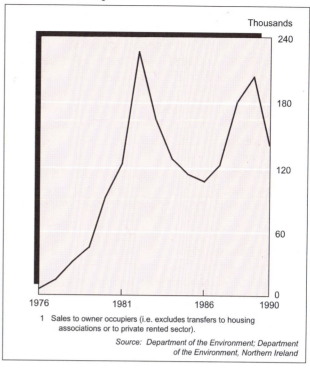

1 Sales to owner occupiers (i.e. excludes transfers to housing associations or to private rented sector).

Source: Department of the Environment; Department of the Environment, Northern Ireland

smaller homes have been built as "starter homes" for people setting up their own home for the first time.

Local authorities let their homes to tenants for a variety of reasons - including to those who have had their name on the waiting list. In England and Wales in 1989-90, 56 per cent of new local authority tenants were from ordinary waiting lists, a slight fall since 1988-89 (Table 8.6). However, the proportion housed on secure tenancies because their local authority accepted them as statutorily homeless, increased from only 16 per

8.5 Housebuilding completions: by sector and number of bedrooms

England & Wales	Percentages and numbers			
	1976	1981	1986	1990
Private enterprise				
(percentages)				
1 bedroom	*4*	*7*	*12*	*14*
2 bedrooms	*23*	*23*	*28*	*28*
3 bedrooms	*58*	*50*	*40*	*33*
4 or more bedrooms	*15*	*21*	*20*	*25*
All houses and flats				
(= 100%) (numbers)	138,477	104,001	155,204	137,792
Housing associations				
(percentages)				
1 bedroom	*44*	*58*	*60*	*43*
2 bedrooms	*34*	*28*	*28*	*36*
3 bedrooms	*21*	*12*	*10*	*17*
4 or more bedrooms	*1*	*2*	*1*	*4*
All houses and flats				
(= 100%) (numbers)	14,618	17,363	10,986	14,697
Local authorities and New				
Towns *(percentages)*				
1 bedroom	*32*	*39*	*66*	*41*
2 bedrooms	*26*	*28*	*30*	*35*
3 bedrooms	*38*	*28*	*21*	*21*
4 or more bedrooms	*4*	*5*	*2*	*3*
All houses and flats				
(= 100%) (numbers)	124,512	58,413	20,539	14,428

Source: Department of the Environment; Welsh Office

8.6 Allocation of local authority housing

England & Wales	Percentages and thousands			
	1981 −82	1986 −87	1988 −89	1989 −90
New tenants *(percentages)*				
Displaced through slum clearance, etc	*5*	*3*	*2*	*2*
Homeless[1]	*16*	*24*	*26*	*28*
Key workers and other priorities	*9*	*7*	*6*	*6*
Ordinary waiting list	*67*	*62*	*60*	*56*
On non-secure tenancies[2]	*3*	*4*	*6*	*9*
Total	*100*	*100*	*100*	*100*
Lettings (thousands)				
To new tenants	265	257	249	239
To tenants transferring or exchanging	173	194	181	168
Total	438	451	431	408

1 Households housed under the homelessness provisions of the *Housing (Homeless Persons) Act 1977* and the *Housing Act 1985*.
2 As defined in Schedule 1, *Housing Act 1985*. Non-secure tenancies in Wales are included under the other categories listed.

Source: Department of the Environment; Welsh Office

cent in 1981-82 to 26 per cent in 1988-89 and to 28 per cent in 1989-90. In addition, some homeless households are housed on non-secure tenancies meaning that in 1989-90 35 per cent of those housed on both secure and non-secure tenancies were homeless. The total number of homes let to new tenants and to existing tenants transferring or exchanging was 408 thousand in 1989-90, 30 thousand fewer than in 1981-82 and 23 thousand fewer than in 1988-89.

Completions of specialised dwellings for the elderly in England fell by a third between 1981 and 1990 (Table 8.7). Over this period, dwellings built by the private sector increased substantially but were offset by a 63 per cent decrease in the number built by local authorities and new towns. In 1990, three-quarters of all specialised dwellings built for the elderly were for sheltered housing.

Housing standards

Chart 8.8 uses the results of the 1986 English House Conditions Survey, the fifth in a quinquennial series undertaken by the Department of the Environment. The survey provided three measures of dwellings in poor condition; dwellings lacking basic amenities, unfit dwellings and dwellings in a state of serious disrepair. Basic amenities were those which qualified for a mandatory grant under the Home Improvement Grant system in place at the time of the survey. These were a kitchen sink, a bath or shower in a bathroom, a wash hand basin, each with hot and cold water supply and an indoor WC. An unfit dwelling is one which is unsuitable for human habitation as defined in section 604 of the *Housing Act 1985*. To be classified unfit, the dwelling must be so far defective in one or more of nine specified matters as to be unsuitable for occupation. The nine matters were: repair, stability, freedom from damp, internal arrangement, natural lighting, ventilation, water supply, drainage and sanitary conveniences and facilities for the preparation and cooking of food and for the disposal of waste water. There is no statutory definition of dwellings in a state of serious disrepair, for this survey these were defined as dwellings requiring repairs costing more than £7,000 at 1981 prices. Since the survey, the system of home improvement grants and the statutory definition of unfitness has been amended by the *Local Government and Housing Act 1989*.

Between 1971 and 1986 the number of dwellings lacking amenities fell by over 80 per cent. Over the same period, the number of unfit dwellings fell, although much less dramatically and the number in serious disrepair actually increased. Similar surveys of housing conditions are also done in Northern Ireland and in Wales although not always in the same year. In Northern Ireland, the number of dwellings lacking amenities fell by 77 per cent between 1974 and 1987, and the number of unfit dwellings fell by 52 per cent. In Wales, between 1973 and 1986, these falls were 77 and 46 per cent respectively.

8.7 Completions of new specialised dwellings for the elderly: by sector

England	Number of dwellings			
	1981	1986	1989	1990
Sheltered housing				
Private enterprise	130	850	3,262	1,942
Housing associations	1,929	1,916	1,099	1,858
Local authorities/New Towns	5,558	3,722	2,578	2,627
Other housing				
Private enterprise	62	193	556	304
Housing associations	261	597	339	418
Local authorities/New Towns	4,636	1,778	1,007	1,109
All dwellings for the elderly	12,576	9,056	8,841	8,258

Source: Department of the Environment

8.8 Unsatisfactory housing[1]

England

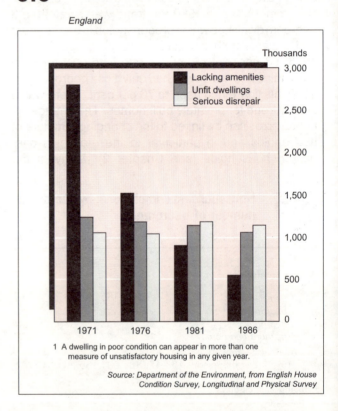

1 A dwelling in poor condition can appear in more than one measure of unsatisfactory housing in any given year.

Source: Department of the Environment, from English House Condition Survey, Longitudinal and Physical Survey

These trends in improvements in amenities can also be seen from the General Household Survey (GHS) which shows that only 1 per cent of households in Great Britain did not have access to a bath or shower by 1989-90 (Table 8.9). This compares with 9 per cent in 1971 and 2 per cent in 1981. Between 1971 and 1989-90, the proportion of households without central heating fell from 65 per cent to 22 per cent.

Bedroom standard is one measure of overcrowding derived by comparing the actual number of bedrooms with a standard number of bedrooms needed based on the number, age and sex of the people in each household

Social Trends 22, © Crown copyright 1992

8.9 Availability of amenities and prevalence of overcrowding

Great Britain		Percentages and numbers	
	1971	1981	1989 −90
Percentage with bath or shower			
Sole use	88	96	98
Shared	3	2	1
None	9	2	1
Percentage with W.C.			
Sole use inside the accommodation	85	95	98
None	1	—	—
Percentage with central heating			
Night storage heating only	8	6	7
Other central heating only	26	52	71
Both kinds	1	—	—
Neither kind	65	41	22
Percentage below bedroom standard[1]	9	5	3
Sample size (= 100%) (numbers)	11,852	11,855	9,973

1 See Appendix, Part 8: Bedroom standard.

Source: General Household Survey

8.10 Rooms per person: by ethnic group of head of household, 1988

England			Percentages and thousands	
	Under 1	1 to 2	Over 2	All house-holds (=100%) (thou-sands)
Ethnic group of head of household				
White	1	49	50	17,830
Non-white of which:	10	65	26	740
Indian	9	69	21	210
Pakistani/Bangladeshi	33	60	8	100
West Indian	3	62	35	190
Other or mixed	5	65	30	240
Not stated	—	51	50	80
All ethnic groups	1	49	49	18,660

Source: Department of the Environment, from the Labour Force Survey Housing Trailer

(see Appendix: Part 8). The percentage of households with fewer bedrooms than the standard is shown in Table 8.9. Overcrowding is becoming less of a problem. Between 1971 and 1989-90 the percentage of households below this bedroom standard fell from 9 per cent to only 3 per cent.

Table 8.10 shows some striking differences in room occupancy by ethnic group of head of household in England. Across all groups, nearly half of all households enjoyed the space of two or more rooms per person in 1988. At the other end of the scale, only 1 per cent of all households were so crowded that they had less than one room per person. However, 10 per cent of households with a non-white head were so crowded that they had less than one room per person. The differences were even more pronounced for households with a head from the Pakistani or Bangladeshi ethnic groups. About one third of all such households had less than one room per person.

Renovation grants are one way of promoting improvements in housing standards. Chart 8.11 shows those renovation grants paid to private owners and tenants under the *Housing Act 1985*. This system of grants was replaced by a new system of mandatory and discretionary grants under the *Local Government and Housing Act 1989* which came into operation in England and Wales during 1990. Although no more grants were approved under the earlier *Housing Act 1985* after June 1990, payments continued after this date for grants which have already been approved.

Under the new system grants take one of five forms: minor works assistance grants, renovation grants, houses in multiple occupation grants, common part grants, and disabled facilities grants. More details

about the new scheme can be found in a free booklet entitled *House Renovation Grants* produced by the Department of the Environment in June 1990.

In 1990, 137 thousand grants were paid to private owners and tenants in Great Britain for renovations, over 8 thousand fewer than in 1989. The high number of grants paid in 1984 reflected temporary measures which made intermediate and repairs grants available at an increased maximum rate of 90 per cent for applications approved by local authorities after 12 April 1982 or submitted to them before 1 April 1984.

8.11 Renovation grants paid to private owners and tenants[1]

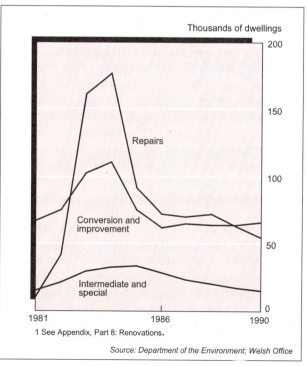

Great Britain

1 See Appendix, Part 8: Renovations.

Source: Department of the Environment; Welsh Office

Homelessness

8.12 Homeless households found accommodation by local authorities: by priority need category[1]

Great Britain	Percentages and thousands		
	1986	1989	1990
Priority need category *(percentages)*			
Household with dependent children	65	67	65
Household member pregnant	13	13	13
Household member vulnerable			
because of:			
Old age	7	6	5
Physical handicap	3	3	3
Mental illness	2	2	3
Other reasons	6	7	7
Homeless in emergency	3	2	3
All categories[2]			
(= 100%) (thousands)	112.0	134.5	155.7
In addition, number			
accommodated who were not in			
priority need (thousands)	10.2	13.2	13.8

1 Households for whom local authorities accepted responsibility to secure accommodation under the *Housing Act 1985* which defines 'priority need'. Data for Wales include some households given advice and assistance only.
2 Includes actions where priority need category is not known.

Source: Department of the Environment; Welsh Office; The Scottish Office

Local authorities (that is London boroughs and district councils in England, Wales and Scotland) have the primary responsibility for dealing with homeless people. Under legislation (Part III of the *Housing Act 1985* and the Scottish equivalent) they are required to help homeless people in defined categories of "priority need" - essentially these are: families with young children, women expecting babies, and those vulnerable through old age, physical disability, mental handicap or illness. They may also help others not in one of these priority need categories, either by securing accommodation or by providing advice and assistance to help them find accommodation themselves.

A council's first responsibility is to satisfy themselves that the applicant is homeless or threatened with homelessness. Once satisfied the council must determine whether the applicant has a priority need. If this is the case, the council have some responsibility to provide accommodation. The legislation does not require councils to provide local authority homes, as it allows them to make arrangements for the homeless to be housed by a housing association or to help them find a private sector tenancy.

In 1990, local authorities in Great Britain accepted responsibility, under the homelessness legislation, to secure accommodation for 170 thousand households. This was an increase of 15 per cent on 1989 (Table 8.12). Of these, 156 thousand were in a priority need category, two-thirds of these households contained dependent children.

8.13 Homeless households[1] found accommodation by local authorities': by reason[2] for homelessness, 1981 and 1990

Great Britain

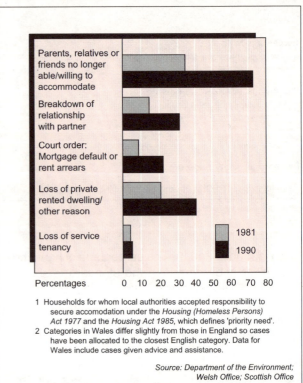

1 Households for whom local authorities accepted responsibility to secure accomodation under the *Housing (Homeless Persons) Act 1977* and the *Housing Act 1985*, which defines 'priority need'.
2 Categories in Wales differ slightly from those in England so cases have been allocated to the closest English category. Data for Wales include cases given advice and assistance.

Source: Department of the Environment; Welsh Office; Scottish Office

Chart 8.13 shows the main reasons for statutory homelessness in Great Britain for 1981 and 1990. In both years, the most frequent reason was that parents, friends or relatives were no longer able or willing to accommodate them. In 1990, this reason accounted for 42 per cent of all cases - about the same as in 1981. Between 1981 and 1990, statutory homelessness as a result of a court order following mortgage default or rent arrears increased by 2.5 times.

8.14 Local authority enquiries under the homelessness legislation: by outcome

Great Britain	Thousands		
	1986	1989	1990
Households applying as homeless			
Accepted — in priority need[1]	112	135	156[2]
— not in priority need	10	13	14
Given advice and assistance only	59	65	85
Found not to be homeless	68	71	83
Total enquiries	249	284	338[2]

1 Households for whom local authorities accepted responsibility to secure accommodation under the homelessness provisions of the *Housing Act 1985*.
2 Includes an estimate of 2,000 households made homeless in Colwyn as a result of the major flooding incident in February 1990.

Source: Department of the Environment; Welsh Office; The Scottish Office

Social Trends 22, © Crown copyright 1992

In addition to the 170 thousand households accepted as homeless (or threatened with homelessness), 85 thousand households outside the priority need categories were given advice and assistance in 1990 - 20 thousand more than in 1989 (Table 8.14). In addition, and following enquiries, a further 83 thousand households who had applied to local authorities were found not to be homeless.

If necessary, local authorities have to provide temporary accommodation (in a hostel, bed and breakfast hotel or a house not suitable for a long-term tenancy) while the case is being assessed and until long-term accommodation can be arranged. At the end of 1990, 48 thousand households in Great Britain who had applied to local authorities as homeless were in temporary accommodation provided by the authority - 8 thousand more than in 1989 but more than double the number in 1986 (Table 8.15). In England alone in 1989-90, total expenditure by local authorities on bed and breakfast accommodation was £147 million. At the end of 1990, about 60 per cent of households in temporary accommodation were in London.

8.15 Homeless households in temporary accommodation[1,2]: by type of accommodation

Great Britain			Thousands
	1986	1989	1990
Bed and breakfast	9	12	12
Hostels, including women's refuges	5	9	10
Short life tenancies and other accommodation	8	20	27
Total in temporary accommodation	23	40	48

1 At end of year.
2 Includes households awaiting outcome of homelessness enquiries.
Source: Department of the Environment; Welsh Office; The Scottish Office

For the first time ever, the 1991 Census of Population counted the number of people sleeping rough on Census day (21 April 1991). The count was designed to cover those people sleeping rough in the open air rather than those in shelters, hostels, or squats. Local authorities, voluntary groups and churches were enlisted to help with the count and to identify possible locations. Overall, more than 2,700 people were counted as sleeping rough in England and Wales on Census night and nearly half of those were in London.

Housing costs and expenditure

The retail prices index (RPI), the most widely used measure of price change, is made up of a large number of component parts, some of which relate to housing.

Charts 8.16 and 8.17 compare the change in housing prices with other selected components of the RPI and look at some of the individual parts of the housing

8.16 Housing and other selected components of the Retail Price Index

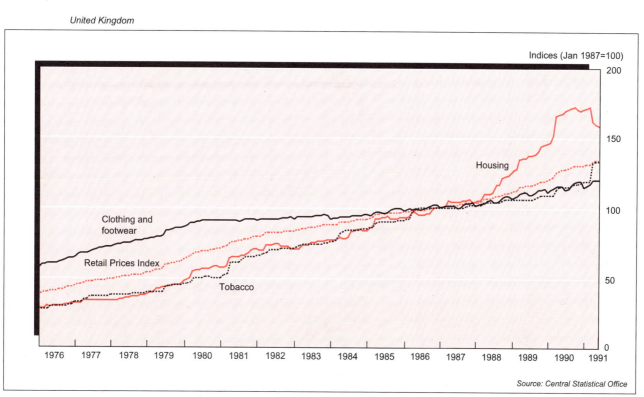

United Kingdom

Indices (Jan 1987=100)

Source: Central Statistical Office

8.17 Selected components of the housing group Retail Prices Index

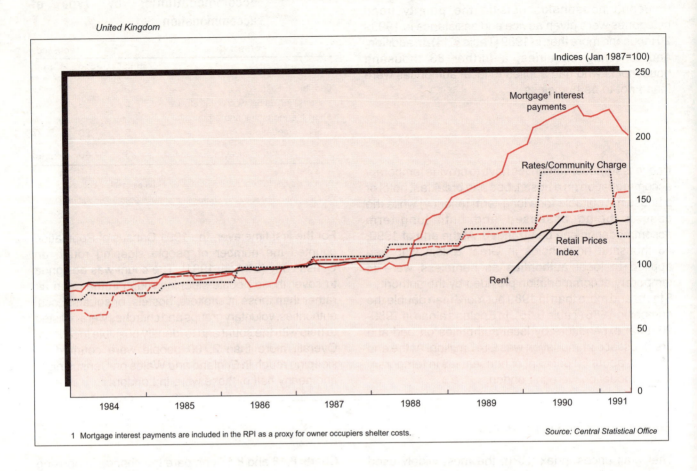

United Kingdom

Indices (Jan 1987=100)

1 Mortgage interest payments are included in the RPI as a proxy for owner occupiers shelter costs.

Source: Central Statistical Office

index. Chart 8.16 compares price changes for the housing group of items in the RPI and with those for two other RPI groups - clothing and footwear and tobacco.

These groups are included not because of any links with housing but because they give a simple indication of how housing prices have moved in comparison with

8.18 Building societies' mortgage interest rates

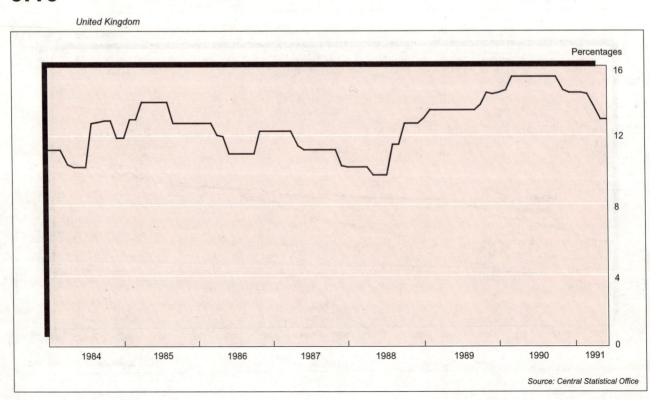

United Kingdom

Percentages

Source: Central Statistical Office

Social Trends 22, © Crown copyright 1992

8.19 Mortgage and rent payments[1]: by tenure, 1989

United Kingdom   Percentages and numbers

| | Payments (£ per annum) | | | | | | | | | Sample size |
	Under £250	£250 −£499	£500 −£749	£750 −£999	£1,000 −£1,499	£1,500 −£1,999	£2,000 −£2,499	£2,500 −£2,999	£3,000 and over	(=100%) (numbers)
Tenure of household										
Owner occupied										
Buying with a mortgage	2	4	6	8	15	15	12	9	29	3,013
Rented										
Local authority/new town	35	10	7	9	20	16	3	1	—	1,833
Housing association	33	8	9	15	25	9	1	—	—	161
Privately, furnished	13	3	8	7	23	11	8	5	23	226
Privately, unfurnished	26	7	12	12	24	10	3	3	3	250

1 Rent payments are gross rent less any rent rebate (Housing benefit) received. Rent payments include rates and/or service charges where these were given as part of the rent figure and they could not be deducted (usually where the tenant only pays a combined amount).

Source: Family Expenditure Survey, Central Statistical Office

other prices in the RPI. Between 1976 and June 1991, the housing group index increased more than five-fold - much more than the all-items index which increased three-fold.

Chart 8.17 shows three components of the housing group index: mortgage interest payments, rates/community charge and rent. On the advice of the Retail Prices Index Advisory Committee, the RPI has included the community charge in place of local authority domestic rates since the introduction of the charge.

Between 1986 and June 1991, the all items index rose by 37 per cent. Over the same period the rent index rose by 60 per cent and the rates/community charge index rose by 24 per cent. The rates/community charge index rose sharply between March and April 1990 when the community charge replaced rates in England and Wales. However, it dropped back again in April 1991 to a level below that of March 1990 when the Government reduced the proportion of local authority receipts which have to be raised through the community charge in favour of more central funding.

The index of mortgage interest payments increased by 122 per cent between 1986 and June 1991 reflecting both higher mortgage interest rates and larger mortgage balances. The index of mortgage interest payments rose in every month between May 1988 and October 1990 and has fallen back since. In the more recent period between June 1990 and June 1991, the mortgage interest payments index fell by 6 per cent.

Chart 8.18 shows how building society mortgage interest rates changed between February 1984 and June 1991. The lowest rate in this period was 9.8 per cent between May and July 1988 although by May the following year the mortgage rate had risen to 13.5 per cent. The highest rate was 15.4 per cent between March and October 1990. The increases in interest rates during late-1988, 1989 and early-1990 resulted in a declining demand for mortgages and in a number of borrowers experiencing difficulty in repaying their loans.

Table 8.19 uses the 1989 Family Expenditure Survey to look at annual mortgage and rent payments for different tenure types. These figures show that those buying a property with a mortgage and those renting a private furnished property have much higher annual payments compared to the other categories. Only 6 per cent of households buying with a mortgage had low annual payments of £500 or less compared with 45 per cent of households renting from a local authority or new town. At the other end of the scale, 29 per cent of households buying with a mortgage had annual payments of at least £3,000 compared with less than 1 per cent of households renting from a local authority, new town or housing association.

8.20 Dwelling price[1]: by region, 1991[2]

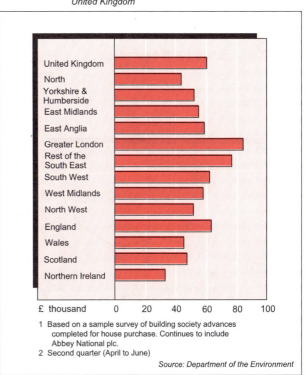

United Kingdom

1 Based on a sample survey of building society advances completed for house purchase. Continues to include Abbey National plc.
2 Second quarter (April to June)

Source: Department of the Environment

8.21 Dwelling price indices[1,2]

Indices (1985=100)

	1981	1985	1989	1990	1991[3]
United Kingdom	73	100	202	199	195
North	79	100	170	193	193
Yorkshire &					
Humberside	78	100	194	211	222
East Midlands	74	100	207	207	200
East Anglia	72	100	221	197	186
Greater London	66	100	203	199	191
Rest of South East	70	100	216	198	186
South West	74	100	219	198	188
West Midlands	81	100	219	223	224
North West	80	100	184	212	215
England	73	100	207	203	198
Wales	77	100	193	201	187
Scotland	74	100	144	161	170
Northern Ireland	81	100	124	131	134

1 Based on a sample survey of building societies advances completed for house purchase. Continues to include Abbey National plc from quarter 3 1989.
2 Indices have been adjusted to take account of changes in the mix of dwellings being bought with building societies mortgages. They also exclude those dwellings bought at non-market prices.
3 Second quarter (April to June).

Source: Department of the Environment

8.22 Mortgage lenders[1]: number of mortgages, arrears and possessions

United Kingdom — Thousands

	Number of mortgages	Loans in arrears at end-period		Properties taken into possession in period
		By 6–12 months	By over 12 months	
1981	6,336	21.5	. .	4.9
1982	6,518	27.4	5.5	6.9
1983	6,846	29.4	7.5	8.4
1984	7,313	48.3	9.5	12.4
1985	7,717	57.1	13.1	19.3
1986	8,138	52.1	13.0	24.1
1987	8,283	55.5	15.0	26.4
1988	8,564	42.8	10.3	18.5
1989	9,125	66.8	13.8	15.8
1990	9,415	123.1	36.1	43.9
1991[1]	9,628	162.2	59.7	36.6

1 Council of Mortgage Lenders estimates as at 31 December in each year except 1991, 30 June. Estimates only cover members of the Council, these account for 90 per cent of all mortgages outstanding.

Source: Council of Mortgage Lenders

In the second quarter of 1991, the average dwelling price in the United Kingdom was £61 thousand although between the regions average prices ranged from £33 thousand in Northern Ireland to £85 thousand in Greater London. Greater London, the rest of the South East and the South West were the only three regions where average prices were higher than the United Kingdom average (Chart 8.20).

Table 8.21 shows indices of dwelling prices in the United Kingdom with 1985 as the base year. These indices take account of the fact that different types of dwellings were bought in different areas in different years. Between 1981 and 1990, the South East had the

8.23 Repossession of properties: warrants issued and executed

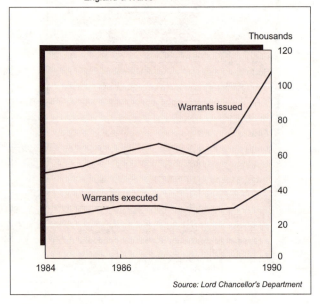

England & Wales

Source: Lord Chancellor's Department

largest rise in average dwelling prices. However, in the first six months of 1991, the average price in some regions (including the South East) fell back - in only Yorkshire and Humberside, the West Midlands, the North West, Scotland, and Northern Ireland did average prices increase.

The number of mortgage repossessions in the United Kingdom nearly trebled between 1989 and 1990 to 43.9 thousand (Table 8.22) and the indication is that the 1991 figure will be even higher. In the first half of 1991, there were 36.6 thousand repossessions compared with only 16.6 thousand in the same period of 1990. The number of mortgage loans in arrears followed the same pattern as repossessions. By the end of June 1991, there were 222 thousand loans in arrears by at least six months compared with 159 thousand at the end of December 1990 and only 81 thousand at the end of December 1989.

Chart 8.23 details the number of warrants issued by the courts in England and Wales for the repossession of residential premises and the number of these warrants actually executed. In 1990, 107 thousand warrants were issued (47 per cent more than in 1989) and 42 thousand warrants were executed - including some which will have been issued in previous years.

Housing benefit is the main source of assistance with housing costs and can be received in the form of rent rebates or allowances. Rate rebates were also paid under the housing benefit scheme until April 1989 in Scotland, and April 1990 in England and Wales, when domestic rates were replaced by the community charge. The housing benefit scheme underwent a major structural reform in April 1988, five years after its introduction. Between 1987-88 and 1988-89 there was

8.24 Recipients of housing benefit[1] and community charge benefit: by type of benefit[2] and tenure

Great Britain   Thousands and percentages

	1987–88		1988–89		1989–90[6]		1990–91	
	Certific-ated[3]	Standard[4]	Certific-ated[3]	Standard[4]	Income support[3]	Non-income support[4]	Income support[3]	Non-income support[4]
Rent rebate and allowance								
Rent rebate and allowance (thousands)	2,690	2,140	2,390	1,600	2,330	1,580	2,300	1,650
Of which pensioners[5] (percentages)	35	65	45	70	40	70	40	65
Rate rebate								
All households (= 100%) (thousands)	3,430	3,420	2,980	2,130	2,540	1,800	.	.
Of which pensioners[5] (percentages)	40	70	45	75	45	80		
Community charge rebate								
Community charge rebate (thousands)	.	.	.	.	440	440	3,280	3,450
Of which pensioners[5] (percentages)	.	.	.	.	. .	. .	45	70

1 Housing benefit and community charge benefit are payable to those responsible for paying rent and rates and community charge respectively. See Appendix Part 8: Housing benefit and community charge benefit.
2 There is some overlap, most households receiving rent assistance will also be in receipt of a rate rebate or a community charge rebate.
3 Recipients of housing benefit (and from April 1990, community charge benefit) who are themselves, or whose partners are, in receipt of supplementary benefit/income support.

4 Recipients of housing benefit (and from April 1990, community charge benefit) who are not in receipt of supplementary benefit/income support.
5 From April 1988 persons are given pensioner status if they or their partners are aged 60 and over.
6 Rate rebate data for 1989–90 are for England and Wales only while community charge rebate data are for Scotland only. The CCB figures for 1990–91 understate the position for the year due to initial backlogs in the processing of CCB claims.

Source: Department of Social Security

a fall in the number of householders receiving benefit, reflecting one of the main aims of these reforms to concentrate help on those most in need. There was also a fall in unemployment which further reduced the numbers receiving housing benefit. In 1990-91, over half of all households receiving housing benefit were pensioner households (Table 8.24). Tax relief is available on a loan to purchase a property in the United Kingdom, providing that the house is used as the borrower's main residence. In 1990-91, tax relief was available on the interest paid on the first £30,000 of a mortgage loan. In that year, 9.4 million single people and married couples benefited from a total of £7.7 billion in mortgage interest tax relief (Table 8.25). The average value of relief per mortgage was £820, although it increased with income.

8.25 Mortgage interest tax relief: by income range, 1990–91

United Kingdom

	Numbers[1] receiving mortgage interest tax relief (thousands)	Average value of relief per mortgage (£ per annum)	Total cost of relief (£ million)
Annual income[2]			
Under £5,000	490	550	270
£5,000 but under £10,000	1,050	610	640
£10,000 but under £15,000	2,060	740	1,520
£15,000 but under £20,000	2,110	800	1,670
£20,000 but under £25,000	1,530	810	1,240
£25,000 but under £30,000	850	880	750
£30,000 but under £40,000	710	1,090	770
£40,000 and over	600	1,400	840
All ranges	9,400	820	7,700

1 Single people and married couples
2 Excludes non-taxable income such as certain social security benefits.

Source: Inland Revenue

Chart 8.26 shows, in real terms, the estimated cost of this mortgage interest relief between 1961-62 and 1990-91. Over the period, the real cost of mortgage interest relief increased more than ten-fold from £740 million to £7,700 million. There was a steady increase over most of the period although there were reductions in the real cost during the late 1970s, in the early 1980s, and again in the second half of the 1980s. Between 1981-82 and 1990-91, the real cost of relief nearly doubled from £3.9 billion to £7.7 billion. In 1991-92, the cost of mortgage interest relief is likely to fall, following the restriction of relief to the basic rate of income tax and reductions in interest rates. It should be noted that changes in the cost of mortgage interest relief reflect changes in many factors including the number of mortgagors, interest rates, mortgage balances and tax rates.

8.26 Total cost of mortgage interest tax relief[1]

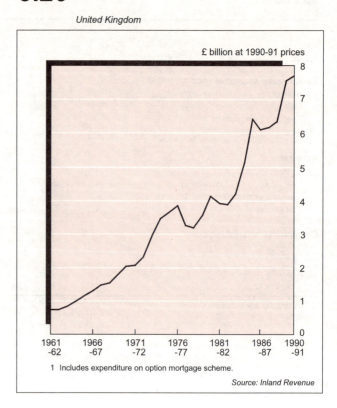

United Kingdom

£ billion at 1990-91 prices

1 Includes expenditure on option mortgage scheme.

Source: Inland Revenue

Characteristics of occupants

8.27 Tenure: by socio-economic group of head of household, 1989-90

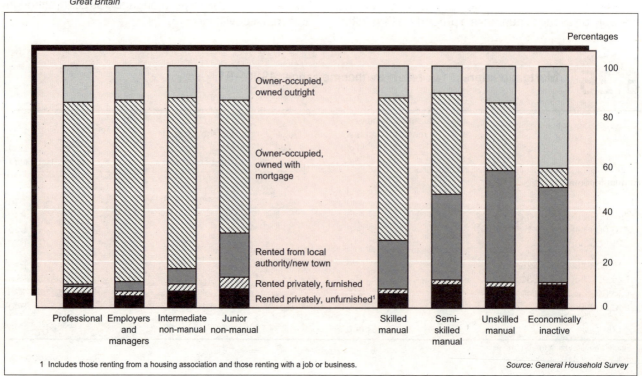

Great Britain

Percentages

- Owner-occupied, owned outright
- Owner-occupied, owned with mortgage
- Rented from local authority/new town
- Rented privately, furnished
- Rented privately, unfurnished[1]

Professional | Employers and managers | Intermediate non-manual | Junior non-manual | Skilled manual | Semi-skilled manual | Unskilled manual | Economically inactive

1 Includes those renting from a housing association and those renting with a job or business.

Source: General Household Survey

8.28 Tenure: by ethnic group of head of household, 1987–1989-90[1]

Great Britain   Percentages and numbers

| Ethnic group of head of household | Owner occupied | | Rented | | Sample size (= 100%) (numbers) |
	Owned outright	With mortgage	Local authority/ new town	Privately[2]	
White	24	40	25	10	29,454
Non-white, of which:					
Indian	16	68	8	9	277
Pakistani/Bangladeshi	18	49	17	17	136
West Indian	5	42	42	11	274
Other or mixed	8	41	21	30	377
All ethnic groups[3]	24	40	25	11	30,594

1 Combined date for 1987, 1988-89, and 1989-90.
2 Includes those renting from a housing association and those renting with a job or business.

3 Total includes those who gave no answer to the ethnic group question.

Source: General Household Survey

Chart 8.27 shows that, in 1989-90, households headed by professionals and employers and managers were the most likely to own their own home or to be buying with a mortgage, whilst households headed by unskilled manual workers were the most likely to rent their accommodation (57 per cent). Just under half of households headed by unskilled manual workers were renting from local authorities and new towns in 1989-90. Over the period 1987-1989, higher proportions of households headed by those from the West Indian ethnic group rented from a local authority or new town than in any other ethnic group. They were five times more likely to rent such accommodation than their Indian counterparts (Table 8.28).

BIBLIOGRAPHY

The following list contains selected publications relevant to Chapter 8: Housing. Those published by HMSO are available from the addresses shown on the back cover of Social Trends.

English House Condition Survey, 1986, HMSO
General Household Survey, HMSO
Housebuilding in England by Local Authority Areas, HMSO
Housing and Construction Statistics (Great Britain), annual and quarterly, HMSO
Housing Finance, Council of Mortgage Lenders
Inland Revenue Statistics, HMSO
Labour Force Survey Housing Trailer, HMSO
Local Housing Statistics: England and Wales, HMSO

Northern Ireland Housing Statistics, HMSO
Regional Trends, HMSO
Rent Officer Statistics, Department of the Environment
Scottish Development Department Statistical Bulletins on Housing, The Scottish Office
Social Security Statistics, HMSO
Welsh House Condition Survey, 1986, Welsh Office
Welsh Housing and Dwelling Survey, Welsh Office
Welsh Housing Statistics, Welsh Office
1988 Private Renters Survey, HMSO

HMSO Publications

Housing and Construction Statistics Annual

Most of the tables in this reference book on housing and construction topics show how things have changed over the last eleven years; others give detailed analyses for the latest year. The quantity and type of housing built each year and the size of stock, improvements and energy conservation, slum clearance, rents rebate, house prices and mortgage payments can all be derived from this publication. It also contains figures on the volume and type of construction work and new orders in Great Britain, the labour, and the use of materials. Detailed analyses of the activities of private contractors and local authorities direct labour departments are given for recent years.

Housing and Construction Statistics - Quarterly

Produced in two parts each quarter designed to supplement the annual volume by making the latest figures available as quickly as possible.

Local Housing Statistics - Quarterly

This publication gives regular statistics on the progress of housebuilding, house renovations and council house sales in individual local authorities in England and Wales. Statistics on homeless households, slum clearance and homes specially designed for the chronically sick and disabled are included as they become available.

Digest of Environmental Protection and Water Statistics - Annual

This Digest provides information on the main trends in environmental protection. Its explanatory text and commentary highlights the trends, gives information on some of the factors likely to influence them and, where appropriate, links series together. It has sections on air quality, water quality, radioactivity, noise, blood lead concentrations, solid wastes, landscapes and nature conservation. A separate section updates the series on water supply and use.

Local Government Financial Statistics - Annual

This publication presents details of local authority expenditure on income during the last financial year. The main figures relate to local authorities in England, but summary figures are also shown separately for the various types of authority (counties and districts, metropolitan and non-metropolitan) in both England and Wales. Further tables set the total of local authority expenditure in the context of the whole of the national economy, and relate present levels of expenditure with those recorded in earlier years.

Government Statistical Service
Further information can be obtained from:
Department of the Environment
Room P1/OO1, 2 Marsham Street
LONDON SW1P 3EB
071-276 4003

Chapter 9: Environment

Attitudes to the environment
●   Many people are prepared to do their bit for the environment. For example over two thirds of people claim to be already using ozone friendly aerosols. *(Chart 9.3)*

Air - global issues
●   Carbon dioxide, which is the most damaging greenhouse gas, comes mainly from power generation and industry - one third of all emissions in 1989 came from power stations and a further quarter from industry. *(Table 9.5)*

Air - national/local issues
●   Despite increases in the sales of unleaded petrol and the increasing awareness of environmental issues, more car owners (58 per cent) still use leaded petrol or diesel than use unleaded (39 per cent). *(Chart 9.12)*

Water
●   Water is a precious resource. It takes 30 thousand litres of water to build a car and 8 pints to brew a pint of beer. Average domestic consumption is around 136 litres per person per day. *(Page 166)*

Waste
●   More and more recycled glass is being used - the amount recycled doubled between 1984 and 1989. The number of bottle banks increased ten-fold between 1980 and 1989. *(Table 9.23)*

Noise
●   During the mid 1980s, one third of all domestic noise complaints were about loud music and a further third were about barking dogs. *(Chart 9.27)*

Nature conservation
●   Many of our native species are rare or endangered. Three of our 43 species of dragonfly have become extinct since 1953 and a further 12 are vulnerable or declining. *(Table 9.32)*

9.1   Air pollution: emissions of black smoke, sulphur dioxide and nitrogen oxides[1]

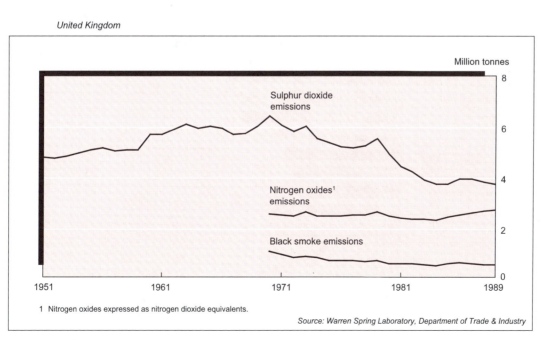

United Kingdom

Million tonnes

Sulphur dioxide emissions

Nitrogen oxides[1] emissions

Black smoke emissions

1951   1961   1971   1981   1989

1 Nitrogen oxides expressed as nitrogen dioxide equivalents.

Source: Warren Spring Laboratory, Department of Trade & Industry

Attitudes to the environment

Over recent years there has been growing concern about environmental problems. Opinion surveys carried out by the Department of the Environment showed that in 1989 about a third of respondents said, without being prompted, that the environment and pollution were among the most important issues with which the government should deal. This was a much greater proportion than three years earlier. Chart 9.2 illustrates the results of EC surveys in 1986 and 1988 on environmental problems and shows that there has been a general increase in the level of concern on most issues. The issues can generally be grouped into local and global problems. People expressed much more concern about national and world issues than about local issues. Damage to the landscape was the cause of greatest concern at local level, with damage to sea life and disposal of industrial waste causing the most concern in global terms. Many people recognise that, given the concerns about the environment, it is possible to change their personal behaviour by (for example) conserving energy or purchasing environmentally friendly goods. Chart 9.3 shows public attitudes to some of these personal actions that help the environment. The figures, which are based on a Department of the Environment survey in 1989, show that the most popular action to help the environment was to use ozone friendly aerosols - almost two-thirds of those asked said they already used them and a further quarter said they would consider using them. Of the other personal actions, four in ten people said that they took used bottles to a bottle bank and a large proportion of the remainder said that they would consider doing so.

9.2 EC public opinion on environmental concerns

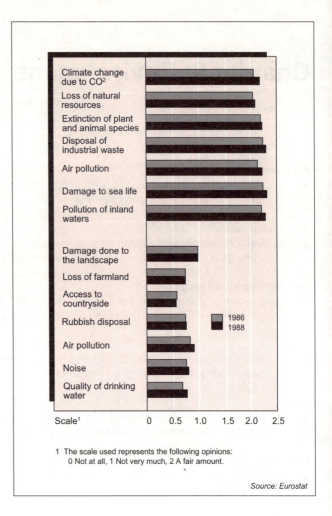

Scale[1]

1 The scale used represents the following opinions:
0 Not at all, 1 Not very much, 2 A fair amount.

Source: Eurostat

9.3 Public attitudes to personal actions to improve the environment, 1989

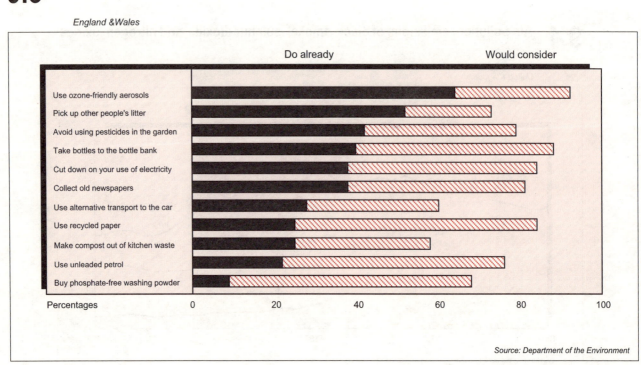

Social Trends 22, © Crown copyright 1992

The consistent growth in membership of voluntary environmental organisations reflects this growing awareness of the environment. The National Trust with just over 2 million members was the largest environmental organisation in 1990 (Table 9.4) and between 1981 and 1990 membership almost doubled.

Membership of Friends of the Earth also showed a remarkable growth with an increase of 92 thousand members between 1981 and 1990 to reach 110 thousand. Young people are also becoming more environmentally aware; membership of the Royal Society for the Protection of Birds included 116 thousand children. Echoing the growing concern over global issues membership of the Royal Society for Nature Conservation (RSNC The Wildlife Trusts Partnership) increased substantially between 1971 and 1990 to stand at 250 thousand members.

On 25 September 1990 the Government published the White Paper *This Common Inheritance, Britain's Environmental Strategy* - Britain's first comprehensive survey of all aspects of environmental concern. It describes what the Government has done and proposes to do. It covers general principles and objectives and the Government's approach to the environmental problems facing Britain, Europe and the World. The White Paper reviews policies and identifies steps that businesses, local government, schools, voluntary bodies and individuals can take to improve the environment for the future.

9.4 Membership of selected voluntary environmental organisations

Great Britain			Thousands
	1971	1981	1990
Civic Trust[1]	214	. .	293[4]
Conservation Trust[2]	6	5	3
Council for the Protection of Rural England	21	29	40[4]
Friends of the Earth[3]	1	18	110
National Trust	278	1,046	2,032
National Trust for Scotland	37	110	218
Ramblers Association	22	37	81
Royal Society for Nature Conservation	64	143	250
Royal Society for the Protection of Birds	98	441	844
Woodland Trust	. .	20	66
World Wide Fund for Nature	12	60	247[5]

1 Members of local amenity societies registered with the Civic Trust.
2 In 1987 the Conservation Society was absorbed by the Conservation Trust.
3 England and Wales only. Friends of the Earth (Scotland) is a separate organisation founded in 1978.
4 Data are for 1989.
5 Excludes an additional 1 million 'other' supporters and donors, ie non-members.

Source: Organisations concerned

Air - global issues

9.5 Emissions of selected gases and smoke: by emission source, 1989

United Kingdom							Percentages and million tonnes
	Carbon monoxide (CO)	Sulphur dioxide (SO$_2$)	Black smoke	Nitrogen oxides (NO$_x$)[1]	Methane (CH$_4$)	Carbon dioxide (CO$_2$)	Volatile organic compounds
Percentage from each emission source							
Domestic[2]	5	4	37	3	3	14	2
Commercial/public service[3]	—	2	1	2	—	5	—
Power stations	1	71	5	29	—	33	1
Refineries	—	3	—	1	—	3	2
Agriculture	—	—	—	—	—	—	—
Other industry	5	16	17	10	—	23	—
Railways	—	—	—	1	—	—	—
Road transport	88	2	39	48	—	19	37
Civil aircraft	—	—	—	1	—	—	—
Shipping	—	2	1	5	—	1	1
Deep mined coal	—	—	—	—	27	—	—
Open cast coal	—	—	—	—	—	—	—
Oil and gas venting	—	—	—	—	5	—	—
Gas leakage[4]	—	—	—	—	10	—	2
Landfill	—	—	—	—	21	—	—
Cattle	—	—	—	—	23	—	—
Sheep	—	—	—	—	10	—	—
Other animals[5]	—	—	—	—	1	—	—
Processes and solvents	—	—	—	—	—	—	51
Other emission sources	—	—	—	—	—	—	4
All emission sources (= 100%) (Million tonnes)	6.55	3.69	0.51	2.69	3.45	157	2.06

1 Expressed as nitrogen dioxide equivalent.
2 Includes Sewage sludge disposal.
3 Includes miscellaneous emission sources.
4 Gas leakage is an estimate of losses during transmission along the distribution system.
5 Pigs, poultry, horses, humans.

Source: Warren Spring Laboratory; Department of Trade and Industry

Air pollution comes from a wide variety of man-made and natural sources. Information is therefore required on the source of emissions, the amounts emitted and the damage caused. Air pollution is measured by a network of monitoring sites, most of which are managed by Warren Spring Laboratory, the government's environmental technology agency which provides impartial and independent information on environmental pollution. The number and location of monitoring sites is reviewed periodically to ensure that they provide a representative coverage of the whole of the United Kingdom. Table 9.5 gives a summary of major United Kingdom air pollutants and where they come from. Carbon dioxide comes mainly from industry. The three major sources of methane were deep-mined coal (27 per cent), cattle (23 per cent) and landfill, a method of waste disposal, (21 per cent). The table illustrates the wide variety of sources of air pollutants.

9.6 Relative contribution[1] to the greenhouse effect of the various gases

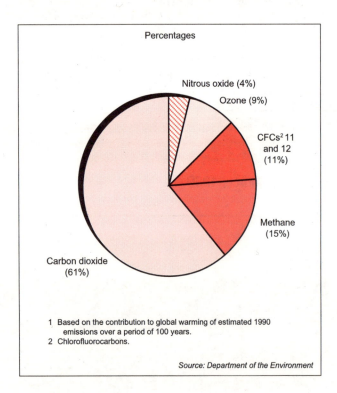

Percentages

Nitrous oxide (4%)

Ozone (9%)

CFCs[2] 11 and 12 (11%)

Methane (15%)

Carbon dioxide (61%)

1 Based on the contribution to global warming of estimated 1990 emissions over a period of 100 years.
2 Chlorofluorocarbons.

Source: Department of the Environment

In the 1989 Department of the Environment survey, about a third of people questioned were very worried about fumes and smoke from factories and a further third said they were quite worried. There was similar concern about acid rain (caused by sulphur and nitrogen oxides). Chart 9.1 shows the trends in emissions of black smoke, nitrogen oxides and sulphur dioxide. After remaining relatively stable throughout the 1960s and early 1970s total emissions of sulphur dioxide in the United Kingdom fell by 42 per cent between the 1970 peak (6.4 million tonnes) and 1989, due largely to industrial decline. Some gases contribute to the greenhouse effect. Heat from the sun passes through the earth's atmosphere and some of this heat is reflected

back. The greenhouse gases trap this reflected heat and the atmosphere acts like a blanket, reducing the rate of heat loss. The phrase greenhouse gases is used because they behave in the same way as the glass in a greenhouse. These greenhouse gases are essential to the earth's climate but as their concentration in the atmosphere rises, less and less heat can escape and so the earth's temperature rises. The concentration of greenhouse gases in the atmosphere has increased in the recent past because of man's activities. The burning of fossil fuels and deforestation has increased the concentration of carbon dioxide, one of the major greenhouse gases, by a quarter since the industrial revolution.

Some greenhouse gases are very efficient at trapping heat but have very low concentrations in the atmosphere. On the other hand, some gases are much less efficient at trapping heat but have very high concentrations. Chart 9.6 shows the contribution of each major gas to the greenhouse effect - determined by the level of efficiency and the atmospheric concentration of each gas. The highest contribution to the greenhouse effect is made by carbon dioxide (61 per cent). One single molecule of carbon dioxide traps little heat whereas one single molecule of chlorofluorocarbons (CFCs) traps far more heat. As an illustration, a CFC 12 molecule is estimated to trap the same amount of heat as 25 thousand carbon dioxide molecules. However, there are far more carbon dioxide molecules in the atmosphere than there are CFC molecules - 800 thousand for every one CFC 12 molecule. So although CFCs are extremely good at trapping heat, their low concentration in the atmosphere means that their overall contribution to the greenhouse effect is only 11 per cent.

Because carbon dioxide (the major greenhouse gas) comes from power stations when they burn coal, oil or gas to produce electricity, one way to help tackle global

9.7 Carbon dioxide emissions[1]: EC comparison

	Million tonne carbon dioxide		
	1980	1986	1989
United Kingdom	528.7	525.9	530.1
Belgium	120.0	95.4	99.1
Denmark	58.4	56.3	47.7
France	459.2	353.2	360.6
Germany (Fed.Rep.)	767.5	675.3	647.9
Greece	48.1	57.4	71.5
Irish Republic	24.5	27.1	28.4
Italy	355.6	343.2	386.1
Luxembourg	12.2	9.9	10.5
Netherlands	151.0	144.8	148.7
Portugal	25.8	27.4	37.7
Spain	196.2	176.1	194.9
European Community	2,747.1	2,492.0	2,562.9

1 All fossil fuels.

Source: Statistical Office of the European Communities

SOCIAL TRENDS 22, © Crown copyright 1992

warming is to use energy more efficiently. In the White Paper on the environment the Government sets out the strategy for energy efficiency. The Government are working towards 1,000 megawatts of renewable electricity generating capacity by the year 2000, about a tenfold increase over present capacity (apart from Scottish hydroelectricity).

European Community emissions of carbon dioxide in 1989 were 2,563 million tonnes (Table 9.7). The United Kingdom with 530 million tonnes was the second largest producer, with the Federal Republic of Germany producing the most. The least emissions came from Luxembourg, the smallest member country.

The ozone layer protects the earth from harmful ultraviolet radiation. It shields the earth from ultraviolet-C radiation, and substantially reduces the amount of ultraviolet-B reaching the earth's surface. An increase in ultraviolet-B would increase the incidence of skin cancer and have serious effects on agricultural crops and marine life. In recent years, there has been

concern that the ozone layer is becoming thinner, or even that holes are developing, allowing more ultraviolet radiation through.

Chart 9.8 shows the contribution to the destruction of the ozone layer by each of the gases considered to be responsible. It shows that the major CFCs (ie CFC 11, 12 and 13), that is those used mainly in aerosols, do the most damage (82 per cent). Carbon tetrachloride (8 per cent), methyl chloroform and other CFCs and halons (used in fire extinguishers) are the other contributors.

Chart 9.9 shows sales of CFCs and what they are used for within the European Community. In 1976, EC sales of CFCs used in aerosols totalled 177 thousand tonnes, by 1981 this figure had been reduced by a third to 116 thousand tonnes. Sales rose in each year between 1982 and 1987 due to the increase in the number of EC member states. Total EC sales of CFCs in 1987 were 137 thousand tonnes.

9.8 Relative contribution of various gases[1] to depletion of the ozone layer, 1988

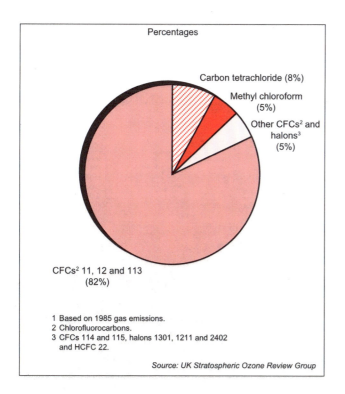

9.9 EC sales of CFCs[1]: by use

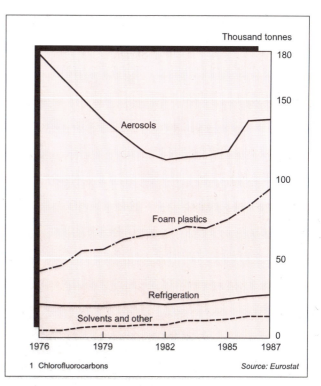

Air - national/local issues

The amount of acid which actually reaches the ground in rain depends both on the acidity of the rain and the amount of rain that falls. Although, in certain parts of the country the rain that does fall is very acidic, because

rainfall is light not much acid actually reaches the ground. However, in other parts of the country where the rain is only weakly acidic, because rainfall is heavy much more acid reaches the ground.

Chart 9.10 shows both the concentration of acid in rain (labelled 'Acidity of rain, 1989') and the amount of acid which actually falls in rain (labelled 'Wet deposited acidity, 1989'). The areas with high concentrations of acid in rain (which tend to be on the eastern side of the country) are not always the areas of high wet deposited acidity. Because of high rainfall, these are in the mountain and hill regions of Wales, Western Scotland and Cumbria. Rain is naturally slightly acidic because carbon dioxide dissolves in rainwater to form carbonic acid. Increases in acidity are due to oxides of sulphur and nitrogen dissolving to form dilute sulphuric and nitric acids. Near those power stations which are burning coal with a high chloride content, hydrochloric acid is also found in rainfall. Acid rain has a long term effect on freshwater, soil and buildings and in forest and crop damage. Acid rain is a global issue - deposits and damage may occur hundreds of miles away from the source of acid pollutants.

The effects of acid rain from sulphur and nitrogen emissions have been studied for many years. The damage done by acid rain depends both on the amount of acid reaching the ground and on the sensitivity of the environment to damage. Over the period 1986-1988 the sensitivity of soils to acid rain was measured. This survey found that a quarter of all soils in Great Britain were particulary sensitive to damage from acid rain. However, a further third were found to be fairly resistant to damage. Of course, it may be that in the areas with particularly sensitive soils, very little acid rain is falling and therefore very little damage is being done. Overall the study found that the sensitivity level was being exceeded in 44 per cent of cases, mainly in the uplands of the north and west.

Lead in the air is a concern, mainly because of its effects on health, particularly children's health. It is estimated that three quarters of the lead in the air comes from petrol. While the consumption of petrol in the United Kingdom rose between 1975 and 1989 the emissions of lead from petrol-engined road vehicles fell by two thirds from 8.0 thousand tonnes to 2.6 thousand tonnes (Chart 9.11). This was because of major reductions in the maximum permitted lead content of petrol at the beginning of 1981 and the end of 1985 and because more unleaded petrol is being used.

9.10 Acidity of rain and wet deposited acidity, 1989

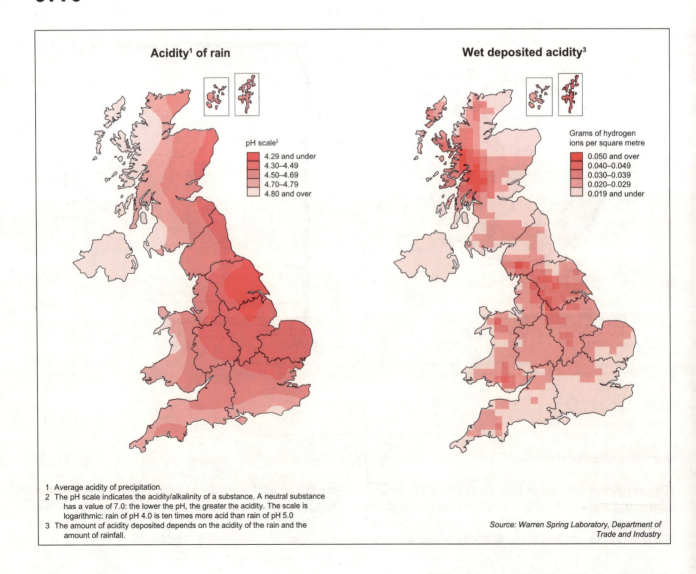

1 Average acidity of precipitation.
2 The pH scale indicates the acidity/alkalinity of a substance. A neutral substance has a value of 7.0: the lower the pH, the greater the acidity. The scale is logarithmic: rain of pH 4.0 is ten times more acid than rain of pH 5.0
3 The amount of acidity deposited depends on the acidity of the rain and the amount of rainfall.

Source: Warren Spring Laboratory, Department of Trade and Industry

9.11 Consumption of petrol and emissions of lead from petrol-engined road vehicles

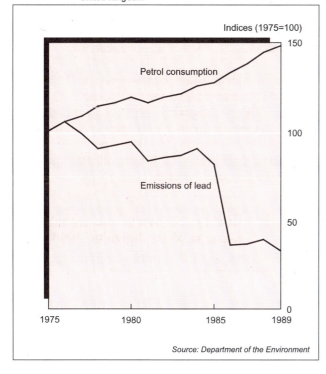

United Kingdom

Source: Department of the Environment

Unleaded petrol was first sold in the United Kingdom in 1986 and the number of petrol stations selling unleaded has risen rapidly. Only 11 per cent sold unleaded petrol in October 1988 compared to 80 per cent in September 1989 and 98 per cent in September 1990. In line with the growth of stations selling unleaded, but following a slow start, sales of unleaded petrol have also increased (Chart 9.12). The dramatic increase in sales between March and April 1989 followed the reduction in duty on unleaded petrol. By May 1991 sales of unleaded petrol had risen to 40 per cent of total United Kingdom sales.

Despite the increase in sales of unleaded petrol, and the increasing awareness of environmental concerns (see Chart 9.3) more car owners still use leaded petrol (58 per cent) than use unleaded (39 per cent). Many cars are unsuitable but some drivers who can use unleaded petrol prefer not to. A Department of the Environment survey in February 1991 found that 7 per cent of drivers with cars that could use unleaded petrol still used leaded petrol. The main reasons given were performance-related.

Estimates are that about 20 per cent of cars on the road in the United Kingdom were immediately able to use unleaded petrol without adjustment at the end of 1989, against 10 per cent at the end of 1988. At the end of 1989, an additional 50 per cent were estimated to be capable of using unleaded petrol following adjustment. All new cars produced after October 1990 must be capable of running on unleaded petrol. Impending EC legislation aimed at cutting car emissions means that all new petrol driven cars will have to be fitted with catalytic converters from 1993 onwards. Therefore, the vast majority of cars will be running on unleaded petrol by the year 2000. Diesel fuel does not contain lead, but its use contributes to emissions of black smoke (see Chart 9.2).

9.12 Deliveries of unleaded petrol

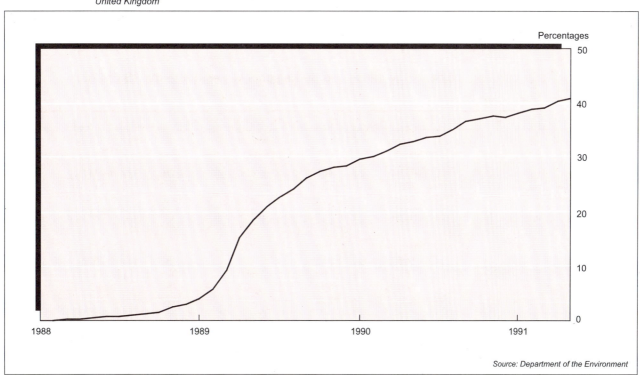

United Kingdom

Source: Department of the Environment

Water

9.13 Average household water use

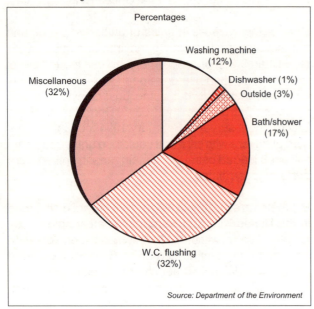

England & Wales

Percentages

- Washing machine (12%)
- Dishwasher (1%)
- Outside (3%)
- Bath/shower (17%)
- W.C. flushing (32%)
- Miscellaneous (32%)

Source: Department of the Environment

Water is an important and vital natural resource. In 1989 total water abstraction (excluding abstractions from tidal sources) was some 33 thousand megalitres a day. The water abstracted is used in industry, in generating electricity, in agriculture and as piped mains water. Due to more efficient use of water there has been a steady decrease in water abstractions by industry over the decade 1979 to 1989 with abstractions falling by almost 58 per cent. As examples of the amounts of water used by industry, it takes 30 thousand litres to build the average car, and 8 pints to brew a pint of beer. Although abstractions by electricity generating companies fluctuate from year to year, total average abstraction per day is around 12 thousand megalitres. Abstractions for water supply increased by 10 per cent between 1979 and 1989 and since the early 1980s have accounted for half of all abstractions.

Average domestic water consumption in 1989 was around 136 litres per person per day. Chart 9.13 shows how this water is used by the average household. Studies by the water industry estimate that an automatic washing machine uses 110 litres per load and a dishwasher 55 litres; a bath uses 80 litres while a shower will use only 35 litres.

9.14 Quality of rivers and canals: by Regional Water Authority, 1989-90[1]

England & Wales Percentages and kilometres

	Good quality	Fair quality	Poor quality	Bad quality	Total length (= 100%) (kilo-metres)
North West	55	25	16	4	5,900
Northumbrian	88	10	2	0	2,785
Severn Trent	52	37	9	1	6,678
Yorkshire	73	14	11	3	6,034
Anglian	57	35	7	1	4,453
Thames	80	16	4	0	3,831
Southern	59	31	9	1	2,137
Wessex	61	34	4	1	2,275
South West	51	36	12	1	2,788
Welsh	80	14	5	0	4,802
England & Wales	65	25	9	1	41,683

1 Data are based on the financial year 1989-90.
2 Data for the Welsh region do not include all water or regional boundaries as regional boundaries are based on river catchment areas not national or County borders.

Source: National Rivers Authority

9.15 Water pollution incidents: by cause and by Regional Water Authority, 1989-90[1,2]

England & Wales Numbers

	Cause of pollution incident					
	Industrial	Farm	Sewage/sewerage	Other	Total[3]	Prosecutions
North West	841	466	695	1,476	3,478	47
Northumbrian	240	57	335	160	792	5
Severn Trent	2,422	292	810	2,480	6,004	35
Yorkshire	822	262	703	677	2,464	34
Anglian	777	182	505	267	1,731	18
Thames	1,616	169	726	1,062	3,573	10
Southern	505[5]	113	454	688	1,760[5]	12
Wessex	167	360	966	1,028	2,521	44
South West	566	663	603	756	2,588	50
Welsh[4]	475	292	574	473	1,814	54
England & Wales	8,431	2,856	6,371	9,067	26,725	309

1 This information has been collated by the National Rivers Authority (NRA) and includes data collected before its formation by the Regional Water Authorities.
2 Data are based on the financial year 1989-90.
3 Incidents reported where pollution was found.

4 Data for Welsh region do not include all incidents and prosecutions for Wales as regional boundaries are based on river catchment areas and not County borders.
5 Data are incomplete.

Source: National Rivers Authority

9.16 Sewage treatment works - non compliance[1]: by Regional Water Authority

England & Wales   Numbers and percentages

	Number sampled			Percentage of works tested that were in breach of consent		
	1986	1988	1989[2]	1986	1988	1989[2]
North West	458	439	378	14	10	4
Northumbrian	196	181	179	19	13	7
Severn Trent	762	785	786	23	12	4
Yorkshire	380	346	346	23	14	8
Anglian	774	788	710	40	27	14
Thames	374	400	410	18	13	5
Southern	282	463	463	19	40	38
Wessex	272	272	272	14	5	4
South West	188	228	384	29	5	18
Welsh[3]	668	753	729	17	17	27
England & Wales	4,354	4,655	4,657	23	23	14

1 See accompanying text.
2 Data are based on the financial year 1989-90.
3 Data for the Welsh region do not include all Wales as regional boundaries are based on river catchment areas not national or county borders.

Source: Water Authorities and National Rivers Authority

Water may become polluted by discharges (for example from industry or sewage works), from run-off (for example from roads and industrial sites) or from incidents such as spillages. In England and Wales discharges to watercourses require the formal consent of the National Rivers Authority (NRA), which has wide powers designed to safeguard water quality. The NRA was established on 1 September 1989 as an independent regulatory body. The NRA took over the responsibility for the control and monitoring of water pollution from the former water authorities which have now been privatised.

Despite the many concerns expressed about water pollution, river quality in the United Kingdom is of generally high quality. Table 9.14 shows that, in 1989-90, 90 per cent of total river and canal length in England and Wales was of good or fair quality, that is capable of supporting reasonably good coarse fisheries and suitable for drinking after treatment. Only 1 per cent was of bad quality. The Northumbrian region had the highest proportion of good quality rivers and canals (88 per cent) and the South West the lowest (51 per cent).

Table 9.15 shows that there were 26,725 reported pollution incidents in 1989-90. It is clear that there has been a increasing awareness of environmental issues in recent years and this may well account for some of the rise in the number of incidents reported. In 1989-90, 32 per cent of incidents were caused by industry, 11 per cent by farm pollution, and 24 per cent by sewage problems. Table 9.15 also shows the number of prosecutions for pollution incidents. The Northumbrian water authority had the fewest prosecutions with the Welsh and South West water authorities the most. Farm pollution incidents attracted the highest number of prosecutions (188).

The North Sea is one of the most closely studied regional seas in the world. The most recent comprehensive survey of the North Sea (the 1985 Quality Status Report) showed that generally it is in good health. Problem areas are largely confined to the slow moving shallow waters of the Wadden Sea which take a heavy load of pollutants from continental rivers. The Rhine, Meuse and Elbe together contribute about two thirds of total riverborne contaminants to the North Sea. Important measures agreed at the Third North Sea Conference in the Hague in March 1990 included the reduction of nutrient inputs to the sea; reducing inputs from rivers, estuaries and the air, and ending sea dumping and incineration.

9.17 Bathing water - compliance with EC Bathing Water Directive[1] coliform standards[2]: by coastal region, 1988 and 1990

United Kingdom   Numbers and percentages

	Identified bathing waters[3] (numbers)		Percentage complying	
	1988	1990	1988	1990
United Kingdom	403	446	66	77
North West	33	33	18	30
Northumbria	19	32	47	66
Yorkshire	22	22	95	77
Anglian	28	29	68	93
Thames	2	3	0	100
Southern	65	66	42	73
Wessex (south coast)	27	28	96	100
Wessex (Bristol Channel)	11	11	36	100
South West	109	133	84	89
Welsh	48	50	77	70
England & Wales	364	407	66	78
Scotland	23	23	52	52
Northern Ireland	16	16	88	94

1 76/160/EEC.
2 At least 95 per cent of samples must have counts not exceeding the mandatory limit values for total and faecal coliforms (see text).
3 The increase in 1990 is due to subdivision of some bathing waters.

Source: Former Water Authorities; National Rivers Authority; Scottish Development Department; Department of the Environment (Northern Ireland)

Considerable attention has been focused over the past few years on discharges by sewage treatment works into rivers, and also on bathing waters which fail to meet EC standards. Table 9.16 shows that in 1989-90 14 per cent of sewage treatment works sampled were failing to meet the standards set in the discharge consents granted by the authorities. However, that proportion represented a significant improvement on the position in 1986 (23 per cent). Table 9.17 shows that the proportion of bathing waters complying with EC standards had reached 77 per cent by 1990.

Oil pollution from tankers, oil rigs and other sources, causes great damage to the marine environment and results in the death of birds, fish and plants. In 1989, and for the fourth consecutive year, there was an increase in the number of oil spills with 764 separate incidents reported, the largest number over the past decade (Table 9.18). Although most spillages are small and no clean-up action is required, 1989 also saw a rise in the number of larger oil spills (by 20 per cent). Clean-

9.18 Oil spills reported: by size, effect and cost

United Kingdom			Numbers and £ thousand	
	1986	1987	1988	1989
Number of incidents	436	500	559	764
Spills over 100 gallons	103	126	110	132
Spills requiring clean-up	126	105	120	160
Costs incurred (£ thousand)	134	198	217	234

Source: Department of the Environment

up action was necessary in the case of 160 spills and the cost of these clean-up operations was £234 thousand in 1989. Illegal discharge of oil pollutants can lead to prosecution by port authorities. These offences include deliberate discharges of oil and ballast water in harbours and coastal waters. There is a rising trend in convictions and in 1989 there were 29 convictions, double the number in 1988, and fines totalling £48,400 were imposed.

Waste

In the United Kingdom each year it is estimated that we produce around 700 million tonnes of waste - only about 3 per cent of this is classified as household waste, while about 37 per cent is agricultural (Chart 9.19). Mining and quarrying waste and agricultural waste are excluded from Chart 9.20 which shows the different means by which the remaining waste,

amounting to some 140 million tonnes, is disposed of each year. Most is disposed of by landfill which is the deposit of waste on land in a way that is intended to prevent pollution or harm to the environment. Through restoration, this land may subsequently be used for other purposes.

9.19 Annual average waste arisings[1]: by type of waste, late 1980s

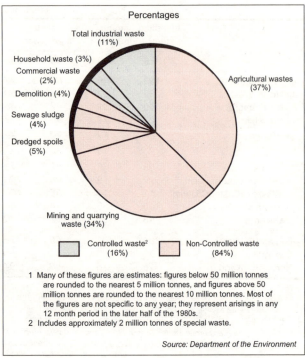

United Kingdom

Percentages

- Total industrial waste (11%)
- Household waste (3%)
- Commercial waste (2%)
- Demolition (4%)
- Sewage sludge (4%)
- Dredged spoils (5%)
- Agricultural wastes (37%)
- Mining and quarrying waste (34%)

Controlled waste[2] (16%)   Non-Controlled waste (84%)

1 Many of these figures are estimates: figures below 50 million tonnes are rounded to the nearest 5 million tonnes, and figures above 50 million tonnes are rounded to the nearest 10 million tonnes. Most of the figures are not specific to any year; they represent arisings in any 12 month period in the later half of the 1980s.
2 Includes approximately 2 million tonnes of special waste.

Source: Department of the Environment

9.20 Annual controlled waste disposal[1]: by disposal route[2], late 1980s

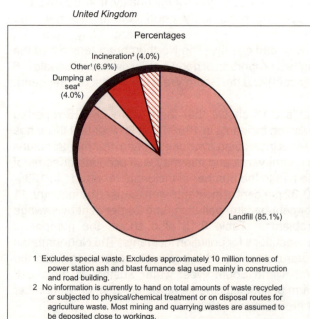

United Kingdom

Percentages

- Incineration[3] (4.0%)
- Other[1] (6.9%)
- Dumping at sea[4] (4.0%)
- Landfill (85.1%)

1 Excludes special waste. Excludes approximately 10 million tonnes of power station ash and blast furnace slag used mainly in construction and road building.
2 No information is currently to hand on total amounts of waste recycled or subjected to physical/chemical treatment or on disposal routes for agriculture waste. Most mining and quarrying wastes are assumed to be deposited close to workings.
3 Includes 2-2.5 million tonnes municipal waste & approximately 2 million tonnes of sewage sludge.
4 Includes 35-40 million tonnes municipal waste and approximately 2 million tonnes of sewage sludge.

Source: Department of the Environment

Social Trends 22, © Crown copyright 1992

Special waste is defined in the *Control of Pollution (Special Waste) Regulations 1980* as controlled waste which consists of, or is contaminated by, substances which are dangerous to life. Prescription drugs are also classed as special waste. The movement and disposal of special waste must be notified and recorded, and its storage, treatment and disposal must be licensed. Special regard must be paid to the best environmental option for disposal. It is estimated that there were between 2.0 - 2.5 million tonnes of special waste arising in the United Kingdom in 1989-90; this represented a very small proportion of total waste. Chart 9.21 shows the disposal methods of this waste, with landfill the main method used.

9.21 Special waste: by disposal route

United Kingdom

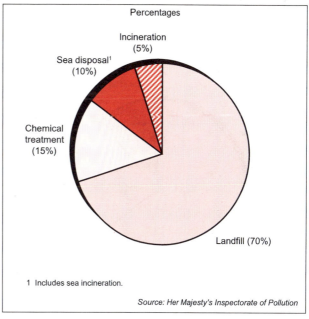

1 Includes sea incineration.

Source: Her Majesty's Inspectorate of Pollution

9.22 Recycled scrap as a percentage of total consumption for selected materials

United Kingdom

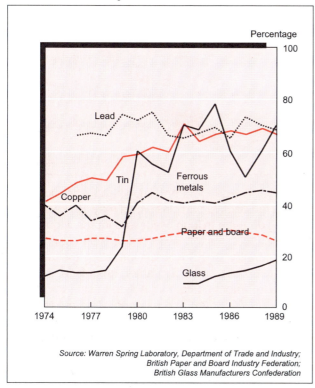

Source: Warren Spring Laboratory, Department of Trade and Industry; British Paper and Board Industry Federation; British Glass Manufacturers Confederation

Reclaimed glass used in manufacture doubled between 1984 and 1989 to 310 thousand tonnes. One way of collecting glass for recycling is the use of bottle banks (Table 9.23). By May 1990 there were 4,648 bottle banks in the United Kingdom which had recovered 130 thousand tonnes of glass in the past year. The number of local authorities participating in bottle bank schemes has risen from 119 in 1980 to 431 in 1989; and the number of sites has increased tenfold, from 433 to 4330 over the same period.

One way of handling certain types of waste is to recycle it back into the manufacturing process. Chart 9.22 shows, for a selection of materials, how much recycled scrap is used in manufacture. Reclamation and recycling of waste not only reduces the amount of waste for disposal, but also helps to conserve energy. In 1974 recycled tin amounted to 12 per cent of total consumption. This rose to 23 per cent by 1979 and then rose sharply to 60 per cent the following year. A target for recycling half of all domestic waste that can be recycled by the year 2000 has been set by the Secretary of State for the Environment.

9.23 Bottle banks: by number of sites and tonnage collected, 1989-1990

United Kingdom	Numbers and tonnage		
	Number of sites		Tonnage collected
	Public	Commercial	
United Kingdom	4,648	3,093	132,700
England	3,894	949	114,300
Wales	137	10	2,000
Scotland	580	2,110	15,200
Northern Ireland	37	24	1,200

Source: British Glass Manufacturers Confederation; Department of the Environment, Northern Ireland

Radioactivity

9.24 Radiation exposure of the UK population: by source

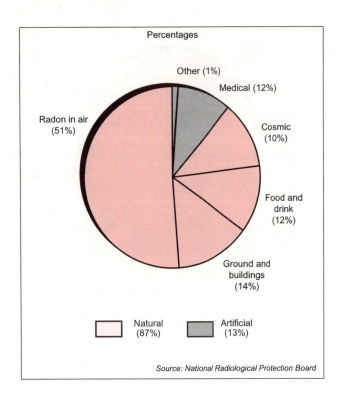

Source: National Radiological Protection Board

9.25 Percentage of homes with radon concentrations of over 200 Bq/m³

United Kingdom

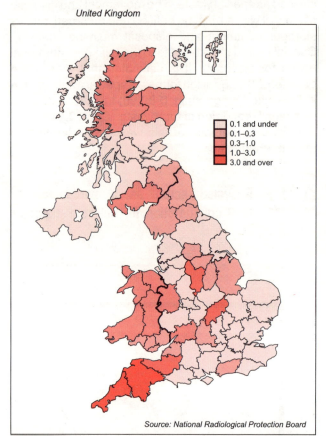

Source: National Radiological Protection Board

Public concern about radiation levels from artificial sources is frequently expressed in the United Kingdom. However, most of the radiation we are exposed to occurs naturally. Chart 9.24 shows that only 13 per cent of radiation exposure of the United Kingdom population in 1989 was due to artificial sources. Naturally occurring sources provide by far the greater proportion of the total dose of radiation in the United Kingdom and radon which occurs naturally in the air accounts for half of the total dose. The radiation dose from nuclear weapons fallout, nuclear waste disposal and other non-medical artificial sources accounts for only 1 per cent of the total. Most of the artificial exposure to radiation comes from medical uses. Radon, the most important source of radiation exposure, comes from the breakdown of uranium which is present in minute quantities in all soils and rocks. Radon can mix with air in the soil and seep out of the ground. In the open air it is diluted to low levels, but higher levels can collect in

buildings. The danger from radon is that it breaks down to form radioactive particles which may be breathed in causing damage to lung tissue and increasing the risk of lung cancer. Radon levels are higher in some parts of the country than in others because the uranium content of rocks and soils varies from place to place. The Government has set an Action Level for radon in houses of 200 Bq/m³ and has published guidance to householders. Chart 9.25 shows the problem is concentrated in particular areas of the country. In Devon and Cornwall as many as 60 thousand homes may have radon concentrations above the Action Level. In Somerset, Northamptonshire and Derbyshire possibly 10 thousand homes could be affected in the same way. The Government advises that householders should take measures to reduce levels of radon in houses above the Action Level.

Noise

Public concern about noise is increasing. In the EC survey on the environment concern over noise came very high in the list of local issues. In England and Wales the number of complaints about noise received by Environment Health Officers more than trebled in ten years to reach 3 complaints for every thousand people by 1988-89. Chart 9.26 shows those categories which are controlled by section 58 of the *Control of Pollution Act 1974*. In 1988-89 nearly two-thirds of

complaints received were due to domestic noise, compared to only three tenths in 1975. There were a total of 2,624 complaints about domestic noise over the two year period mid-1984 to mid-1986, Two thirds of these concerned loud music and barking dogs (Table 9.27). Amplified music was the main source of complaint from people in flats, with barking dogs being the main cause of complaint from people in detached houses.

9.26 Noise - complaints received by Environmental Health Officers: by source[1]

England & Wales

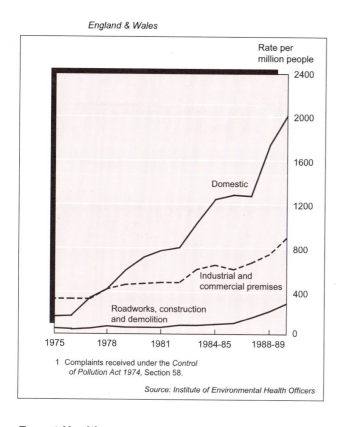

1 Complaints received under the *Control of Pollution Act 1974*, Section 58.

Source: Institute of Environmental Health Officers

9.27 Domestic noise complaints: by type of source

England & Wales

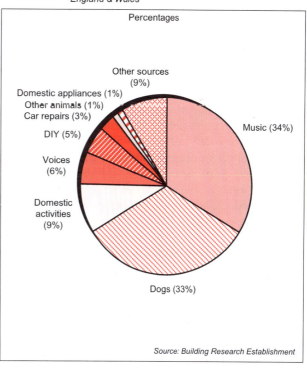

Percentages

- Other sources (9%)
- Domestic appliances (1%)
- Other animals (1%)
- Car repairs (3%)
- DIY (5%)
- Voices (6%)
- Domestic activities (9%)
- Music (34%)
- Dogs (33%)

Source: Building Research Establishment

Forest Health

9.28 Forest crown density

United Kingdom

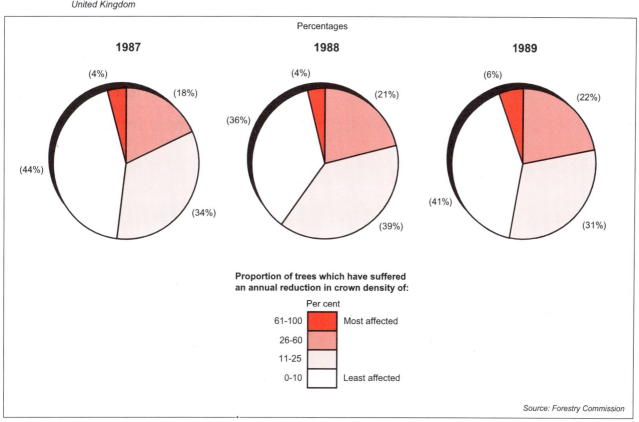

Percentages

1987
- (4%)
- (18%)
- (36%) — *[44%]*
- (44%)
- (34%)

1988
- (4%)
- (21%)
- (36%)
- (39%)

1989
- (6%)
- (22%)
- (41%)
- (31%)

Proportion of trees which have suffered an annual reduction in crown density of:

Per cent
- 61-100 — Most affected
- 26-60
- 11-25
- 0-10 — Least affected

Source: Forestry Commission

Surveys carried out across Europe have shown a decline in tree health in several countries, including Britain (Chart 9.28). They are carried out using two criteria to assess damage - the amount of light passing through the foliage (crown density) and leaf discoloration. Although it is possible that air pollution may be a factor in tree damage - these surveys cannot distinguish between the effects of air pollution and the effects of drought, frost, insect and fungal attack and root disturbance.

Nature Conservation

With environmental issues coming so strongly to the fore in recent years, protection of the environment is something that many people feel strongly about. Nature conservation is an area of particular concern and the rapid growth of the newer conservation organisations such as Friends of the Earth, the Woodland Trust and the Worldwide Fund for Nature (see Table 9.4) indicates more active involvement.

Forests and woodlands occupy one tenth of the land in the United Kingdom and provide one of the most effective ways by which carbon dioxide, one of the main contributors to global warming, can be removed from the atmosphere. However, they are also an important economic resource in that they provide timber and since 1985 the Forestry Commission has had a duty to balance the interests of forestry and those of the environment. Since 1985 grant schemes have been in operation aimed at encouraging the maintenance and enhancement of broadleaved woodlands for timber production, landscape, recreation and nature conservation. Chart 9.29 shows the switch between 1983-1984 and 1989-1990 in the use of broadleaves for new planting and restocking.

9.29 Tree planting and restocking: by area and species

Great Britain

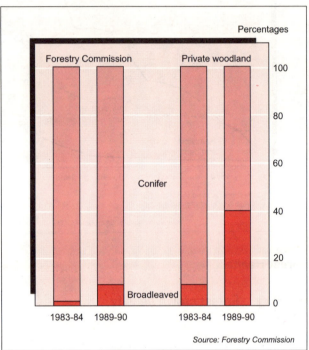

Source: Forestry Commission

People visit the countryside for a variety of reasons. In 1989 a survey by the Countryside Commission showed that 18 per cent of trips were to go on long walks, 17 per cent were for drives, outings and picnics, 13 per cent to visit the coast (excluding resorts) and 12 per cent to visit historic houses, country and wildlife parks and nature reserves.

For many years areas of outstanding beauty or particular environmental value have been identified in order to protect and preserve them for greater public enjoyment. There are 10 National Parks in England and Wales covering nearly one tenth of the country (Table 9.30). Thirty-eight areas of Outstanding Natural Beauty cover an additional 13 per cent of the total area of England and Wales with over half concentrated in the south of England. Green Belt areas are designed to check the growth of large built-up areas, safeguard the surrounding countryside, prevent merging of neighbouring towns, preserve the special character of historic towns and assist in urban regeneration. The area of Green Belts in England more than doubled between 1979 and 1989.

9.30 Designated areas[1] as a percentage of total area: by region, 1990[2]

United Kingdom   Percentages and kilometres

	National Parks	Areas of Out- standing Natural Beauty[3]	Green Belt areas[4]	Defined Heritage Coasts Length (km)
North	23	15	504	111
Yorkshire & Humberside	21	2	2,480	80
East Midlands	5	3	615	—
East Anglia	—	7	108	119
South East	—	23	6,052	73
South West	7	27	818	576
West Midlands	2	8	2,458	—
North West	2	11	2,451	—
England	7	14	15,435	959
Wales	20	4	—	501
Scotland	—	13	—	—
Northern Ireland	—	20	—	—

1 Some areas may be in more than one category.
2 At 31 March.
3 National Scenic Areas in Scotland.
4 1989.

Source: Department of the Environment

9.31 Non-statutory protected areas: by protecting body, 1990[1]

United Kingdom	Number and area	
	Number	Area (sq km)
Royal Society for the Protection of Birds	118	747
Royal Society for Nature Conservation and Local Nature Conservation Trusts	2,000	674
National Trust[2]	88	129
Woodland Trust	414	53
Wildfowl and Wetlands Trust	9	17
Field Studies Council	2	14

1 At 31 March.
2 Properties specifically managed as nature reserves.

Source: Organisations involved

9.32 Native species at risk, 1990

Great Britain				Numbers
	Number endangered[1]	Number vulnerable[2]	Number rare[3]	Number of native species
Mammals	2	12	5	76
Birds	61	2	12	519
Reptiles	2	—	—	11
Amphibians	1	1	—	6
Freshwater fish[4]	3	4	2	34
Marine fish[5]	—	—	—	310
Dragonflies/damsel-flies	4	2	3	41
Grasshoppers/crickets	3	2	1	30
Beetles	142	84	266	3,900
Butterflies/moths	27	22	55	2,400
Spiders[6]	22	31	26	622
Crustaceans[6]	2	1	3	2,742
Bryozoans[6]	—	—	1	280
Molluscs[6]	10	7	13	1,044
Worms/leeches	—	—	1	837
Cnidarians[6]	1	—	1	374

1 Species in danger of extinction and whose survival is unlikely, if the causal factors continue operating.
2 Species believed likely to move into endangered category in the near future, if the causal factors continue operating.
3 Species with small world populations that are not at present endangered or vulnerable but are at risk.
4 Includes fish which leave the sea to breed in freshwater, eg salmon.
5 Includes fish which leave the freshwater to breed in the sea, eg eels.
6 Numbers at risk relate to terrestial, freshwater and brackish species only.

Source: Nature Conservancy Council

Nature conservation measures are not limited to designated areas. Many protected areas are owned or managed by voluntary bodies (Table 9.31) and include Sites of Special Scientific Interest and some National Nature Reserves. Between them the Royal Society for Nature Conservation and Local Nature Conservation Trusts and the Royal Society for the Protection of Birds are responsible for the largest number of areas protected by voluntary bodies, accounting for over four-fifths of the total.

The Nature Conservancy Council use a classification devised by the International Union for the Conservation of Nature to assess rare and endangered species in the United Kingdom. Many species have declined or become rare during this century (Table 9.32). Insects have suffered substantial falls in their population, 3 of our 43 species of dragonflies have become extinct since 1953 and a further 12 are vulnerable or declining. Most of our 55 resident species of butterfly have declined significantly since 1950. Plants, too, are at risk, 14 of the 1,425 species of native seed-bearing plants have become extinct since 1930.

BIBLIOGRAPHY

The following list contains selected publications relevant to Chapter 9: Environment. Those published by HMSO are available from the addresses shown on the back cover of Social Trends.

Digest of Environmental Protection and Water Statistics, HMSO
Environmental Digest for Wales, Welsh Office
Scottish Environmental Statistics, Scottish Office

Statistical Bulletins (Supplement to Digest of Environmental Protection and Water Statistics), HMSO
"This Common Inheritance, Britain's Environmental Strategy" White Paper, HMSO

Department of the Environment Publications

Land Use Change in England

This bulletin presents the results of the Department's statistics on changes in Land Use, based on data recorded by Ordnance Survey as part of its work on Map revision.

Statistical Bulletins

Air Quality   1991 **£3**   *Radioactivity 1990* **£3**

Water Quality 1990 **£3**

These annual bulletins provide additional detailed tables for most of the chapter topics in the Digest of Environmental Protection and Water Statistics (see HMSO Publications).

1985-2001 **£25**

The latest is an occasional series of publications giving summary results of the Department's household estimates for England, the regions, counties, metropolitan districts and London Boroughs. Estimates are given for the years 1985 to 2001 and a series of appendices describe the methods of calculation.

Development Control Statistics 1989/90 **£5**

This publication provides statistics of decisions on planning applications handled by local planning authorities in England. Information about planning appeals is also included.

The above publications are available from the
Department of the Environment
Publications Sales Unit
Building 1, Victoria Road
Ruislip, Middlesex HA4 ONZ

All The Latest Statistics
from the
Central Statistical Office

0839-338-PLUS

Retail Price Index 337
Monthly Trade Figures 338
Balance of Payments (quarterly) 339
Public Sector Borrowing Requirement 340
Index of Output of the Production Industries 341
Producer Prices 342
Retail Sales 343
Credit Business 344
Gross Dometic Product 345

CSO
STATCALL

**Calls charged at 33p per minute cheap rate,
44p per minute at all other times**

Chapter 10: Leisure

Availability of leisure time
- Working women have much less free time than working men. Women in full-time employment have 37 hours of free time each week, 10 hours less than men. *(Chart 10.1)*

- Manual employees work shorter basic hours and get more paid holiday than ever before. In 1991, 92 per cent of manual employees were entitled to four or more weeks paid holiday. *(Chart 10.3)*

Home-based leisure activities
- Three out of every five households have a video cassette recorder. In 1990, we rented 374 million video tapes. *(Table 10.4)*

- People are watching less television. Despite longer broadcasting hours and more choice of channels, in 1991 viewers watched an average of just under 24 hours per week compared to almost 26 hours in 1986. *(Table 10.5)*

Social and cultural activities
- Blackpool Pleasure Beach was the most popular tourist attraction in 1990, with 6.5 million visitors. *(Table 10.17)*

Sporting activities
- In the 1990/91 season, attendances at Football League Division One games increased for the third successive year to reach an average of 22,681. *(Table 10.19)*

Holidays and travel
- Two out of every five adults do not take a holiday, a proportion which has remained more or less unchanged since 1971. *(Chart 10.21)*

Resources
- In 1989, households spent an average of 16 per cent of their total expenditure on leisure. *(Table 10.27)*

10.1 Leisure time in a typical week: by sex and employment status, 1990-91

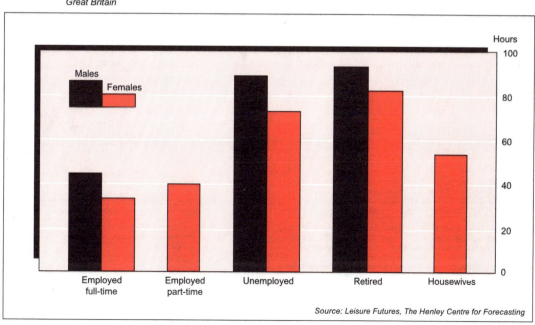

Great Britain

Source: Leisure Futures, The Henley Centre for Forecasting

Availability of leisure time

10.2 Time use in a typical week: by employment status and sex, 1990–91

Great Britain   Hours

	Full-time employees		Part-time employees		
	Males	Females	Females	Housewives	Retired
Weekly hours spent on:					
Employment and travel[1]	48.3	42.6	20.9	0.3	0.7
Essential activities[2]	24.1	39.6	52.1	58.4	33.0
Sleep[3]	49.0	49.0	49.0	49.0	49.0
Free time	46.6	36.8	46.0	60.3	85.3
Free time per weekday	4.5	3.3	5.4	8.4	11.6
Free time per weekend day	12.1	10.3	9.5	9.3	13.6

1 Travel to and from place of work.
2 Essential domestic work and personal care, including essential
shopping, child care, cooking, personal hygiene and appearance.
3 An average of 7 hours sleep per night is assumed.

Source: The Henley Centre for Forecasting

This chapter describes the amount of leisure time that people have and how they spend it. Chart 10.1 (on the previous page) shows the leisure time people had in a typical week in 1990-91. Of all the people shown in the chart, retired men had the most leisure time with 93 hours, followed by unemployed men with 86 hours. Women in full-time employment enjoyed 37 hours of leisure time per week, 10 hours less than similarly employed men. This was because when they were not at work, women spent more time on essential activities such as looking after the children, cleaning, cooking and shopping (Table 10.2). Despite the fact that they spend less time at work, women working part-time actually have less free time than men who work full-time.

10.3 Weekly hours of work and entitlement to annual paid holidays[1]

United Kingdom

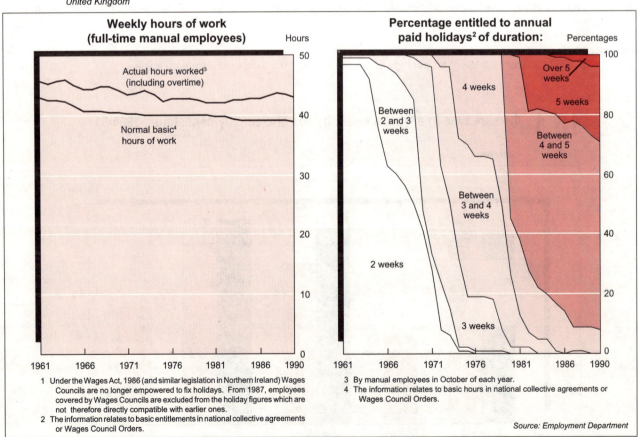

1 Under the Wages Act, 1986 (and similar legislation in Northern Ireland) Wages Councils are no longer empowered to fix holidays. From 1987, employees covered by Wages Councils are excluded from the holiday figures which are not therefore directly compatible with earlier ones.
2 The information relates to basic entitlements in national collective agreements or Wages Council Orders.
3 By manual employees in October of each year.
4 The information relates to basic hours in national collective agreements or Wages Council Orders.

Source: Employment Department

Not surprisingly the retired had the most free time, both during the week and at the weekend. Housewives had, on average, 5 hours more free time on every weekday than women who worked full-time. However, at weekends, women who worked made up for their lack of leisure time during the week and had more free-time than housewives.

The trend over the past 25 years or so has been towards a reduction in basic working hours and an increase in holiday entitlement (Chart 10.3). The actual hours worked over this period, which include overtime, decreased from 45 hours in 1961 to 42 hours in 1980, but increased slightly between 1981 and 1988. Since then they have fallen back.

Average paid holiday entitlement has been steadily increasing since the 1960s. In 1961, 97 per cent of full-time manual employees had a basic entitlement of only 2 weeks. By 1971 two-thirds had an entitlement of 3 weeks or more and by 1981 the majority of these employees had between 4 and 5 weeks paid annual leave. In 1990, nine out of ten were entitled to more than 4 weeks, with three out of ten to at least 5 weeks.

Home-based leisure activities

10.4 Leisure based consumer durables: by household type, 1989-90

Great Britain   Percentages

	1 adult aged 16-59	2 adults aged 16-59	Small family[1]	Large family[2]	Large adult house-hold[3]	2 adults 1 or both aged 60 and over	1 adult aged 60 and over	All house-holds
Percentage of households with								
Television	94	99	99	99	100	99	98	99
Video cassette recorder	48	78	81	82	84	39	11	60
Home computer	10	15	37	46	31	4	1	19
Compact disc player	15	21	17	21	28	7	2	15

1 One or 2 persons aged 16 and over and 1 or 2 persons aged under 16.
2 One or more persons aged 16 and over and 3 or more persons aged under 16, or 3 or more persons aged 16 and over and 2 persons aged under 16.

3 Three or more persons aged 16 and over, with or without 1 person aged under 16.

Source: General Household Survey

The most popular home-based leisure activities are watching television, visiting or entertaining friends or relations and listening to the radio. In 1989-90, almost all households had a television (Table 10.4), video cassette recorders and home computers were less common (60 per cent and 19 per cent respectively) although the proportion with video cassette recorders was 7 percentage points higher than in 1988-89. The rapid rise in sales of compact discs (see later Chart 10.9) meant that in one in seven households owned a compact disc player.

The larger the household the more likely they are to own leisure-based consumer durables, particularly when there are children in the household. Only 10 per cent of one person households owned a home computer compared to 46 per cent of large families. There was also a noticeable reluctance among households made up of older people to purchase the newer goods such as a home computer or compact disc player.

Generally people spend far more time watching television than listening to the radio (Tables 10.5 and

10.5 Television viewing[1]: by social class

United Kingdom   Hours and minutes and percentages

	1986	1987	1988	1989	1990
Social class[2]					
(hours:mins per week)					
ABC1	20:47	20:54	20:14	19:48	19:31
C2	25:18	24:40	25:25	25:00	24:13
DE	33:11	31:47	31:44	30:57	30:13
All persons	25:54	25:25	25:21	24:44	23:51
Reach[3]					
(percentages)					
Daily	78	76	77	78	77
Weekly	94	93	94	94	94

1 Viewing of live television broadcasts from the BBC, ITV and Channel 4.
2 See Appendix, Part 10: Social class.
3 Percentage of UK population aged 4 and over who viewed TV for at least three consecutive minutes.

Source: Broadcasters' Audience Research Board;
British Broadcasting Corporation; AGB Limited

10.6 Radio listening: by age

United Kingdom
Hours and minutes and percentages

	1986	1987	1988	1989	1990
Age group					
(hours:minutes per week)					
4 – 15 years	2:12	2:07	2:13	2:21	2:26
16 – 34	11:24	11:18	11:40	12:07	12:28
35 – 64	9:56	10:16	10:33	11:10	11:42
65 years and over	8:27	8:44	8:49	9:00	9:18
All aged 4 years and over	8:40	8:52	9:12	9:46	10:12
Reach[1]					
(percentages)					
Daily	43	43	43	44	45
Weekly	75	74	73	74	74

1 Percentage of UK population aged 4 and over who listened to radio for at least half a programme a day.

Source: British Broadcasting Corporation

10.6). In 1990, on average, people watched television for almost 24 hours each week, and listened to the radio for just over 10 hours each week.

Although the amount of television we can watch increased substantially from 1986, following the introduction of breakfast and all-night television, the average time spent watching the four network channels fell each year between 1986 and 1990. On average, people watched over two hours less television per week in 1990 than in 1986.

Around the world, there has been a trend towards wider choice for the television viewer. Sixteen million homes in America now have a pay-per-view system in which

10.7 Television viewing: by type of programme, 1990

United Kingdom

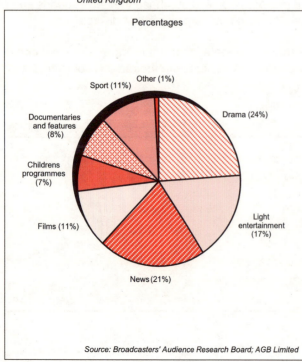

Percentages

Sport (11%), Other (1%), Documentaries and features (8%), Childrens programmes (7%), Films (11%), News (21%), Light entertainment (17%), Drama (24%)

Source: Broadcasters' Audience Research Board; AGB Limited

they must pay to watch a specific event or programme. Over one million homes in the United Kingdom now receive satellite or cable television, many paying monthly subscriptions to view certain channels. Sporting events feature heavily on American pay-per-view. However, in the United Kingdom, certain sporting events are deemed to be in the national interest and broadcasting rights cannot currently be sold to satellite or cable authorities. The current list of events include the Derby and Grand National horse races, the FA Cup Final and the Boat Race.

Whereas television viewing is declining, radio listening is increasing, by 18 per cent between 1986 and 1990 (Table 10.6). There were increases at all age groups shown in the table. In 1990 those aged 16-34 spent the most time listening to the radio - twelve and a half hours per week.

The number of independent radio stations broadcasting in Great Britain increased from 49 to 78 between 1986 and 1990. In spite of this wider choice, the proportion of people who listen to the radio has remained fairly constant at around 43 per cent.

The programmes people watch on television are clearly dependent on what is broadcast. Chart 10.7 gives the proportion of viewing time spent watching each type of programme in 1990. A quarter of all viewing time is spent watching drama programmes.

One reason for the decline in television viewing is that viewers are watching videos instead, either rented, recorded from earlier broadcasts or bought. Ownership of video cassette recorders increased rapidly during the 1980s. In 1990 14.8 million households were estimated to have at least one video recorder, (Table 10.8). Of these households a quarter hired a video cassette tape in the week prior to being interviewed, 4 percentage points lower than in 1989.

10.8 Hiring of pre-recorded VCR tapes

United Kingdom

	1986	1988	1989	1990
Domestic video population[1]				
(millions)	9.66	12.20	13.80	14.80
Hiring of video tapes[2]				
Percentage hiring tapes during previous 7 days	30	29	30	26
Average number of tapes per hiring	2.24	2.02	1.94	1.90
Number of tapes hired per week (millions)	6.5	7.2	8.0	7.3

1 Estimated number of households in possession of at least one video cassette recorder based on a survey of 13,000 households per quarter.
2 Figures refer to households in possession of a video cassette recorder.

Source: British Videogram Association

The British Videogram Association estimates that there were 374 million rentals in 1990 and that a further 38 million video tapes were purchased by the public. Sales to the public doubled in each year between 1985 and 1989 and have been growing at a faster rate than tape rental.

Other statistics produced by the British Videogram Association using quarterly surveys show that in 1990 nearly three quarters of tapes were rented from specialist video shops with the remainder rented from other outlets such as newsagents, garages, and off-licences.

In 1989, sales of compact discs (CDs) exceeded sales of long-play albums (LPs) for the first time. By 1990 CD sales were more than double those of LPs (Chart 10.9). Cheaper CD players and the introduction of mid-price and budget price discs have been partly responsible for the increase in CD sales.

Sales of LPs fell by 35 per cent between 1989 and 1990 to less than 25 million and cassette sales also fell. Despite this, cassettes still accounted for over a third of all items sold. Their continued popularity is partially due to the increase in ownership of personal stereos.

The age of readers of magazines with the highest readership is given in Table 10.10. Generally, younger women are more likely to read the most popular women's magazines than older women. In 1990, one in eight women aged between 15 and 24 read *Bella*, compared to one in sixteen women aged 65 and over. However, the readership of *Women's Weekly* did not follow this trend, with women aged 65 and over more likely to be a reader than any other age group.

10.9 Trade deliveries of LPs, cassettes, compact discs and singles[1]

United Kingdom

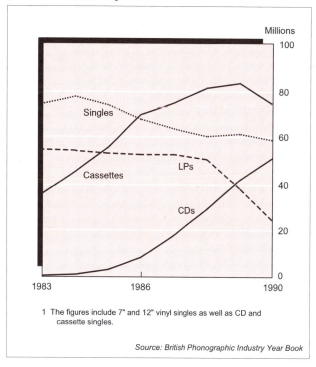

1 The figures include 7" and 12" vinyl singles as well as CD and cassette singles.

Source: British Phonographic Industry Year Book

In 1990, the *Radio Times* and *TV Times* were the most popular of the general weeklies, both with an average issue readership of one-fifth of the adult population. On average 16.5 million people read a general monthly magazine in 1990 - this represented over one third of the adult population. The readership of most popular women's magazines fell substantially between 1971 and 1989. *Woman's Own*, for example, had an average issue readership figure of 7.2 million in 1971 which had fallen to 4.3 million by 1990. During the 1980s European

10.10 Reading of the most popular magazines: by sex and age, 1971 and 1990

Great Britain

	Percentage of adults reading each magazine in 1990			Percentage of each age group reading each magazine in 1990				Readership[1] (millions)		Readers per copy (numbers)
	Males	Females	All adults	15 – 24	25 – 44	45 – 64	65 and over	1971	1990	1990
General magazines										
Radio Times	18	19	19	20	20	18	17	9.5	8.5	2.9
TV Times	18	19	19	21	19	18	15	9.9	8.4	3.0
Reader's Digest	14	13	13	8	13	17	14	9.2	6.1	3.9
What Car	7	1	4	6	5	3	1	.	1.8	12.2
National Geographic	5	3	4	4	4	4	2	1.1	1.7	. .
Exchange and Mart	5	2	3	5	4	3	1	.	1.5	8.2
Women's magazines[2]										
Woman's Own	3	16	10	10	11	9	8	7.2	4.3	4.2
Bella	3	15	10	12	11	8	6	.	4.3	. .
Woman's Weekly	2	11	7	4	5	9	10	4.7	3.1	2.6
Woman	2	11	7	6	8	6	5	8.0	3.0	3.2
Best	2	11	6	9	8	5	3	.	2.9	3.1
Prima	2	10	6	7	8	5	2	.	2.6	3.0

1 Defined as the average issue readership and represents the number of people who claim to have read, or looked at, one or more copies of a given publication during a period equal to the interval at which the publication appears.

2 The age analysis for women's magazines includes male readers.

Source: National Readership Surveys, Joint Industry Committee for National Readership Surveys; Circulation Review, Audit Bureau of Circulation

10.11 Reading of national newspapers: by sex and age, 1971 and 1990

Great Britain

	Percentage of adults reading each paper in 1990			Percentage of each age group reading each paper in 1990				Readership[1] (millions)		Readers per copy (numbers)
	Males	Females	All adults	15–24	25–44	45–64	65 and over	1971	1990	1990
Daily newspapers										
The Sun	25	20	23	29	24	21	16	8.5	10.2	2.6
Daily Mirror	22	17	19	20	18	21	18	13.8	8.7	2.8
Daily Mail	10	9	9	7	8	11	11	4.8	4.2	2.5
Daily Express	10	8	9	7	7	10	11	9.7	3.9	2.5
Daily Star	8	5	6	8	8	5	3	.	2.8	3.0
The Daily Telegraph	6	4	5	3	4	7	7	3.6	2.3	2.2
Today	5	3	4	5	5	3	1	.	1.7	3.0
The Guardian	4	2	3	3	4	3	1	1.1	1.3	3.1
The Times	3	2	3	2	3	3	2	1.1	1.2	2.7
The Independent	3	2	2	3	3	2	1	.	1.1	2.7
Financial Times	2	1	2	1	2	2	—	0.7	0.7	3.6
Any daily newspaper [2]	69	59	64	63	62	68	63	..	..	..
Sunday newspapers										
News of the World	31	28	29	37	32	27	21	15.8	13.2	2.6
Sunday Mirror	22	19	21	23	21	21	17	13.5	9.3	3.2
The People	17	15	16	15	16	18	15	14.4	7.4	2.9
The Mail on Sunday	13	11	12	14	14	13	7	.	5.6	2.9
Sunday Express	10	9	10	6	7	13	14	10.4	4.4	2.6
The Sunday Times	9	7	8	8	9	8	4	3.7	3.5	3.0
Sunday Telegraph	5	4	4	3	3	6	5	2.1	1.9	3.2
The Observer	5	4	4	4	5	4	3	2.4	1.8	3.3
Independent on Sunday	3	2	3	3	3	2	1	.	1.2	3.2
Any Sunday newspaper [3]	74	69	71	73	70	75	67	..	..	..

1 Defined as the average issue readership and represents the number of people who claim to have read or looked at one or more copies of a given publication during a period equal to the interval at which the publication appears.

2 Includes the above newspapers plus the Daily Record.
3 Includes the above newspapers plus the Sunday Post, Sunday Mail, Scotland on Sunday and Sunday Sport.

Source: National Readership Surveys, Joint Industry Committee for National Readership Surveys; Circulation Review, Audit Bureau of Circulation

publishers entered the British women's magazine market and introduced a number of new magazines. Of these, *Bella*, which was launched in 1987, was the most popular women's monthly magazine in 1990. Similarly, *Prima*, which was launched in 1986, was also among the most popular.

Men are more likely to read newspapers than women (Table 10.11), and a higher proportion of people in the 45-64 age group read a daily newspaper than in any other age group.

In 1990 the most widely read newspaper in Great Britain was *The Sun*, which was read by one quarter of all men and one fifth of all women. It was particularly popular amongst those aged 15-24. Although readership of *The Sun* increased by 20 per cent between 1971 and 1990, readership of most other newspapers fell during the same period. Readership of *The Daily Express* fell by 60 per cent.

Readership of Sunday newspapers also fell between 1971 and 1990 despite the introduction of larger newspapers, more colour supplements and a number of new Sunday newspapers. The most popular Sunday newspaper in 1990 was *The News of the World* which had an average issue readership of 13.2 million.

Social and cultural activities

Libraries offer their visitors a number of services which can range from the borrowing of books to the use of a photocopier. Many public libraries are now also a focus of local community work and information services.

In 1989-90 over 8 million children's books were borrowed from public libraries (Table 10.12), 40 per cent more than in 1980-81. Borrowings of adult fiction remained the most popular, with over 17 million books borrowed in 1989-90.

10.12 Libraries: material on loan

United Kingdom			Thousands
	1980 −81	1983 −84	1986 −87	1989 −90[1]
Adult fiction	14,992	16,162	15,801	17,349
Adult non-fiction	7,580	8,332	8,652	9,824
Children's books	5,703	6,265	6,472	8,034
Sound and video recordings	633	1,048	977	2,088

1 Figures for 1989−90 are not comparable with earlier years.

Source: Public Library Statistics,
Chartered Institute of Public Finance and Accountancy

10.13 Methods of obtaining current book

Great Britain					Percentages
	1981	1984	1986	1988	1990
Bought (including book clubs)	31	35	34	37	38
Library	38	33	33	33	32
Borrowed from friend or relative	17	17	19	17	15
Gift	9	9	7	7	8
Already in home	4	4	4	4	4
Don't know	1	2	3	2	3

Source: The Book Report, *Euromonitor*

The 1987 General Household Survey (GHS) asked a number of questions on the use of library services. Of those interviewed, 26 per cent had visited a public library in the four weeks before the interview. Women were more likely to visit than men (29 per cent compared with 22 per cent) although those men visiting were likely to do so slightly more frequently than women.

Borrowing from a library is one way of obtaining a book to read. However, in 1990, the most popular method of obtaining a book was to buy it, either from a shop or through a book club, rather than to borrow it or receive it as a gift (Table 10.13).

The number of West End theatre attendances increased in every year between 1981 and 1990 except in 1986 (Chart 10.14). In 1990 the total audience figure was 11.3 million, up slightly on 1988 but 39 per cent higher than in 1981.

Data compiled by City University through three major West End audience surveys estimate that the highest proportion of theatregoers were in the 25-34 age group in 1982, 1986 and 1990/91.

The expansion in choice for the television viewer (see Table 10.5) and the large increase in the use of video cassette recorders (see Table 10.9) has not reduced cinema attendance in the United Kingdom. The percentage of people visiting the cinema at least once a year has increased rapidly during the late 1980s (Table 10.15). In 1990, 64 per cent of the population visited the cinema, compared to only 38 per cent in 1984. Of those aged 15-24, 87 per cent attended the cinema at least once in 1990.

10.14 Attendances at West End theatre performances

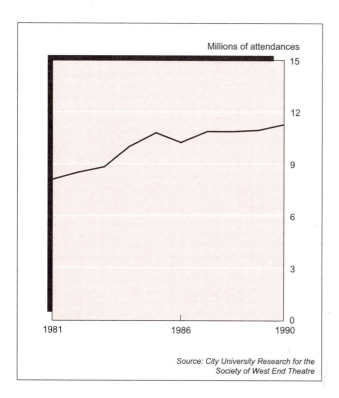

Millions of attendances

*Source: City University Research for the
Society of West End Theatre*

Seating capacity in cinemas increased during the late 1980s to around 400 thousand by 1990. The increase was due almost entirely to the increase in the number of multi-screen cinema complexes. Cinemas with five or more screens accounted for 30 per cent of all screens in the United Kingdom in 1990 compared to 12 per cent in 1988.

10.15 Attendance at cinemas[1]: by age

United Kingdom					Percentages
	1984	1986	1988	1989	1990
Aged					
7-14	73	87	84	85	85
15-24	59	82	81	86	87
25-34	49	65	64	72	79
35-44	45	60	61	67	70
45 and over	13	25	34	35	41
All persons aged 7 and over	38	53	56	60	64

1 Percentage attending at least once in any given year.

Source: Cinema and Video Audience Research

10.16 Cinema attendance: selected countries

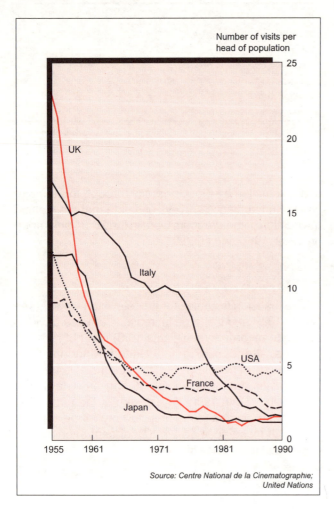

Number of visits per head of population

Source: Centre National de la Cinematographie; United Nations

In 1990 the Americans were the most prolific cinema attenders with over 4 visits per person, this was nearly four times the attendance rate in Japan and double the rate in France.

Blackpool Pleasure Beach was the most popular tourist attraction in 1990 (Table 10.17), with 6 1/2 million visitors. Other popular attractions with free admission included the Albert Dock in Liverpool where the attendance of 6 million was 43 per cent higher than in 1988. Madame Tussaud's continued to be the most popular attraction in 1990 amongst those with an admission charge. Admissions to the Science Museum nearly halved between 1988 and 1990 following the introduction of admission charges, falling from 2.4 million in 1988 to 1.3 million in 1990.

In 1990 there were around 2 1/2 thousand museums in the United Kingdom. There are many types of museum. Some house personal collections, many record local history and artistic achievement. Others, like the Theatre Museum, reflect the performing arts.

10.17 Attendances at the most popular tourist attractions

Great Britain				Millions
	1981	1986	1988	1990
Attractions with free admission				
Blackpool Pleasure Beach	7.5	6.5	6.5	6.5
Albert Dock, Liverpool	..	2.0	4.2	6.0
British Museum	2.6	3.6	3.8	4.8
Strathclyde Country Park, Motherwell	..	..	..	4.2
National Gallery	2.7	3.2	3.2	3.7
Palace Pier, Brighton	..	..	..	3.5
Pleasure Beach, Great Yarmouth	..	..	2.3	2.6
Tate Gallery, London	0.9	1.1	1.6	1.6
Pleasureland, Southport	..	..	1.5	1.5
Bradgate Park	1.2	1.2	1.2	1.3
Frontierland, Morecambe	..	..	1.0	1.3
Attractions charging admission				
Madame Tussaud's[1]	2.0	2.4	2.7	2.5
Tower of London	2.1	2.0	2.2	2.3
Alton Towers[2]	1.6	2.2	2.5	2.1
Natural History Museum[3]	3.7	2.7	1.4	1.5
Chessington World of Adventures	0.5	0.8	1.2	1.5
Blackpool Tower	..	1.4	1.5	1.4
Royal Academy, London	0.7	0.6	1.0	1.3
Science Museum[4]	3.8	3.0	2.4	1.3
London Zoo	1.1	1.2	1.3	1.3
Kew Gardens	0.9	1.1	1.2	1.2

1 1988 and 1990 figures not comparable with previous years.
2 1990 figures not comparable with previous years.
3 Admission charges were introduced in April 1987.
4 Admission charges were introduced in 1989.

Source: British Tourist Authority

Cinema attendances are increasing (see Chart 10.16), the video market is expanding (see Table 10.9) and television, in particular satellite film channels, show 3 thousand films per year. Despite this, production of films in Great Britain dropped to a low of fewer than 30 films in 1990, mainly with very small budgets. By comparison, the French film industry made 130 films in the same year.

Although the percentage of people visiting the cinema has increased recently (Table 10.15), the average number of visits per person fell considerably between 1955 and 1990 for each of the countries shown in Chart 10.16. In the United Kingdom in 1955 the annual rate of visits stood at 23 per person, higher than in any of the other countries. However, by 1984 the United Kingdom rate was the lowest (below 1), and well below the rates in the United States (5) and France (3). Between 1984 and 1990 the number of visits per person in the United Kingdom rose, to reach 1.5 in 1990 when there were 88.7 million visitors to United Kingdom cinemas.

Sporting Activities

Sport plays a fundamental role in promoting good health and physical fitness, and has the potential to reduce the burden on health services. Furthermore, provision of sporting and recreational facilities has been recognised by the police, probation officers and social workers as being beneficial in reducing crime, particularly in inner cities. The Sports Council estimate that around 21 million adults and 7 million children take part in sport or active recreation in Great Britain.

The 1987 General Household Survey (GHS) included questions on sports and physical exercises, the results of which are shown in Table 10.18. In the GHS, informants were asked about participation in sports during the four week period before the interview. Since these interviews were carried out throughout the year, the survey results represent participation in a four-week period averaged over the whole year.

Snooker, pool and billiards were the most popular sports, with 15 per cent of people participating. They were particularly popular among skilled manual workers, with 22 per cent participating. Professionals were more likely than other socio-economic groups to participate in most of the sports in the table, particularly cycling, jogging or running and swimming or diving.

10.18 Participation in sports and physical exercise: by socio-economic group, 1987

Great Britain   Percentages and numbers

	Pro-fessional	Employers and managers	Inter-mediate and junior non-manual	Skilled manual and own account non pro-fessional	Semi-skilled manual and personal service	Unskilled manual	All groups[1]
Percentage in each group participating in each activity in the 4 weeks before interview							
Pedal cycling	12	7	8	8	8	6	8
Track and field athletics	—	—	—	—	—	—	—
Jogging, cross-country/road running	11	5	5	5	3	2	5
Soccer	6	4	2	7	4	3	5
Rugby Union/League	—	—	—	—	—	—	—
Cricket	2	2	1	1	1	0	1
Tennis	4	2	2	1	1	1	2
Netball	—	—	1	—	—	—	—
Basketball	—	—	—	—	—	—	1
Golf, pitch and putt, putting	10	9	3	4	2	1	4
Swimming or diving	21	16	16	11	8	5	13
Fishing	2	2	1	4	2	1	2
Yachting or dinghy sailing	2	1	1	1	—	—	1
Other water sports	3	2	1	1	—	—	1
Horse riding, show jumping pony trekking	1	1	1	—	1	—	1
Badminton	7	4	4	2	2	1	3
Squash	9	4	2	2	1	1	3
Table tennis	3	3	2	2	1	1	2
Snooker, pool, billiards	18	16	10	22	11	11	15
Darts	7	8	6	13	9	8	9
Tenpin bowls or skittles	3	2	2	2	1	1	2
Lawn or carpet bowls	2	2	2	2	1	1	2
Boxing or wrestling	0	—	—	—	—	—	—
Self defence	1	1	1	1	1	—	1
Weight training/lifting	6	5	4	5	3	2	5
Gymnastics	0	—	—	—	—	—	—
Keep fit, yoga, aerobics, dance exercise	9	8	13	4	7	3	9
Skiing	2	1	—	—	—	—	—
Ice skating	1	—	1	1	1	—	1
Curling	—	0	—	—	—	0	—
Motor sports	1	—	—	1	—	—	—
Sample size (= 100%) (numbers)	705	2,465	6,012	4,051	3,830	1,265	19,529

1 Includes full-time students, members of the Armed forces, people who have never worked, and inadequately described occupations.

Source: General Household Survey

10.19 Average attendances[1] at football matches[2]

England & Wales and Scotland   Numbers

| | Football League (England & Wales) | | | | Scottish Football League | | |
	Division 1	Division 2	Division 3	Division 4	Premier Division	Division 1	Division 2
1961/62	26,106	16,132	9,419	6,060	.	11,147	1,686
1966/67	30,829	15,701	8,009	5,407	.	9,270	1,068
1971/72	31,352	14,652	8,510	4,981	.	10,236	1,416
1976/77	29,540	13,529	7,522	3,863	11,844	2,331	765
1980/81	24,660	11,202	6,590	3,082	9,777	2,202	609
1986/87	19,800	9,000	4,300	3,100	11,720	1,524	662
1987/88	19,300	10,600	5,000	3,200	13,949	1,339	745
1988/89	20,600	10,600	5,500	3,200	15,708	2,455	504
1989/90	20,800	12,500	5,000	3,400	15,576	2,064	761
1990/91	22,681	11,457	5,208	3,253	14,424	2,369	489

1 Football league attendances are rounded to the nearest hundred between 1986/87 and 1989/90.

2 League matches only until 1985/86. From 1986/87, Football League attendances include promotion and relegation play-off matches.

Source: Football League; Scottish Football League

During the 1990/91 football season average attendances at Football League Division One (England and Wales) games rose for the third successive year, to 22,681 (Table 10.19). Manchester United had the highest average attendance in the Football League, at 43,218, followed by Arsenal, at 36,864. Sheffield Wednesday were the best supported team in Division Two with an average attendance of 26,605.

In Scotland, Glasgow Rangers and Glasgow Celtic again attracted the biggest crowds. In League matches Rangers attracted an average attendance of almost 36 thousand. Average attendances in the Scottish Premier Division have risen by almost half since 1980/81, despite a fall of 7 per cent between 1989/90 and 1990/91.

Nearly 19 million spectators attended Football League games in England & Wales in 1990/91 (Table 10.20). There were over 5 million attendances at greyhound racing meetings and although this was one million fewer than in 1981/82 it was still the second most popular of the sports shown. Attendance at horseracing meetings continued to be popular in 1990/91. Attendances at the fifty-nine racecourses in Great Britain totalled 4.7 million, 27 per cent higher than in 1981/82.

10.20 Spectator attendance[1] at selected sporting events

Thousands

	1971/72	1981/82	1990/91
Football League (England & Wales)	28,700	20,006	18,828
Greyhound racing	8,800	6,100	5,121
Horse racing	4,200	3,700	4,698
Scottish Football League	4,521	2,961	3,377
Rugby Football Union (England)	700	750[6]	1,250
Motor sports[2]	..	1,300	2,275
Rugby Football League[3]	1,170	1,226	1,539
Test and County cricket	984	994	..
English basketball	2	85	140
Motorcycle sports[4]	250	250	250
Scottish basketball[5]	9	14	9

1 Estimated.
2 Car and kart racing only, not including rallying.
3 League matches only.
4 Excluding speedway.
5 National league and cup matches only.
6 1982 season.

Source: Organisations concerned

Holidays

The proportion of adults who do not take a holiday has remained much the same since 1971 (Chart 10.21). However, there has been a slow increasing trend for people to take more than one holiday each year. Holiday-taking varies considerably by social class; in 1990, 42 per cent of adults in the lower social classes D and E took at least one holiday compared with 79 per cent in classes A and B.

The number of overseas holidays taken by Great Britain residents increased by over a half between 1981 and 1990, to 20.5 million, although this was half a million less than in 1989 (Table 10.22). Research in America suggests that during economic recession people travel smaller distances, use their cars instead of flying, visit friends and relatives less, and leave the children at home more.

10.21 Number of holidays[1] per year: by social class

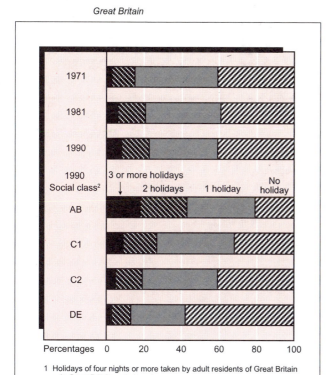

Great Britain

1 Holidays of four nights or more taken by adult residents of Great Britain in Great Britain and abroad.
2 See Appendix, Part 10: Social Class.

Source: British National Travel Survey, British Tourist Authority

10.22 Holidays[1] taken by Great Britain residents: by destination

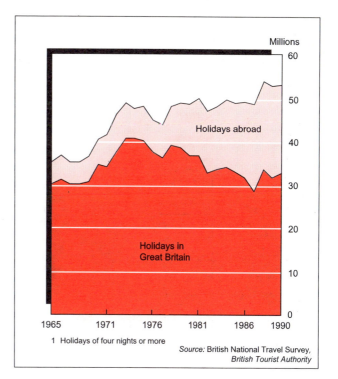

1 Holidays of four nights or more

Source: British National Travel Survey, British Tourist Authority

In 1990 United Kingdom residents took 14 million holidays in other European Community (EC) countries (Table 10.23). The most popular destinations were

10.23 Foreign holidays[1] by United Kingdom residents: by destination

Thousands and percentages

	1981	1986	1989	1990	Percentage change 1981-1990
Belgium/Luxembourg	199	348	278	365	84
Denmark	97	70	62	42	-57
France	2,209	2,572	3,767	4,012	82
West Germany	342	415	599	653	91
Greece	881	1,472	1,566	1,551	76
Irish Republic	471	356	580	612	30
Netherlands	310	373	559	593	91
Italy	763	786	891	733	-4
Portugal	362	882	903	885	145
Spain	2,841	5,556	5,717	4,637	63
European Community	8,474	12,830	14,922	14,083	66
Other Europe	1,579	2,303	3,114	3,226	104
Middle East	87	76	78	85	-2
North Africa	175	239	345	278	59
South Africa	29	15	60	46	61
Other Africa	62	83	154	173	178
Australia and New Zealand	27	54	99	101	274
Commonwealth Carribean and Latin America	142	133	269	288	104
United States	717	450	1,221	1,248	74
Canada	123	86	139	172	40
All countries[2]	11,664	16,556	20,777	20,164	73

1 A visit of one or more nights where a holiday is the main purpose. Business trips and visits to friends or relatives are excluded.
2 Including others not given in the table.

Source: Employment Department

10.24 Domestic holidays taken by United Kingdom residents: by region, 1990

United Kingdom

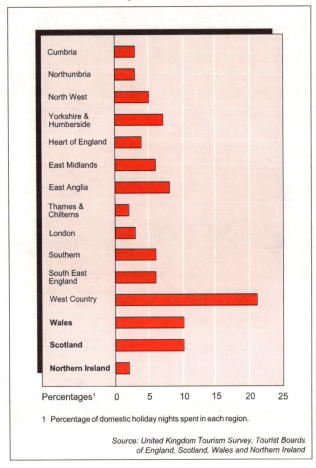

Percentages[1]

1 Percentage of domestic holiday nights spent in each region.

Source: United Kingdom Tourism Survey, Tourist Boards
of England, Scotland, Wales and Northern Ireland

nights were spent in the region covered by the West Country Tourist Board than in any other (21 per cent). Scotland and Wales were next (10 per cent each).

10.25 Leisure day visits[1]: number of visits and expenditure, 1988-89

Great Britain — Millions and £ million

	Visits (millions)		Expenditure (£ million)	
	20 miles and over	40 miles and over	20 miles and over	40 miles and over
Attractions				
Park, garden, common	14	8	154	130
Temporary show or carnival	16	12	87	72
Zoo, aquarium, bird sanctuary, safari park	13	10	83	62
Theme park	9	7	58	43
Museum or art gallery	9	6	68	50
Castle, ancient monument	8	5	57	43
Stately home	6	5	49	39
Cathedral or church	4	2	21	15
Historic ship or steam railway	3	2	21	17
Outdoor activities				
Taking part in outdoor sport	23	13	384	325
General tour, sightseeing	66	52	245	211
Walking, hiking, rambling, climbing	22	12	130	85
Swimming, sunbathing	20	11	69	47
Watching outdoor sport	21	16	74	60
Fishing	7	5	41	35
Picnicking	8	6	6	4
Horse riding or pony-trekking	1	1	19	18
Canoeing, rowing, sailing, windsurfing	3	3	22	18
Power or motor-boating, water skiing	3	1	11	8
Other activities				
Party, celebration, anniversary	27	12	248	96
Dance or disco	13	5	132	56
Visits or meetings with friends or relatives	144	92	582	422
Theatre, opera, cinema, ballet, concert	25	13	296	166
Bingo or casino	1	0	12	1
Public house or wine bar	18	5	141	44
Restaurant or cafe	27	11	400	157
Taking part in indoor sport	14	5	73	32
Watching indoor sport	1	1	6	4
Shopping trip (not routine)	64	37	1,458	880
Other	36	24	266	218
Total[2]	630	379	5,212	3,358

1 Round trips from home of 3 hours or more, excluding work related trips and routine shopping trips.
2 Includes 4 million visits where purpose was not given.

Source: Leisure Day Visits Survey, Employment Department;
English Tourist Board

Spain and France each with over 4 million holidays. However, the number of holidays has not increased to all European destinations. Denmark has steadily decreased in popularity since 1981 and holidays to Italy in 1990 fell below the 1981 levels despite steady growth throughout the 1980s. The United States was the most popular destination outside the EC with 1.2 million visits in 1990. Between 1981 and 1990 holidays by United Kingdom residents to Australia and New Zealand, more than trebled.

The British Tourist Authority coordinated the United Kingdom activities to mark 1990 - the European Year of Tourism. The Year, held under the auspices of the European Commission, involved a total of 18 European countries and was aimed at heightening the awareness of the political, economic and social importance of tourism. Over 2 thousand events were held in the United Kingdom under the banner of the Year.

Results from the United Kingdom Tourism Survey show that in 1990 there were 294 million nights spent by United Kingdom residents on domestic holidays, 9 per cent less than in 1989 (Chart 10.24). More of these

Social Trends 22, © Crown copyright 1992

In 1990, 43 per cent of all holiday nights spent in the United Kingdom by foreign tourists (excluding those from the Irish Republic) were spent in London. Conversely only 3 per cent of domestic holiday nights were spent in London which shows markedly different preference between domestic and overseas tourists. Other regions popular with foreign tourists were Scotland (10 per cent of holiday nights) and the West Country (7 per cent of holiday nights).

During 1988-89 over 630 million day visits were made from home in Great Britain (Table 10.25). Spending on day trips totalled £5.2 billion, nearly half of domestic tourism expenditure in the United Kingdom. The most popular single reason for making a day trip was to visit friends or relatives, accounting for 23 per cent of day visits. General tours or sightseeing was second most popular, at 10 per cent of trips. The weekend is the most popular time for day visits, over half were made at weekends in 1988-89.

In 1990 there were 1.5 million employees in employment in tourism-related industries in Great Britain, 29 per cent more than in 1981.

Resources

10.26 Arts Council expenditure

United Kingdom	Percentages and £ thousand			
	1971 −72	1981 −82	1986 −87[1]	1990 −91
National companies[2]	29	27	24	22
Regional Arts Associations	5	11	19	19
Art	5	6	5	4
Drama	20	18	15	13
Music	20	19	17	16
Dance	4	4	5	5
Literature	2	2	1	1
Other [3]	15	12	15	19
Total (= 100%) (£ thousand)	12,096	83,028	136,870	181,843

1 Great Britain only.
2 Includes the English National Opera in London and on tour, the National Theatre (in three auditoria), the Royal Opera and the Royal Ballet Companies in London and on tour, and the Royal Shakespeare Company in Stratford-on-Avon and in London.
3 Includes arts centres and community projects (including the South Bank Board) training in the arts, incentive funding and general operating costs.

Source: Annual Report, Arts Council of Great Britain;
Arts Council of Northern Ireland

In August 1991 the major football pools companies began funding a new Arts and Sports Foundation. The money will be divided between the sport and the arts and is expected to be around £70 million per year. The income for sport will be primarily used for building sports centres and stadiums, and will be about equal to the annual Sports Council received from the government grant. The money will have less effect on the Arts as the Arts Council already receives far greater assistance from central government (Table 10.26).

The Arts Councils of Great Britain and Northern Ireland were established to develop and improve the knowledge, understanding, and practise of the arts, to increase their accessibility to the public and to advise and co-operate with government departments, local authorities and other organisations. The table shows how the Arts Councils allocate their government grant-in-aid.

Total expenditure amounted to over £181 million in 1990-91, of which 22 per cent went to National Companies (theatre, ballet and opera). The proportion going to regional arts associations increased four-fold between 1971-72 and 1989-90 to 19 per cent of the total.

10.27 Household expenditure on selected leisure items

United Kingdom	£ and percentages		
	1981	1986	1989
Average weekly household expenditure (£)			
Alcoholic drink consumed away from home	5.39[2]	5.93	6.92
Meals consumed out[1]	..	4.38	5.51
Books, newspapers, magazines, etc	2.00	2.73	3.31
Television, radio and musical instruments	3.26	4.85	5.65
Purchase of materials for home repairs, etc	1.57	3.06	2.89
Holidays	3.08	5.39	7.76
Hobbies	0.08	0.06	0.09
Cinema admissions	0.14	0.10	0.16
Dance admissions	0.12	0.12	. .[4]
Theatre, concert, etc admissions	0.17	0.29	0.35
Subscription and admission charges to participant sports	0.43	0.71	0.85
Football match admissions	0.06	0.08 }	0.20
Admissions to other spectator sports	0.02	0.04 }	
Sports goods (excluding clothes)	0.26	0.37	0.62
Other entertainment	0.24	0.41	0.70[4]
Total weekly expenditure on above	16.82[3]	28.52	35.01
Expenditure on above items as a percentage of total household expenditure	13.4	16.0	15.6

1 Eaten on the premises, excluding state school meals and workplace meals.
2 Including home consumption.
3 The total for 1981 is not comparable with later years since the figure for the category "Meals consumed out" is not available.
4 For 1989, "Dance admissions" have been included with "Other entertainment."

Source: Central Statistical Office

The Arts Council of Great Britain operate a parity policy with local authorities for the theatre, which requires local authorities to match their grants. Regional theatre, in particular, is subsidised to enable it to pursue a sound artistic policy, but without the threat of closure should a production fail to attract audiences.

Business sponsorship is making an increasing contribution to the funding of the arts. In 1975-76 only a handful of major businesses sponsored the arts and the level of sponsorship was estimated at just over £0.5 million. However, more businesses were encouraged to sponsor following the establishment in 1976 of the Association for British Sponsorship of the Arts, an independent organisation dedicated to raising more commercial sponsorship for the arts. The government introduced its Business Sponsorship Incentive Scheme (BSIS) in 1984. This offers matching grants for new sponsorship and has encouraged over 900 businesses into sponsorship.

In 1989, households in the United Kingdom spent 15.6 per cent of their total expenditure on the leisure-based items shown in Table 10.27. This was slightly lower than in 1986. In 1989, holidays accounted for 22 per cent of all expenditure on the leisure-based items shown. Average household expenditure on materials for home repairs fell from £3.06 per week in 1986 to £2.89 in 1989. This was the only one of the listed items where expenditure fell between the two years.

BIBLIOGRAPHY

The following list contains selected publications relevant to Chapter 10: Leisure. Those published by HMSO are available from the addresses shown on the back cover of Social Trends.

Annual Reports of the Sports Council, Sports Council for Northern Ireland, Sports Council for Wales, and the Scottish Sports Council, available from the individual Councils
Arts Council of Great Britain Annual Report and Accounts, Arts Council of Great Britain
Arts Council of Northern Ireland Annual Report and Accounts, Arts Council of Northern Ireland
BBC Handbook, BBC
British National Travel Survey, British Tourist Authority
British Phonographic Industry Year Book, British Phonographic Industry
Business Monitor MQ6 - Overseas Travel and Tourism

Cinema and Video Industry Audience Research, CAA
Digest of Tourist Statistics, British Tourist Authority
Employment Gazette, HMSO
Family Expenditure Survey, HMSO
Film and Year Book, British Film Institute
General Household Survey, HMSO
Independent Broadcasting Authority Annual Report and Accounts, IBA
United Kingdom Tourist Statistics 1990, Tourist Boards of England, Northern Ireland, Scotland and Wales.
Visits to Tourism Attractions, British Tourist Authority and National Tourist Boards

Chapter 11: Participation

Charity
●   Three out of every ten people do not give to charity.   *(Page 190)*

Religion
●   While church membership is falling, membership of other religions, such as Muslims and Sikhs, is increasing.
    (Table 11.4)

Voluntary sector
●   People who live in the South East and the South West are more likely to do organised voluntary work than those in other parts of the country.   *(Chart 11.10)*

●   The RNLI are attending an increasing number of callouts - in 1990, they attended nearly five thousand callouts, two thirds more than in 1981.   *(Table 11.13)*

Politics
●   The British public are more apathetic at European Parliament elections than they are at General Elections. In the 1989 EC election, turnout was 36 per cent - the lowest turnout in Europe.   *(Table 11.16)*

Other participation

●   Trade Union membership and the number of unions continues to fall. Membership has fallen by a quarter from the 1979 peak of 13.3 million to 10.2 million in 1989.   *(Table 11.19)*

●   The most common reason for belonging to a Trade Union was that it protected members if any problems arose at work (cited by 93 per cent of respondents).   *(Table 11.20)*

●   Alcoholics Anonymous had 15 thousand more clients in 1990 than 1981.   *(Table 11.21)*

11.1   Trade Union membership

United Kingdom

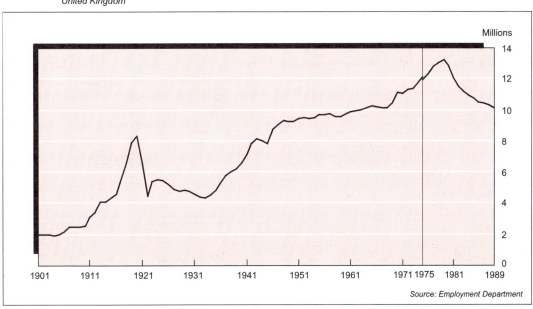

Source: Employment Department

Participation

This chapter looks at how people participate in the life of the community. Participation can take various forms such as: membership of organisations; voting in elections; charity work; voluntary rescue work; and helping others in the community.

Charity

Table 11.2 shows the total income and voluntary income of the larger charities. In 1989 there were 25 charities whose total income was over £10 million. Charities raise their income in a variety of ways, not just through contributions from the public - although this is the way that most people participate in charitable work. In 1989 Charity Projects Ltd, a fund-raising organisation which raises money through organised events such as Comic Relief and distributes the money to other charities for use on particular projects, raised nearly all its income by voluntary contributions. This was followed by Tear Fund (an overseas relief and development organisation) and Help the Aged who raised nearly 90 per cent of their total income by voluntary income. Not all charities have such high proportions of income from voluntary contributions. Barnardo's for example, raised only 42 per cent of total income from contributions and the Spastics Society just over 43 per cent. In 1989, the National Trust remained the charity with the highest total income, but Oxfam had the highest voluntary income.

The different ways charities raise income are described in Chart 11.3 which shows that 57 per cent of the total income of the top 200 charities came from voluntary gifts in 1989, four percentage points higher than in 1988. These voluntary gifts include voluntary fund raising, legacies and covenants. Of the remaining income, 18 per cent came from local and central government grants and fees. The chart also shows the different types of charities to which money is going. Medical and health charities received just under one-third of the total income of the top 200 charities in the United Kingdom in 1989. A further one-fifth of the total income of these top 200 charities was given to charities working on international aid.

The Charity Household Survey carried out by the Charities Aid Foundation in 1989/90 found that the average amount given by all respondents (including non-donors) in the month prior to interview was £7.73.

11.2 Total income and voluntary income of selected[1] charities, 1989[2]

United Kingdom		£ million cash
	Total income	Total voluntary income
National Trust	89.1	43.4
Oxfam	66.7	49.3
Barnardo's	61.3	25.8
Salvation Army	56.6	29.6
Save the Children Fund	51.9	36.5
Spastics Society	51.3	22.3
Imperial Cancer Research Fund	48.6	40.3
Royal National Lifeboat Institution	47.4	40.5
British Red Cross Society	40.9	19.4
Cancer Research Campaign	38.2	31.7
Royal National Institute for the Blind	36.8	16.8
Guide Dogs for the Blind Association	36.3	21.5
National Society for the Prevention of Cruelty to Children	28.8	22.9
Christian Aid	28.1	18.5
Charity Projects Limited	27.8	27.6
Royal Society for the Prevention of Cruelty to Animals	27.2	20.5
British Heart Foundation	24.7	20.7
Help the Aged	24.5	21.7
Marie Curie Memorial Foundation	19.1	14.3
Action Aid	17.9	14.2
Royal British Legion	17.7	11.4
Tear Fund	15.4	13.7
Royal Society for the Protection of Birds	15.4	11.1
Peoples' Dispensary for Sick Animals	15.1	12.6
Cancer Relief Macmillan Fund	14.2	12.2

1 Fund raising charities with a voluntary income of £10.0 million or over in the year.
2 Accounting periods ending in 1989; although 12 month periods covered may differ.

Source: Charity Trends 13th Edition, *Charities Aid Foundation*

However, the survey also found that a large number of people do not donate or donate only small amounts whereas a much smaller number of people donate much larger amounts. Three in ten of those interviewed had not donated to charity in the previous month and over half had donated less than £2.

Under the *1986 Finance Act* it became possible for those who are part of a PAYE system to authorise donations to charities as a tax free deduction from pay. The maximum amount of these donations rose to £480 in 1989-90 and to £600 in 1990-91. In the year to 5 April 1990, £7.3 million was donated by 181 thousand people.

11.3 Total income of the top 200 charities: by source and major sector, 1989

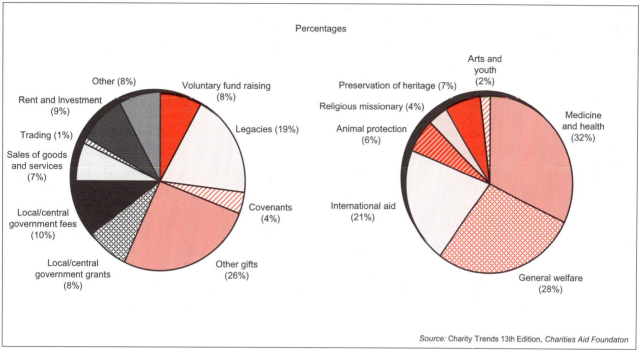

United Kingdom

Percentages

Source: Charity Trends 13th Edition, *Charities Aid Foundaton*

Religion

11.4 Church membership, ministers and buildings: estimates

	Adult members (millions)		Ministers (thousands)		Buildings (thousands)	
United Kingdom	1975	1990	1975	1990	1975	1990
Trinitarian Churches						
Anglican	2.27	1.84	15.9	14.1	19.8	18.3
Presbyterian	1.65	1.29	3.8	3.1	6.4	5.6
Methodist	0.61	0.48	4.2	2.3	9.1	7.5
Baptist	0.27	0.24	2.4	2.9	3.6	3.4
Other Protestant Churches	0.53	0.70	7.1	9.0	8.0	11.3
Roman Catholic	2.53	1.95	8.0	7.6	4.1	4.6
Orthodox	0.20	0.27	0.1	0.2	0.1	0.2
Total	8.06	6.77	41.6	39.2	51.2	50.9
Non-Trinitarian Churches						
Mormons	0.10	0.15	5.3	9.8	0.2	0.4
Jehovah's Witnesses	0.08	0.12	7.1	12.7	0.6	1.3
Spiritualists	0.06	0.06	0.2	0.4	0.6	0.6
Other Non-Trinitarian	0.09	0.13	0.9	1.5	1.1	1.1
Total	0.33	0.46	13.5	24.4	2.5	3.4
Other religions						
Muslims	0.40	0.99	1.0	2.3	0.2	1.0
Sikhs	0.12	0.39	0.1	0.2	0.1	0.2
Hindus	0.10	0.14	0.1	0.2	0.1	0.1
Jews	0.11	0.11	0.4	0.4	0.3	0.3
Others	0.08	0.23	0.4	1.2	0.1	0.4
Total	0.81	1.86	2.0	4.3	0.8	2.0

Source: UK Christian Handbook 1992/1993 Edition, *MARC Europe*

Table 11.4 shows that while membership of Trinitarian churches (that is those who believe in the unison of the Holy Trinity in one Godhead) is falling, membership of other religions, such as Muslims and Sikhs is increasing. It is estimated that between 1975 and 1990 the total adult membership of Trinitarian churches fell by 16 per cent to 6.8 million. However, membership of some non-Trinitarian churches including Mormons and Jehovah's Witnesses increased over the same period. The greatest increase in religious membership was within the other religions category including Muslims, Sikhs, Hindus and Jews where it is estimated that total membership more than doubled over the period with a corresponding growth in the number of religious leaders.

The population census was held in 1991, but two years before on 15 October 1989 tens of thousands of churches across England contributed to the English Church Census organised by MARC Europe. On Church Census day 3.7 million adults attended church, a decrease of 8 per cent since 1979, together with 1.2 million children under 15. Of the individual denominations, the number of adults attending Roman Catholic churches were down 14 per cent, Methodist churches were down 11 per cent and Anglican churches were down 9 per cent. However, there was an increase of 42 per cent in the numbers attending the Independent Church, and increases of 8 per cent and 4 per cent for the Pentecostal and Afro-Caribbean churches.

11.5 Percentage of the population attending church services: by age, 1979 and 1989

England

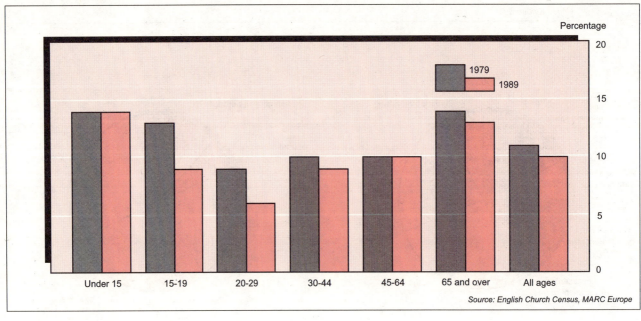

Source: English Church Census, MARC Europe

11.6 Marriages: religious and civil ceremonies, 1971 and 1989

Great Britain   Thousands and percentages

	1971	1989		
	All marri-ages	First marri-ages[1]	Second or sub-sequent[2]	All marri-ages
Manner of solemnisation				
Religious ceremony				
Church of England/ Church in Wales	160	111	3	119
Church of Scotland	20	12	1	14
Roman Catholic	48	26	0	28
Other Christian	37	17	7	37
Jews and other non-Christian	2	2	0	2
Civil ceremonies	180	76	52	181
Total marriages	447	243	63	382
Civil marriages as a percentage of all marriages				
England & Wales	*41*	*31*	*83*	*48*
Scotland	*31*	*28*	*78*	*41*
Great Britain	*40*	*31*	*82*	*47*

1 First marriage for both partners.
2 Remarriage for both partners.

Source: Office of Population Censuses and Surveys;
General Register Office (Scotland)

Fewer young people are attending church than they did in the late 1970s. Chart 11.5 uses the English Church Census figures to look at church attendance for different age groups in 1979 and in 1989. Over this period, the proportion of the overall population attending church fell only slightly from 11 per cent to 10 per cent, with the proportions of those aged under 15 and those aged over 30 being remarkably similar for the two years. However, the proportion of those aged between 15 and 19 years attending church fell from 13 to 9 per cent and the proportion of those aged between 20 and 29 fell from 9 to 6 per cent.

For many people who are not regular churchgoers, baptisms, weddings and funerals may be the only time they attend church. In Great Britain 130 thousand fewer people married in 1989 than in 1971; a drop of nearly 15 per cent (Table 11.6). Of the 382 thousand weddings in 1989, nearly two-thirds were between couples where both partners were marrying for the first time. In 1971 around 4 in 10 marriages were civil rather than religious marriages; by 1989, this proportion had risen to just under 5 in 10, but there are regional differences. In both years the percentage of all marriages which were civil ceremonies was smaller in Scotland than it was in England and Wales. Marriages where one or both partners were remarrying were much more likely to be solemnised with a civil ceremony than those where both partners were marrying for the first time.

Voluntary Sector

The Women's National Commission (WNC) was formed in 1969 as an advisory committee to the Government, with a small secretariat in the Cabinet Office. Its terms of reference are to ensure by all possible means that the informed opinions of women are given their due weight in the deliberations of government. The Commission consists of 50 women, elected or appointed by mainly national organisations which have a large and active female membership and which have been invited by Government to send a representative. These include women's voluntary organisations, political parties, trade unions, religious groups, professional and business organisations and women participating in voluntary service and caring organisations. Although varying greatly in size and age the 50 constituent organisations of WNC represent a broad spectrum of women's experience and views in the United Kingdom today. The Commission works by responding to government papers and by setting up *ad hoc* working groups to study, report and make recommendations to government on issues of its own choosing. The Commission has two Co-Chairpersons, one a minister appointed by the Prime Minister and one elected from among the members.

Membership of many of the larger women's voluntary organisations has fallen during the 1980s. Table 11.7 shows the membership of some of these larger organisations; the Women's Institutes were the organisations with the highest membership in 1990 with 319 thousand members. While membership of many organisations fell between 1981 and 1990, the Association of Inner Wheel Clubs and Soroptomist International both attracted more members. There were also many new women's organisations formed, often to meet a specific need or interest.

The National Federation of Women's Institutes (NFWI) was founded in Canada by Adeline Hunter Hoodless in the 1890s as a direct result of the death of her fourth child from what she believed to be her own ignorance of hygiene standards and child care. From these beginnings the NFWI movement evolved. The first United Kingdom meeting was held at Llanfairpwll, North Wales in 1915 at the instigation of a Canadian WI member.

Between the first United Kingdom meeting and 1928 detailed membership records were not kept although records of the numbers of institutes do exist. In 1915 there were 12 institutes and by 1928 this had risen to 4,244. In 1929 there were nearly 271 thousand members (Chart 11.8). Membership increased steadily (apart from a short period during the Second World War) to a peak of 467 thousand members in 1954. Since then, membership has declined to only 319 thousand in 1990, although the number of institutes has actually increased by 853.

11.7 Membership of selected women's voluntary organisations

United Kingdom			Thousands
	1971	1981	1990
Mothers Union[1,2]	308	210	177
National Federation of Women's Institutes[1]	440	378	319
National Women's Register	15	24	20
National Union of Townswomen's Guilds[1]	216	155	105
Royal British Legion (Women's Section)	162	165	112
Church of Scotland Women's Guild[1]	127	86	69
Scottish Women's Rural Institutes	58	50	38
Association of Inner Wheel Clubs	30	34	35
Soroptomist International of GB and Ireland[1,2]	13	14	16
National Council of Women[1,3]	6	3	2
Wales Assembly of Women[1,3,4]	..	..	100
Women's Forum Northern Ireland[1,3,4]	..	..	100

1 Members of the Women's National Commission.
2 Includes the Republic of Ireland.
3 Umbrella organisations.
4 Includes members of affiliate organisations.

Source: Women's National Commission

11.8 Membership of the National Federation of Women's Institutes

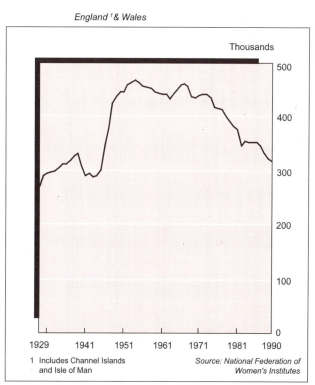

England [1] & Wales

1 Includes Channel Islands and Isle of Man

Source: National Federation of Women's Institutes

11.9 Selected voluntary organisations: membership and branches, 1971 and 1990

United Kingdom	Membership (thousands)		Branches/centres (numbers)	
	1971	1990	1971	1990
Abbeyfield Society[1]	6	12	345	600
Age Concern England	..	180	..	1,100
British Red Cross Society	172	82	917	1,200
Confederation of Indian Organisations	.	260	52	77
Disablement Income Group	..	5	..	..
Lions Club of the British Isles and Ireland	8	21	302	897
National Association of Leagues of Hospital Friends	250	350	835	1,249
National Association of Round Tables of Great Britain and Ireland	29	22[7]	1,072	1,220[7]
National Federation of Community Organisations[2]	.	1	564	26
National Federation of Gateway Clubs	8	40	200	723
National Federation of Self-Help Organisations	.	.	400	2,500
National Society for the Prevention of Cruelty to Children[3]	20	21	217	220
PHAB (Physically Handicapped and Able Bodied)	2	20	50	480
Retirement Pensions Association	600	40	1,500	600
Rotary International in Great Britain and Ireland	50	65	1,106	1,735
Royal British Legion	750	660	4,135	3,284
Royal Society for Mentally Handicapped Children and Adults	40	75	400	600
Royal Society for the Prevention of Cruelty to Animals[4]	..	21	207	207
St John Ambulance Brigade[5]	..	55	..	3,209
Toc H[6]	15	5	1,046	427

1 Data relate to 1 January 1972 and 1 January 1991 respectively.
2 Figures refer to member organisations.
3 England, Wales, and Northern Ireland only. The branches are responsible for over 4 thousand district committees.
4 England and Wales only.
5 England and Northern Ireland only. Not including over 20 thousand members of youth organisations.
6 Owing to changes in the method of recording, the 1990 figures are not comparable with those for 1971.
7 Figures are for 1991

Source: Organisations concerned

Many organisations depend and rely on voluntary help and on people giving their time and energy. This is one way in which people can participate in and contribute to the life of the community. Table 11.9 gives the membership figures for some of the major voluntary organisations. Many organisations operate at a local level, responding to needs in their particular areas. Their activities include fund-raising, visiting and helping lonely, elderly, sick and disabled people, providing transport, arranging holidays, running rest homes and canteens, shops and trolley services in hospitals.

One of the organisations shown in the table, the Abbeyfield Society, is a federation of 600 Local Voluntary Societies, which set up and manage family size houses which can accommodate seven to nine elderly people who would otherwise be alone and at risk; residents furnish their own rooms and although they come together for main meals they essentially lead their own lives. Details of environmental organisations can be found in Chapter 9.

A study on voluntary work was carried out for the Home Office as part of the 1987 General Household Survey. Voluntary work was defined as unpaid work which is done through a group or on behalf of an organisation and is of service or benefit to other people or the community and not only to one's family or personal friends. Informal caring or helping by individuals was not included.

People are more likely to do organised voluntary work in the South East and South West of England than they are in other parts of the country (Chart 11.10). As well as differences between the different parts of the country, there are also differences between the sex and socio-economic group of the people who participate in voluntary work (Chart 11.11). For all socio-economic groups, women were more likely than men to participate in voluntary work. Overall, 25 per cent of women participated compared with 21 per cent of men.

11.10 Participation in voluntary work: by region, 1987

Great Britain

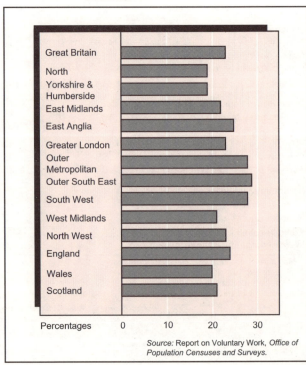

Source: Report on Voluntary Work, *Office of Population Censuses and Surveys.*

11.11 Participation in voluntary work: by sex and socio-economic group, 1987

Great Britain

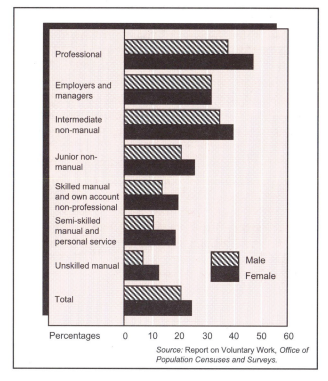

Source: Report on Voluntary Work, *Office of Population Censuses and Surveys.*

However, for both sexes, it was those in the professional, employers and managers, and intermediate non-manual socio-economic groups who were most likely to participate. The higher levels of participation by women in all groups meant that the highest proportion of volunteers, nearly a half, was among women professionals and the lowest participation rate was for men in the unskilled manual group. However, as there are comparatively few women in the professional group, they comprise only 2 per cent of all women volunteers.

Trends in the number of youngsters joining organisations are obviously going to be affected by trends in the birth rate. As 1964 was a peak year for births in the United Kingdom (see Table 1.13) organisations catering for the 14-18 year age group could have been expected to reach their peak membership around 1980. This is borne out in Table 11.12 with most organisations showing a decline in membership since 1981. Despite the falls, the Girl Guides and Scout Associations continue to have a large membership and now include younger members. In 1990 there were over 30 thousand Rainbow Guides aged between 4 and 7 and 115 thousand Beaver Scouts aged between 6 and 8.

The Duke of Edinburgh's Award Scheme, inaugurated in 1956, is not an organisation with members but a programme of activities for young people aged between 14 and 25, and is run by volunteers. Any organisation which is concerned with young people within the age range may apply to the National Award Office to be licensed as an Operating Authority. Since the Scheme began over 2 million young people from all parts of the world have taken part. In 1990, 200 thousand young people were participating in the scheme and gained 39 thousand awards. The number of youngsters taking part rose between 1971 and 1990, increasing by almost 40 per cent between 1971 and 1981 by 18 cent between 1981 and 1990.

11.12 Membership of selected organisations for young people

United Kingdom			Thousands
	1971	1981	1990
Membership			
Cub Scouts	265	309	359[8]
Brownie Guides	376	427	356[9]
Scouts[1]	215	234	197
Girl Guides[2]	316	348	233
Sea Cadet Corps	18	19	15
Army Cadet Force	39	46	40
Air Training Corps	33	35	35
Combined Cadet Force	45	44	41
Boys Brigade[3]	140	154	106
Girls Brigade[3]	97	94	91
Methodist Association of Youth Clubs	115	127	50
National Association of Boys Clubs	164	186	156
Youth Clubs UK — Boys	179	430[7]	322[7]
— Girls	140	341[7]	245[7]
National Federation of Young Farmers Clubs[4]			
— Males	24	28	20
— Females	16	23	16
Young Men's Christian Association[5] Registered members			
— Males	35	36	890
— Females	13	19	778
Registered participants[6]	154	151	1,667
Duke of Edinburgh's Award Participants	122	170	200
Awards gained			
Bronze	18	23	23
Silver	7	10	10
Gold	3	5	6

1 Includes Venture Scouts (15½-20 years).
2 Includes Ranger Guides (14-18 years) and Young Leaders (15-18 years). In addition to the United Kingdom figures also include the Channel Islands and the Isle of Man and British Guides in Foreign Countries.
3 Figures relate to British Isles.
4 Figures relate to England, Wales, and the Channel Islands and to young people aged between 10 and 25 in 1971, and between 10 and 26 in 1981.
5 Figures relate to persons aged under 21.
6 The 1990 figure is not comparable with earlier years because of a change in definition.
7 Figures include membership of clubs affiliated to four local associations.
8 Includes Beaver Scouts (6 – 8 years).
9 Inclues Rainbow Guides (4 or 5 – 7 years).

Source: *Organisations concerned*

11.13 Voluntary rescue work

United Kingdom   Numbers

	1971	1981	1990
Royal National Lifeboat Institution			
Volunteer crew members	5,000	5,000	5,000
Callouts	2,789	3,017	4,937
Lives rescued	1,438	1,076	1,601
Mountain Rescue Committee of Great Britain			
Volunteer team members	2,340	2,804	3,486
Callouts	277	485	929
Persons assisted	207	541	1,167
British Cave Rescue Council			
Volunteer team members	. .	900	920
Callouts	21	48	73
Persons assisted	66	101	154

Source: Organisations concerned

Perhaps one of the greatest commitments a person can make to participating in society is to put their own lives at risk to save others. Five thousand volunteer members formed the crews of lifeboats in the Royal National Lifeboat Institution (RNLI) in 1990 and they attended a total of nearly five thousand callouts. This was two-thirds more callouts than in 1981 and three quarters more than in 1971 although there was no increase in the number of volunteer crew members (Table 11.13). Between 1981 and 1990 the number of volunteer team members of the Mountain Rescue Committee of Great Britain rose by 24 per cent and they attended 444 more callouts in 1990 than in 1981. These rescue teams are being increasingly used for what are not strictly mountaineering incidents such as hanggliding, parascending, mountain biking, horseriding and animal rescue. Many rescue teams also assist the authorities with searches for missing persons on lowland areas, victims of crime or misadventure. In Scotland, which is of course very mountainous, rescue teams were called out on 254 incidents in 1990 which involved such diverse activities as snow climbing, ice climbing, off-piste skiing, summer hill walking, rock climbing, mountain biking and hot air ballooning.

Politics

The right to free and secret ballot to choose our elected representatives is one of the most important aspects of participating in the democratic process. Table 11.14 shows that 75.3 per cent of the electorate exercised this right in the United Kingdom General Election held on 11 June 1987. This turnout was higher than in the 1983 election (72.7 per cent) but roughly comparable with the 1979 election (76.0 per cent). In 1987 the outgoing Government was returned with 42.3 per cent of the votes cast and an overall majority of 101 seats, the second largest majority since the 1945 General Election. Labour won 229 seats with 30.8 per cent of

11.14 Votes recorded in parliamentary General Elections and by-elections: by party

United Kingdom   Percentages and thousands

	General Election 3/5/79	May 1979 to June 1983	General Election 9/6/83	June 1983 to June 1987	General Election 11/6/87	June 1987 to Sept 1991
Number of by-elections	.	20	.	31	. .	21
Turnout *(percentages)*[1]	*76.1*	*61.2*	*72.7*	*62.4*	*75.3*	*57.4*
Votes recorded, by party *(percentage of all votes)*						
Conservative	*43.9*	*23.8*	*42.4*	*16.0*	*42.3*	*22.8*
Labour	*36.9*	*25.7*	*27.6*	*14.9*	*30.8*	*39.5*
Social Liberal Democrats[2]	*13.8*	*9.0*	*13.7*	*15.0*	*12.8*	*17.6*
Social Democratic Party[2]	*0*	*14.2*	*11.6*	*5.6*	*9.7*	*3.7*
Plaid Cymru	*0.4*	*0.5*	*0.4*	*0.3*	*0.4*	*2.6*
Scottish National Party	*1.6*	*1.7*	*1.1*	.	*1.3*	*5.0*
Northern Ireland Parties	*2.2*	*23.3*	*2.5*	*47.4*[4]	*2.2*	*4.3*
Green Party[3]	*0.1*	*0.3*	*0.2*	—	*0.3*	*1.9*
Others	*1.1*	*1.6*	*0.5*	*0.8*	*0.2*	*2.7*
Total (= 100%) (thousands)	31,221	715	30,671	1,979	32,530	759

1 Estimated by dividing the number of votes cast by the number of people on the electoral registers in force at the time of the elections.
2 The Social Democratic Party (SDP) was launched on 26 March 1981. A SDP candidate contested a Parliamentary seat for the first time in the by-election held at Warrington on 16 July 1981. In the 1983 and 1987 General Elections the Liberals and SDP contested seats as the Liberal-SDP Alliance. In 1988 the Social and Liberal Democrats formed, after which the Democrats and the SDP contested elections separately. In June 1990 the SDP decided to disband and the last by-election they contested was at Bootle on 24 May 1990.
3 Known as the Ecology Party before 1987.
4 On 17 December 1985 all 15 Ulster Unionist MPs resigned their seats and sought re-election as a protest against the Anglo-Irish agreement. The 15 by-elections were held on 23 January 1986 thus accounting for the high figure shown here.

Source: Home Office

11.15　Women in the House of Commons at general elections: by party

United Kingdom

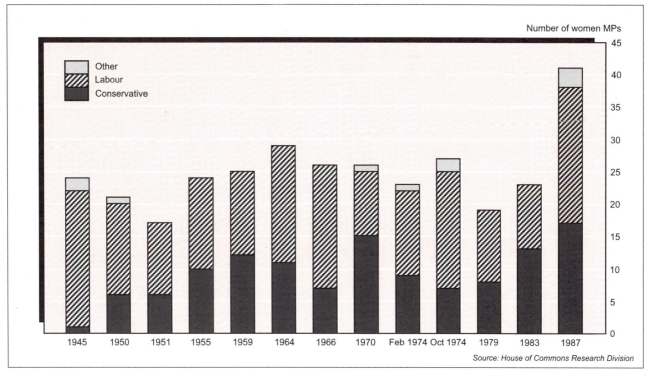

Source: House of Commons Research Division

the votes cast while the Liberal-Social Democratic Party (SDP) Alliance polled 22.5 per cent of the votes, but won only 22 seats, one less than in 1983. The fact that Plaid Cymru, the Scottish National Party and the Northern Ireland Parties had such a low percentage of the total votes cast is a reflection of the fact that they only contest seats in certain areas - their share of the vote is of course much higher in these areas. It is clear that fewer people exercise their right to vote in by-elections with a turnout between June 1987 and September 1991 of less than 58 per cent.

The highest intake of female MPs at a General Election was in 1987, when 41 women were elected to Parliament - 6.3 per cent of the total (Chart 11.15). With the election of three more women at by-elections in Vauxhall (June 1989) Mid-Staffordshire (March 1990) and Paisley North (November 1990) the number has risen to 44 (6.8 per cent) At the 1987 general election there were 329 women candidates (14.2 per cent of the total); in 1945 there were only 86 (5.2 per cent).

With membership of the European Community, the United Kingdom electorate have more opportunity to exercise their democratic rights. However, they seem less willing to participate in European elections than they are in their own General Elections and less willing

to participate than their European neighbours. In each of the 1979, 1984 and 1989 elections, the lowest percentage of voters turning out was in the United Kingdom, 32.8, 32.5 and 36.0 per cent respectively (Table 11.16). In the same three years the percentage of the electorate participating in Belgium was over 91 per cent. However, it should be noted that voting is compulsory in certain member states for European as well as national elections.

11.16　Rates of participation in EC elections

			Percentages
	1979	1984	1989
United Kingdom	32.8	32.5	36.0
Belgium	91.4	92.1	93.0
Denmark	47.8	54.0	46.0
France	61.2	57.4	50.4
Germany (Fed.Rep.)	65.7	56.8	61.5
Greece	.	78.4	77.7
Irish Republic	63.6	47.6	68.5
Italy	86.0	83.4	81.5
Luxembourg	88.9	88.8	87.0
Netherlands	58.2	50.9	47.2
Portugal	.	.	51.2
Spain	.	.	54.8
EUR 12	62.5[1]	59.4[2]	58.5

1 EUR 9.
2 EUR 10.

Source: European Parliament

This low level of participation in European elections is consistent with further figures on attitudes to membership of the European Communities (EC). In a survey conducted by the European Commission in the spring of 1991, participants were asked about their attitudes to membership (Chart 11.17). Membership of the EC was most unpopular in Denmark and the United Kingdom where 18 and 14 per cent of people considered it a bad thing compared with only 2 per cent in the Netherlands. In the Netherlands 91 per cent were in favour of membership closely followed by Luxembourg (86 per cent). Only 59 per cent of those interviewed in the United Kingdom considered it a good thing.

11.17 Attitudes to membership of the EC, 1991

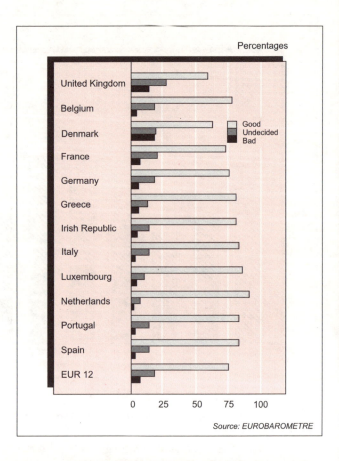

Source: EUROBAROMETRE

"Women's National Commission,

"Directory of Women's Organisations 1991-1992".

Copies are available free of charge from: The Women's National Commission, Room 50A/4, Government Offices, Horse Guards Road, London, SW1P 3AL."

Social Trends 22, © Crown copyright 1992

Other participation

As well as voting at elections, people can participate in government by appealing against the administrative decisions of government departments. The means of appeal is to complain to the Parliamentary Ombudsman - the Parliamentary Commissioner for Administration (PCA) - through Members of Parliament. In 1990 there were 23 per cent fewer complaints than in 1981. Of the total of 724 complaints dealt with in 1990, three-quarters were rejected; 177 full investigations were completed and reported to MPs and 42 per cent of these were found to be justified and having involved maladministration leading to injustice (Table 11.18).

The Health Service Commissioners (HSC), who are statutory independent officers, deal with complaints about services and administration within the National Health Service. The number of complaints received rose by 44 per cent between 1981 and 1990. In 1990,

487 complaints were reported on and just under half were found to have involved failures in service, or maladministration leading to injustice.

Local Government Ombudsmen - Commissioners for Local Administration - deal with complaints against local authorities and certain other authorities in Great Britain. There are separate Commissions for England and Wales and a Commissioner for Scotland. The number of complaints received by all the Commissioners more than doubled between 1986 and 1990. In 1990, 416 complaints were reported on and almost 66 per cent of these were found to have involved maladministration leading to injustice.

Chart 11.1 and Table 11.19 show that trade union membership and the number of unions continued to fall in 1989. Membership has fallen by a quarter from its 1979 peak of 13.3 million to 10.2 million in 1989. The number of unions also fell but this trend is partly a result

11.18 Complaints to Ombudsmen[1]

Great Britain   Numbers

	1971	1976	1981	1986	1990
Complaints to the Parliamentary Commissioner for Administration					
Received during the year	548	815	917	719	704
Dealt with during the year[2]					
Rejected	295	505	694	549	535
Discontinued after partial investigation	39	29	7	2	12
Reported upon					
Maladministration leading to injustice found	67	139	104	82	74
Other	115	190	124	86	103
Total dealt with during the year	516	863	929	719	724
Complaints to the Health Commissioner[3,4,5]					
Received during the year	.	582	686	883	990
Dealt with during the year[2]					
Rejected[6]	.	413	583	684	420
Discontinued after partial investigation	.	13	15	16	16
Reported upon					
Containing failures in service/ maladministration leading to injustice found	.	61	152	290	236
Other	.	59	255	193	251
Total dealt with during the year	.	546	699	831	1,006
Complaints to the Commissioners for Local Administration[3,7]					
Received during the year[8]	.	1,335	3,293	5,159	10,892
Dealt with during the year[2]					
Rejected/discontinued after partial investigation	.	772	2,621	4,438	10,036
Reported upon					
Maladministration leading to injustice found	.	143	203	266	274
Other	.	142	204	185	142
Total dealt with during the year	.	1,057	3,028	4,889	10,452

1 See Appendix, Part 11: Parliamentary Commissioner for Administration, Health Service Commissioner, Commissioners for Local Administration.
2 Some complaints will have been received during the previous year.
3 The Health Service Commissioner and the Commissioners for Local Administration report annually from April to the following March. The 1990-91 figures appear under 1990 etc.
4 The Health Service Commissioner started operating on 1 October 1973.
5 From 1981 the figures refer to the number of individual grievances rather than reports issued.

6 Includes cases referred back to complainant for more information and no response received.
7 The Commissioners for Local Administration for England started operating on 1 April 1974, for Wales in September 1974, and for Scotland on 1 January 1976.
8 In Wales includes complaints brought forward from previous year because complaint accepted for investigation but report not issued or complaint under consideration.

Source: Annual Reports: The Parliamentary Commissioner for Administration; The Health Service Commissioner; The Commissioners for Local Administration in England, Scotland, and Wales

11.19 Trade unions: numbers and membership

United Kingdom

	Number of unions	Total membership Millions	As a percentage of civilian workforce in employment[1]	Percentage change in membership since previous year
1975 [2]	501	12.2	49.4	+ 3.6
1975	470	12.0	48.6	
1976	473	12.4	50.5	+ 3.0
1977	481	12.8	52.4	+ 3.7
1978	462	13.1	52.6	+ 2.1
1979	453	13.3	52.8	+ 1.3
1980	438	12.9	52.9	− 2.6
1981	414	12.1	51.0	− 6.5
1982	408	11.6	49.8	− 4.2
1983	394	11.2	47.4	− 3.1
1984	375	11.0	45.6	− 2.2
1985	370	10.8	44.6	− 1.6
1986	335	10.5	43.2	− 2.6
1987	330	10.5	41.5	− 0.6
1988	315	10.4	39.8	− 0.9
1989	309	10.2	37.9	− 2.1

1 As at December for years 1978 onwards, previously based on mid-year estimates.\
2 Thirty one organisations previously regarded as trade unions are excluded from 1975 onwards because they failed to satisfy the statutory definition of a trade union in Section 28 of the *Trade Union and Labour Relations Act, 1974.*

Source: Employment Gazette, *Employment Department*

11.20 Reasons given for belonging to a trade union, 1989

Percentages

	Very/fairly important	Not very/not at all important/does not apply to me
To protect me if problems come up	93	6
To get higher pay and better working conditions	80	20
To get members' benefits	71	29
To help other people I work with	76	23
I believe in them in principle	67	33
Most of my colleagues are members	55	45
It's a tradition in my family	15	84
It's a condition of having my job	38	62

Source: British Social Attitudes Survey, Social and Community Planning Research

given was that it protected members if any problems arose at work (93 per cent). A smaller proportion, 80 per cent, said they were members in order to obtain higher pay and improved working conditions. Only 15 per cent gave family tradition as a reason. During the 1970s a substantial range of advisory and counselling services were developed providing general information and advice through largely volunteer-based advice centres (Table 11.21). The number of clients who visited Relate, formerly the National Marriage Guidance Council, for counselling on marriage or intimate personal relationships, nearly trebled between 1971 and 1990. The number of clients using the Disablement Information and Advice Lines has also more than trebled between 1981 and 1990. There has been a substantial growth in the work of organisations dealing with alcohol-related problems. Alcoholics Anonymous had 15 thousand more clients in 1990 than 1981 and Al-Anon, which provides support for the families of those who suffer from alcohol dependence, dealt with over 5 thousand more clients in 1990 than in 1981.

of a tendency towards larger unions, with some unions merging together. There is a large concentration of members in a small number of unions; 80 per cent of all members in 1989 were concentrated in just 7 per cent of unions. Smaller trade unions with less than 500 members accounted for 39 per cent of all unions but less than half a per cent of all members at the end of 1989. Table 11.20 shows the results of a survey conducted in 1989 giving varying reasons why people belong to Trade Unions. The most common reason

11.21 Selected advisory and counselling services[1]

United Kingdom

Numbers and thousands

	Branches/centres (Numbers)			Clients (Thousands)		
	1971	1981	1990	1971	1981	1990
Al-Anon Family Groups	135	612	1,070	1.2	7.3	12.8
Alcoholics Anonymous	420	1,550	2,800	6.3	30.0	45.0
Catholic Marriage Advisory Council	63	68	80	2.5	3.3	15.8
Citizens Advice Bureaux	512	914	1,413	1,500.0	4,514.6	7,665.7
Cruse Bereavement Care	13	73	180	5.0	9.1	21.0
Disablement Information and Advice Lines	.	44	120	.	40.0	150.0
Law Centres	1	41	59	1.0	155.0	295.0
Leukaemia Care Society	1	21	40	0.2	1.7	5.2
Relate[2]	141	178	145	21.6	38.3	60.0
Samaritans	127	180	185	89.0	314.7	451.0
Young People's Counselling and Advisory Service	. .	55	125	. .	30.0	113.0

1 See Appendix, Part II: Selected advisory and counselling services.
2 Including Marriage counselling in Scotland.

Source: Organisations concerned

In 1990 the Citizens Advice Bureau dealt with over 7.5 million clients, an increase of 70 per cent over 1981. In England and Wales and Northern Ireland over 23 per cent of all enquiries in 1990-91 were about social security with a further 21 per cent concerned with consumer, trade and business, which includes enquiries regarding consumer debt (Table 11.22). Scottish Citizens Advice Bureaux statistics were collected on a broadly similar basis to those of other Bureaux in the United Kingdom in 1980-81 but the system changed before the statistics for 1985-86.

11.22 Citizens Advice Bureaux: by type of enquiry

England & Wales and Northern Ireland and Scotland — Percentages

	England & Wales and Northern Ireland			Scotland		
	1980-81	1985-86	1990-91	1980-81	1985-86	1989-90
Types of enquiry (percentages)						
Consumer, trade and business[1]	18.6	17.8	21.7	19.4	22.2	24.0
Housing, property and land	15.8	15.1	10.4	15.1	11.1	9.7
Social security	9.7	19.5	23.5	11.7	23.0	21.2
Family and personal	14.8	10.7	9.3	12.3	9.8	8.2
Employment	10.0	9.9	10.9	10.1	13.4	12.0
Taxes and Duties	2.7	2.5	5.4	2.7	. .	. .
Administration of justice	8.5	8.3	7.3	7.7	1.0	0.9
Holidays, travel and leisure	4.6	2.8	1.9	3.0	0.7	0.7
Health	3.6	3.0	2.3	3.6	. .	1.5
Other	11.7	10.4	7.3	14.4	18.9	21.8

1 Includes consumer debt.

Source: National Association of Citizens Advice Bureaux; Citizens Advice (Scotland)

BIBLIOGRAPHY

The following list contains selected publications relevant to Chapter 11: Participation. Those published by HMSO are available from the addresses shown on the back cover of Social Trends.

Annual Report of the Commission for Local Administration in England
Annual Report of the Commission for Local Administration in Wales
Annual Report of the Commission for Local Administration in Scotland
Annual Report of the Council on Tribunals, HMSO
Annual Report of the Parliamentary Commission for Administration, HMSO
Annual Report of the Registrar General for Northern Ireland, HMSO
Annual Report of the Registrar General for Scotland, General Register Office (Scotland)
British Electoral Facts 1832-1987, Gower
British Social Attitudes Survey, SCPR
Britain Votes, Gower

Charity Commissioner's Report, HMSO
Charity Household Survey, Charities Aid Foundation
Charity Trends, Charities Aid Foundation
Christian England, MARC Europe
Eurobarometre, EC
Marriage and Divorce Statistics (Series FM2), HMSO
Men and Women in Great Britain, HMSO
Official Handbook to the European Parliament, EC
Report on Voluntary Work, HMSO
The Lifeboat Service: Annual Report and Accounts, RNLI
The Times Guide to the House of Commons, Times Books Ltd
UK Christian Handbook, MARC Europe
Women's Organisations in the United Kingdom, WNC

HOME OFFICE

Statistics of offences against prison discipline and punishments,

England & Wales 1989

Presents information on offences against prison discipline and associated punishments.

price **£7.95**

CMND1236 ISBN 010 112362 0
Available from HMSO

HOME OFFICE

Criminal statistics
England & Wales 1989

Criminal statistics England and Wales is produced annually by the Home Office and published by HMSO as a Command Paper. It brings together statistics on recorded crime, the criminal workload of the courts, sentencing and the use of remand, with a commentary on the tables and charts. Detailed information is included on homicides and on offences involving the use of firearms. The five supplementary volumes provide more detailed tables by police force areas, offence and petty sessional division.

HMSO **£17.60**

CMND 1322 ISBN 010 113222 0

Chapter 12: Crime and Justice

Offences
- Crimes against property, that is theft and handling stolen goods, fraud and forgery and criminal damage account for around nine-tenths of offences.
  (Table 12.2)

Victims
- The risk of being a victim of crime is higher among the ethnic minority groups than among the white population.
  (Table 12.9)

- Most homicide victims know their attacker. Around two thirds of male victims and three quarters of female victims were related to or knew their attacker.
  (Chart 12.10)

Offences cleared up
- Police clear up rates have fallen in England and Wales during the 1970s and 1980s. In 1990, 32 per cent of recorded offences were cleared up, compared to 45 per cent in 1971.
  (Table 12.13)

Offenders
- Reconviction rates are high - 44 per cent of adult males released from prisons in England and Wales are reconvicted within two years.
  (Table 12.23)

Prisons and probation service
- The United Kingdom has a higher number of people in prison per head of population than any other EC country.
  (Chart 12.25)

Resources
- The strength of the police force has increased significantly during the last 30 years - by 70 per cent between 1961 and 1990.
  (Table 12.34)

Northern Ireland
- The number of deaths due to the security situation in Northern Ireland increased slightly between 1989 and 1990 from 62 to 76.
  (Chart 12.38)

12.1 Notifiable offences[1] recorded by the police

England & Wales, Scotland and Northern Ireland

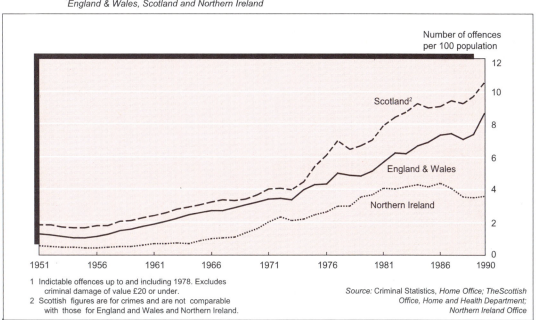

1 Indictable offences up to and including 1978. Excludes criminal damage of value £20 or under.
2 Scottish figures are for crimes and are not comparable with those for England and Wales and Northern Ireland.

Source: Criminal Statistics, *Home Office; The Scottish Office, Home and Health Department; Northern Ireland Office*

In this chapter England and Wales, Scotland and Northern Ireland are generally discussed separately because of their different legal systems.

Offences

Chart 12.1 and Table 12.2 cover notifiable offences. These are the more serious offences which generally require trial by a jury. Although the name of the series has changed over the years, the offences which are covered have remained more or less the same. A list of notifiable offences is published in the annual Home Office publication *Criminal statistics: England and Wales*. Crime statistics in Northern Ireland cover indictable offences. These are broadly comparable to the notifiable offences in England and Wales.

In Scotland, crimes and offences are divided into two classes. Crimes are more serious, and are roughly comparable with notifiable offences in England and Wales - offences are less serious. Despite some degree of comparability, the definitions of crime are different in different parts of the United Kingdom, and comparisons should only be made with care.

The number of notifiable offences recorded by the police provides a measure of the amount of crime with which the police are faced. It does not measure the number of offences actually committed as many are either not reported to the police or not recorded by them. The extent to which crimes are reported is covered by Chart 12.7.

Before the 1920s, the police recorded fewer than 100 thousand offences each year in England and Wales. By 1950 this had reached half a million, by 1980 2.5 million and by 1990, this total reached 4.4 million (Table 12.2). This means that nine offences are recorded annually by the police for every 100 people (Chart 12.1). In Scotland, there were 10.5 crimes recorded by the police per 100 population in 1990, the corresponding rate for Northern Ireland was only 3.5 offences for every 100 people.

The recorded crime rate in Northern Ireland was lower than the rate for any police force area in England and Wales where the rate ranged from 4.5 offences per 100 population in Dyfed-Powys to over 14 in Northumbria.

Crimes against property, that is theft and handling stolen goods, burglary, fraud and forgery and criminal damage account for the vast majority of offences (around 90 per cent). Theft (particularly vehicle thefts) and handling stolen goods alone accounted for over half of all recorded offences in England and Wales in 1990 (Table 12.2).

Between 1989 and 1990, the number of vehicle thefts recorded by the police in England and Wales increased by over a quarter. The only fall in England and Wales was for sexual offences, by 2 per cent. The biggest year-on-year change in the table is for drug trafficking in Scotland which increased by a third between 1989 and 1990, reflecting increased police activity.

12.2 Notifiable offences[1] recorded by the police: by type of offence

England & Wales, Scotland and Northern Ireland   Thousands

	England & Wales			Scotland			Northern Ireland		
	1971	1989	1990	1971	1989	1990	1971	1989[2]	1990[2]
Notifiable offences recorded									
Violence against the person	47.0	[3] 177.0	184.7	5.0 [3]	14.0	13.6[7]	1.4 [3]	3.3	3.4
Sexual offences, of which	23.6	29.7[6]	29.0[6]	2.6	3.1	3.2	0.2	0.9	0.8
rape and attempted rape	..	3.3	3.4	0.2	0.5	0.5	..	0.1	0.1
Burglary	451.5	825.9	1,006.8	59.2	93.7	101.7	10.6	14.7	14.8
Robbery	7.5	33.2	36.2	2.3	4.4	4.7	0.6	1.7	1.6
Drugs trafficking	..	9.2	10.0	..	2.1	2.8	..	—	—
Theft and handling stolen goods	1,003.7	2,012.8[5]	2,374.4[5]	104.6	234.7	255.2	8.6	27.1	29.3
of which, theft of vehicles	167.6	393.4	494.2	17.1	29.1	36.1	..	6.4	7.0
Fraud and forgery	99.8	134.5	147.9	9.4	24.1	25.0	1.5	4.4	4.2
Criminal damage	27.0[4]	465.6[4]	553.5[4]	22.0	79.1	86.4	7.4[8]	2.0	2.2
Other notifiable offences	5.6[5]	18.5	21.1	5.0	40.3	46.0	0.5	1.0	1.0
Total notifiable offences	1,665.7[4]	3,706.2[4]	4363.6[4]	211.0	493.4	535.8	30.8[8]	55.1	57.2

1 Offences which in 1978 and earlier years were 'indictable'. Scottish figures of 'crime' have been recompiled to approximate to the classification of notifiable offences in England & Wales and Northern Ireland. However, because of differences in the legal system, recording and counting practices, and classification problems, Scottish figures are not comparable with those for England & Wales and Northern Ireland.

2 Figures for 1989 and 1990 no longer include 'assault on police' and communicating false information regarding a bomb hoax. These offences have been removed from the categories 'Violence against the person' and 'Other notifiable offences.'

3 Figures for 1989 and 1990 are not precisely comparable with those for 1971

4 Excludes offences of criminal damage valued at £20 or less.

5 Offences of 'abstracting electricity', of which there were 4,477 cases in 1989 and 3,770 cases in 1990 are included among 'Other offences' in 1971 and 'Theft and handling stolen goods' in 1989 and 1990.

6 Includes offences of 'gross indencency with a child.'

7 The definition changed in January 1990. It is estimated that there would have been one thousand fewer cases recorded in 1989, using the revised definition.

8 Figures for 1971 exclude criminal damage valued at £25 or less. Figures for 1989 and 1990 exclude criminal damage valued at £200 or less.

Source: Criminal Statistics, Home Office; The Scottish Office Home and Health Department; Northern Ireland Office

Of the 4.4 million offences recorded by the police in England and Wales in 1990, only 10 thousand involved firearms (Chart 12.3). This was an increase of 9 per cent on 1989 but was five times the number recorded in 1972. The biggest increases in the use of firearms have been in criminal damage and robbery.

In 1990, firearms were issued to the police in England and Wales on 2,874 operations in which criminals or other persons were believed to be armed (Chart 12.4). In Scotland, there were 51 operations in which firearms were issued to the police in 1990. Comparisons over time are difficult. Before 1983 in England and Wales and 1984 in Scotland the figures are for the number of occasions on which firearms were issued to the police not the number of operations.

The total number of drug offences identified by police and Customs officers has increased. In 1990, 45 thousand people were found guilty of drug offences, cautioned for drug offences, or paid a fine to HM Customs and Excises in cases involving the importation of small quantities of drugs (Table 12.5). This was 21 thousand more than in 1986 and 27 thousand more than in 1981. The vast majority of people (39 thousand) were dealt with for unlawful possession of drugs.

Statistics of offences recorded by the police provide only a partial picture of crime committed. The crime recording process starts when someone reports to the police that an offence has been committed, or when the police themselves discover an offence. However, many offences are not reported to the police and therefore cannot be recorded. Moreover some offences which

12.3 Notifiable offences[1] involving firearms recorded by the police[2]: by type of offence

England & Wales

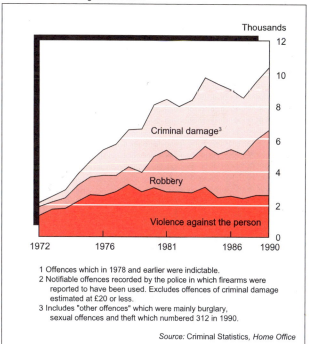

1 Offences which in 1978 and earlier were indictable.
2 Notifiable offences recorded by the police in which firearms were reported to have been used. Excludes offences of criminal damage estimated at £20 or less.
3 Includes "other offences" which were mainly burglary, sexual offences and theft which numbered 312 in 1990.

Source: Criminal Statistics, Home Office

are reported to the police are not recorded because, for example, the complainant may decide not to proceed, or the police may decide there is insufficient evidence of an offence having been committed.

The British Crime Survey (BCS) relies on interviews with the public to give a fuller count of the number of offences than the number recorded by the police. Some crimes such as company fraud and shoplifting are crimes against organisations rather than people - they are not covered by the survey. The survey also excludes so-called victimless crimes, for example, drug abuse. The most recently available data are from the 1988 survey in England and Wales, which provides estimates of crimes committed in 1987.

12.4 Operations[1] on which guns were issued to the police

Great Britain

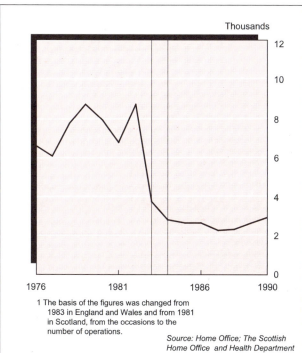

1 The basis of the figures was changed from 1983 in England and Wales and from 1981 in Scotland, from the occasions to the number of operations.

Source: Home Office; The Scottish Home Office and Health Department

12.5 Drug offences, persons found guilty, cautioned or dealt with by compounding[1]: by offence

United Kingdom				Numbers
	1976	1981	1986	1990
Unlawful production[2]	785	1,603	944	629
Unlawful supply	836	1,000	1,876	2,151
Possession with intent to supply unlawfully	496	699	1,858	2,751
Unlawful possession	11,097	14,850	20,052	39,350
Unlawful import or export	366	1,357	1,525	2,478
All drug offences[3]	12,754	17,921	23,905	44,922

1 Includes H.M. Customs and Excise cases dealt with by the payment of a penalty in lieu of prosecution.
2 Includes offences of cultivation of cannabis plants.
3 As the same person may appear in more than one category, rows cannot be added together to produce totals or sub-totals.

Source: Home Office

12.6 Percentage of offences recorded by the police: by type of offence, 1987

England & Wales

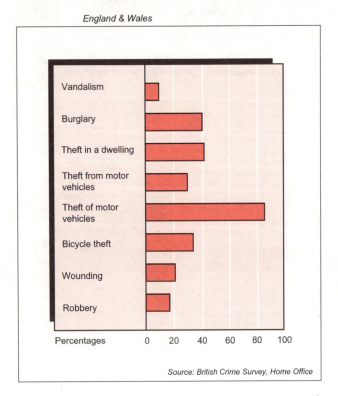

Percentages: 0 20 40 60 80 100

(categories from top: Vandalism, Burglary, Theft in a dwelling, Theft from motor vehicles, Theft of motor vehicles, Bicycle theft, Wounding, Robbery)

Source: British Crime Survey, Home Office

12.7 Number of crimes committed and offenders dealt with, 1987

England & Wales

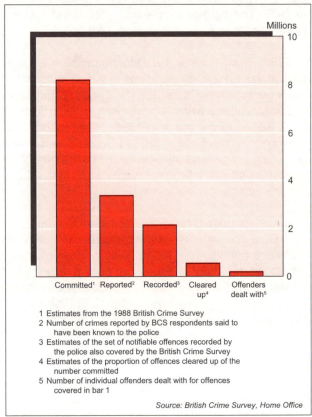

Millions
10
8
6
4
2
0

Committed[1] Reported[2] Recorded[3] Cleared up[4] Offenders dealt with[5]

1 Estimates from the 1988 British Crime Survey
2 Number of crimes reported by BCS respondents said to have been known to the police
3 Estimates of the set of notifiable offences recorded by the police also covered by the British Crime Survey
4 Estimates of the proportion of offences cleared up of the number committed
5 Number of individual offenders dealt with for offences covered in bar 1

Source: British Crime Survey, Home Office

Chart 12.6 compares crime figures from the BCS with notifiable offences recorded by the police. In this way, the proportion of offences recorded by the police can be estimated. Theft of motor vehicles were the most likely to be recorded (86 per cent of offences committed in 1987). The police recorded 41 per cent of burglaries, but only 17 per cent of robbery offences, and 10 per cent of vandalism. The gap between offences committed and recorded is mainly because many offences are not reported to the police. Nearly half of the survey respondents who did not report incidents to the police said it was because the incident was too trivial, or involved no loss or damage; a further fifth said they felt the police would not have been able to do anything about the incident.

Using all offences which are covered by both the British Crime Survey and notifiable offences, Chart 12.7 shows the fall-off from the number of offences committed as estimated by the survey, to the number of offences recorded by the police, to the number of these which are cleared up. For these offences comparable between the BCS and the police statistics, only 7 per cent of offences committed were cleared-up. This should not be seen as a measure of police performance. The BCS shows that many crimes were not reported to the police - clearly if a crime is not reported, the police cannot clear it up.

Victims

It is difficult to compare levels of crime in different countries using only statistics on offences recorded by the police. Differences in legal systems and police recording practices make comparisons hazardous, and there may also be differences in the willingness of victims to report crimes to the police in different countries. In 1989, a number of countries (including the United Kingdom) participated in a standard international survey in which levels of crime were measured by asking a sample of people about their experience of crime. The results of this survey have to be regarded cautiously as the samples used were limited in size (2 thousand in most countries), and response rates were variable.

Chart 12.8 uses the results of this international survey to show the percentage of people who had experienced one or more of the offences covered. Those in the United States of America were the most likely to experience crime in 1988 (29 per cent) whereas those in Switzerland and Finland were the least likely (both 16 per cent).

For England and Wales, the 1988 British Crime Survey compared the risk of being a victim of crime between different ethnic groups. Table 12.9 shows that both

12.8 Victims of one or more crimes: international comparison, 1988

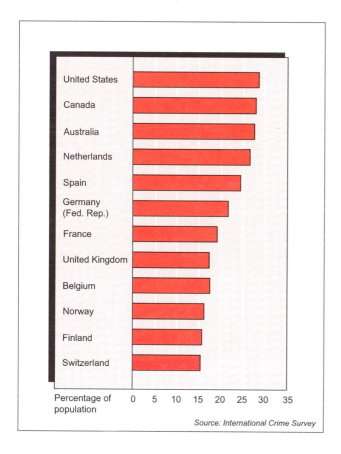

Percentage of population

Source: International Crime Survey

12.9 Victims of one or more crimes[1]: by ethnic origin and type of offence, 1987

England & Wales			Percentages
	Ethnic origin of victim		
	White	Afro-Caribbean	Asian
Percentage who were victims of each offence			
Household vandalism	5	4	8
Burglary	6	10	6
Vehicles (owners)			
Vandalism	9	9	14
All thefts[2]	18	26	20
Bicycle theft (owners)	4	8	2
Other household theft	6	6	8
Assault	3	7	4
Threats	2	4	5
Robbery/theft from person	1	3	3
Other personal thefts	4	6	3
Sample size (numbers)	9,874	733	996

1 Based on incidents occurring over the full recall period.
2 Includes theft of and from vehicles and attempted theft.

Source: British Crime Survey, Home Office

than whites for many types of crime. This is largely explained by social and demographic factors, particularly the areas in which they live. However, even after taking account of this, the risk of being a victim of crime still tends to be higher among the ethnic minority groups, with Asians particularly at greater risk of vandalism and robbery/theft from the person. Afro-Caribbeans and Asians see many offences against them as being racially motivated. Being threatened and assaulted because of race is common. For Asians, evidence or suspicion of a racial element in offences against property is relatively frequent.

12.10 Relationship between homicide victim and principal suspect[1]: by sex of victim, 1990

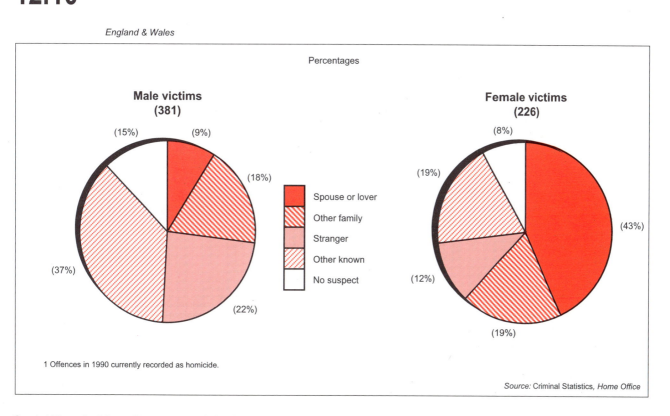

England & Wales

1 Offences in 1990 currently recorded as homicide.

Source: Criminal Statistics, Home Office

12.11 Criminal injuries compensation

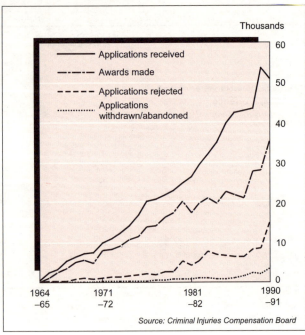

Great Britain

Source: Criminal Injuries Compensation Board

12.12 Victim support

England & Wales

	1981 −82	1986 −87	1989 −90	1990 −91
Victim Support schemes (numbers)	114	305	350	384
Referrals (thousands)	28	257	506	597
Volunteers (thousands)	..	4.2	6.7	7.2
Funding for Victim Support (£ thousands)				
Current prices	15	286	3,910	4,703
Constant 1989-90 prices	23	344	3,910	4,355

Source: Home Office

introduced on 1 April 1964, the number of new applications increased every year until 1989-90, followed by a slight fall to 50,820 in 1990-91 (Chart 12.11). The 35,190 awards made in 1990-91 was a quarter higher than in 1989-90.

Victim Support is an association of more than 380 local, independent charitable schemes which provide advice and assistance to victims of crime in England and Wales, largely through voluntary workers.

The Home Office pays a grant to the Victim Support national office which co-ordinates the service and provides training. Part of the grant goes to local schemes to meet salaries and running costs. The numbers of schemes, referrals and volunteers have all increased during the last ten years (Table 12.12). In particular, the number of referrals to Victim Support increased more than twenty fold.

Homicide victims often knew their attacker. Chart 12.10 shows the relationship between homicide victims and the offenders. Around two thirds of male victims and four fifths of female victims were related to, or knew, their attacker.

The continuing rise in crimes of violence is reflected in an increase in applications to the Criminal Injuries Compensation Board (CICB). Since the scheme was

Offences cleared up

12.13 Clear-up rates for notifiable offences[1]: by type of offence

England & Wales, Scotland and Northern Ireland   Percentages

	England & Wales			Scotland			Northern Ireland		
	1971	1989	1990	1971	1989	1990	1971	1989[2]	1990[2]
Notifiable offences recorded									
Violence against the person	82	[3] 77	77	87	[3] 81	82[8]	28	[3] 58	62
Sexual offences, of which	76	75[6]	76[6]	77	77	79	87	85	92
rape and attempted rape	..	74	74	81	79	79	..	90	88
Burglary	37	27	25	26	17	16	30	27	22
Robbery	42	26	26	21	29	28	18	22	18
Drugs trafficking	..	99	98	..	100	99	..	100	100
Theft and handling stolen goods	43	31[5]	30[5]	37	26	24	43	43	36
of which, theft of vehicles	..	27	26	36	26	24	..	46	31
Fraud and forgery	83	66	61	80	72	69	79	79	74
Criminal damage	34[4]	23[4]	22[4]	32	21	20	43	34	36
Other notifiable offences	92[5]	96[7]	95[7]	85	97	97	42	79	79
Total notifiable offences	45[4]	34[4]	32[4]	38	33	32	32	43	38

1 See Table 12.3 footnote 1.
2 Figures since 1989 no longer include 'assault on police' and 'communicating false information regarding a bomb hoax'. These offences have been removed from the categories 'Violence against the person' and 'Other notifiable offences'.
3 Figures for 1989 and 1990 are not precisely comparable with those for 1971.
4 Excludes criminal damage valued at £20 or less.
5 Includes offences of 'abstracting electricity'.

6 Includes offences of 'gross indecency with a child'.
7 Includes offences of 'trafficking in controlled drugs', recorded only from the beginning of 1983.
8 The definition of serious assault changed in January 1990. It is esttimated there would have been one thousand fewer cases recorded in 1989, using the revised definition.

Source: Criminal Statistics, Home Office; The Scottish Office Home and Health Department; Northern Ireland Office

12.14 Clear up rates for recorded notifiable offences: by police force area, 1990

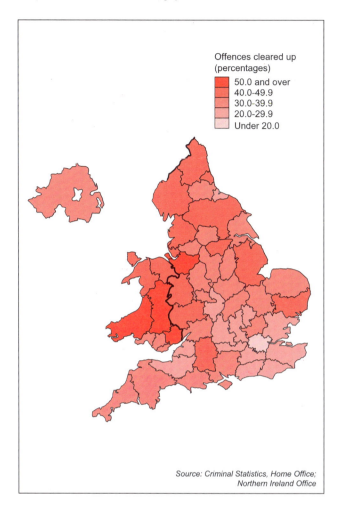

Offences cleared up
(percentages)

- 50.0 and over
- 40.0-49.9
- 30.0-39.9
- 20.0-29.9
- Under 20.0

*Source: Criminal Statistics, Home Office;
Northern Ireland Office*

12.15 Notifiable offences cleared up by the police: by method of clear-up, 1990

England , Wales & Northern Ireland

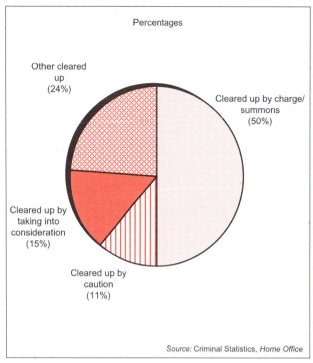

Percentages

Other cleared up (24%)

Cleared up by charge/ summons (50%)

Cleared up by taking into consideration (15%)

Cleared up by caution (11%)

Source: Criminal Statistics, Home Office

An offence can be cleared up by the police in a number of ways. These are: if a person is charged (whether or not they are subsequently found guilty), summonsed, or cautioned for the offence, if the offence is admitted and is taken into consideration by the court (not in Scotland), or if there is sufficient evidence to charge a person but the case is not proceeded with. Examples of this last point would include where the offence is attributed to a child under the age of criminal responsibility, where the offender is already serving a long sentence for another offence, or because the victim is unable to give evidence. In 1990, half of all cleared-up offences were through a charge or summons

(Chart 12.15). In 1990, in England and Wales, 32 per cent of recorded offences were cleared up compared to 45 per cent in 1971 (Table 12.13).

Although in the country as a whole, just under one-third of recorded offences were cleared up in 1990, the clear-up rate varied considerably between different offence groups and police force areas. For example, only a quarter of robberies, burglaries and criminal damage offences recorded by the police in England and Wales were cleared up compared to three quarters of offences of violence against the person and sexual offences. Between the different police force areas, the clear-up rate ranged from only 17 per cent in the Metropolitan police force area to 51 per cent in the Gwent police force area (Chart 12.14). In 1990, the overall clear-up rate in England and Wales was similar to that in Scotland, but lower than that in Northern Ireland.

Police and courts action and sentencing

This section looks at the action of the police and courts in England and Wales. Following a crime and the detection of the alleged offender, the police can take no action, issue a formal caution or refer the case to the Crown Prosecution Service who will decide whether or not to prosecute. The first two options may be used when the offender is below the age of criminal responsibility or where there is insufficient evidence. There are no central statistics for the number of offenders dealt with in these ways but they are thought to be used increasingly for juveniles.

In Scotland, it is the procurator fiscal who decides whether or not to prosecute. The fiscal may prosecute, or issue a fiscal warning, offer a fixed penalty (for some motoring offences and for certain other minor offences), divert the alleged offender to another agency (eg social work) or may decide not to proceed.

For some minor offences where guilt is admitted, the police may deal with an offender by means of a formal caution by a senior police officer. In 1990, 166 thousand people were cautioned in England and Wales for

12.16 Defendants proceeded against, persons cautioned and persons given written warnings or fixed penalty notices

England & Wales   Thousands

| | Indictable offences | | Summary offences | | | | |
| | | | Motoring offences | | | Other offences | |
	Defendants proceeded against	Persons cautioned	Defendants proceeded against[1]	Persons given written warnings	Fixed penalty notices[1,2]	Defendants proceeded against	Persons cautioned
1971	374	77	1,026	209	1,997	395	32
1977	[4] 474	115	1,222	198	2,831	[4] 466	34
1977	470	101	1,166	198	2,831	458	38
1981	523	104	1,299	253	4,317	472	50
1982	539	111	1,214	236	4,481	469	49
1983	530	115	1,252	235	4,619	521	51
1984	521	124	1,181	215	4,419	482	66
1985	520	145	1,158	205	4,522	469	73
1986	463	137	1,199	208	5,059	508	77
1987	488	150	850	165	5,814	505	87
1988	494	141	826	173	6,175	543	95
1989[3]	449	136	847	156	6,272	568	102
1990[3]	..	166	..	154	6,298	..	103

1 For notices issued up to 1 October 1986 some persons were prosecuted following non-payment of a fixed penalty. The extended fixed penalty system was introduced on 1 October 1986. It allowed the police to issue fixed penalty notices for a much wider range of offences than hitherto, and to register fines automatically in the event of non-payment without the need for court proceedings.
2 Number of notices, not persons.

3 Reclassification of certain indictable offences as summary following *Criminal Justice Act 1988.*
4 Series adjusted from 1977 following the implementation of the *Criminal Law Act 1977,* and a new procedure for counting court proceedings See Appendix, Part 12: Criminal courts in England and Wales.

Source: Home Office

indictable offences and 103 thousand for summary offences (excluding motoring offences) (Table 12.16). Of the 166 thousand offenders cautioned for indictable offences, 60 per cent were cautioned for theft or handling stolen goods (Table 12.17). The proportion of offenders cautioned for drug offences has increased from negligible levels in 1981 to 11 per cent by 1990.

For some minor motoring offences, the police have other options available. Depending on the type and seriousness of the offences, they have discretion on whether to give a fixed penalty or vehicle defect rectification scheme (VDRS) notice, or to give a written warning. On 1 October 1986, the extended fixed penalty system, covered in Part III of the *Transport Act*

12.17 Offenders cautioned: by type of indictable offence

England & Wales   Percentages and thousands

	1971[1]	1981	1989	1990
Percentage of all offenders cautioned				
Violence against the person	3.0	5.4	10.8	10.1
Sexual offences	5.0	2.7	2.6	2.0
Burglary	16.0	10.8	8.8	8.6
Robbery	0.3	0.1	0.3	0.3
Theft and handling stolen goods	69.2	76.2	60.2	60.0
Fraud and forgery	1.3	1.3	2.9	2.8
Criminal damage	4.7	2.0	2.7	2.5
Drug offences	..[3]	0.3	9.6	11.2
Other (excluding motoring offences)[2]	0.4	1.3	2.1	2.4
Total offenders cautioned (= 100%) (thousands)	77.3	103.9	136.0	166.3

1 Adjusted to take account of the *Criminal Damage Act 1971.*
2 Offenders cautioned for going equipped for stealing etc were counted against "burglary offences" until 1986 and against "others" from 1987. Historical data provided in this table have been amended to take account of this change. Includes drug offences in 1971.
3 Separate figures are not available for 1971; included with "others".

Source: Criminal Statistics, Home Office

12.18 Persons proceeded against or given fixed penalty notices

Scotland   Thousands

| | Crimes | Offences | | |
| | | Motoring | | Other |
	Persons proceeded against	Persons proceeded against	Fixed penalty notices[1]	Persons proceeded against
1971	45	100	74	80
1977	49	85	158	80
1981	59	103	401	84
1982	69	92	402	75
1983	71	100	410	75
1984	69	73	408	69
1985	72	71	454	68
1986	70	67	491	67
1987	69	67	542	64
1988	64	66	542	66[2]
1989	63	67	599	62[2]

1 Includes conditional offers of a fixed penalty by the procurator fiscal introduced in 1983. The number of fixed penalty notices issued by the police and traffic wardens for 1986 and 1987 have been estimated from figures to November 1986 and from December 1986.
2 From January 1988 procurators fiscal made conditional offers of a fixed penalty for some minor offences; these totalled some 15,600 in 1989.

Source: The Scottish Office Home and Health Department

12.19 Offenders sentenced for indictable offences: by type of offence and type of sentence, 1989

England & Wales   Percentages and thousands

	Discharge	Probation/ Supervision	Fine	Community service order	Fully suspended sentence	Immediate custody			Total sentenced (= 100%) (thousands)
						under 5 years	5 years and over	Other	
Offences									
Violence against the person	17	7	37	7	9	15	1	7	55.7
Sexual offences	11	13	33	1	8	25	8	2	7.3
Burglary	10	19	14	13	7	31	—	5	43.3
Robbery	4	10	2	7	2	55	14	6	4.6
Theft and handling stolen goods	20	13	42	7	6	10	—	3	134.3
Fraud and forgery	18	12	35	8	12	13	—	2	22.4
Criminal damage	19	17	29	6	5	12	—	11	9.4
Drug offences	8	5	62	3	5	13	3	—	22.6
Motoring	4	3	77	4	3	9	—	1	11.3
Other	11	3	57	5	6	14	—	3	28.1
Total notifiable offences	16	12	40	7	7	15	1	4	339.0

Source: Home Office

1982 and now contained in the *Road Traffic Offenders Act 1988*, was introduced in England and Wales. This allows the police in England and Wales to issue fixed penalty notices for a much wider range of minor traffic offences, such as speeding and neglect of traffic directions. Since April 1990 the penalties have been £16 for non-endorsable offences and £32 for endorsable offences. In Scotland it is the procurator fiscal who may decide to make an offer of a fixed penalty for endorsable offences on receiving a report of an offence from the police. The arrangements for dealing with unpaid notices were also changed so that the courts could automatically register an unpaid notice as a fine without any court appearance. The fine imposed was set at 50 per cent higher than the original fixed penalty.

In 1990 the number of fixed penalty notices for motoring offences issued in England and Wales increased to 6.3 million from 4.5 million in 1985. Over the same period, the number of people given written warnings for motoring offences fell from 205 thousand to 154 thousand. In Scotland the number of fixed penalty notices increased by 11 per cent between 1988 and 1989 to 599 thousand (Table 12.18). Over the same period, the number of people proceeded against for crimes and non-motoring offences fell slightly while those proceeded against for motoring offences showed little change from the previous three years.

If the case is not dealt with by any of the above methods, then the Crown Prosecution Service in England and Wales will decide whether or not to prosecute. If they do decide to prosecute, the case will be heard in either a Magistrates' court or a Crown Court (the latter being used for the most serious offences). Following a conviction, the magistrate or judge decides upon the most appropriate sentence although a magistrate cannot sentence an offender to custody for longer than six months.

The majority of offenders sentenced for indictable offences in England and Wales are fined - 40 per cent in 1989 (Table 12.19). However, the percentage varied between offences and ranged from 2 per cent of offenders sentenced for robbery to 77 per cent of offenders sentenced for motoring offences. Only 16 per cent of offenders were sentenced to immediate custody, although the percentage was much higher for robbery (69 per cent) and sexual offences (33 per cent).

12.20 Male defendants aged 21 and over sentenced to immediate custody for indictable offences: by average sentence length[1] and offence group

England & Wales   Months

	1981	1986	1989
Magistrates' court			
Violence against the person	3.2	2.9	3.0
Sexual offences	3.1	3.8	3.9
Burglary	3.7	3.6	3.4
Theft and handling stolen goods	2.9	2.7	2.5
Fraud and forgery	3.1	3.0	2.8
Criminal damage	2.8	2.1	2.0
Drug offences	3.2	2.9	2.6
Other (excluding motoring offences)	1.8	1.6	1.9
Motoring offences	3.6	3.3	3.7
All offences	3.1	3.0	2.7
Crown Court			
Violence against the person	16.7	18.2	19.9
Sexual offences	28.5	32.2	37.3
Burglary	16.6	16.1	17.2
Robbery	38.6	46.6	48.2
Theft and handling stolen goods	10.6	10.5	10.3
Fraud and forgery	15.6	14.8	15.2
Criminal damage	19.1	22.2	21.8
Drug offences	26.4	29.8	32.3
Other (excluding motoring offences)	11.3	13.3	12.3
Motoring offences	6.3	6.1	7.9
All offences	16.7	18.1	20.5

1 Excludes life sentences.   *Source: Criminal Statistics, Home Office*

In Scotland, fines were imposed on four out of every five people who had a charge proved against them in court (including motoring and other minor offences) in 1990. Custody accounted for a further 7 per cent.

Table 12.20 shows the average sentence length for men aged 21 and over who were sentenced to immediate custody. The highest average sentence length received in Magistrates' courts in England and Wales in 1989 was for sexual offences (3.9 months). Between 1981 and 1989 the average sentence length received in Magistrates' courts fell for all but three offence groups (sexual offences, motoring offences, and other offences)

The average sentence length was much higher in the Crown Court which sentences the more serious cases. In 1989, the average sentence length was 20.5 months although for individual offences the average ranged from 7.9 months for motoring offences to 48.2 months for robbery.

Unlike sentences at Magistrates' courts, the average length of sentence in the Crown Court increased between 1981 and 1989 (by over 20 per cent).

Offenders

This section looks at the age of offenders and the extent to which sentenced offenders commit further crimes following release.

In 1989, 77 thousand people were sentenced to custody in Great Britain, 9 thousand fewer than in 1988 (Chart 12.21). Of these, 70 per cent were aged 21 and over, 26 per cent were aged between 17 and 20, and 4 per cent aged between 14 and 16. During the 1970s, the proportion sentenced who were aged between 14 and 16 increased to 12 per cent, however, during the 1980s this proportion fell steadily to the 1989 level.

Chart 12.22 concentrates on young offenders and shows the age at which they were found guilty of, or cautioned for, indictable offences in England and Wales. The peak age for male offenders in 1961 was 14 years. Between 1961 and 1971, the rate of offenders increased at all ages from 11 upwards and the peak age changed to 17 years - by 1989 the peak age had increased to 18 years.

12.21 Persons sentenced to custody: by age

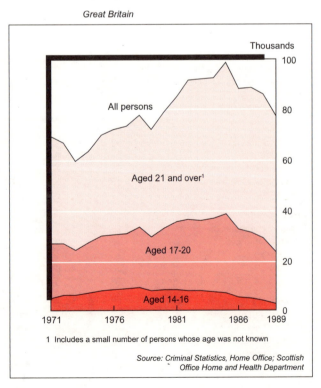

Great Britain

1 Includes a small number of persons whose age was not known

Source: Criminal Statistics, Home Office; Scottish Office Home and Health Department

12.22 Offenders aged under 21 found guilty of, or cautioned for, indictable offences: by sex and age

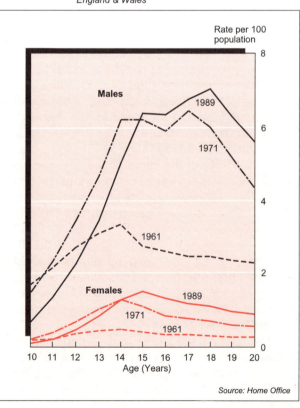

England & Wales

Source: Home Office

Table 12.23 shows the proportion of adult male offenders in England and Wales who were discharged during 1986 and who were subsequently reconvicted within two years. The greatest proportion of reconvictions was amongst those offenders discharged from sentences of up to 3 months with over half being reconvicted within 2 years of release. Thirty-seven per cent of adult males discharged during 1986 and subsequently reconvicted received a sentence of unsuspended imprisonment on first reconviction.

12.23 Reconvictions within two years of discharge during 1986: by length of sentence from which discharged

England & Wales			Numbers and percentages	
	Length of sentence from which discharged			
	Up to 3 months	Over 3 months up to 18 months	Over 18 months up to and excluding Life	Life
Number discharged[1]	7,940	18,579	8,170	30
Percentage reconvicted within 12 months[2]	37.0	26.9	18.7	3.3
Percentage reconvicted between 12 – 24 months[2]	14.1	16.4	19.6	0.0

1 Number of adult male prisoners discharged from unsuspended imprisonment during 1986.
2 The percentages are estimates based on a sample of discharges. The number reconvicted includes only those reconvicted for 'standard list offences'.

Source: Home Office

Prisons and probation service

The total prison population in England and Wales is projected to continue to increase, reaching between 56 and 57 thousand in 1999 (Chart 12.24). Between the end of the Second World War and the late 1980s, the average prison population increased in almost every year rising from only 16 thousand in 1946 to 50 thousand in 1988. However, this figure fell back slightly in 1989 and fell further in 1990 to stand at 46 thousand.

Comparisons between prison populations in different countries are fraught with problems. The number of people in prison is affected by the crime rate, police success in detecting crime and prosecuting and sentencing policy in each country. There are also technical differences about what constitutes a prisoner. Therefore, a country with a high prison population per head may not necessarily have a high crime rate, just a tougher sentencing policy. No one measure is sufficient when making international comparisons.

Two possible analyses are the number of people in prison for every 100 recorded crimes and per head of population. In 1985, a United Nations survey showed Sweden to have the lowest prison population per 100 recorded crimes (under 5). The rate in the United Kingdom was more than three times higher but was still less than the rates in Austria and Italy which were both higher than 20.

12.24 Average population in custody[1]: by type of prisoner

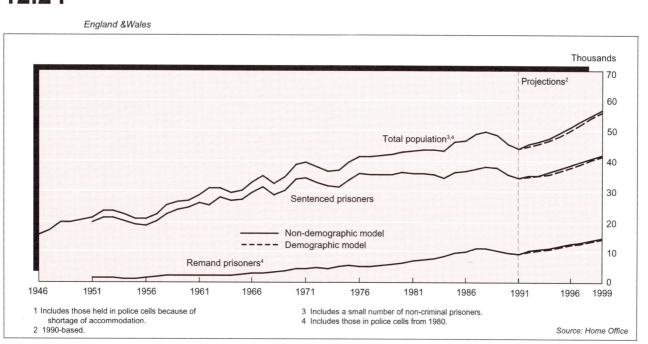

England &Wales

1 Includes those held in police cells because of shortage of accommodation.
2 1990-based.
3 Includes a small number of non-criminal prisoners.
4 Includes those in police cells from 1980.

Source: Home Office

Prison population per 100,000 head of population is shown in Chart 12.25. Of the countries shown, the Netherlands had the lowest rate at September 1989 (45 in prison for every 100,000 people) and the United Kingdom had the highest rate (96).

The ethnic minority groups make up a higher proportion of the prison population than they do in the population as a whole. A small part of the difference is due to the different age distribution of the ethnic minority populations. Of the 28 thousand prisoners (aged 21 and over) under sentence in England and Wales at the end of June 1990, 17 per cent were known to be from ethnic minority groups. The majority of these were of West Indian, Guyanese or African ethnic origin (Table 12.26).

12.25 **Prison population [1]: international comparison, 1989**

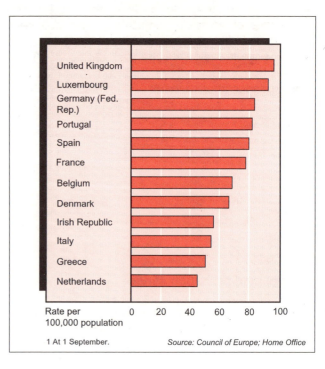

Rate per 100,000 population

1 At 1 September.   Source: Council of Europe; Home Office

12.26 **Population under sentence on 30 June 1990: by ethnic origin, age and offence group**

England & Wales   Percentages and numbers

	White	West Indian/ Guyanese/ African	Indian/ Pakistani/ Bangladeshi	Chinese/ Arab/ Mixed origin	Others[1]	All persons (= 100%) (numbers)
Males						
Prisoners aged under 21						
Violence against the person	84.6	8.7	2.7	2.8	1.2	1,019
Rape	74.8	15.7	7.6	1.3	0.6	159
Other sexual offences	89.7	5.2	1.7	1.7	1.7	58
Burglary	93.2	2.7	0.9	2.7	0.5	1,653
Robbery	71.4	19.0	4.8	3.7	1.1	900
Theft and handling	87.1	6.8	2.4	2.6	1.1	650
Fraud and forgery	65.2	8.7	8.7	17.4	—	23
Drug offences	72.2	21.1	3.4	1.1	2.2	90
Other offences	89.2	4.1	4.0	1.9	0.8	629
Offence not recorded	77.5	7.1	3.3	2.0	10.1	953
In default of payment of a fine	95.6	1.8	—	—	2.6	113
All prisoners aged under 21	84.4	7.9	2.8	2.6	2.3	6,247
Total population aged 15-20 [2]	93.0	1.3	3.3	1.1	0.3	2,476,000[3]
Prisoners aged 21 and over						
Violence against the person	85.8	8.6	3.0	1.9	0.7	6,458
Rape	78.4	15.4	3.7	1.5	1.0	1,282
Other sexual offences	94.1	3.4	1.5	0.5	0.5	1,519
Burglary	91.8	5.6	0.7	1.4	0.5	4,232
Robbery	80.4	14.9	2.0	1.7	1.0	3,152
Theft and handling	89.5	7.4	1.4	1.3	0.4	2,392
Fraud and forgery	82.0	10.9	3.8	2.3	1.0	772
Drug offences	54.8	29.0	9.9	2.6	3.7	2,739
Other offences	86.6	8.1	2.7	1.5	1.1	2,651
Offence not recorded	75.5	11.9	2.7	1.4	8.5	2,195
In default of payment of a fine	91.8	4.3	1.5	0.3	2.1	328
All prisoners aged 21 and over	82.7	11.0	3.0	1.6	1.7	27,720
Total population aged 21-64 [2]	94.8	1.2	2.2	0.7	0.3	15,503,000[3]

1 Includes offenders whose ethnic origin was not recorded.
2 Based on combined data for 1987, 1988 and 1989.
3 Rounded to nearest thousand.

Source: Prison Statistics, Home Office; Labour Force Survey, Office of Population Censuses and Surveys

12.27 Prisoners: by sex and length of sentence

United Kingdom   Numbers and rates

	1985	1986	1987	1988	1989	1990
Males						
Prisoners aged 21 and over serving:						
Up to 18 months	12,302	11,480	10,771	9,911	9,265	8,397
Over 18 months and up to 4 years	8,878	9,878	10,617	11,308	11,488	10,059
Over 4 years less than life	6,047	6,835	7,989	9,073	10,011	10,505
Life sentences	2,511	2,680	2,852	3,019	3,178	3,299
All sentenced male prisoners	29,738	30,873	32,229	33,311	33,943	32,260
Rate per 100,000 male population aged 21 and over	155	160	165	170	171	162
Females						
Prisoners aged 21 and over serving:						
Up to 18 months	623	618	576	507	465	423
Over 18 months and up to 4 years	245	306	404	406	381	314
Over 4 years less than life	96	125	172	218	284	330
Life sentences	63	72	77	82	92	97
All sentenced female prisoners	1,027	1,121	1,229	1,213	1,222	1,164
Rate per 100,000 female population aged 21 and over	5	5	6	6	6	5

Source: Home Office; The Scottish Office Home and Health Department; Northern Ireland Office

However, this proportion varied between the different types of offence from only 6 per cent for non-rape sexual offences to 45 per cent for drug offences. There are a wide range of explanatory factors involved that can affect the apparent distribution of offences between different ethnic groups and this should be borne in mind before attempting to draw comparisons.

The total sentenced adult male prison population in the United Kingdom fell slightly in 1990 (Table 12.27) following increases in each of the previous 4 years. The number of prisoners serving up to 18 months dropped by about a quarter between 1986 and 1990. This was due in part to the increase in remission from 13 August 1987 to a half for those prisoners sentenced to up to 12 months. The number of male prisoners serving life sentences increased by a quarter between 1986 and 1990.

The average number of people in prison in England and Wales and Northern Ireland fell in 1990 for the second successive year to stand at 47 thousand. This was over 3 thousand less than in 1989 (Table 12.28). In 1990, one in five prisoners in England and Wales and Northern Ireland was being held on remand, either untried or convicted awaiting sentence. The number of young offenders serving sentences fell considerably between 1981 and 1990 mainly because of the increased use of cautioning by the police resulting in fewer young offenders being dealt with by the courts.

12.28 Receptions[1] into prison establishments and population in custody

England & Wales and Northern Ireland   Thousands

	1981	1986	1988	1989	1990
England & Wales and Northern Ireland					
Average population					
Males	44.5	47.1	49.0	48.5	45.2
Females	1.5	1.6	1.8	1.8	1.6
Total	45.9	48.6	50.8	50.3	46.8
Remand prisoners	7.4	10.3	10.8	10.7	9.8
Untried prisoners	5.3	8.8	9.1	8.9	8.0
Convicted prisoners awaiting sentence[2]	2.1	1.4	1.7	1.8	1.8
Sentenced prisoners[3]	38.1	38.2	39.8	39.3	36.8
Adults	26.8	28.5	31.0	31.8	30.2
Young offenders[4]	11.4	9.7	8.7	7.5	6.6
Other sentences	—	—	—	—	—
Non-criminal prisoners	0.4	0.2	0.2	0.2	0.2
Receptions[1]					
Untried prisoners	49.6	57.7	59.8	60.6	54.4
Convicted prisoners awaiting sentence[2]	24.1	16.6	17.3	17.8	18.2
Sentenced prisoners	90.5	89.9	85.3	79.9	70.4
Non-criminal prisoners	4.8	3.7	3.1	3.1	2.3
England & Wales					
Highest number of inmates sleeping:					
Two in a cell	11.3	13.5	13.4	12.8	12.0
Three in a cell	5.6	4.9	5.7	5.0	3.5

1 Figures of receptions contain an element of double counting as individuals can be received in more than one category of prisoner.
2 Includes persons remanded in custody while social and medical inquiry reports are prepared prior to sentence. Prisoners in Northern Ireland are not committed for sentence but are sentenced at the court of conviction.
3 See Appendix, Part 12: Young offenders.
4 Northern Ireland figures for young prisoners are not available separately before 1980, they are included with adults.

Source: Prison Statistics, Home Office; Northern Ireland Office

12.29 Receptions into prison establishments and population in custody for Scotland

	1981	1986	1988	1989	1990
					Numbers
Average population					
Males	4,383	5,394	5,057	4,838	4,587
Females	135	194	172	147	137
Total	4,518	5,588	5,229	4,986	4,724
Remand prisoners	746	1,017	844	770	751
Untried prisoners	564	796	690	639	592
Convicted prisoners awaiting sentence	182	221	153	131	160
Sentenced prisoners	3,769	4,570	4,385	4,216	3,973
Adults	2,556	3,448	3,434	3,341	3,201
Young offenders[1]	1,174	1,074	902	813	708
Other sentences	41	49	48	61	63
Non-criminal prisoners	1	1	1	1	1
Receptions[2,3]					
Untried prisoners	10,663	15,295	13,310	12,177	12,826
Convicted prisoners awaiting sentence	2,887	2,812	1,690	2,104	2,343
Sentenced prisoners	15,539	23,220	20,540	19,484	17,134
Non-criminal prisoners	14	13	7	15	21

1 Includes Detention Centre receptions prior to 1989 and Borstal receptions prior to 1984.
2 A reception is counted if one or more warrants arrive for the same person from the same court on the same day, thus if a person is already held in custody and a warrant arrives for that person a further reception is counted. (In England, Wales and Northern Ireland, reception for sentenced prisoners are counts of first receptions).
3 Total receptions cannot be calculated by adding together receptions in each category because there is double counting. Thus, a person received on remand and then under sentence in relation to the same set of charges, is counted in both categories.

Source: The Scottish Office Home and Health Department

12.30 Persons supervised by the probation service : by type of supervision[1]

England & Wales

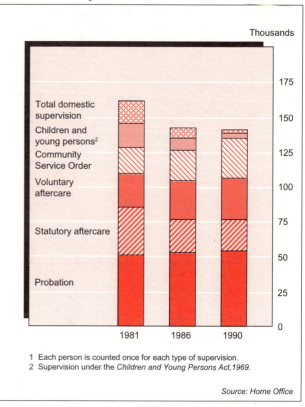

1 Each person is counted once for each type of supervision.
2 Supervision under the *Children and Young Persons Act, 1969.*

Source: Home Office

Table 12.29 shows that the average population of prison establishments in Scotland continued to fall between 1989 and 1990, by 5 per cent. In contrast to England and Wales, remand prisoners were fewer in 1989 than in 1986.

In 1975 the Home Secretary made a statement encouraging the more widespread use of parole and its granting at an earlier stage. Before 1 July 1984 prisoners might be considered for release on parole licence after serving a third of their prison sentence or a minimum qualifying period of twelve months after sentence, whichever was longer. On 1 July 1984, the minimum qualifying period for parole in England and Wales was reduced from 12 to 6 months from sentence, although the overriding requirement to serve a third of the sentence if this was longer remained unchanged. As a result of this change there was a large rise in England and Wales in the number of prisoners recommended for parole and between 1983 and 1984 the number of cases considered for parole more than

doubled. The proportion of persons recommended for parole rose to 61 per cent of cases considered in 1986 but has since shown a slight decline and in 1989 it was 58 per cent. Compared to England and Wales, the proportion in Scotland has always been far lower; for example, only 35 per cent in 1989.

Chart 12.30 shows that 141 thousand people were under the supervision of the probation service in England and Wales at the end of 1990; this was 13 per cent lower than in 1981 although similar to the figure in 1986. Much of this fall is accounted for by the decrease in the numbers under domestic supervision and the supervision of children and young persons. Domestic supervision results from a court order for young people under 18 where either their parents or guardians are unable to provide suitable home circumstances. The fall in the number of persons receiving supervision under the *Children and Young Persons Act* reflects the much greater use by the police of cautioning of juvenile offenders and the large fall in the numbers dealt with in the courts. Many of those supervised in 1990 were either on probation or subject to a community service order.

Legal Aid

12.31 Legal aid[1] and legal advice and assistance: by type of case

England & Wales   Thousands and percentages

	1971 −72	1976 −77	1981 −82	1984 −85	1985 −86	1986 −87	1987 −88	1988 −89	1989 −90	1990 −91
Civil legal aid: certificates issued (thousands)										
Matrimonial proceedings										
— issued to men	36[4]	32	112	36	37	36	34	31	128	138
— issued to women	118	123		86	87	90	91	88		
Other cases	49	56	79	100	108	119	122	128	131	158
Total	202	211	191	222	232	245	247	247	259	296
Criminal legal aid: applications granted										
Total, all criminal proceedings and appeals[2] (thousands)	167	362	443	515	571	620	628	652	643	658
Legal advice and assistance[3]										
Type of case (percentages)										
Matrimonial and family	.	*56*	*48*	*43*	*41*	*41*	*40*	*40*	*40*	*38*
Criminal	.	*15*	*23*	*27*	*26*	*23*	*22*	*22*	*22*	*22*
Other	.	*29*	*29*	*30*	*33*	*36*	*38*	*38*	*38*	*40*
Claims paid (thousands)	.	292	649	953	1,039	981	1,077	995	1,029	1,041

1 See Appendix, Part 12: Legal aid.
2 Calendar years. 1971 is shown under 1971-72, etc. Includes care
   proceedings.
3 Scheme began on 2 April 1973.

4 After 1975-76 data refer to offers of certificates accepted, some of
   which will have been issued in an earlier year.

Source: Legal Aid Annual Reports, *Lord Chancellor's Department*

The Legal Aid scheme aims to provide legal advice, assistance and representation to people who would otherwise be unable to pay, or would find it difficult to pay, for such a service.

Legal Aid comes in three forms. Firstly, Legal Advice and Assistance. This allows for a solicitor to give advice and assistance and provides legal representation (principally in domestic proceedings in magistrate's courts). Secondly, Civil Legal Aid. This allows for representation by a solicitor or barrister in most proceedings in civil courts for people who have reasonable grounds for taking, defending, or being party to proceedings. Thirdly, Criminal Legal Aid. This is granted by the courts to people who require assistance in meeting the costs of their defence in cases where the court considers it to be in the interests of justice that such assistance is provided. The system is broadly the same in Scotland, except that applications for legal aid for summary criminal cases are determined by the Scottish Legal Aid Board, not by the courts.

The total number of certificates for civil legal aid issued in England and Wales in 1990-91 was 296 thousand (Table 12.31). This was 37 thousand more than in the previous year and more than all other years shown in the table. There was a substantial fall between 1976-77 and 1977-78 because of the withdrawal of legal aid for undefended divorce cases. There was also a fall between 1979-80 and 1980-81 because of the introduction in 1980 of the assistance by way of representation scheme which allows for representation of a parent or guardian in certain child care proceedings.

The number of criminal legal aid applications granted in England and Wales in 1990-91 was 658 thousand, again, more than any of the other years in the table and nearly four times greater than the number granted in 1971-72.

The number of claims paid for legal advice and assistance increased sharply in the early years after introduction and has since risen to over 1 million in England and Wales in 1990-91.

There have also been changes in the type of case on which legal advice and assistance is sought; in 1973-74 (the first year the scheme was in operation), around 60 per cent of the cases involved marriage or family matters and only about 10 per cent related to criminal affairs, but by 1990-91 these proportions had changed to 38 per cent and 22 per cent respectively.

In Scotland, 21 thousand certificates for civil legal aid were issued in 1990-91 - a small increase over the previous year. Over half of these were for husband and wife actions (mainly divorce). The number of criminal legal aid applications granted in 1990-91 was 65 thousand - an increase of 6 thousand over the previous year. Finally, 180 thousand claims for legal advice and assistance were paid in Scotland in 1990-91.

Almost all defendants appearing at the Crown Court for trial or sentence were legally aided in 1990. Where an appeal against a decision in a Magistrates' court was heard at the Crown Court, only half of all people were legally aided (Table 12.32). In Magistrate's courts, only 28 per cent of adults tried for indictable offences were legally aided in 1971, although this had risen to 71 per cent by 1989.

12.32 Percentage of defendants on criminal charges who were legally aided[1]: by type of proceedings

England & Wales   Percentages

| | Magistrates' court proceedings | | | | Crown Court proceedings | | |
| | Trials of adults for | | Proceedings relating to committal for trial[2] | All criminal proceedings at juvenile courts | Trials at the Crown Court | Appearances for sentencing following conviction at magistrates' court | Appeals against a decision of a magistrates' court |
	Indictable offences	Summary offences					
1971	28	1	71	5[3]	94	94	65
1976	53	2	70	21	96	98	64
1981	65	2	57	31	97	97	67
1986	92	3	76	55	97	94	61
1989	71	5	80	74	98	91	54
1990	..	..	..	..	98	92	52

1 See Appendix, Part 12: Legal aid.
2 Figures should be treated with caution since they are based on estimated data.
3 Figure includes some care proceedings.

Source: Lord Chancellor's Department

Resources

Table 12.33 shows how public expenditure on justice and law has risen steadily over the period 1981 to 1990. In 1990, it accounted for 5.2 per cent of general Government expenditure compared with only 3.7 per cent in 1981. Around a half of all expenditure was on the police.

Between 1961 and 1990, the strength of the police force in the United Kingdom increased by 70 per cent from 88 thousand to 149 thousand (Table 12.34). Over the same period, the proportion of women in the police-force increased from 3 per cent to 11 per cent.

Table 12.35 shows data on manpower in prison department establishments in Great Britain. These include borstals, youth custody centres, detention centres, and young offender institutions.

At 1 January 1991, there were 35 thousand staff, nearly 2 thousand more than a year earlier and over 8 thousand more than at the beginning of 1981. Prison officers form the majority of staff in post accounting for three quarters of total manpower in 1991 - slightly higher than in 1981.

12.33 Public expenditure on justice and law[1]

United Kingdom   £ million and percentages

	1981	1986	1989	1990
Police	2,433	3,691	4,695	5,351
Prisons	613	1,071	1,331	1,722
Legal Aid	160	345	524	613
Probation	102	148	201	220
Parliament	243	530	708	664
Law Courts	757	1,219	2,295	2,640
Total	4,308	7,004	9,754	11,210
As a percentage of general Government expenditure	3.7	4.3	4.9	5.2

1 Costs are not included for social work staff employed in Scotland on aspects related to the criminal justice system which in England and Wales are undertaken by the probation service.

Source: Central Statistical Office

12.34 Police force and police auxiliaries manpower[1]: by sex

United Kingdom   Thousands

	1961	1971	1981	1989	1990
Police Force					
Men	85.2	107.9	127.8	132.5	132.7
Women	2.7	4.3	12.1	15.7	16.5
Total	87.9	112.2	139.9	148.2	149.1
Police auxiliaries					
Total	84.2	76.6	67.4	50.4	52.3

1 As at 31 December each year.

Source: Home Office; The Scottish Office Home and Health Department; Northern Ireland Office

12.35 Prison service: manpower[1]

Great Britain			Numbers and rates	
	1971	1981	1990	1991
Prison officer class	13,087	19,441	25,174	26,762
Governor class	532	614	908	928
Other non-industrial staff	3,027	4,358	4,932	5,047
Industrial staff	1,825	2,426	2,503	2,497
Total staff in post	18,471	26,839	33,517	35,234
Number of inmates per prison officer[2]				
Male establishments	3.5	2.6	2.3	1.9
Female establishments	2.3	1.7	1.7	1.3

1 At 1 January each year.
2 Prison officer class excluding prison officers under training or prison
  auxiliaries who are not directly involved in the supervision of inmates.

Source: Home Office; The Scottish Office Home and Health Department

The growth in prison officer manpower has meant that, despite the increase in the average population in prison establishments since 1981, the ratio of inmates to prison officers has fallen substantially. However, because the officers work in shifts, the number of inmates per prison officer on duty at any one time are higher than the overall rates given in the table. In England and Wales the number of staff on duty at any time is also affected by the phased reduction in working hours which began in 1987 (as a result of the Fresh Start agreement on pay and conditions which covered most staff working in prisons).

In 1990, there were 6,573 full-time established probation officers (Table 12.36). In addition, there were a further 581 part-time probation officers in 1990, seven-times the number in 1971. The number of full-time ancillaries

12.36 Probation service manpower: by type and sex

England & Wales				Numbers
	1961	1971	1981	1990
Full-time				
Established				
Male	1,762	2,547	3,537	3,703
Female		1,061	1,952	2,870
Temporary				
Male	13	42	9	14
Female	14	39	15	18
Trainees[1]				
Male	..	..	4	4
Female	..	..	7	3
Ancillaries[2]	..	..	891	1,646
Part-Time				
Probation Officers				
Male	21	20	18	89
Female	28	60	114	492
Ancillaries[2]	..	..	99	272

1 Trainees figures are not available prior to 1979.
2 Ancillaries figures are not available by sex or prior to 1975. The figures prior
  to 1983 do not include day care centre ancillaries.

Source: Home Office

at the end of 1990 was 1,646. Ancillaries have a variety of duties including work in community service schemes, day centres and other work in support of probation officers.

Table 12.37 shows trends in the size of the Judiciary and the numbers of legal representatives in England and Wales, Scotland and Northern Ireland. Unfortunately, figures are not directly comparable due to differences in the legal system and composition of the Judiciary. In England and Wales High Court Judges try High Court civil work and the serious criminal cases in the Crown Court. Circuit Judges try the great majority of Crown Court cases and also sit in the county court to try civil actions. Recorders and Assistant Recorders are barristers or solicitors who undertake to

12.37 The Judiciary, and legal representatives

England & Wales, Scotland and Northern Ireland			Numbers
	1972	1981	1990
England & Wales			
The Judiciary			
Judges[1,2]			
Lord Justices	14	18	27
High Court Judges	70	74	83
Circuit Judges	233	334	427
Recorders	325	446	752
Assistant Recorders	.	..	421
District Judges[2]	134	150	223
Magistrates[3]	20,539	25,435	27,011[10]
Legal representatives			
Barristers[4]	2,919	4,685	6,645
Solicitors[5]	26,327	39,795	55,685
Scotland[2]			
The Judiciary			
Judges	19	21	24
Sheriffs[6]	..	78	101
Stipendiary Magistrates	3	3	4
Justices of the Peace[7]	.	..	904
Legal representatives[8]			
Advocates	48	134	276
Solicitors	3,374	5,065	7,087
Northern Ireland[9]			
The Judiciary			
Judges			
High Court Judges	..	8	10
County Court Judges	5	10	13
Circuit Registrars	0	4	4
Resident Magistrates	17	15	17
Legal representatives			
Barristers	88	203	308
Solicitors	..	888	1,295

1 Excludes deputy judges and, for 1972 and 1981, assistant recorders.
2 Figures relate to 31 December each year.
3 Figures relate to 1 January each year.
4 Figures relate to 1 October each year.
5 Number who applied for a practising certificate in year ending 31 October.
6 Numbers not available before local government reorganisation in 1975.
7 On rota for court duty, 31 March 1990.
8 Practising.
9 Figures are at 1971, 1981 and 1990.
10 Figures are for 1989.

Source: Lord Chancellor's Department; The Magistrates' Association;
The Law Society; The General Council of the Bar;
The Scottish Office Home and Health Department;
Northern Ireland Office

sit in the Crown Court for a minimum of 20 days a year and who perform similar duties to Circuit Judges but usually deal with the less serious cases. District Judges are former solicitors who act as judicial officers in civil cases, dealing with matter arising between the start of proceedings in an action up until the trial.

In Scotland, greater use is made of full-time legally qualified judges. The Court of Session, consisting of 22 judges, is the supreme civil court. The most serious criminal cases are dealt with in the High Court, where the judges are the same persons as in the Court of Session, or under solemn procedure in the Sheriff

court. The Sheriff court is the principal local court of both civil and criminal jurisdiction. Sheriffs are qualified as advocates or solicitors. Sheriffs principal are full-time judges resident in their Sheriffdom. In Northern Ireland High Court Judges try High Court civil work and the serious criminal cases in the Crown Court. County Court Judges try the great majority of Crown Court cases and also sit in the County Court to try civil actions. Deputy Court Judges are drawn mainly from Senior and Junior Counsel - in addition, four Circuit Registrars, three Resident Magistrates and one practising Solicitor fulfil the same role which covers only the civil courts.

Northern Ireland

The number of deaths due to the security situation in Northern Ireland increased slightly between 1989 and 1990 with 27 members of the security services and 49 civilians killed (Chart 12.38). The greatest number killed was in 1972, the year when terrorist activity was at its peak, when there were 467 deaths. The deaths in 1990 bring the total number of security service personnel killed since 1969 to 895 and the total number of civilians to 1,953.

12.38 Northern Ireland: deaths due to the security situation

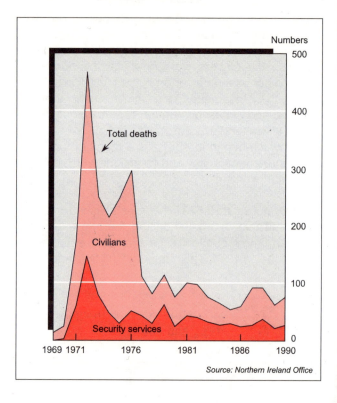

Source: Northern Ireland Office

BIBLIOGRAPHY

The following list contains selected publications relevant to Chapter 12: Crime and Justice. Those published by HMSO are available from the addresses shown on the back cover of Social Trends.
Annual Report of the Law Society of Scotland on the Legal Aid Scheme, HMSO
Civil Judicial Statistics, Scotland, HMSO
Criminal Injuries Compensation Board Report and Accounts, HMSO
Criminal Statistics, England and Wales, HMSO
Criminal Statistics, Scotland, HMSO
Experiences of Crime Across the World, Key Findings of the 1989 International Crime Survey, Kluwer
Home Office Statistical Bulletins Series, Home Office
Judicial Statistics, England and Wales, HMSO

Legal Aid Annual Reports, (England and Wales), HMSO
Legal Aid Reports, (Northern Ireland), HMSO
Police Statistics, England and Wales, CIPFA
Prison Statistics, England and Wales, HMSO
Prisons in Scotland Report, HMSO
Probation Statistics, England and Wales, Home Office
Report of the Parole Board for England and Wales, HMSO
Report of the Parole Board for Scotland, HMSO
The Scottish Office Statistical Bulletins Series, The Scottish Office
Statistics of the Misuse of Drugs: Seizures and Offenders Dealt With, United Kingdom, Home Office
Ulster Year Book, HMSO
Victim Support: Annual Report, Home Office

Chapter 13: Transport

Transport - general

●   Over the last 30 years, use of public transport has fallen and the use of private vehicles has increased four-fold.

(Chart 13.1)

●   Around 1.1 million people commute into Central London every day - 84 per cent of them use public transport.

(Chart 13.3)

●   As a nation, we are spending more and more on transport and vehicles. Between 1963 and 1990, the proportion of consumers' expenditure on transport and vehicles increased from 8.9 per cent to 11.7 per cent.   *(Table 13.7)*

Road

●   Two car families are on the increase - the proportion of households with at least two cars has increased from just 2 per cent of households in 1961 to 22 per cent by 1989.   *(Chart 13.9)*

Rail

●   British Rail is carrying more passenger traffic in fewer carriages - the 12 thousand carriages used in 1990-91 covered 20 per cent more passenger kilometres than the 17 thousand carriages used in 1976.   *(Table 13.13)*

Air

●   The number of flights to and from United Kingdom airports increased by 92 per cent between 1976 and 1990 to reach 1.1 million.   *(Chart 13.17)*

Transport casualties

●   In 1990, British roads were most dangerous between 5pm and 6pm on weekdays, when casualty rates reached 4,319 per hour.   *(Chart 13.18)*

●   The United Kingdom has one of the lowest rates of road deaths among western countries, with less than 10 deaths per 100,000 population in 1989.   *(Table 13.21)*

13.1   Road and rail passenger transport use

Great Britain

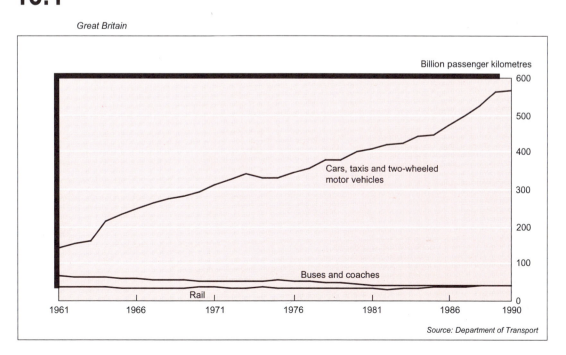

Source: Department of Transport

Transport - general

13.2 Passenger transport use and prices

Billion passenger kilometres and price indices

	1981	1986	1989	1990
Use (Great Britain)				
Billion passenger kilo- metres travelled by:				
Air[1]	3	4	5	5
Rail[2]	34	37	40	40
Road				
Buses and coaches	42	41	41	41
Cars, taxis, and two- wheeled motor vehicles[3]	409	471	563	567
Bicycles	5	5	5	5
Total	493	558	654	658
Retail price indices[4] **(United Kingdom)**				
(January 1987 = 100)				
Fares and other travel costs	69	97	115	123
Bus and coach fares[5]	69	98	119	126
Rail fares	69	96	117	128
Other travel costs[6]	..	..	110	118
Motoring expenditure	82	98	114	121
Purchase of motor vehicles	84	97	115	117
Maintenance of motor vehicles	72	98	116	128
Petrol and oil	91	100	107	120
Vehicle tax and insurance[7]	..	..	123	128
Retail price index (all items)	75	98	115	126

1 Revenue passenger kilometres on scheduled and non-scheduled services. Includes Northern Ireland and Channel Islands. Excludes air taxi services, private flying and passengers paying less than 25 per cent of the full fare on scheduled and non-scheduled services.
2 British Rail, plus London Regional Transport, Strathclyde PTE, and Tyne and Wear PTE.
3 Based on statistics of vehicle-kilometres derived from traffic counts and estimates of average number of persons per vehicle derived from the National Travel Survey.
4 Because of rounding there may be slight differences between percentage changes calculated using the above figures and those calculated using the definitive series published at the time. Where no figures are given, it is because these groups have no direct counterpart in earlier series.
5 Coach fares have only been included since 1987.
6 Prior to 1987, an index for other travel costs is not available on a comparable basis.
7 Between 1978 and 1986, indices for vehicle licences and motor insurance are only available separately.

Source: Department of Transport; Central Statistical Office

The bottom part of Table 13.2 shows selected retail price indices for transport. The all items retail prices index rose by 68 per cent between 1981 and 1990. Bus and coach fares rose by more than this rate of inflation (83 per cent), whilst motoring expenditure (48 per cent) and the price of petrol and oil (32 per cent) rose by less.

13.3 Central London commuter traffic[1]: by mode of transport, 1990

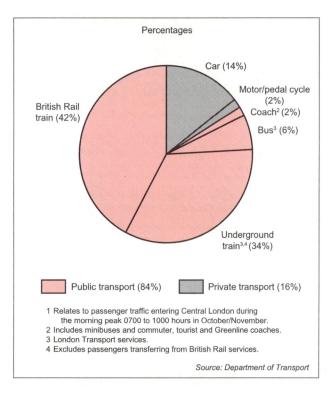

Percentages

British Rail train (42%)

Car (14%)

Motor/pedal cycle (2%)

Coach[2] (2%)

Bus[3] (6%)

Underground train[3,4] (34%)

Public transport (84%)   Private transport (16%)

1 Relates to passenger traffic entering Central London during the morning peak 0700 to 1000 hours in October/November.
2 Includes minibuses and commuter, tourist and Greenline coaches.
3 London Transport services.
4 Excludes passengers transferring from British Rail services.

Source: Department of Transport

Since 1961 there has been a decline in the use of public transport, while the use of private road vehicles has increased to four times the earlier level (Chart 13.1 and Table 13.2). In 1990, 88 per cent of the total distance travelled in Great Britain was in cars, taxis and motorcycles, compared to only 57 per cent in 1961. A quarter of all travel in 1961 was by bus or coach but by 1990 this share had fallen to about one-sixteenth. The amount of rail travel declined slightly in the sixties and seventies but by the end of the 1980s it had increased back to its 1961 level, although the railway's share of total distance travelled fell from 16 per cent in 1961 to 6 per cent in 1990.

Chart 13.3 shows the methods of travel used by commuters to Central London during the morning rush hour (between 7 and 10 am). Around 1.1 million people travel into the centre of London each day - 14 per cent travel by car and 2 per cent by motorcycle or pedal cycle. The remaining 84 per cent use public transport. The largest proportion (42 per cent) use British Rail and the second largest proportion (34 per cent) use the underground. There are nearly 16 thousand licensed taxis operating in London - around one for every 450 people living in the capital. By comparison, Paris has one licensed taxi for every 400 people and in Tokyo there is one taxi for every 250 people.

13.4 Number of journeys and distance travelled per person per week: by purpose[1] and age, 1988-1990

Great Britain   Number of journeys and miles travelled

	To or from work	In course of work	Education	Escorting		Shopping	Other personal business	Social or entertain- ment	Holidays/ day trips/ other	All purposes
				Work	Education					
Number of journeys per person per week										
0 – 15 years	0.1	—	2.2	0.3	0.4	1.4	1.0	3.2	2.5	11.0
16 – 59 years										
Males	6.8	1.7	0.3	0.6	0.2	2.6	2.0	3.9	1.7	19.9
Females	3.9	0.5	0.3	0.3	0.7	3.5	1.7	3.7	1.8	16.5
60 years and over	0.7	0.2	—	0.1	—	3.3	1.6	2.7	1.4	10.0
All ages	3.2	0.6	0.6	0.4	0.3	2.8	1.6	3.4	1.8	14.9
Distance travelled per person per week (miles)										
0 – 15 years	0.3	0.2	7.8	1.6	0.9	7.0	4.9	25.9	21.1	69.8
16 – 59 years										
Males	63.8	34.6	2.1	2.7	0.9	13.6	12.9	38.3	21.9	190.9
Females	24.0	5.0	2.2	1.7	1.9	17.6	10.1	35.3	22.6	120.7
60 years and over	4.9	2.5	—	0.6	0.2	13.9	7.7	23.1	18.7	71.6
All ages	26.0	11.7	2.9	1.7	1.1	13.4	9.3	31.5	21.4	119.0

1 See Appendix, Part 13: Journey purpose.

Source: National Travel Survey, Department of Transport

People make journeys for differing reasons, and as work, shopping and leisure patterns change they affect journeys made and distances travelled. Figures from the National Travel Survey (NTS) show that a quarter of all journeys made during the period 1988-1990 were either to or from work, or in the course of work (Table 13.4). These journeys account for a third of total mileage travelled. Over the period 1988-1990, people were making an average of 15 journeys per week compared with only 11 in 1965 and the average single journey length increased from about 6.5 miles in 1965 to 8 miles in 1988-1990. Men travel further to work than women, the average journey distance travelled to or from work in 1988-1990 was 6 miles for women and 9 miles for men.

Table 13.5 shows the increase since 1971 in travel between the United Kingdom and the rest of the European Community (EC). The number of visits to the EC by residents of the United Kingdom trebled between 1971 and 1990, increasing by much more than the number of visits made in the opposite direction by EC visitors. Air travel is still the most popular form of transport between the United Kingdom and the rest of the European Community although the percentage of journeys made by air increased only slightly between 1971 and 1990 (from 55 per cent to 59 per cent).

13.5 Overseas travel[1] between the United Kingdom and the rest of the European Community[2]: by mode of travel

			Thousands of visits		
	1971	1976	1981	1986	1990
Visits to the UK by EC visitors[3]					
Air	1,641	2,372	2,462	3,081	5,023
Sea[4]	1,770	3,364	3,560	3,861	3,835
All	3,411	5,736	6,022	6,941	8,858
Visits to the EC by UK residents[3]					
Air	4,192	4,802	6,869	11,221	13,057
Sea[4]	3,090	3,907	7,090	7,899	8,975
All	7,282	8,709	13,959	19,120	22,032

1 The number of visits, not visitors. Anyone entering or leaving more than once in the same period is counted on the occasion of each visit.
2 Includes Irish Republic, Denmark, Greece, Portugal and Spain throughout.
3 See Appendix, Part 13: EC visitor.
4 Includes passengers travelling across the land border between the UK and the Irish Republic.

Source: International Passenger Survey, Employment Department

Table 13.6 gives an international comparison of overland passenger traffic for 1979 and 1989. Obviously the amount of traffic is heavily dependent on the population. In 1989, people travelled 630 billion kilometres in Great Britain. The country with the largest amount of traffic was the USA with nearly 4,200 billion passenger kilometres in 1989. The largest increase in passenger traffic between 1979 and 1989 shown in the table was in Portugal (52 per cent), followed by Italy (41 per cent) and Japan and Great Britain (both around 39 per cent). The smallest increase in passenger traffic over the

13.6 Passenger traffic — by mode: international comparison[1], 1979 and 1989

Billion passenger kilometres

	Cars and taxis		Buses and coaches		Rail excluding metro systems		All modes	
	1979	1989	1979	1989	1979	1989	1979	1989
Great Britain	372.0[1]	556.0	48.0	41.0	30.7	33.3	450.7	630.21
Belgium	60.2[2]	73.0[2,3]	9.4	10.5[3]	7.0	6.4	76.5	89.9
Denmark	40.4	52.1	7.0	8.9[3]	3.8	4.8[3]	51.2	65.8
France	440.0	570.0[3]	34.0	43.0[3]	53.6	64.3	527.6	677.3
Germany (Fed Rep.)	467.4	565.0[3]	64.3[4,5]	53.0[3,4,6]	39.4	42.1	571.1	660.1
Greece	..	..	5.8	5.0[3]	1.5	2.0	..	..
Irish Republic	..	..	..	..	1.1	1.2[3]	..	..
Italy[1]	320.4	485.0[3]	71.6	80.0[3]	39.7	44.4	431.7	609.4
Luxembourg	..	—	..	..	0.3	0.2[3]	..	..
Netherlands	109.5	128.0[3]	11.1	10.0[3]	8.5	10.2	129.1	148.2
Portugal	38.8	62.0[3]	7.4	10.6[3]	5.6	5.9	51.8	78.5
Spain	125.6	157.0	32.1	39.0	13.2	16.1	170.9	212.1
Austria[1]	46.8	62.2	12.9	14.0	7.4	7.1	67.2	83.3
Czechoslavakia	..	..	32.1	39.7	15.4	19.7	..	..
Finland	33.5	45.8	8.3	8.5	3.0	3.2	44.8	57.5
German DR	..	..	25.6[1]	23.1[1]	22.3	23.8	..	..
Hungary	..	..	..	..	14.6	12.7	..	..
Norway[1]	28.5	40.0[3]	4.1	4.0[3]	2.2	2.1	34.8	46.1
Sweden[1]	69.1	86.8	7.0	9.0	6.2	6.2	82.3	102.0
Switzerland	64.7	64.0[3]	4.2	5.8[3]	8.3	11.0	77.2	80.8
Yugoslavia	..	..	29.2	30.0[3]	10.1	11.7	..	..
Japan	338.5	530.0[3]	89.7	110.0[3]	312.5	390.0[3]	740.7	1,030.0
USA	3,405.1	4,100.0[3]	44.6[7]	37.0[3,7]	18.3	21.0	3,468.0	4,158.0
USSR	..	..	376.0	490.0[3]	335.3	410.7	..	..

1 National and foreign vehicles.
2 Excludes taxis.
3 Estimated.
4 Includes public transport vehicles abroad.
5 Break in series.
6 Excludes firms with less than 6 coaches or buses.
7 Intercity transport only.

Source: Department of Transport

period was in Switzerland (only 5 per cent). The use of buses and coaches increased in a number of the Eastern European countries shown. In the USSR, for example, the use of buses and coaches increased by 30 per cent and in Czechoslovakia use increased by 24 per cent - while in Britain and the Federal Republic of Germany passenger traffic on buses decreased by 15 and 18 per cent respectively. The proportion of total passenger traffic using the railways varied between the countries, but was highest in Japan at 38 per cent of total distance travelled in 1989.

Between 1963 and 1990 the proportion of consumers' expenditure spent on transport and vehicles increased from 8.9 to 11.7 per cent (Table 13.7). In 1963, 14 per cent of transport and vehicle expenditure was on the maintenance and running of motor vehicles; by 1990 this had increased to 25 per cent. Conversely, the proportion spent on bus and coach fares fell from 31 per cent in 1963 to 6 per cent in 1990. These figures reflect the changing patterns of transport use and costs shown earlier in Chart 13.1 and Table 13.2

13.7 Consumers' expenditure per head[1] on transport

United Kingdom

£ per week at 1985 prices and percentages

	1963	1971	1976	1981	1984	1985	1986	1990
Net purchase of motor vehicles, spares and accessories	1.44	2.54	2.43	2.86	3.34	3.51	3.82	4.33
Maintenance and running of motor vehicles	0.60	0.94	1.36	1.53	1.64	1.71	1.84	2.68
Railway fares[2]	0.48	0.47	0.43	0.46	0.49	0.50	0.52	0.55
Bus and coach fares[2]	1.33	0.99	0.91	0.69	0.65	0.67	0.62	0.62
Other travel and transport[3]	0.45	0.73	0.89	1.40	1.52	1.59	1.83	2.55
All transport and vehicles	4.30	5.67	6.01	6.93	7.65	7.98	8.64	10.73
Expenditure on transport and vehicles as a percentage of total consumers' expenditure	*8.9*	*10.2*	*9.9*	*10.4*	*10.7*	*10.8*	*11.0*	*11.7*

1 Average weekly expenditure per head of population.
2 Includes purchase of season tickets.
3 Includes purchase and maintenance of other vehicles and boats.

Source: Central Statistical Office; Office of Population Censuses and Surveys

Road

13.8 Cars and car ownership: by region, 1981 and 1989

	1981					1989				
	Percentage of house-holds with-out the regular use of a car[1]	Percentage of house-holds with regular use of[1]		Cars per 1,000 pop.	Average vehicle age (years)	Percentage of house-holds with-out the regular use of a car[1]	Percentage of house-holds with regular use of[1]		Cars per 1,000 pop.	Average vehicle age (years)
		One car only	Two or more cars				One car only	Two or more cars		
Great Britain	39	45	15	281	6.1	34	41	22	355	5.9
North	48	41	10	227	5.4	42	42	16	285	5.5
Yorkshire & Humberside	46	43	12	245	5.5	41	44	15	313	5.5
East Midlands	37	47	15	273	6.0	31	47	22	344	6.0
East Anglia	31	51	18	321	6.3	29	47	24	412	6.0
South East	36	46	19	316	6.3	30	43	27	391	6.0
Greater London	45	42	14	287	6.1	39	43	18	350	5.9
Rest of South East	30	48	22	336	6.4	24	44	32	416	5.8
South West	31	51	18	329	7.1	26	49	25	404	6.8
West Midlands	38	46	16	290	6.0	33	43	24	375	5.9
North West	45	42	13	250	5.7	38	42	20	327	5.6
England	39	45	16	288	6.1	33	44	23	365	5.9
Wales	38	47	15	271	6.3	30	50	20	327	6.2
Scotland	49	40	11	217	5.0	45	41	14	281	5.1
Northern Ireland	40	46	14	237	. .	. .	. .	. .	. .	. .

1 Includes cars and light vans normally available to the household.

Source: Department of Transport

The earlier Chart 13.1 highlights the increasing importance of car travel, and Table 13.8 summarises car ownership in each region for 1981 and 1989. Households in Scotland are the least likely to own a car - about half of all Scottish households had no regular use of a car in both 1981 and 1989. The region with the highest proportion of households with regular use of two or more cars was the South East (excluding Greater London) with 32 per cent in 1989, compared with 22 per cent for Great Britain as a whole. In 1989 there were around 355 cars per 1,000 population - an increase of 26 per cent since 1981. The largest regional increase over the same period was 31 per cent in the North West. Vehicle age differs between regions - the oldest cars are in the South West (6.8 years), which also has a higher proportion of older people than other regions of the country.

Chart 13.9 illustrates how the rapid growth in car ownership during the 1960s has subsequently slowed down. In 1961, fewer than a third of households had the regular use of a car. This had increased to over a half by 1969 and had reached two thirds by 1989. Two car families are also on the increase. Despite the fall in average household size (see Chapter 2), the proportion of households with at least two cars has continued to rise steadily - from 2 per cent of all households in 1961 to 22 per cent in 1989. In 1989, 2.2 million private cars were registered for the first time, 56 per cent more than in 1981. Between these two years, the proportion of newly registered cars which were registered by companies rose from 40 per cent to 51 per cent.

13.9 Households with and without regular use of a car[1]

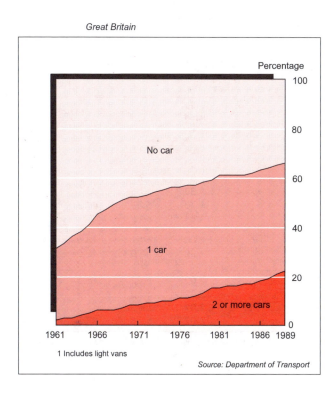

Great Britain

1 Includes light vans

Source: Department of Transport

13.10 Households with regular use of a car: by socio-economic group, 1989

United Kingdom   Percentages and numbers

	No car	One or more cars	One car only	Two or more cars	Sample size (= 100%) (numbers)[1]
Socio-economic group					
Professional	4	95	43	52	585
Employers and managers	5	95	41	54	1,680
Intermediate non-manual	15	85	56	30	820
Junior non-manual	27	73	55	18	737
Skilled manual[2]	17	83	56	26	2,806
Semi-skilled manual[3]	45	55	44	11	1,214
Unskilled manual	57	43	35	8	389
Retired	56	44	38	6	3,299
Others	69	31	26	5	1,194
All groups[4]	35	65	44	21	13,068

1 Combined sample for General Household Survey and Continuous Household Survey.
2 Includes foremen, farm managers and own account workers.
3 Includes personal service workers and farm workers.

4 Includes 0.8 million households headed by armed forces, inadequately described, never worked, housewives and other inactive.

Source: General Household Survey;
Continuous Household Survey;
Northern Ireland Office;

Although car ownership has increased over recent decades, those in the employers, managerial and professional groups are still the most likely to own a car (Table 13.10). Only 4 per cent of those in the professional group had no use of a car, compared with an all-groups average of 35 per cent. For households in the unskilled manual group, 57 per cent had no use of a car.

About 2 million driving tests are taken each year in the United Kingdom (Table 13.11). Each year since 1983 women have taken more tests than men but men have a significantly better pass rate. During the period 1980 to 1990 the pass rates for both men and women rose consistently to reach 58 per cent for men and 47 per cent for women by 1990. Data from the Department of

Transport from 1985 show that a fifth of driving test failures occur due to the omission of precautions before starting the engine, improper use of foot pedals and gears and lack of control on or before moving off.

With a greater increase in car ownership than in road building, roads have become considerably busier (Table 13.12). The average daily flow is the number of vehicles passing a particular point on a road in a 24 hour period. This flow is high on busy roads such as motorways (55 thousand vehicles per day) and low on minor roads (only 1.4 thousand per day). The largest increase in traffic between 1976 and 1990 was on trunk roads outside built-up areas (where traffic flow almost doubled) and the smallest increase was on principal roads in built-up areas (up by a third).

13.11 Driving test pass rates: by sex

Great Britain   Millions and percentages

	Tests conducted (millions)	Pass rate (percentages)		
		Men	Women	All
1980	1.96	53.0	41.5	47.3
1981	2.03	52.9	42.5	47.6
1982	2.01	53.1	42.9	48.1
1983	1.89	53.8	43.7	48.7
1984	1.78	54.3	44.2	49.1
1985	1.84	54.2	43.7	48.6
1986	2.00	54.1	43.8	48.6
1987	1.98	56.0	46.0	50.0
				[1]
1987	2.03	56.2	46.3	50.3
1988	2.09	58.2	47.3	52.3
1989	2.07	58.3	47.3	52.3
1990	2.02	58.3	47.3	52.3

1 From 1987 onwards coverage is for the United Kingdom.

Source: Department of Transport;
Northern Ireland Vehicle Inspection
Driving Test Headquarters

13.12 Average daily flow of motor vehicles[1]: by class of road

Great Britain   Thousands

	1971	1976	1981	1986	1990
Type of road					
Motorways	28.5	30.8	30.4	38.1	54.6
Built up roads					
Trunk	..	12.6	13.9	16.7	17.6
Principal	..	11.5	12.2	12.8	14.8
Non built-up roads					
Trunk	..	7.3	9.0	11.6	14.2
Principal	..	4.3	4.5	5.5	6.7
All minor roads	..	0.9	1.1	1.2	1.4
All roads	1.8	2.0	2.2	2.6	3.1

1 Flow at an average point on each class of road.

Source: Department of Transport

Rail

13.13 British Rail: passenger business, and investment

Great Britain

Passenger business	1976	1981	1986–87	1990–91
Passenger carriages (thousands)	17.1	16.2	13.7	12.5
Passenger kilometres per passenger carriage (millions)	1.66	1.84	2.27	2.67
Passenger receipts per passenger kilometre (pence)[1]	5.39	5.76	5.81	6.20
PSO and PTE grant per passenger kilometre (pence)[1]	3.74	4.28	3.04	2.11
Operating expenses per train kilometre (£)[1]	11.7	12.7	10.5	9.3
Investment (£ million)	568	463	509	858

1 Adjusted for general inflation by the GDP market price deflator (1990-91 prices).

Source: Department of Transport

13.14 British Rail: performance indicators

Great Britain   Percentages

	1986-87[1]	1988-89	1990-91[1]
Percentage of trains arriving within punctuality target			
InterCity sector (10 mins)	85	87	85
Network SouthEast sector (5 mins)	91	92	90
Regional sector			
Express and long rural (10 mins)	91	90	90
Urban and short rural (5 mins)			90
Percentage of trains cancelled			
InterCity sector	0.8	1.0	2.2
Network SouthEast sector	1.6	1.4	2.1
Regional sector			
Express and long rural	0.5	1.2	1.8
Urban and short rural			2.9

1 Severe winter weather affected some services.

Source: Department of Transport

Table 13.13 presents a summary of British Rail's (BR) passenger business and investment between 1976 and 1990-91. British Rail is increasingly carrying more passenger traffic in fewer carriages. Between 1976 and 1990-91, British Rail reduced it's stock of passenger carriages by one quarter. The 12.5 thousand carriages used in 1990-91 covered over 20 per cent more passenger kilometres than the 17 thousand carriages in use in 1976 (Chart 13.1). Over the same period, British Rail's (Group) operating expenses fell by 21 per cent in real terms although the cost to passengers increased by 15 per cent.

The rail network in Great Britain is made up of the InterCity network, local stopping services, commuter services, and freight and parcel services. The performance of the rail system may be measured by the punctuality of the train services and by the number of train cancellations, as well as by the use people make of trains (see Chart 13.1 and Table 13.2). One of BR's objectives is to achieve a punctuality standard which requires that 90 per cent of trains on InterCity and longer Regional services arrive within 10 minutes of their scheduled time and 92 per cent of trains on Network SouthEast and 90 per cent on the shorter Regional services arrive within 5 minutes of their scheduled time (Table 13.14). A second objective is a cancellations standard of 1 per cent of current timetabled services for Network SouthEast and shorter Regional and 0.5 per cent for InterCity and longer Regional. In recent years, the first objective has not been achieved for Network South East and InterCity services, though it has for Regional services. The second objective has not been met and in 1990-91 over 2 per cent of trains on all networks were cancelled.

Water

13.15 Roll-on roll-off ferry traffic[1]: passenger cars

Great Britain

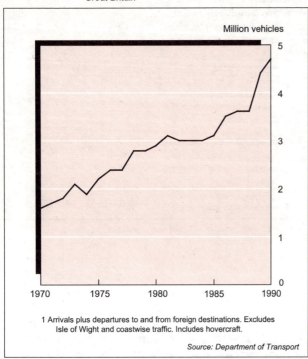

Million vehicles

1 Arrivals plus departures to and from foreign destinations. Excludes Isle of Wight and coastwise traffic. Includes hovercraft.

Source: Department of Transport

Chart 13.15 and Table 13.16 show that in 1990, 4.7 million accompanied passenger cars were carried by roll-on/roll-off ferries and hovercraft between Great Britain and foreign ports. Of the 4.5 million which travelled by ship, 65 per cent were travelling to or from French ports, two-thirds of them across the Dover Straits. Between 1976 and 1990 accompanied car traffic nearly doubled, reflecting the growth in motoring holidays abroad. The number of accompanied buses and coaches using roll-on/roll-off ferry services increased from 37 thousand in 1970 to 185 thousand in 1990. The Channel Tunnel, which is due to open in mid-1993, will compete with the ferry services.

As well as transporting people to the continent, ferries also take people to other parts of the United Kingdom and to the Isle of Man and Channel Isles. In 1990 nearly a half of all passenger cars travelling on these domestic routes were going to or from Northern Ireland and a tenth were travelling to or from the Isle of Man. The total number of cars travelling on these domestic routes increased by a half between 1981 and 1990.

13.16 Accompanied passenger car arrivals at, and departures from, Great Britain ports using foreign and coastwise routes: by overseas country

Thousand vehicles

	1976	1981	1986	1989	1990
Belgium	495	591	478	492	482
Denmark	54	112	45	52	64
Scandinavia and Baltic			67	44	32
France	1,019	1,402	1,944	2,642	2,900
Germany (Fed Rep)	} 265	} 22	21	26	29
Netherlands		259	325	346	356
Irish Republic	246	378	345	507	551
Spain and Portugal	29	20	27	38	45
All overseas routes by ship	2,106	2,784	3,252	4,148	4,460
Hovercraft services (France)	259	287	218	245	230
All overseas routes	2,365	3,071	3,470	4,393	4,690
Coastwise routes by ship					
Northern Ireland	191	210	286	355	364
Isle of Man	..	95	55	69	72
Orkneys and Shetlands[1]	..	52	64	97	102
Channel Islands	..	89	96	95	100
Other[2]	..	65	90	119	124
All coastwise routes by ship	398	511	592	735	761
All cars	2,764	3,582	4,062	5,128	5,452

1 Includes traffic recorded at both Great Britain mainland and island ports.
2 Ferry services to the islands of Arran and Lewis counted at the mainland ports only. Services to the Isle of Wight are excluded.

Source: Department of Transport

Air

The number of flights to and from United Kingdom airports increased by 92 per cent between 1976 and 1990 to reach 1.1 million (Chart 13.17). Over this period domestic flights increased by 91 per cent, international scheduled flights by 99 per cent and international non-scheduled flights by only 79 per cent following a reduction of 6 per cent between 1989 and 1990. The number of air passengers is expected to double again in the next 20 years.

13.17 Landings or take-offs at airports: by type of service

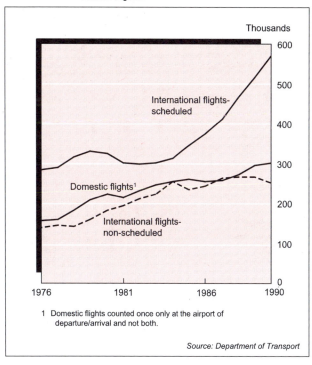

United Kingdom

1 Domestic flights counted once only at the airport of departure/arrival and not both.

Source: Department of Transport

Transport casualties

13.18 Road casualties per hour: by day of week, 1990

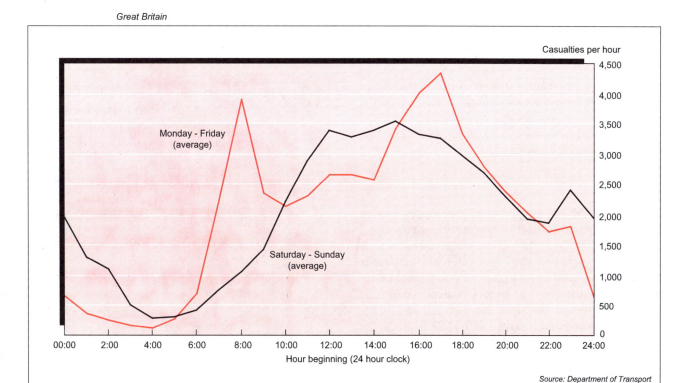

Great Britain

Source: Department of Transport

In Great Britain in 1990, the most likely time of day for a road casualty at weekends was between 3 pm and 4 pm (3,537 casualties per hour), on a weekday it was between 5 pm and 6 pm (4,319 casualties per hour). At weekends road casualties were more than three times as likely between the hours of midnight and 4 am as they were in the same period during weekdays (Chart 13.18). The rate of road casualties for children is highest between 8 am and 9 am and between 3 pm and 5 pm, the times when children are travelling to and from

13.19 Passenger casualty rates: by mode of transport

United Kingdom   Rate per billion passenger kilometres

	1978	1979	1981	1983	1986	1988	1989	Average 1980 – 1989
Air[1]								
Deaths	—	0.2	0.2	0.3	0.5	—	0.4	0.4
Total casualties	—	0.3	0.4	0.6	0.7	—	1.0	0.6
Rail[2]								
Deaths	1.3	1.4	1.0	0.8	0.8	1.7	0.8	0.9
Total casualties	63	65	70	72	72	83	75	74
Bus or coach[2]								
Deaths	1.0	0.6	0.4	0.8	0.6	0.3	0.5	0.6
Total casualties	231	218	223	235	220	218	233	226
Car[3]								
Deaths	6.9	6.5	5.7	4.9	4.8	4.1	4.4	4.9
Total casualties	424	401	366	317	344	330	332	340
Two-wheeled motor vehicles[3]								
Deaths	175	168	118	107	100	114	100	110
Total casualties	10,499	9,731	7,192	7,186	6,847	7,291	6,246	7,144
Pedal cyclists[2,4]								
Deaths	62	70	57	50	49	46	57	51
Total casualties	4,345	5,163	4,635	4,778	4,768	5,203	5,515	4,779
Water[5]								
Deaths	0.5	1.8	0.4	0.9	0.5	0.5	23	10
Total casualties	..	..	..	..	..	..		
Foot[2,4]								
Deaths	97	85	75	77	74	70	68	73
Total casualties	2,812	2,669	2,430	2,467	2,436	2,354	2,403	2,429

1 World passenger carrying services of UK airlines for fixed and rotary wing craft over 2,300 kilograms. Passenger kilometres relate to revenue passengers only.
2 Great Britain only.
3 Drivers and passengers in Great Britain.
4 For pedal cyclists distance travelled is used as 'passenger kilometre'.

For travel on foot distance walked is used as 'passenger kilometre'.
5 Domestic and international passenger services of UK registered vessels. The 1989 figure includes passengers on the River Thames pleasure boat "Marchioness". Passengers on the "Herald of Free Enterprise" (1987) are included in the 1980 – 89 average.

Source: Department of Transport

school. At weekends the rate of road casualties for adults and children is similar during the main part of the day, but after 7 pm on Saturdays until around 5 am the following Sunday morning the rate for adults is much higher than that for children.

Table 13.19 shows transport casualty rates by type of travel. Casualties are least likely to occur on air transport and are most likely to occur whilst travelling by motorcycle. Between 1981 and 1989, casualty rates for all types of road travel except by pedal cycle either fell or remained at the 1981 level. However, it is difficult to interpret trends because the year to year rates fluctuate considerably. The 1980-1989 average for water fatalities is largely dominated by the deaths resulting from the capsize of the roll-on/roll-off ferry 'Herald of Free Enterprise' in 1987 and the sinking of the Marchioness on the River Thames in 1989. Although the casualty rate for air travel is substantially below that for other types of travel, a much higher percentage of the casualties result in death. The rate for air travel is affected by the proportions of long and short distance flights since the greatest risk is at landing and takeoff.

13.20 Percentage of drivers and riders killed in road traffic accidents who were over the legal blood alcohol limit

Great Britain

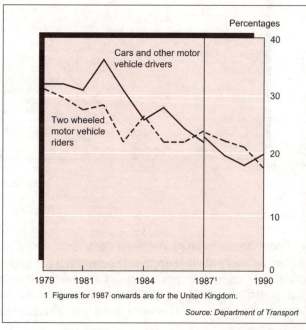

1 Figures for 1987 onwards are for the United Kingdom.

Source: Department of Transport

13.21 Road vehicles, road deaths[1] and car user deaths: international comparison, 1989

				Rates
	Road vehicles	Rate of road deaths		Rate of car user deaths
	per 1,000 popu-lation	per 100,000 popu-lation	per 100,000 motor vehicles	per billion car kilo-metres
United Kingdom	427	9.7	23	7.4[3]
Belgium	452	20.1	44	25.3
Denmark	396	13.1	33	10.3
France	532	20.4	38	22.9
Germany (Fed. Rep.)	541	12.9	24	11.3
Greece	251	19.0	76	. .
Irish Republic	265	13.1	49	. .
Italy	582	11.9	20	13.9
Luxembourg	507[2]	17.7	35	19.7
Netherlands	438	9.8	22	8.8
Portugal	283[2]	31.0	109	40.0
Spain	376[2]	24.0	64	68.5
Austria	492	20.6	42	27.8
Czechoslovakia	237[2]	10.3	43	. .
Finland	470	14.8	31	10.8
German DR	336	10.9	32	. .
Hungary	200[2]	20.4	102	. .
Norway	503	9.0	18	9.5
Sweden	462[2]	10.6	23	10.3
Switzerland	598	13.2	22	12.4
Yugoslavia	157	19.5	124	80.7
Japan	595	11.7	20	. .
USA	854	18.7	22	10.4

1 See Appendix, Part 13: Road deaths.
2 Excludes mopeds.
3 Great Britain.

Source: Department of Transport

The distance travelled in between carries a much lower risk. Data averaged over the period 1980-1989 show that 67 per cent of air casualties resulted in death compared to only 3 per cent for pedestrians; 1.5 per cent for cars and motorcycles; 1 per cent for pedal cyclists and rail travel, and less than 1 per cent for bus or coach transport.

Chart 13.20 looks at the relationship between road accidents and drinking. The chart only includes people subject to coroners' reports who died within 12 hours of an accident. The percentage of drivers killed in road accidents who were over the legal blood alcohol limit fell from around 31 per cent in 1981 to 20 per cent in 1990. These figures are consistent with other indicators that the level of drinking and driving has fallen over this period. There are differences at different times of the day. About 70 per cent of pedestrians aged 16 and over killed between 10 pm and 4 am have high blood alcohol levels and approximately half of car drivers, motor cycle riders and passengers killed during the night have blood alcohol levels above the legal limit. During the 12

13.22 Car and driver accidents and casualties: by model of car[1], 1989

Great Britain   Rates and percentages

		Accidents resulting in injury per 10,000 licensed vehicles	Injuries to driver or passengers per 10,000 licensed vehicles	Percentage of accidents[2] resulting in fatal or serious injury to driver
Size[3] and model of car				
Small cars				
Citreon	AX	125	87	6
Fiat	Panda	118	81	8
Fiat	UNO	143	90	10
Ford	Fiesta	142	97	8
Nissan	Micra	121	85	9
Peugeot	205	122	82	9
Renault	5	123	88	9
Rover	Metro	117	81	8
Rover	Mini	113	89	10
Vauxhall	Nova	131	89 ·	8
Volkswagen	Polo	106	58	7
All small cars		126	86	8
Small/Medium cars				
Ford	Escort	155	99	8
Ford	Orion	167	99	6
Lada	Riva	124	72	13
Lada	Samara	137	81	8
Mazda	323	103	57	6
Nissan	Sunny	133	71	8
Peugeot	309	127	87	7
Renault	11	118	82	10
Rover	200 Series	113	61	9
Rover	Maestro	123	70	9
Skoda	Estelle 2	97	59	6
Toyota	Corolla	107	59	9
Vauxhall	Astra	154	84	7
Vauxhall	Belmont	123	58	5
Volkswagen	Golf	106	62	5
All small/medium cars		134	80	8
Medium cars				
BMW	3 Series	118	64	7
Citreon	BX	146	66	5
Ford	Sapphire	170	96	8
Ford	Sierra	179	97	7
Peugeot	405	165	76	8
Rover	Montego	149	76	6
Vauxhall	Cavalier	158	88	6
Volvo	340	88	47	9
All medium cars		138	73	7
Large cars				
Ford	Granada	171	78	5
Rover	800 Series	145	58	6
Volvo	740	98	42	5
All large cars		114	52	6

1 Privately owned cars registered since 1 January 1987, excluding high performance version.
2 Accidents involving a collision with another vehicle or hard object where at least one person was injured. Both private and company owned cars are included.
3 As an approximate guide small cars are between 11 feet 8 inches and 12 feet 6 inches long, small/medium cars are between 12 feet 11 inches and 13 feet 9 inches long, medium cars are between 14 feet 2 and 15 feet long and large cars are over 15 feet long. The sub-totals include models not separately identified.

Source: Department of Transport

months up to September 1989, 541 thousand breath tests were carried out, of which 432 thousand were carried out because there was a suspicion of consumption of alcohol or suspicion of a moving traffic offence. The remaining 109 thousand were carried out after an accident had occurred.

In 1989 the United Kingdom (9.7), the Netherlands (9.8) and Norway (9.0) had the lowest rates of road deaths per 100,000 population of the countries shown in Table 13.21. The highest rate was in Portugal - 31.0 per 100,000 population. Norway, Japan and Italy had the lowest rate of road deaths per 100,000 motor vehicles for all the countries shown in 1989, the highest was in Yugoslavia (124 deaths per 100,000 vehicles).

On 1 January 1989, the standard report prepared by the police on any traffic accident resulting in personal injury was modified to include the registration number of any vehicles involved. By linking these registration numbers with data held at the Driver and Vehicle Licensing Agency, it is possible to obtain more information about the car involved (model, age, etc), but not about the people involved.

The Department of Transport subsequently published the data in a report which showed injury accident involvement rates for common types and models of car. The report also contained information on car user casualty rates and the percentage of drivers who were killed or injured. Some of these data are shown in Table 13.22.

There is some variability between models of car for each of the rates shown. However, it is important to remember that the rates, particularly those in the first two columns, are influenced by the level and type of use, and by the characteristics of the driver. The percentage injury rates in the last column give a better indication of the inherent safety record of the model.

BIBLIOGRAPHY

The following list contains selected publications relevant to Chapter 13: Transport. Those published by HMSO are available from the addresses shown on the back cover of Social Trends.

Annual Vehicle Census Great Britain, Department of Transport
Bus and Coach Statistics Great Britain, HMSO
Car and Driver: Injury Accident and Casualty Rates Great Britain: 1989, HMSO
International Passenger Survey, Employment Department
International Passenger Transport, HMSO
London Traffic Monitoring Report, HMSO
Merchant Fleet Statistics, HMSO
Motor Vehicle Registrations, Department of Transport
National Road Maintenance Condition Survey Report, HMSO
Overseas Travel and Tourism, HMSO
Ports Statistics, Department of Transport/British Ports Federation
Quarterly Transport Statistics, Department of Transport
Regional Trends, HMSO

Road Accidents Great Britain - The Casualty Report, HMSO
Road Accidents, Scotland, Scottish Office
Road Accidents Statistics English Regions, HMSO
Road Accidents: Wales, Welsh Office
Road Casualties Great Britain, Department of Transport
Road Lengths in Great Britain, HMSO
Scottish Transport Statistics, Scottish Office
Statistics of Road Traffic Accidents in Europe, United Nations
Traffic in Great Britain, Department of Transport
Transport of Goods by Road in Great Britain, HMSO
Transport Statistics for London, HMSO
Transport Statistics Great Britain, HMSO
International Comparisons of Transport Statistics, Parts I, II and II, HMSO
UK Airports - Annual Statement of Movements, Passengers and Cargo, Civil Aviation Authority
Welsh Transport Statistics, Welsh Office

APPENDIX: Definitions and Terms

Major surveys used in *Social Trends*

	Frequency	Sampling frame	Type of respondent	Location	Set sample size (most recent survey included in *Social Trends*)	Response rate (percentages)
Census of Population	Decennial	Detailed local	Household head	UK	Full count	100
British Social Attitudes Survey	Annual	Electoral Register	Adult in household	GB	4,402 addresses	64
British National Travel Survey—Yearly[1]	Annual	Electoral Register	Individual adult	GB	4,440 individuals[5]	55
British Crime Survey	Intermittent	Electoral Register	Adult in household	EW	11,400 addresses	77
Charity Household Survoy	Annual	Quota sample	Individual in Household	GB	1,000 individuals	7
Continuous Household Survey	Continuous	Rating valuation list	All adults in household	NI	4,500 addresses	71
Family Expenditure Survey	Continuous	Postcode Address File	Household	UK	11,675 addresses[6]	70
General Household Survey	Continuous	Postcode Address File	All adults in household	GB	11,838 addresses	84
International Passenger Survey	Continuous	International passengers at ports and airports	Individual traveller	UK	165,000 individuals	84
Labour Force Survey	Continuous	Postcode Address File	Adult in household[2]	GB	60,000 addresses	83
National Food Survey	Continuous	Postcode Address File	Housewife	GB	12,238 addresses	59
National Readership Survey	Continuous	Electoral Register	Individual in home	GB	28,319 individuals	65
National Travel Survey	Continuous	Postcode Address File	Individual in household	GB	5,000 households per year	80
New Earnings Survey	Annual	Inland Revenue PAYE records	Employee[3]	GB	[3]	[3]
Survey of Personal Incomes	Annual	Inland Revenue	Tax unit[4]	UK	68,500 tax units	89
Share Survey	Annual	Stock Exchange List	Share holders and companies	UK	80,000 shareholders 220 companies	8
Leisure Day Visits Survey	Continuous	Postcode Address File	All adults in household	UK	12,000 households	74
Smoking among secondary school children	Biannual	DES and SOED[9] records	School pupils (aged 11 – 15)	GB	9,728 pupils	87

1 Previously known as the British Tourism Survey, yearly.
2 Includes some proxy information.
3 In the New Earnings Survey employers supply data on a 1 per cent sample of employees who are members of PAYE schemes. 226 thousand were selected for the 1991 sample and there was a 95.5 per cent response but some 44 thousand returned questionnaires did not contain data.
4 In the Survey of Personal Incomes local tax offices supply data on tax units to a central point in Inland Revenue.

5 Basic sample only; in 1989 a further 4,302 individuals were contacted in connection with holidays abroad.
6 Effective sample only. Set sample includes ineligible households.
7 Not applicable; quota sample.
8 Taken from share registers.
9 Department of Education and Science and The Scottish Office Education Department.

The **Census of Population** is described in the article "The 1991 Census of Great Britain: plans for content and output" in *Social Trends 21* (page 13).

The first **British Social Attitudes Survey** was conducted in 1983 by Social and Community Planning Research. Technical details of the survey, which is conducted annually, were contained in the Appendix to the article *'Recent Trends in Social Attitudes'* in *Social Trends 19* (page 22).

A description of the **British Crime Survey** was contained in the Appendix to *Social Trends 21* (page 213).

A description of the **General Household Survey** was contained in the Appendix to *Social Trends 12* (page 253). In 1984 the sampling frame of the General Household Survey was changed from the Electoral Register to the Postcode Address file. The **Continuous Household Survey** in Northern Ireland is a similar survey to the General Household Survey in Great Britain.

A description of the **Labour Force Survey** was contained in the Appendix to *Social Trends 16* (page 204).

A description of the **National Food Survey** was contained in the Appendix to *Social Trends 12* (page 255). In 1984 the sampling frame of the National Food Survey changed from the Electoral Register to the Postcode Address File, selecting the sample by means of a stratified random sampling scheme from 52 local authority districts.

Descriptions of these surveys were contained in the Appendix to *Social Trends 12* (pages 253, 255 and 256):
British National Travel Survey
Family Expenditure Survey
International Passenger Survey
New Earnings Survey
National Readership Survey

A description of the 1985-86 **National Travel Survey (NTS)** was contained in the Appendix to *Social Trends 18* (page 197).

PART 1: POPULATION

Population and population projections
The estimated population of an area includes all those usually resident there, whatever their nationality. Members of HM and non-UK armed forces are taken to be resident at their stationed address. Students are taken to be resident at their term-time address. Population projections are on the same basis.

The current series of estimates are updated annually: starting with those derived from the 1981 Census of Population they allow for subsequent births, deaths and migration.

National population projections have recently been made every two years from the 1981-based to the 1989-based projections. Further details of the 1989-based projections were published in *Population Projections 1989-2029: Series PP2 No. 17 (HMSO).*

The principal projections are supplemented by variants assuming higher or lower fertility or mortality rates to provide some measure of the uncertainties present in the principal projections. Sub-national projections are also made.

Refugees
The basis for the determination of refugee status and the subsequent granting of asylum is the 1951 United Nations Convention relating to the Status of Refugees, extended in its application by the 1967 Protocol relating to the Status of Refugees. The United Kingdom is party to both. The Convention defines a refugee as a person who 'owing to a well-founded fear of being persecuted for reasons of race, religion, nationality, membership of a particular social group or political opinion, is outside the country of his nationality and unable or, owing to such fear, is unwilling to avail himself of the protection of that country '. In addition, the United Kingdom is prepared to grant, to applicants who do not fully meet the requirements of the Convention, exceptional leave to stay here for an appropriate period, if it would not be right, in all the circumstances of their cases, to insist on their leaving the United Kingdom.

PART 2: HOUSEHOLDS AND FAMILIES

Households
A household: a single person or a group of people who have the address as their only or main residence and who either share one meal a day or share the living accommodation.

Size of household: is *de jure* household size and counts those people who are usually resident in the household irrespective of whether or not they are present on census night. In the General Household Survey the size of the household is the number of people who normally live there.

Families
A family: is a married couple, either with or without their never-married child or children (of any age), or a lone parent together with his or her never-married child or children. A lone parent (in the Census) is a married parent whose spouse does not reside in the same household, or any single, widowed, or divorced parent.

A lone parent family (in the General Household Survey): consists of a lone parent, living with his or her never-married dependent children, provided these children have no children of their own. Married lone mothers whose husbands are not defined as resident in the household are not classified as lone parents because evidence suggests the majority are separated from their husband either because he usually works away from home or for some other reason that does not imply the breakdown of the marriage (see OPCS's *GHS Monitor 82/1).* Couples describing themselves as married (or common-law married) but who are in fact cohabiting are coded and counted as married.

Children: are never-married people of any age who live with one or both parent(s). They also include step-children and adopted children (but not foster children) and also grandchildren (where the parents are absent).

Dependent children: in the 1961 Census, dependent children were defined as children under 15 years of age, and persons of any age in full-time education.

In the 1971 Census, dependent children were defined as never-married children in families who were either under 15 years of age, or aged 15-24 and in full-time education. However, for direct comparison with the General Household Survey (GHS) data, the definition of dependent children used for 1971 in Table 2.6 has been changed to include only never-married children in families who were either under 15 years of age, or aged 15-18 and in full-time education.

In the 1981 Census and the GHS dependent children are never-married children in families who are aged under 16, or aged 16-18 and in full-time education.

Divorce
A decree of divorce or of nullity of marriage may be granted on certain grounds as set out in the *Matrimonial and Family Proceedings Act 1984.* A divorce is a dissolution of marriage granted if the marriage has irretrievably broken down. Annulled marriages are either void (for example if it was bigamous) or voidable (for example if it has not been consummated). A decree nisi is granted by the Court at the time of the hearing, and normally becomes absolute after six weeks on the application of the party granted the decree nisi. The parties are then legally free to remarry. The law in Scotland did not change until the coming into effect of the *Divorce Reform Act (Scotland) 1976* on 1 January 1977.

PART 3: EDUCATION

Main categories of educational establishments

Educational establishments in the United Kingdom may be administered and financed in one of five different ways:

Public sector: by local education authorities, which form part of the structure of local government;

Assisted: by governing bodies which have a substantial degree of autonomy from public authorities but which receive grants direct from central government sources; or

Grant maintained: since 1988 all local education authority maintained secondary, middle and primary schools can apply for Grant Maintained status and receive direct grants from the department of Education and Science. The governing body of such a school is responsible for all aspects of school management, including the deployment of funds, employment of staff and provision of most of the educational support services staff and pupils. In January 1991 there were 50 Grant Maintained schools in England and Wales.

Independent: by the private sector, including individuals, companies, and charitable institutions.

Local Management of Schools (LMS): Under LMS, which was introduced in Northern Ireland in 1991, all public sector and assisted secondary schools have delegated responsibility for managing their school budgets and staff numbers, and this delegation is beingextended to primary schools in these sectors.

Stages of education

There are three stages of education: primary (including nursery), secondary, and further (including higher) education. The first two stages are compulsory for all children between the ages of five and sixteen years (fifteen before 1972/73); and the transition from primary to secondary education is usually made between ten and a half and twelve years but is sometimes made via middle schools (see below) after age twelve. The third stage of education is voluntary and includes all education provided after full-time schooling ends.

Primary education

Primary education includes three age ranges: nursery, under five years of age; infant, five to seven or eight years; and junior, seven or eight to eleven or twelve years. The great majority of public sector primary schools take both boys and girls in mixed classes. In Scotland the distinction between infant and primary schools is generally not made.

The pattern for Nursery and Primary education in Northern Ireland is nursery education (age 3-4) and primary schools (age 4-11).

Nursery education is provided in either nursery schools or nursery classes in primary schools. It is compulsory for children who attain the age of 4 on or before 1 July to commence primary school the following September.

The usual age for transfer to secondary education is 11 as in England and Wales.

Middle schools

In England and Wales middle schools take children from first schools and generally lead on, in turn, to comprehensive upper schools. They cover varying age ranges between eight and fourteen. Depending on their individual age range they are deemed either primary or secondary.

Secondary education

Provision of maintained secondary schools in an area may include any combination of types of school. The pattern is a reflection of historical circumstance and of the policy adopted by the local education authority. Comprehensive (including middle deemed secondary) schools account for about 90 per cent of pupils in a variety of patterns as to forms of organisation and the age range of the pupils attending. Comprehensive schools normally admit pupils without reference to ability and aptitude, and cater for all the children in a neighbourhood; but in some areas they co-exist with modern, grammar, and technical schools.

In Northern Ireland secondary education normally begins when pupils reach the age of 11. Under current transfer arrangements from primary to secondary education parents have the choice as to whether their children take the Transfer Procedure tests which are compiled and marked by the Department of Education. The Education Reform Order 1989 introduced new open enrolment arrangements whereby all secondary schools are rquired to admit pupils who have indicated a preference for the school provided there is room at the school. Where schools receive more applications for admission than places available then pupils must be admitted on the basis of published criteria prepared by the schools.

Special schools

Special schools, either day or boarding, provide education exclusively for children who are so seriously handicapped, physically or mentally, that they cannot profit fully from education in normal schools.

Further education

The term 'further education' may be used in a general sense to cover all non-advanced education after the period of compulsory education. More commonly it excludes those staying on at secondary school, and those studying higher education at universities, polytechnics and some other colleges. The figures in Chart 3.19 cover all courses taken in public sector and assisted establishments of further education.

Higher education

The term 'higher education' as used in this chapter (Tables 3.20, 3.24 and 3.26) covers all courses (including teacher training courses) in universities, polytechnics and some courses in other colleges (including Scottish Central Institutions), that is those leading to qualifications above General Certificate of Education 'A' level, Scottish Certificate of Education 'H' grade, and BTEC National Diploma Certificate, or their equivalents.

'A' level 'score'

The GCE examining boards, classify the results of candidates who have passed at 'A' level in five grades, ranging from A (the highest) to E (the lowest). As a convenient indication of the overall 'A' level qualification of candidates applying through the Universities Central Council on Admissions (UCCA) for a place at university, UCCA translate the 'A' level grades into a 'score' by means of the following simple scale:

$$A = 5, B = 4, C = 3, D = 2, E = 1, Fail = 0$$

No more than three subjects are counted, and no score is allotted to a candidate who passed in only one subject. The candidate's best performance in each subject, whenever obtained, is used. The $AAA = 15$, the maximum score; $EE = 2$, the lowest pass score. No distinction is made between candidates obtaining say, a score of 8 on two 'A' levels (eg BB) and those obtaining the same score on three 'A' levels (eg BDD).

Due to inherent differences betwen the two systems, direct comparisons between GCE and SCE 'scores' are not valid. Chart 3.22 shows GCE 'A' level scores only and does not include SCE 'Highers'.

School-leaving qualifications

In England, Wales and Northern Ireland, the two main examinations for school pupils at the minimum school leaving age are the Certificate of Secondary Education (CSE) and General Certificate of Education (GCE) 'O' level. Both CSE and 'O' level examinations are taken in a wide range of subjects. The CSE is awarded at grades 1 to 5 and 'O' level at grades A to E. Grade 1 CSE results are deemed equivalent to higher graded results (grades A-C) at 'O' level and both are considered to be at the standard required for the GCE 'O'-level pass grade, which operated up to 1974. In 1987 (1988 in Northern Ireland), the GCE 'O' level and CSE examinations were replaced by the GCSE examination. The GCSE examination is awarded at grades A to G. GCSE grades A to C are equivalent to 'O' level grades A to C or CSE grade 1. The GCE is also offered at 'A' level and usually taken after a further two years of study in a sixth-form, or equivalent. These examinations are awarded at grades A-E.

In Scotland, the Scottish Certificate of Education (SCE) Ordinary ('O') grade course leads to an examination (of approximately equivalent standard to the GCSE examination at the end of the fourth year of secondary schooling. Secondary schooling in Scotland starts at age 11.5 to 12.5 years approximately. In 1986 the first phase of the new Standard Grade examinations was introduced. These examinations, which are aimed at a wider ability range, will replace 'O' grades by the early 1990s. From 1973 to 1985 'O' grades were awarded in a 5-band, A to E, structure; awards in bands A to C correspond to what were previously rated passes. From 1986 Standard grades are being awarded on 1-7 scale, with 'O' grades being awarded on a comparable 1-5 scale; grades 1-3, in total, are approximately equivalent to the previous A-C. The examination of the Higher (H) grade requires, basically, one further year of study and may be taken at the end of the fifth or sixth year. For the better 'H' grade candidates the range of subjects covered may be almost as wide as for the 'O' grades - it is not unusual for candidates to study five or six subjects spanning both arts and science. The breadth of study inevitably means that an individual subject in the 'H' grade course is not taken to the same depth as the more specialised GCE 'A' level course.

Pupil/teacher ratios

The pupil/teacher ratio within schools is the ratio of all pupils on the school register to all teachers employed in schools on the day of the annual count. Part-time teachers are included on a full-time equivalent basis, with part-time service calculated as a proportion of a full-time school week. Part-time pupils are counted as 0.5 (except in Scotland where they are counted as 1.0).

PART 4: EMPLOYMENT

Labour force

The civilian labour force includes people aged 16 and over who are either in employment (whether as an employee, self-employed or on work-related government employment and training programmes, but excluding those in the Armed Forces) or unemployed. The ILO definition of unemployment refers to people without a job who were available to start work within two weeks and had either looked for work in the previous four weeks or were waiting to start a job they had already obtained. Estimates on this basis are not available before 1984, as the Labour Force Survey did not then collect information on job search over a four week period. The former GB Labour Force definition of unemployment, the only one available for estimates up to 1984, counted people not in employment and seeking work in a reference week (or prevented from seeking work by a temporary sickness or holiday, or waiting for the results of a job application, or waiting to start a job they had already obtained), whether or not they were available to start (except students not able to start because they had to complete their education).

Workforce

Workforce in employment plus the unemployed.

Workforce in employment

Employees in employment, self-employed, HM Forces and participants on work-related government training programmes.

GHS definition of unemployed

The unemployed consist of those who, in the week before interview, were looking for work, would have looked for work if they had not been temporarily sick, or were waiting to take up a job they had already obtained. In this context temporary sickness refers to illness lasting 28 days or less. These definitions apply whether or not the person was registered as unemployed or claiming unemployment benefit.

From 1985 full-time students were classified according to their own reports of what they were doing in the reference week; in previous years they were classified as 'inactive'. Also, from 1985 people on the Youth Training Scheme were classified as 'working' if they were with an employer providing work experience in the reference week and as 'inactive' if they were at college. From 1989 all those on schemes YTS, ET and JTS were classified as 'working'.

Sector classification

The Post Office has been included in public corporations from 1961 onwards although employees were still civil servants until 1969. In 1974 water services (previously undertaken by local authorities) passed to Regional Water Authorities classified to public corporations; trust ports were reclassified from local authorities to public corporations; and most local authority health services were transferred to the Regional and Area Health Authorities which form part of the central government sector. From 1970 employees of some local authority transport under-takings were taken over by passenger transport authorities classified to public corporations. Most of the steel industry was nationalised in 1967, and the aircraft and shipbuilding industries in 1977. The Royal Ordnance Factories, Royal Mint, Property Services Agency (Supplies Division) (now the Crown Suppliers), and Her Majesty's Stationery Office were established as trading funds and reclassified to public corporations from 1974, 1975, 1976, and 1980 respectively. British Aerospace and part of Cable and Wireless Ltd (operating mainly overseas) were reclassified to the private sector in 1981. The National Freight Company Ltd, formerly the National Freight Corporation, and Britoil were reclassified to the private sector in 1982, and Associated British Ports were transferred to the private sector in 1983. Enterprise Oil was reclassified to the private sector in June 1984. British Telecom plc was reclassified to the private sector in November 1984, and Trust Ports (Great Britain) in April 1985. Between 1984 and 1986 British Shipbuilders were transferred to the private sector. In April 1986 both United Kingdom Atomic Energy Authority and English Industrial Estates Corporation were reclassified from central government to public corporations. In December 1986 the British Gas Corporation was reclassified to the private sector as was British Airways plc in February 1987 and Royal Ordnance plc in April 1987. British Airports Authority plc was transferred to the private sector in July 1987, as were subsidiaries of the National Bus Company at various dates between July 1986 and April 1988. British Steel plc was privatised in December 1988, as were polytechnics (previously in the local authority sector) in April 1989.

Industrial disputes

Statistics of stoppages of work owing to industrial disputes in the United Kingdom relate to disputes connected with terms and conditions of employment. Small stoppages involving fewer than 10 workers or lasting less than one day are excluded from the statistics except where the aggregate number of working days lost in the dispute exceeds 100. Disputes not resulting in a stoppage of work are not included in the statistics.

Workers involved and working days lost relate to persons both directly and indirectly involved (unable to work although not parties to the dispute) at the establishments where the disputes occurred. People laid off and working days lost at establishments not in dispute, due for example to resulting shortages of supplies, are excluded.

There are difficulties in ensuring complete recording of stoppages, in particular near the margins of the definition; for example short disputes lasting only a day or so, or involving only a few workers. Any under-recording would affect the total number of stoppages much more than the number of working days lost.

The Unemployed

Definition of unemployment — claimant counts

People claiming benefit (that is unemployment benefit, supplementary benefits, or national insurance credits) at Unemployment Benefit Offices on the day of the monthly count, who on that day that they are unemployed and that they satisfy the conditions for claiming benefit. (Students claiming benefit during a vacation and who intend to return to full-time education are excluded.)

Social Trends 22, © Crown copyright 1992

Unemployment rate

Unemployment rates, available down to to the level of travel-to-work areas, are calculated by expressing the number of unemployed claimants as a percentage of the mid-year estimate of the total workforce (the sum of employees in employment, unemployed claimants, self employed, HM forces and participants on work-related government training programmes).

Narrower rates (as a percentage of employees in employment and the unemployed only) are also available down to the level of travel-to-work areas.

Definition of unemployment — OECD concepts

The unemployment figures used in these standardised rates are estimated by the OECD to conform, as far as possible, with the definition of unemployment in the guidelines of the International Labour Organisation (ILO), and the rates are calculated as percentages of the total labour force, again as defined in the ILO guidelines. According to these guidelines the unemployed covers all persons of working age who, in a specified period, are without work, who are available for work, and who are seeking employment for pay or profit. The total labour force consists of civilian employees, the self-employed, unpaid family workers, professional and conscripted members of the armed forces, and the unemployed. The standardised rates will therefore differ from the unemployment rates published in national sources whenever the national definition of unemployment differs from that indicated above, or the denominator used to calculate the national rates is other than the total labour force.

Employment and training measures

Current Employment Department schemes and programmes include:

Job-Share Scheme
Jobstart
Youth Training
Employment Training
Employment Action
Enterprise Allowance Scheme

Past schemes and programmes

Temporary Short-Time Working Compensation Scheme, which replaced the Short-Time Working Compensation Scheme in the textiles, clothing, and footwear industry
Temporary Employment Subsidy
Small Firms Employment Subsidy

Adult Employment Subsidy
Job Release Scheme (full-time and part-time schemes)
Young Workers Scheme (applications approved)
New Workers Scheme
Youth Employment Subsidy
Youth Training Scheme
Community Industry
Youth Opportunities Programme
Job Creation Programme
Community Enterprise Programme
Special Temporary Employment Programme
Job Introduction Scheme
Work Experience Programme
Training in Industry
Community Programme
Voluntary Projects Programme
Old Job Training Scheme
New Job Training Scheme
Training for Enterprise
Access to Information Technology
Local Grants to Employers
Wider Opportunities Training Programme
Open Technology Programme
National Priority Skills Service
Industrial Language Training Service

Participants in work related government training programmes

These comprise participants in Youth Training (and previously Youth Training Scheme) and Employment Training who receive work experience except those who have contracts of employment (who are included in employees in employment). In Northern Ireland they consist of those on Youth Training Programme, Job Training Programme, and Attachment Training participants and other management training scheme participants training with an employer.

PART 5: INCOME AND WEALTH

The household sector

The household sector includes private trusts and individuals living in institutions as well as those living in households. It differs from the personal sector, as defined in the national accounts, in that it excludes unincorporated private businesses, private non-profit-making bodies serving persons, and the funds of life assurance and pension schemes. More information is given in an article in *Economic Trends*, September 1981.

Household disposable income is equal to the total current income of the household sector *less* payments of United Kingdom taxes on income, employees' national insurance contributions, and contributions of employees to occupational pension schemes. It is revalued at constant prices by a deflator implied by estimates of total household expenditure at current and constant prices. This deflator is a modified form of the consumers' expenditure deflator.

Regional Accounts

Estimates of household income by region and county were published in *Economic Trends* (April 1991), together with brief notes on changes to sources and methods. A full description of sources and methods was published in *Economic Trends* (July 1989)

Social security benefits

The National Insurance Fund provides insurance against loss of income in the event of unemployment, sickness and invalidity, widowhood or retirement. These are generally known as contributory benefits. Non-contributory benefits include income-related support to people or families with low income (income support and family credit). Payments, often in the form of loans, may also be made from the social fund to assist people with exceptional expenses which they would find difficult to pay out of their regular income. Non-income-related support is available through child benefit and, for the long-term sick or disabled, through severe disablement allowance, attendance allowance and mobility allowance and the various industrial injury benefits. A separate war pensions scheme pays benefit to people widowed or disabled as a result of wars, or service in HM Forces, since 1914.

For the purpose of the *Social Security Act 1975* there are five classes of contribution to the National Insurance Fund. Class 1 is payable by employed earners and their employers, from 1991/92 Class 1A contributions are payable by employers on the benefit of cars and car fuel provided to their employees, Class 2 and Class 4 are payable by the self-employed, and Class 3 is payable on a voluntary basis by those who are neither employed nor self-employed but who wish to maintain their contribution record. Class 1 contributions are wholly earnings-related, Class 1A contributions are assessed according to the scale rate charges used by the Inland Revenue and Class 4 contributions are related to the level of profits or gains. Class 2 and Class 3 contributions are flat-rate. In general, unemployment benefit and industrial injuries benefits are only payable to Class 1 contributors.

The weekly standard rates of benefits and personal allowances for income support are:

Rates of benefits, April 1991 £

	Stand-ard rate	Adult depend-ant	Each child
Retirement pension			
(single person)	52.00	31.25	10.70
Widow's pension	52.00		10.70
Unemployment benefit	41.40	25.55	10.70[2]
Invalidity pension	52.00	31.25	10.70
Industrial disablement			
benefit (100%)	84.90		
Invalidity allowance[1]			
Age 40	11.10		
Age 50	6.90		
Age 60 (men) (55 women)	3.45		
Sickness benefit	39.60	24.50	
Child benefit			
first child			8.25
subsequent child			7.25
One-parent benefit (first or only child of certain lone (persons)	5.60		

1 Payable with Invalidity pension when incapacity began before each age shown.
2 Child dependancy only payable where beneficiary is over pension age.

Income support personal allowances, April 1990 £

Couple	One aged 18 or over	62.25
	Both under 18	47.30
Single claimant	Aged 25 or over	39.65
	18 – 24	31.15
	under 18	23.65
Lone parent	Aged 18 or over	39.65
	under 18	23.65
Dependent	Child under 11	13.35
	11 – 15	19.75
	16 – 17	23.65
	18	31.15

Income support is income-related and non-contributory. From September 1988 it has not normally been available to people aged below 18. People in full-time education or working more than 24 hours are also excluded. Couples (whether married or not) and any dependent children are assessed as a unit. Claimants with one or more dependent children also receive a family premium of £7.95. Certain 'client groups' are entitled to additional payments:

Additional payments, April 1990 £

	Single	Couple
Disability premium	16.65	23.90
Pensioner premium	13.75	20.90
Enhanced pensioner premium	15.55	23.35
Higher pensioner premuim (80 or over or disabled 60-79)	18.45	26.20
Lone parent premium	4.45	

It is not possible to receive more than one of these. There is also a severe disability premium of £31.25 and a child disability premium of £16.65.

Unemployed claimants

The data for 1983 onwards presented in Table 5.10 are taken from the count of unemployed claimants taken for the Department of Social Security (DSS). This count is different from that taken for the Department of Employment (DE), which is used in Chapter 4. The DE count is designed to produce quick simple figures for all unemployed claimants. In order that the statistics are as accurate a record as possible of the status of claimants on the count date, they are compiled retrospectively 3 weeks later rather than on the count date itself, to take account of later notifications of both new and terminating claims.

The DSS count is more detailed and includes information on the claimant's benefit position on the date of the count. Unlike the DE count, no retrospective adjustment is made to the figures and the DSS count includes only those claimants who declare unemployment for that day or are expected to, given their firm evidence of unemployment during the previous fortnight. Students on vacation and temporarily stopped workers, are included in the DSS count if they are claiming benefit. The differences between the DE and DSS counts reflect the different objectives which the two counts serve.

Independent Taxation

Since the introduction of Independent Taxation on 6 April 1990 all taxpayers are taxed separately on their own incomes and take responsibility for their own tax affairs.

Under Independent Taxation every individual taxpayer is entitled to a personal allowance which can be set against any type of income. A married man is entitled to claim the married couple's allowance in addition to his personal allowance. If his total net income is too small to use the whole of the married couple's allowance he can transfer the unused allowance to his wife.

In 1991-92 taxpayers aged 65 and over are entitled to claim the aged personal allowance and the aged married couple's allowance. The amount of the aged personal allowance depends on the age of the individual taxpayer while the amount of the married couple's allowance depends on the age of the elder of the husband or wife. These aged allowances are subject to an income limit, and for incomes in excess of this limit, the allowances are reduced by £1 for each additional £2 of income until the basic levels of the personal and married couple's allowances are reached.

Redistribution of income

Estimates of the incidence of taxes and benefits on household income, based on the Family Expenditure Survey, are published by the Central Statistical Office in *Economic Trends*. The article covering 1988 appeared in the issue for March 1991, and contains details of the definitions and methods used.

Personal wealth

The estimates of the distribution of the marketable wealth of individuals relate to all adults in the United Kingdom. They are produced by combining estimates of the distribution of wealth identified by the estate multiplier method with independent estimates of total personal wealth derived from the Central Statistical Office personal sector balance sheets. The methods used were described in a article in *Economic Trends* (October 1990) entitled 'Estimates of the Distribution of Personal Wealth'.

Estimates of the distribution of wealth allowing for pension rights cover both rights in occupational pension schemes and rights to state retirement pensions and widows' benefits. Certain assumptions are necessarily involved in the valuation of the rights taken in aggregate, and a description of the main assumptions used in the calculations was given in a further article in *Economic Trends* (November 1991) entitled "Estimates of the distribution of personal wealth." Further assumptions are involved in allocating pension rights to various size holdings of marketable wealth. Below the upper percentiles the distribution estimates vary significantly depending on the allocation assumptions used, and ranges are therefore shown for the 25th and 50th percentiles in Table 5.20. A fuller account of the scope of the estimates is given in *Inland Revenue Statistics, 1986*.

Net wealth of the personal sector

Balance sheet estimates of the net wealth of the personal sector, analysed by type of asset and liability, are published annually in the February issue of *Financial Statistics*. Revised estimates for the personal and other sectors from 1979 were included in the *United Kingdom National Accounts*, 1990 edition.

PART 6: EXPENDITURE AND RESOURCES

Retail prices

The General Index of Retail Prices measures the changes month by month in the level of prices of the commodities and services purchased by all types of household in the United Kingdom, with the exception of certain higher income households and households of retired people mainly dependent on state benefits. These households are:

> (a) the 4 per cent (approximately) where the total household recorded gross income exceeds a certain amount (£700 a week in 1990).

> (b) those in which at least three-quarters of the total income is derived from state pensions and benefits and which include at least one person over the national insurance retirement age.

The weights which are used to calculate the index are based on the pattern of household expenditure derived from the continuing Family Expenditure Survey. Since 1962 the weights have been revised in February of each year.

Expenditure patterns of one-person and two-person pensioner households differ from those of the households upon which the General Index is based. Separate indices have been compiled for such pensioner households since 1968, and quarterly averages are published in the Department of Employment 's *Employment Gazette*. They are chain indices constructed in the same way as the General Index of Retail Prices. It should however be noted that the pensioner indices exclude housing costs.

An explanation of the methods used in calculating the retail prices index is contained in *'A short guide to the RPI'*, published in the August 1987 issue of the *Department of Employment Gazette* and also available as a booklet from HMSO.

Household expenditure

The national accounts definition of household expenditure, within consumers' expenditure, consists of: personal expenditure on goods (durable and non-durable) and services, including the value of income in kind; imputed rent for owner-occupied dwellings; and the purchase of secondhand goods *less* the proceeds of sales of used goods.

Excluded are: interest and other transfer payments; all business expenditure; and the purchase of land and buildings (and associated costs). In principle, expenditure is measured at the time of acquisition rather than actual disbursement of cash. The categories of expenditure include that of non-resident as well as resident households and individuals in the United Kingdom.

For further details see the article entitled *'Consumers' expenditure'* in *Economic Trends*, September 1983.

Household saving

Household saving is the balance of income and expenditure on the current account of households, and is derived from the personal sector account, mainly by subtracting the income and expenditure (and hence saving) of the other parts of the personal sector. The household savings ratio is household saving expressed as a percentage of household disposable income.

Household income comprises:
> Wages and salaries, and forces' pay
> Self-employment income
> Rent, dividends, and interest
> Income in kind
> Pensions and benefits paid by life assurance
>   and pension schemes
> Social security benefits
> Other current transfers

Household disposable income comprises:
> Household income *less*
> United Kingdom taxes on income
> Social security contributions (excluding employers' contributions)
> Employees' contributions to occupational pension schemes

Household expenditure comprises:
> Interest payments
> Expenditure on goods and services
> Life assurance premiums etc paid by individuals
> Other current transfers

(Note that this definition of household expenditure does not accord with that for national accounts purposes — see above.)

Expectation of life

The expectation of life at a given age, shown in Table 7.4 as applying to a particular year, is the average number of years which a person of that age could be expected to live, if the rates of mortality at each age experienced by the population in that year (or in a period including that year) were assumed to be experienced thereafter in all future years. The mortality rates which underlie the expectations of life figures in Table 7.4 are based, up to 1981, on total deaths occurring in a period of years of which the year shown is the middle year, and in the case of 1991 and 2001, on the mortality rates assumed for those years in the Government Actuary's mid-1989-based population projection.

Death Certificates

On 1st January 1986, a new certificate for deaths within the first 28 days of life was introduced in England and Wales. It is not possible to assign one underlying cause of death from this certificate. In Table 7.5, for the sake of consistency, the United Kingdom figures for 1990 exclude deaths at ages under 28 days. In Table 7.23 the 1986 and 1990 figures for England and Wales exclude deaths under 28 days.

Standardised mortality rates

The mortality rates used in Charts 7.5 and 7.6 have been directly standardised — that is, for each year they were calculated by applying observed age-specific rates to a standard population. The standard population used was for the United Kingdom in 1981.

Drinking

A standard unit is equivalent to a half pint of beer, 1/6 gill of spirits (an English single measure), a glass of wine (4 fl oz) or a small glass of fortified wine (2 fl oz). (One unit is roughly equivalent to 8½ grammes of absolute alcohol.)

Notified Addicts

Doctors are required to send to the Chief Medical Officer at the Home Office particulars of persons whom they consider to be addicted to any of 14 controlled drugs (mainly opiates).

Accidental deaths

The data in Table 7.23 exclude deaths where it was not known whether the cause was accidentally or purposely inflicted, misadventure during medical care, abnormal reactions, late complications and late effects of accidental injury. It does however include a small amount of double counting; these are cases where the accident occurred while the deceased was working at home or in residential accommodation. Figures for Scotland comprise accidents occurring on farms and in forests, in mines and quarries, and in industrial places and premises.

Discharges from mental illness and mental handicap hospitals and units

A major change in data collection affected hospital activity statistics from 1 April 1987. Up to 1986 the data for Chart 7.35 were collected through the Mental Health Enquiry (MHE) which covered mental illness and mental handicap hospitals and units and was based on the calendar year. Since April 1 1987 the data has come from the Hospital Episode Statistics (HES) system which covers all NHS hospitals and is based on the financial year. Any interpretation of the data should take into account serious deficiences in both quality and coverage of HES data in its first year (1987/88) as well as differences in coverage of the two systems.

Unrestricted principals

An unrestricted principal is a medical practitioner who provides the full range of general medical services and whose list is not limited to any particular group of persons. In a few cases (about 20), he may be relieved of the liability to have patients assigned to him or be exempted from liability to emergency calls out-of-hours from patients other than his own. Doctors may also practise in the general medical services as restricted principals, assistants or trainees.

In-patient activity

In Table 7.31 in-patient cases treated for 1981 are hospital discharges and deaths taken from the SH3 return. From 1989/90 these are Finished Consultant Episodes (FCE) from the KP70 return. A FCE is a completed period of care of a patient using a bed, under one consultant, in a particular District/Special Health Authority. If a patient is transferred from one consultant to another within the same hospital, this counts as a FCE not a hospital discharge. Conversely, if a patient is transferred from one hospital to another in the same district without changing consultant, this counts as a hospital discharge but not as a FCE. The KP70 includes healthy live born infants whereas the SH3 returns did not.

Manpower

The total of Health Authorities' staff and family practitioners would contain an element of duplication, since some practitioners have been counted under more than one of the categories shown. Figures for England, Scotland and Wales relate as closely as possible to 30 September, except those for ophthalmic family practitioner staff which refer to 31 December. Figures for Northern Ireland relate to 31 December, except those for family practitioner staff which relate to 31 July.

Staff of the Post Graduate Specialist Health Authorities and those Family Practitioner Committee staff on health authority payrolls are included in Regional and District Health Authorities' staff, as are Common Services Agency staff in Scotland. In 1982, due to the restructuring of the NHS in England and Wales, Area Health Authorities were removed and their functions devolved to District Health Authorities.

The figures for medical and dental staff in Regional and District Health Authorities include permanent paid and honorary staff in hospital and community health services, hospital practitioners and part-time medical/dental officers, but exclude locum staff in Great Britain. Northern Ireland figures include all community sessional staff.

Figures for family practitioner staff include General Medical Practitioners (principals, assistants and trainees), General Dental Practitioners (principals and assistants) and staff of the General Ophthalmic Service.

PART 8: HOUSING

Dwellings
Estimates of the stock of dwellings are based on data from the Censuses of Population, with adjustments for enumeration errors and for definitional changes. The figures include vacant dwellings and temporary dwellings occupied as a normal place of residence. Privately rented dwellings include those rented from housing associations, private owners and other tenures; including dwellings rented with farm or business premises and those occupied by virtue of employment.

Renovations
The data for Chart 8.11 are for renovation grants paid under the *Housing Act 1985*. These payments do not include grants paid under the new system under the *Local Government and Housing Act 1989*. No more grants were approved under the *Housing Act 1985* after June 1990 in England and Wales, although payments were made after this date for grants approved before this date. The notes below refer to England and Wales only. Broadly similar schemes operate in Northern Ireland and Scotland.

The new house renovation grants were introduced on 1 July 1990 under Part VIII of the *Local Government and Housing Act 1989*. Under the new scheme, local authorities can give renovation grants of up to 100 per cent of the cost of works for owner occupiers and private sector tenants on the lowest incomes. All applicants for grants are subject to a test of resource. This is based very closely on that used for housing benefit. Grants are mandatory towards the cost of essential works needed to bring a house or flat up to a new standard of fitness for human habitation. About one million home owners may be eligible to apply for mandatory grants. Local Authorities (who are responsible for administering the new grants) are also able to give discretionary grants for other works intended to put homes in a reasonable state of repair. Landlords may also be able to get grants towards the cost of repair and improvements to the properties they own, including common parts of flats and houses in multiple occupation. This may involve grants for the conversion of empty properties with homes for rent. For the first time, a new mandatory disabled facilities grant will be available to all homeowners and tenants for works to enable a disabled person to enjoy comparable facilities in and around a house to those enjoyed by an able-bodied person. In addition, discretionary grants will be available to make a house suitable for the accommodation, welfare or employment of a disabled person. This grant will also be subject to a test of resources.

Bedroom standard
This concept is used to estimate occupation density by allocating a standard number of bedrooms to each household in accordance with its age/sex/marital status composition and the relationship of the members to one another. A separate bedroom is allocated to each married couple, any other person aged 21 or over, each pair of adolescents aged 10-20 of the same sex, and each pair of children under 10. Any unpaired person aged 10-20 is paired, if possible with a child under 10 of the same sex, or if that is not possible, is given a separate bedroom, as is an unpaired child under 10. This standard is then compared with the actual number of bedrooms (including bedsitters) available for the sole use of the household, and deficiences or excesses are tabulated. Bedrooms converted to other uses are not counted as available unless they have been denoted as bedrooms by the informant; bedrooms not actually in use are counted unless uninhabitable.

Housing benefit
From April 1983, housing benefit fully replaced the provision of assistance with rent and domestic rates through supplementary benefit and the former rent and rate rebate and rent allowance schemes. The responsibility for paying housing benefit to all eligible persons was given to local authorities. A new housing benefit scheme was introduced from 1 April 1988 as an integral part of the social security reforms. The two schemes are briefly described below. Further details including the amounts used for assessment are given in the Department of Social Security publication *Social Security Statistics 1989*.

Principles of housing benefit
Under the 1983 and 1988 housing benefit schemes claimants could receive help with rent and rates but not with mortgage interest or water rates. A person may be eligible for housing benefit for rent or rates paid on the dwelling he occupies as his home, but the actual amount of rent and/or rates on which benefit is assessed may be reduced in certain circumstances.

The 1983 scheme
The 1983 scheme had two types of housing benefit, certificated and standard.

Certificated housing benefit
For people who received supplementary benefit the Department of Health and Social Security issued a certificate of entitlement to the appropriate local authority responsible for paying housing benefit. Rent and rates were normally met in full unless the household included non-dependants such as lodgers or adult relatives.

Standard housing benefit
Other householders had to apply for 'standard' housing benefit. Entitlement was assessed by comparing a claimant's gross income from all sources (less any specified disregards) with the housing benefit needs allowance for himself, partner and any dependent children. Additional amounts were allowed for pensioners and handicapped people. Where the claimant's income exactly matched his needs allowance housing benefit amounted to 60 per cent of eligible rent and 60 per cent of eligible rates. If his income was less than or more than his needs allowance, this 60 per cent figure was added to or decreased using a system of six tapers. There were difference tapers for rent and rates; these differed according to whether income was above or below the needs allowance, and for pensioners with income below the needs allowance there were enhanced tapers. Maximum benefit could not exceed the eligible rent and rates, and no benefit was payable if the calculated amount fell below certain minimum levels.

The 1988 scheme
All householders now have to make a specific claim to their local authority for housing benefit. The calculation is aligned with that for income support, using the same system of personal allowances and premiums for special groups such as pensioners and disabled people. Claimants with net incomes at or below income support levels qualify for maximum housing benefit (100 per cent of eligible rent and prior to April 1990 (April 1989 in Scotland) 80 per cent of eligible rates, less any deductions for non-dependents). People with net incomes above income support levels have their maximum housing benefit reduced by a proportion of that excess income using a taper of 65 per cent for rent and prior to April 1990 (April 1989 in Scotland) there was a 20 per cent taper for rates. Specified amounts of certain types of net income are disregarded, and a capital rule provides firstly that no housing benefit is payable if assessed capital exceeds an upper limit of £8,000 (increased to £16,000 from April 1990), and secondly for tariff income to be assumed on each £250 step of assessed capital between £3,000 and the upper limit. No benefit is payable if the calculated amount falls below certain minimum levels.

Community Charge Rebates and Community Charge Benefit
In April 1989, community charge replaced domestic rates in Scotland. Community Charge Rebates were introduced into housing benefit to provide help with the community charge. From April 1990, when community charge was introduced in England and Wales, a new benefit — 'Community Charge Benefit' — was also introduced for the whole of Great Britain. The method of calculation follows closely that described for housing benefit in the 1988 scheme: maximum rebate is 80 per cent of the personal charge, but the taper of excess income is 15 per cent.

General Household Survey

The GHS has periodically included questions about participation in various leisure activities. In 1973, 1977, 1980, 1983 and 1986 these questions covered participation in sports, games and physical activities, watching spectator sports and participation in other non-sport leisure activities. In 1987 several changes were made − new sets of questions on sports participation and the use of public libraries, and forests and woodlands were introduced − the questions on entertainment, outings and sightseeing activities were changed to prompt for visits to specified kinds of arts performances, galleries and museums and historic buildings.

Because of these changes, data on sports participation, entertainment, galleries, museums and historic buildings are not comparable with results for previous years.

Further details of the changes and the effects on results can be found in the *General Household Survey 1987 Report* and the supplementary report for 1987 on sports participation.

The GHS sample is taken continuously throughout the year, but results for a full quarter are a balanced sample, so that although the question refers to the four weeks preceding the week of the interview, the rates and frequencies of participation over any four weeks within a quarter are assumed to be representative of the quarter as a whole. These were aggregated over the year to produce annual figures. More details of this process and of limitations of the data are given in the *General Household Survey, 1973, 1977, 1983, 1986 and 1987* reports along with details of the questionnaires and the coding of leisure activities.

Social class: Institute of Practitioners in Advertising (IPA) definition

Social class categories are based on head of household's occupation as follows:

Class A — Higher managerial, administrative, or professional

Class B — Intermediate managerial, administrative, or professional

Class C1 — Supervisory or clerical, and junior managerial, administrative, or professional

Class C2 — Skilled manual workers

Class D — Semi and unskilled manual workers

Class E — State pensioners or widows (no other earners), casual or lowest grade workers, or long-term unemployed

PART 11: PARTICIPATION

Church membership

Definitions of membership vary according to the church denomination or religious group in question. For the purpose of Table 11.4 adult church membership is defined as appropriate to each particular group, so that for example the Electoral Roll (not to be confused with the Local Authority Electoral Roll) has been used for the Church of England, the Easter communicant figure has been used for the Church in Wales, while mass attendance has been used for the Roman Catholic churches.

Commissioners for Local Administration

The Commissioners investigate complaints from members of the public about injustice caused by maladministration in local government in England, Scotland and Wales.

Examples of faults or failures which the Local Commissioners have treated as maladministration are: neglect and unjustified delay; malice or bias or unfair discrimination; failure to observe relevant rules or procedures; failure to take relevant considerations into account; and failure to tell people of their rights. Commissioners have no power to question the merits of a decision taken without maladministration.

A complaint should be made in writing and may be sent direct to the Local Commissioner or to a member of the authority complained against with a request that it should be sent to the Local Commissioner.

Certain administrative actions are outside the jurisdiction of the Commissioners; these include matters where the complainant has a right of appeal to a tribunal or court of law, personnel matters, contractual and commercial transactions, complaints about public passenger transport, docks, harbours, entertainment, industrial establishments and markets, and the internal affairs of schools and colleges. Where the complainant has the right of appeal to a tribunal, minister or court of law the Commission has a discretion to waive this restriction if he considers it not reasonable for the complainant to have exercised that right.

If a report by a Local Commissioner finds that injustice has been caused by maladministration, the Council must consider the report and tell the Local Commissioner what action they propose to take. A Local Commissioner cannot force a Council to act if they decide not to.

Since 1 January 1985 the statistical records of the Local Commissioner for Wales relate to all complaints, not only to formally referred complaints as hitherto.

Health Service Commissioners

The function of the Health Service Commissioners, who are statutory independent officers appointed by the Crown, is to investigate complaints of failure in provision or in execution of a service provided by a health authority, or maladministration by or on behalf of these authorities. The authorities concerned include Regional Health

Authorities, District Health Authorities, Family Health Service Authorities and NHS Trusts. A complaint may be made directly to the appropriate commissioner, but only after it has been brought to the attention of the relevant health authority and an adequate opportunity given to that authority to investigate it and reply. Matters outside jurisdiction include action taken in the Commissioner's opinion solely in the exercise of clinical judgment and any action taken by family doctors, dentists, pharmacists and opticians who provide services under contract to a health authority.

There are three Health Service Commissioners: one each for England, Scotland and Wales. At present all three posts and that of Parliamentary Commissioner, are held by the same person.

The Commissioners report annually to Parliament for the year to 31 March from April to the following March and otherwise as they see fit.

Parliamentary Commissioner for Administration
The Parliamentary Commissioner is a statutory independent officer appointed by the Crown. His function is to investigate complaints of maladministration brought to his notice by Members of Parliament on behalf of members of the public. His powers of investigation extend to actions taken by central government departments and certain non-departmental public bodies in the exercise of their administrative functions, but not to policy (which is the concern of Government) or legislation (which is the concern of Parliament).

Certain administrative actions are, however, outside his jurisdiction; these include matters affecting relations with other countries, contractual matters, hospitals (but see the note on the Health Service Commissioners) and personnel questions of the armed forces and the civil service. The Commissioner cannot investigate any matter where the complainant has exercised a right of appeal to a tribunal or court of law. However, he may at his discretion conduct an investigation if such a right of appeal exists and it is held that the complainant has, with good reason, not resorted to that right.

In the performance of his duties, the Parliamentary Commissioner has the power to require the production of evidence, including official papers, and the attendance of witnesses. He reports his findings to the Member of Parliament who presented the case. The Commissioner reports annually to Parliament and may submit such other reports as he thinks fit. An all-party Select Committee considers his reports.

Parliamentary elections
A general election must be held at least every 5 years, or sooner if the Prime Minister of the day so decides. The United Kingdom is currently divided into 650 constituencies, each of which returns one member to the House of Commons. To ensure equitable representation, four permanent Boundary Commissions (for England, Wales, Scotland and Northern Ireland) make periodic reviews of constituencies and recommend any change in the number or redistribution of seats that may seem necessary in the light of population movements or for some other reason.

Selected Advisory and counselling services
Al—Anon Family Groups: Support groups for Alcoholics' families. Includes Alateen which is part of Al-Anon. Data also include the Republic of Ireland.
Alcoholics Anonymous: Includes branches in the Channel Isles. The 1981 and 1990 figures exclude Northern Ireland.
Catholic Marriage Advisory Council: Figures are for years ending March 1972, March 1982, and March 1990. They relate to Great Britain only.
Citizens Advice Bureaux: Figures are for years ending December 1971, March 1982, and March 1990. The figures given for 'Clients' represent new enquiries in 1971, and new *plus* repeat enquiries in 1981 and 1990.
Cruse: Cruse Bereavement Care. Figures given for clients exclude many short-term contracts.
Leukaemia Care Society: Figures for 'Clients' represent numbers of families.
Relate: Includes National Marriage Guidance Council (now operating under the name Relate in England, Wales, N. Ireland, Channel Isles and Isle of Man) and Scottish Marriage Guidance Council. Figures given for 'Clients' represent numbers of families and are new cases during the year.

PART 12: LAW ENFORCEMENT

Criminal courts in England and Wales
The courts of ordinary criminal jurisdiction in England and Wales are the magistrates' courts, which try the less serious offences and the Crown Court which deals with the serious cases. Almost all offenders under 17 are dealt with in juvenile courts, which are a special form of magistrates' court. The Crown Court was established by the *Courts Act 1971,* which came into effect on 1 January 1972. From that date the former courts of assize and quarter sessions were abolished.

Part III of the *Criminal Law Act 1977,* which came into effect on 17 July 1978, redefined offences according to three new modes of trial, namely:

   i.   offences triable only on indictment
   ii.   offences triable either on indictment or summarily, but which are triable summarily only with the consent of the accused
   iii.   offences triable only summarily

For statistical purposes the figures for court proceedings and for police cautioning for 1979 to 1986 are shown in two groups; the first group is a combination of i. and ii. above which has been called 'indictable' and covers those offences which must or may be tried by jury in the Crown Court and the second group, 'summary' offences, covers iii. above and can only be tried at magistrates' courts.

Where possible comparable figures have been given for 1977 and 1978 to take account of both these changes in legislation and changes in counting practice (to remove an element of double counting).

Criminal courts in Scotland
The courts exercising criminal jurisdiction in Scotland are the High Court of Justiciary, the Sheriff Court and the District Court.

The High Court is Scotland's supreme criminal court, and deals with the most serious cases and with all appeals. There is no appeal from it to the House of Lords. All cases in the High Court are tried by a judge and jury (referred to as "solemn procedure" or "on indictment").

The Sheriff Court has both solemn and summary jurisdiction and deals with less serious cases. Most prosecutions are dealt with by summary procedure (ie before a sheriff and without a jury). The sentencing powers of the Sheriff Court are more limited than those of the High Court, but where a case merits more severe penalties the sheriff may remit it to the High Court for sentence.

The District Courts were established in 1975 by statute to replace the former Burgh Courts. The District Courts are presided over by lay justices and deal summarily with minor offences. The sentencing power of the District Court is more limited than that of the Sheriff Court, except where it is presided over by a stipendiary magistrate, when it has the same jurisdiction and powers as a sheriff sitting summarily.

Prosecutions in Scotland are brought by procurators fiscal who act in the public interest on behalf of the Lord Advocate. It is the procurator fiscal, advised in serious cases by Crown Counsel, who decides in each case whether to proceed, and if so, in which court to prosecute.

Support for victims of crime
The Criminal Injuries Compensation Scheme provides lump sum compensation based on common law damages for victims of violent crime in Great Britain where the injury is assessed as worth £750 or more. The ex-gratia scheme applies to anyone criminally injured within Great Britain or on a British registered ship or aircraft.

Sentences and orders
The following are the main sentences and orders which can be imposed upon those persons found guilty in 1989 and 1990. Some types of sentence or order can only be given to offenders in England and Wales in certain age groups.

Absolute and conditional discharge
A court may make an order discharging a person absolutely or (except in Scotland) conditionally where it is inexpedient to inflict punishment and a probation order is not appropriate. An order for conditional discharge runs for such period of not more than three years as the court specifies, the condition being that the offender does not commit another offence within the period so specified. In Scotland a court may also discharge a person with an admonition.

Attendance centres
This sentence, available in England, Wales, and Northern Ireland, involves deprivation of free time. The centres are mainly for boys between the ages of 10 and 16 found guilty of offences for which an adult could be sentenced to imprisonment. At the end of 1990, however, in addition to the 95 centres for boys aged 10 to 16, 18 of which also took girls in the same age group, there were 26 centres for males aged 17 to 20. Attendance is on Saturday mornings or afternoons for up to three hours on any one occasion and for a total of not more than 24 hours and (normally) not less than 12. The activities include physical training and instruction in useful skills (eg first aid.)

Probation orders
Probation is designed to assist the rehabilitation of an offender while he remains at liberty and under the supervision of a probation officer (social worker in Scotland), whose duty it is to advise, assist, and befriend him. A cardinal feature of the order is that it relies on the co-operation of the offender. In England and Wales probation orders may only be made on people aged 17 or over; juveniles aged under 17 may receive supervision orders and (up to October 1991) care orders (see below). There is no age limit in Scotland, but children under 16 would normally be dealt with outside the criminal justice system. Probation orders may be given for any period between 6 months and 3 years inclusive.

Community service
An offender aged 17 or over (16 or over in Scotland) who is convicted of an offence punishable with imprisonment may be required to perform unpaid work for not more than 240 hours, and not less than 40 hours. From 24 May 1983 an offender aged 16 in England and Wales may be required to perform unpaid work for not more than 120 hours, and not less than 40 hours. In Scotland the *Law Reform (Miscellaneous Provisions) (Scotland) Act 1990* requires that community service can only be ordered where the court would otherwise have imposed imprisonment or detention. Protection and community service may be combined in a single order in Scotland.

Young offender institutions
Borstal training and imprisonment related to offenders aged under 21 years were abolished by Part 1 of the *Criminal Justice Act 1982* and from 24 May 1983 a new determinate sentence of youth custody for offenders aged 15 and under 21 was introduced in England and Wales, normally of over 4 months, and with a maximum sentence of 12 months for offenders aged under 17. A sentence of custody for life was introduced for offenders aged 17 and under 21 in place of life imprisonment. The range of detention centre orders for males was also changed: the usual sentence became one of between 21 days and 4 months instead of 3 months to 6 months as previously. Section 123 of the *Criminal Justice Act 1988* replaced youth custody and detention centre order by detention in a young offender institution (1 October 1988). Young offenders serving determinate sentences are eligible for remission and parole (see below). In Scotland no person under 21 may be sent to prison. Children under 16 are dealt with by the children's hearings system, which is not part of the criminal justice system. For young offenders (aged 16 – 21) Borstal training was abolished in Scotland by the Criminal Justice (Scotland) Act 1980, and detention centres were abolished by the Criminal Justice Act 1988 and replaced by detention in a young offender institution.

Detention Centres
Until their abolition in October 1988 detention centres were intended to provide a method of custodial treatment for young offenders who committed an offence for which an adult could be sentenced to imprisonment and for whom a long period of residential training did not seem necessary. The sentence was used for offenders aged between 14 (16 in Scotland) and 21 years old. A person released from a detention centre in England and Wales came under the supervision of a probation officer or social worker for a period of 3 months. Those released before 24 May 1983 were subject to 12 months supervision, but their supervision ended on 24 May 1983, or as soon thereafter as the 3 months supervision was completed. Those serving sentences in Detention Centres were eligible for remission (see below).

Imprisonment
The custodial sentence for adult offenders is imprisonment or, in the case of mentally abnormal offenders, hospital orders with or without restrictions on when the offender may be discharged. A third of a prisoner's sentence (half in Northern Ireland) is remitted subject to good conduct and industry. In England and Wales from 13 August 1987 those serving sentences of 12 months or less (including young offenders) became eligible for remission of one half rather than one third of their sentence. This effectively removed all such sentences from the parole scheme. Those serving sentences of over 9 months (18 months in Scotland and prior to 1 July 1984 in England and Wales) may be released under the parole scheme after serving 6 months (12 months in Scotland and prior to 1 July 1984 in England and Wales) or a third of that sentence whichever is the longer. A life sentence prisoner may be released on licence subject to supervision and is always liable to recall.

Fully suspended sentences of imprisonment and suspended sentences with supervision order
In England, Wales and Northern Ireland, sentences of imprisonment of two years or less may be fully suspended. The period for which a sentence may be suspended is between one and two years at the discretion of the court. The result of suspending a sentence is that it will not take effect unless during the period specified the offender is convicted of another offence punishable with imprisonment. The *Criminal Justice Act 1972*, which came into force on 1 January 1973, gave the courts power, on passing a suspended sentence of over 6 months, to impose a 'suspended sentence with supervision order ' placing the offender under the supervision of a probation officer for a specified period not longer than the period of suspension.

Partly suspended sentences of imprisonment
Section 47 of the *Criminal Law Act 1977* was implemented on 29 March 1982. As amended by Section 30 of the *Criminal Justice Act 1982*, this gives the courts the power to suspend not less than a quarter of a sentence of imprisonment of between 3 months and 2 years.

Social Trends 22, © Crown copyright 1992

Deferred Sentence

In Scotland the court may decide to defer sentence after conviction for a period and on conditions determined by the court. At the end of this period the case is considered by the court at the deferred diet, which has the same powers of sentence as at conviction.

Young Offenders Centres: Northern Ireland

On 1 June 1979 provisions in the *Treatment of Offenders (Northern Ireland) Act 1968* were brought into operation so that those under 21 years of age would no longer be sent to prison unless the court wished to impose a sentence of 3 years or more, but would be detained in a Young Offenders Centre.

Fines

Fines may be imposed with or without time to pay the fine. If the fine is not paid in the time allowed imprisonment or detention may result.

Compensation Orders

The *Powers of the Criminal Courts Act 1973* and *Criminal Justice (Scotland) Act 1980* enable criminal courts to help the victims of crime, imposing compensation orders on those found guilty.

Supervision orders and care orders: England and Wales

Under the *Children and Young Persons Act 1969,* which came into force on 1 January 1971, supervision and care orders may be made on people aged under 17 in both criminal and care proceedings. The *Childrens Act 1989* abolishes the courts' power to make care orders in criminal proceedings, with effect from 14 October 1991.

Legal aid

Advice and assistance provided by a solicitor, short of actual representation in court and tribunal proceedings, may be obtained either free or on payment of a contribution by those whose capital and income are within certain financial limits.

Assistance by way of representation covers the cost of a solicitor preparing a case and representing a client in court. It is available (either free or on payment of a contribution to those who are financially eligible) for most civil cases in the magistrates' court, for proceedings before Mental Health Review Tribunals', and for certain proceedings relating to the care of children and young people.

Legal aid in civil cases, such as county court and higher court proceedings, covers all work up to and including court proceedings and representation by a solicitor and a barrister, if necessary. Legal aid in these cases is available free or on a contributory basis to those whose capital and income are within certain financial limits. Applicants must show that they have reasonable grounds for asserting or disputing a claim. Certain types of action, including libel and slander, are excluded from the scheme.

In the criminal courts in England and Wales a legal aid order may be made if this appears desirable in the interest of justice and the defendant's means are such that he requires financial help in meeting the costs of the proceedings in which he is involved. No limit of income or capital above which a person is ineligible for legal aid is specified, but the court must order a legally-aided person to contribute towards the costs of his case where his resources are such that he can afford to do so.

Advice and assistance and civil legal aid in Scotland operate on the same basis. In the case of advice by way of representation (ABWOR), however, this is granted mainly for summary criminal cases rather than civil cases and applies where a plea of guilty is made. Mental health appeals are also covered by ABWOR. Criminal legal aid, which is granted by the Scottish Legal Aid Board, for summary cases and for all appeals, and by the courts for solemn cases, is not subject to a contribution.

Civil courts in England and Wales

The main civil courts in England and Wales are the county courts, which are the courts for the lesser cases, and the High Court, where the more important cases are heard. Magistrates' courts have limited civil jurisdiction covering such matters as matrimonial proceedings for separation and maintenance orders, adoption and affiliation and guardianship orders, and care proceedings. Most appeals in civil cases go to the Court of Appeal (Civil Division) and from there may go to the House of Lords.

County courts are presided over by a judge, who almost always sits alone, although he may in a very limited number of cases sit with a jury consisting of eight persons if either party wishes it and the court makes an order to that effect. The jurisdiction of the county courts covers: actions founded upon contract and tort (except libel and slander) where the amount claimed is not more than £5,000 (increased from £2,000 in 1981); equity matters, such as trusts and mortgages, where the amount does not exceed £30,000; and actions concerning land where the net annual value for rating does not exceed £1,000 (£1,500 in London). Cases outside these limits may be tried in the county court by consent of the parties, or may be transferred to the High Court.

Other matters dealt with by the county courts include adoption cases, bankruptcies (which are dealt with in certain courts outside London), and undefended divorce cases (which are heard and determined by county courts designated as divorce county courts).

Civil courts in Scotland

The Court of Session is the supreme civil court in Scotland. As a general rule it has the original jurisdiction in all civil cases and appellate jurisdiction (that is the power to hear and give decisions on appeals) over all civil courts, unless such jurisdiction, original or appellate, is expressly excluded by statute. The Court is divided into two parts, the Inner House and the Outer House. The Inner House exercises appellate jurisdiction on reclaiming motions from the Outer House and on appeals from the inferior courts. Appeals from the Court of Session may go to the House of Lords.

The Sheriff court is the principal local court of civil, as well as criminal, jurisdiction in Scotland. Its civil jurisdiction is comparable with that of the county courts in England and Wales but is more extensive in certain directions. There is no limit to the sum which may be sued for in the Sheriff court. The Sheriff's jurisdiction now includes actions of divorce, but does not extend to actions of declarator of marriage, or to actions of declarator involving the personal status of individuals or to certain other actions; but, with these exceptions, the civil jurisdiction of the court is generally similar in scope to that of the Court of Session. In addition, the Sheriff deals with a mass of quasi-judicial and administrative business, some of which is similar to that dealt with in county courts in England and Wales, but of which a large part is particular to the Scottish system.

EC visitor

'EC visitor' means a person who, being permanently resident outside the UK, visits the UK for a period of less than 12 months. UK citizens resident in the EC for 12 months or more coming home on leave are included in this category. Visits to the EC similarly are visits for a period of less than 12 months by people permanently resident in the UK (who may be of foreign nationality).

Road deaths

Road deaths are normally counted as those which occur within 30 days of the accident. Figures for countries whose road deaths do not meet this definition have been standardised using the factors below:-

Country	Death within	Correction (percent)
France	6 days	+ 9
Greece	3 days	+ 12
Italy	7 days	+ 7
Spain	24 hours	+ 30
Portugal	at scene	+ 35
Austria	3 days	+ 12
Switzerland	1 year	- 5
Japan	24 hours	+ 30

Social Trends 22, © Crown copyright 1992

Index

The references in this index refer to table and chart numbers, or entries in the Appendix.

REGIONAL TRENDS 26

What the newspapers say about REGIONAL TRENDS

'... provides a fascinating insight into the differing lifestyles of particular regions...' – *Financial Times*

'... the most authoritative source of comprehensive regional comparisons, ranging from the serious to the trivial...' – *Daily Telegraph*

' ... includes district statistics .... providing an intriguing insight into small pockets of the country ...' – *The Times*

' ... the definitive reference book on how parts of Britain differ ...' – *Daily Telegraph*

' ... Regional Trends' 200 pages provide a highly readable snapshot of social and economic conditions in Britain ...' – *Morning Star*

' ... the fullest-ever picture of Britain and modern-day Brits ...' – *Daily Star*

' ... contains some information to confirm stereotyped images of lifestyle around Britain's regions – but also some to challenge them ...' – *Financial Times*

1991 Edition
HMSO £23.00 net

ISBN 0 11 620449 4

Central Statistical Office publications are published by HMSO. They are available from HMSO bookshops and through booksellers.